SECOND EDITION

MODELS FOR CLEAR WRITING

Robert B. Donald
Betty Richmond Morrow
Lillian Griffith Wargetz
Kathleen Werner

Prentice Hall, Englewood Cliffs, New Jersey 07632

Library of Congress Cataloging-in-Publication Data

Models for clear writing.

Bibliography: p.
Includes indexes.
1. English language—Rhetoric. 2. College readers.
I. Donald, Robert B.
PE1408.M583   1989   808′.0427   88-30660
ISBN 0-13-586959-5

Editorial/production supervision: *Bea Marcks/Edith Riker*
Cover Design: *Ben Santora*
Manufacturing buyer: *Laura Crossland*
Cover photo: *James Carmichael, The Image Bank*

To
ROBERT B. DONALD
our colleague, co-author, and friend

 © 1989, 1984 by Prentice-Hall, Inc.
A Division of Simon & Schuster
Englewood Cliffs, New Jersey 07632

Printed in the United States of America

10 9 8 7 6 5 4 3 2 1

ISBN 0-13-586959-5

Prentice-Hall International (UK) Limited, *London*
Prentice-Hall of Australia Pty. Limited, *Sydney*
Prentice-Hall Canada Inc., *Toronto*
Prentice-Hall Hispanoamericana, S.A., *Mexico*
Prentice-Hall of India Private Limited, *New Delhi*
Prentice-Hall of Japan, Inc., *Tokyo*
Simon & Schuster Asia Pte. Ltd., *Singapore*
Editora Prentice-Hall do Brasil, Ltda., *Rio de Janeiro*

CONTENTS

PREFACE   *ix*

Acknowledgments, x

**1   UNDERSTANDING WRITING
      AS A PROCESS**   *1*

Getting Started, 2
Choosing a Topic, 2
Establishing a Purpose, 4, 5
Writing Your Paper, 10
Choosing Effective Titles, 17
Editing and Revising, 17
Editing, 20
Proofreading, 20
Overview, 21

2   NARRATING   *23*

Organization, 23
Models

      Roy Popkin, "Night Watch," 32
      Bob Lancaster, "Eddie Lovett, Polyhistor," 35
      James Thurber, "University Days," 41
      Newman Levy, "A Woman Walks By," 48
      Tom Hritz, "Cold Water on a Hot Shower," 50
      Georgette Walton, "Very Cold and All Alone," 53

Integrating Reading And Writing Skills:
   Having A Clear Purpose, 54
Improving Your Vocabulary:
   The Dictionary And The Thesaurus, 58
Assignment, 60

3 DESCRIBING 62

Organization 62
Models

Frederick Lewis Allen, "The Scopes Trial," 72
John Steinbeck, "The Turtle," 76
James Tuite, "The Sounds of Manhattan," 79
Virginia Woolf, "The Death of the Moth," 82
Daniel Samerin, "Shake, Rattle, or Roll?" 86

Integrating Reading With Writing Skills: Using Details To Form
Generalizations, 88
Improving Your Vocabulary:
Reading The Entire Dictionary Entry, 91
Assignments, 93

4 EXPLAINING BY EXAMPLES 95

Rhetoric, 95
Organization, 98
Models

James Thurber, "The Case against Women," 101
William Safire, "I Led the Pigeons to the Flag," 105
Lewis Thomas, "Death in the Open," 108
Ellen Goodman, "One Season Fits All," 112
Deems Taylor, "The Monster," 115
Mark Pleshenko, "Honeymoon Hints," 120

Integrating Reading With Writing Skills: Identifying Main Ideas
And Supporting Ideas, 122
Improving Your Vocabulary: The Right Word, 127
Assignments, 130

5 EXPLAINING A PROCESS 133

Rhetoric, 133
Organization, 136
Models

S. I. Hayakawa, "How Dictionaries Are Made," 138
Paul Roberts, "How to Say Nothing in Five Hundred Words," 141
Alexander Petrunkevitch, "The Spider and the Wasp," 154
Malcolm X with Alex Haley, "Coming to an Awareness
of Language," 161
Stephen Leacock, "How to Live to be 200," 164
Ernest Hemingway, "When You Camp Out, Do It Right," 167
Robertson Davies, "How to Design a Haunted House," 171

Integrating Reading Skills With Writing Skills:
   Explaining For Clarity/Reading For Comprehension, 174
Improving Your Vocabulary:
   Levels Of Usage, 177
Assignments, 178

6   COMPARING AND CONTRASTING   *181*

Rhetoric, 181
Prewriting, 182
Organization, 184
Introduction and Thesis Statement, 184
Body, 185
Writing the Essay, 187
Providing Adequate Transitions, 188
Concluding the Essay, 188
Analogy, 189
Models

   Paul B. Horton and Chester L. Hunt, "Created Equal?" 191
   Bruce Catton, "Grant and Lee: A Study in Contrasts," 194
   David and Vera Mace, "Marriage East and West," 199
   Melvin Maddocks, "In Praise of Reticence," 202
   Lewis Thomas, "The Deacon's Masterpiece," 206
   Patti Wright, "From Courtship to Dating," 212

Integrating Reading Skills With Writing Skills: Prewriting/
   Prereading, 214
Improving Your Vocabulary: Denotation And Connotation, 218
Assignment, 220

7   DIVIDING AND CLASSIFYING   *223*

Rhetoric, 223
Organization, 225
Models

   George D. Gibson, "Effective Legal Writing and Speaking," 228
   Judith Viorst, "Friends, Good Friends—and Such Good Friends," 233
   Isaac Asimov, from "What Do You Call a Platypus?" 238
   Paul Gallico, "Fans," 241
   Thomas Sowell, "Pink and Brown People," 246
   Bob Swift, "On Reading Trash," 249
   Debbie Lucci, "The TV As Teacher," 252

Integrating Reading Skills With Writing Skills: Recognizing
   Different Patterns Of Organizations, 254
Improving Your Vocabulary: Etymology, 256
Assignments, 260

8   ESTABLISHING CAUSE AND EFFECT   *262*

Rhetoric, 262
Organization, 265
Models

      Russell Baker, "Sometimes Peanuts Are Unwelcome," 267
      Frank Trippett, "The Great American Cooling Machine," 270
      Maurice W. Van Allen, M.D., "The Deadly Degrading Sport," 275
      Joyce Carol Oates, Excerpt from "On Boxing," 279
      William Allen, "Toward an Understanding of Accidental Knots," 283
      Jean E. Mizer, "Cipher in the Snow," 288
      Lola Karnes, "Why I Lost Ho-Hum," 292

Integrating Reading and Writing Skills:
   Recognizing Cause and Effect Relationships, 293
Improving Your Vocabulary: Sources Of New Words, 296
Assignment, 299

9   DEFINING   *301*

Rhetoric, 301
Organization, 308
Models

      Bob Greene, "Fifteen," 309
      Dorothy Thompson, "Concerning Tolerance," 315
      Joseph Wood Krutch, "The Tragic Fallacy," 319
      Leo Rosten, "The Mischief of Language," 321
      Desmond Morris, "Barrier Signals," 329
      Curtis Ulmer, "What is Poverty? Listen," 334

Integrating Reading Skills With Writing Skills: Discovering
   Meaning Through Context, 336
Improving Your Vocabulary, 339
Assignment, 343

10 PERSUADING   *346*

Rhetoric, 346
Organization, 349
Models

Rose Lee Hayden, "The Future is Now," 352
McCrum, Cran, and McNeil, "An English Speaking World," 355
Arthur Ashe, "An Open Letter to Black Parents: Send Your Children
   to the Libraries," 358
H. L. Mencken, "Criminology," 361
Ossie Davis, "The English Language Is My Enemy," 365
Muriel R. Schulz, "Is The English Language Anybody's Enemy?" 369
Robert A. Wolfe, "Escape," 373

Integrating Reading Skills With Writing Skills: Distinguishing
   Between Fact and Opinion, 375
Improving Your Vocabulary: Context, 381
Assignment, 384

11 WRITING ABOUT LITERATURE   *386*

Rhetoric, 387
Organization, 396
Models

Jack Matthews, "The Contest," 405
William Carlos Williams, "The Use of Force," 407
R. F. Dietrich, on "The Use of Force," 411
Mark Twain, "Fenimore Cooper's Literary Offenses," 417
John Ciardi, from "How Does a Poem Mean," 423
Brooks and Warren, "The Organic Nature of Poetry," 428
Robert Statti, "The Maturing of Huckleberry Finn," 432

Integrating Reading Skills With Writing Skills:
   Form and Content, 435
Improving Your Vocabulary: Metaphor, 440
Assignment, 440

AUTHOR INDEX   *443*

SUBJECT INDEX   *444*

PREFACE

Models for Clear Writing, a result of many years of teaching experience, attempts to satisfy three needs: enjoyable learning for the student, effective support for the instructor, and comprehensive direction for the course. To these ends, we have chosen models with as wide a range of topics as possible but still within the students' interests and scope.

Some of the selections are long, some short; some are serious, some are light-hearted; some are simple, some are more complex; some stand alone, some present opposing views.

Models for Clear Writing attempts to improve the students' writing by integrating reading and writing skills. Research clearly indicates that learning how to be a good writer and learning how to be a good reader often require an understanding of the same concepts:

1. Having a clear purpose in mind
2. Understanding various patterns of organization
3. Forming generalizations
4. Separating main ideas from supporting ideas
5. Understanding the function of details
6. Distinguishing between fact and opinion
7. Recognizing the importance of phrases as units of writing
8. Recognizing the importance of key words and word placement
9. Understanding how language affects tone
10. Understanding how tone affects interpretation
11. Understanding how context affects meaning.

In each chapter, the rhetorical pattern and its practical purpose are clearly explained and illustrated, and the professional and student models then show the theory put into practice. The models represent not only a broad spectrum of viewpoints and opinions, but also a wide range of styles and methods of development. After almost every essay, discussion questions follow to stimulate close reading which, in turn, encourages the creative response that leads to worthwhile writing.

Chapter 1 presents writing as a learnable skill and emphasizes a step-by-step procedure for developing clear and effective writing.

Chapters 2 through 8 then deal with a specific mode of development: narration, description, example, process, comparison, division and classification, cause and effect. The final three chapters—on definition, persuasion, and writing about literature—explore various combinations of rhetorical patterns and show how writers may employ more than one method to achieve their purpose. Thus, the student moves in orderly fashion from the simple patterns of organization to the more complex. As students progress systematically from chapter to chapter, the wide-ranging and eclectic selection of models encourages them to expand gradually the range of their own writing and eventually go beyond the confines of the single-mode essay.

ACKNOWLEDGMENTS

We appreciate the generous support we received in writing this book. As always, the college has supported us enthusiastically. Our president, William K. Bauer, was quick to grant our every request, usually even before we made it. We also thank Peggy Williams, our academic vice-president and John Rizzo, our vice-president for business, for their cooperation and support.

Our colleagues in the Community College of Beaver County also deserve our thanks, especially Linda Ciani, our research librarian, whose expertise saved us countless hours. And we thank our secretary, Marsha Spano.

From outside the college, we received perceptive and painstaking criticism from our reviewers.

We also appreciate the generous support of Edie Riker, Jane Bauman, Phil Miller, Carolyn Ruddle, and, for old times sake, Gary Gutchell, all of Prentice Hall.

We thank most warmly our students for contributing their own essays to exemplify our principles: Lola Karnes, Debbi Lucci, Mark Pleshenko, Daniel Samerin, Karen Secrest, Robert Statti, Georgette Walton, Robert A. Wolfe, Patti Wright.

Finally, we thank the authors and publishers who gave permission to reprint the writings used in this book:

p. 32, Roy Popkin, "Night Watch." Reprinted by permission of *The National Observer* © 1964. Dow Jones & Company, Inc. All rights reserved.

p. 35, Bob Lancaster, "Eddie Lovett, Polyhistor." *The Philadephia Inquirer*, April 6, 1975.

p. 41, James Thurber, "University Days," excerpt from *My Life and Hard Times*. New York: Harper & Row, 1933, 1961. Reprinted by permission of Rosemary Thurber.

p. 48, Newman Levy, "A Woman Walks By," from *The Contemporary College Writer: Patterns in Prose*, Second Edition, Harry M. Brown. New York: Van Nostrand, 1977.

p. 50, Tom Hritz, "Cold Water on a Hot Shower," *The Pittsburgh Post Gazette*, September 28, 1987.

p. 53, Georgette Walton, "Very Cold & All Alone."

p. 57, Robert Atwan and William Vesterman, *Effective Writing for the College Curriculum*. New York: McGraw-Hill, 1987. pp. XV, XVI.

p. 65, Henry David Thoreau, excerpt from "Brute Neighbors," *Walden* (New York: Ticknor & Fields, 1854), p. 54–57.

p. 67, Romain Gary, excerpt from *A European Education*. New York: Simon & Schuster, 1960, p. 1. Reprinted with permission.

p. 68, Lawrence Sanders, excerpt from *The Tenth Commandment*. New York: Berkley Book, 1980, p. 349–350. Reprinted by permission of the Putnam Publishing Group.

p. 69, James Clavell, excerpt from *Whirlwind*. Copyright 1986 by James & April Clavell, by permission of Wm. Morrow & Co., Inc.

p. 72, Frederick Lewis Allen "The Scopes Trial," *Only Yesterday*.

p. 76, John Steinbeck, "The Turtle," from *The Grapes of Wrath* by John Steinbeck. Copyright 1939, renewed © 1967 by John Steinbeck. All rights reserved. Reprinted by permission by Viking Penguin, Inc.

p. 79, James Tuite, excerpt from "The Sounds of Manhattan," Copyright © 1966 by the New York Times Company. Reprinted by Permission.

p. 82, Virginia Woolf, "The Death of The Moth," from *Death of a Moth and other Essays*. © 1942 by Harcourt Brace Jovanovitch, Inc. Renewed 1970 by Marjorie T. Parsons. Reprinted by permission of the publisher and Hogarth Press.

p. 86, Daniel Samerin (student), "Shake, Rattle or Roll."

p. 89, Upton Sinclair, excerpt from *The Jungle*. New York: New American Library Signet Classics, 1961, p. 169.

p. 90, Alan Moorehead, excerpt from "A Most Forgiving Ape," *No Room in The Ark*. New York: Harper & Row, 1959, p. 83.

p. 97, Mildred and Edward Hall, excerpt from "The Sounds of Silence," *Playboy* 18 (June, 1971). Reprinted by permission of Playboy.

p. 101, James Thurber, "The Case Against Women," *Let Your Mind Alone*. New York: Harper & Row, 1937, Copyright © 1937 James Thurber, Copyright © 1965 Helen W. Thurber and Rosemary T. Sauers.

p. 105, William Safire, "I Led The Pigeons to the Flag" *New York Times Magazine*, May 27, 1979. Copyright © 1979 by The New York Times Company. Reprinted by permission.

p. 108, Lewis Thomas, "Death in the Open," from *The Lives of a Cell*. Copyright © 1974 by Lewis Thomas. All rights reserved. Reprinted by permission of Viking Penquin, Inc..

p. 109, Newman P. and Genevieve Birk, *Using English Effectively*. Reprinted with permission of MacMillan Publishing Company. Copyright © 1965 by MacMillan Publishing Company.

p. 112, Ellen Goodman, "One Season Fits All," © 1988 The Boston Globe Newspaper Co./Washington Post Writers Group. Reprinted with permission.

p. 115, Deems Taylor, "The Monster," from *Of Men and Music*. New York: Simon & Schuster, 1937.

p. 120, Mark Pleshenko (student), "Honeymoon Hints."

p. 124, John A. Garraty, excerpt from *American Nation* by John A. Garraty, Copyright © 1975, 1979, 1983 by Harper & Row Publishers, Inc. Reprinted by permission of the publisher.

p. 126, Devin Adair, "The Story of the Irish Race."

p. 127, H. W. Fowler, "Love of the Long Word," from *A Dictionary of Modern English Usage* by H. W. Fowler, 2nd ed., revised by Sir Ernest Gowers, 1965. Reprinted by permission of Oxford University Press.

p. 127, Gelette Burgess, excerpt from *Words Words Words*, 2nd ed. by Marvin S. Zuckerman, Encino, Calif.: Glencoe Publishing Co., Inc., 1980, p. 166–172.

p. 136, S. J. Perelman, excerpt from *The Most of S. J. Perelman.* Copyright © 1930, 1958 by S. J. Perelman. Renewed 1986 by Adam and Abbey Perelman. Reprinted by permission of Simon & Schuster, Inc.

p. 138, S.I. Hayakawa, excerpt from "How Dictionaries Are Made," *Language in Thought and Action*, 4th ed., Copyright 1978 by Harcourt Brace Jovanovich, Inc. Reprinted by permission of the publisher and George Allen and Unwin, Ltd.

p. 141, Paul Roberts, "How to Say Nothing in 500 Words," *Understanding English*, New York: Harper & Row, 1958.

p. 154, Alexander Petrunkevitch, "The Spider and the Wasp," *Scientific American*, August 1952. Scientific American, Inc.

p. 161, Malcolm X with Alex Haley, "Coming to an Awareness of Language," *The Autobiography of Malcolm X*, New York: Random House, Inc., 1966 pp. 170–173. Copyright © 1964 by Alex Haley and Malcolm X; © 1965 by Alex Haley & Betty Schabazz. Reprinted by permission of Random House, Inc. and Hutchinson Publishing Group.

p. 164, Stephen Leacock, "How to Live to be 200," *Literary Lapses*. Permission granted by the Ayer Company, successors to Arno Press.

p. 167, Ernest Hemingway, "When You Camp Out—Do it Right," *The Toronto Star*. June 26, 1920.

p. 171, Robertson Davies, "How to Design a Haunted House," *One Half of Robertson Davies*, New York: Viking, 1978. By permission of Robertson Davies.

p. 175, 255, Robert Pirsig, excerpt from *Zen and The Art of Motorcycle Maintenance*, pp. 107–111. Copyright © 1974 by Robert M. Pirsig. Reprinted by permission of Wm. Morrow & Co. and The Bodley Head.

p. 189, Thomas Huxley, excerpt from "Liberal Education," an address given in 1868.

p. 190, W.B. Yeats, excerpt from *Collected Poems*. Copyright 1912 by Macmillan Publishing Co.; renewed 1940 by Bertha Georgia Yeats. Reprinted by permission of Macmillan Publishing Co., Macmillan London Limited, and Michael Yeats.

p. 191, Paul B. Horton and Chester L. Hunt, "Created Equal?" *Sociology*, 3rd ed., New York: McGraw-Hill, 1972, pp. 249–250. Copyright © 1972. Reprinted by permission.

p. 194, Bruce Catton, "Grant and Lee: A Study in Contrasts," in *The American Story* Earl Schenck Miers, ed. Copyright © Broadcast Music, Inc. Reprinted by permission.

p. 199, David and Vera Mace, excerpt from *Marriage East and West* by David and Vera Mace. Copyright © 1959, 1960 by David and Vera Mace. Reprinted by permission of Doubleday, a division of Bantam, Doubleday, Dell Publishing Group, Inc.

p. 202, Melvin Maddocks, "In Praise of Reticence," Copyright 1988 by *Time Inc.* All Rights Reserved. Reprinted by permission from Time.

p. 206, Lewis Thomas, "The Deacon's Masterpiece," *The Medusa and the Snail*, London: Penguin Books, 1981, pp. 109–114. Copyright 1974, 1979 by Lewis Thomas. Originally published in *The New England Journal of Medicine*. Reprinted by permission of Viking Penguin, Inc. and Penguin Books, Ltd.

p. 212, Patti Wright (student), "From Courtship to Dating."

p. 214, Hans Kung, excerpt from *Does God Exist?* Translation Copyright © 1978, 1979, 1980 by Doubleday, a division of Bantam Doubleday, Dell Publishing Group, Inc. Reprinted by permission of the publisher.

p. 220, Otto L. Bettmann, excerpt from *The Good Old Days—They Were Terrible*. Copyright © 1974 by Otto Bettmann. Reprinted by permission of Random House, Inc.

p. 221, A.P. Features, "Problem Student Gets Last Laugh," by permission of The Associated Press.

p. 228, George Gibson, "Effective Legal Writing and Speaking," from *Business Lawyer* (1980). Copyright © 1980 by The American Bar Association and its Section of Corporation, Banking & Business Law.

p. 233, Judith Viorst, "Friends, Good Friends—and Such Good Friends," Copyright © 1977 by Judith Viorst. Originally appeared in *Redbook*.

p. 238, Isaac Asimov, "What Do You Call a Platypus?" *National Wildlife Magazine*, March/April 1972. Reprinted with permission of Dr. Isaac Asimov.

p. 241, Paul Gallico, "Fans," Copyright 1931. Condé Nast Publications. Reprinted by permission of Harold Ober Associates.

p. 355, Robert McCrum, William Cran, and Robert MacNeil, "An English Speaking World," *The Story of English*, New York: Viking, 1986.

p. 358, Arthur Ashe, "An Open Letter to Black Parents: Send Your Children to the Libraries," Copyright © 1977 by the New York Times Company. Reprinted by permission.

p. 361, H. L. Mencken, "Criminology," from *Prejudices: Sixth Series*. Copyright 1927 by Alfred A. Knopf, Inc. and renewed 1955 by H. L. Mencken.

p. 365, Ossie Davis, "The English Language is My Enemy." Copyright by the Association for the Study of Afro-American Life and History.

p. 366, Muriel R. Schulz, "Is the English Language Anyone's Enemy?" *ETC: A Review of General Semantics,"* vol. 32, no. 2. Reprinted by permission of the International Society for General Semantics.

p. 373, Robert A. Wolfe, "Escape."

p. 377, Hyman G. Rickover, "Rescue Foundering Education," *The New York Times,* January 30, 1983, p. E 11. Copyright © 1983 by the New York Times Company. Reprinted by permission.

p. 378, "Courage and Confidence" excerpt from *The Philadelphia Record,* April 13, 1945.

p. 379, William O. Douglas, excerpt from *The Court Years: The Autobiography of William O. Douglas,* New York: Random House, Inc., 1981, p. 339. Copyright © 1981 by Random House, Inc.

p. 379, James Morris, *The Preachers,* New York: St. Martin's Press, Inc., 1973, pp. 3, 4. Copyright © 1973 by James Morris.

p. 393, Logan Pearsall Smith, excerpt from *All Trivia* (N.Y.: Doubleday Page, 1912, 1934).

p. 395, Mark Twain, excerpt from "The War Prayer."

p. 405, Jack Matthews, "The Contest," excerpt from *Archetypal Themes In the Modern Story* (N.Y.: St. Martins Press, 1973) 5, 6.

p. 407, William Carlos Williams, "The Use of Force," from *The Doctor Stories.* Copyright 1938 by William Carlos Williams. Reprinted by permission of New Directions Publishing Corporation.

p. 411, R. F. Dietrich, "The Use of Force," Studies in Short Fiction, vol. 3, no. 4, Summer, 1966, p. 446-50. Revised for Dietrich's Instructor's Manual for *The Realities of Literature,* Waltham, Mass.: Xerox College Publishing Co., 1971, p. 59-65.

p. 417, Mark Twain "Fenimore Cooper's Literary Offenses," *The Portable Mark Twain* New York: Penguin, 1977, 541-557.

p. 423, John Ciardi "How Does a Poem Mean," (Boston: Houghton-Miflin, 1959) 671-674. Copyright © 1959 by Houghton-Mifflin Co. Used by permission.

p. 428, Cleanth Brooks and Robert Penn Warren, "The Organic Nature of Poetry," *Understanding Poetry*, 3rd ed., 16-18. Copyright © 1938, 1950, 1960 by Holt Rinehart & Winston, Inc. Reprinted by permission of Holt Rinehart and Winston, CBS College Publishing.

p. 432, Robert Stratti, "The Maturing of Huckleberry Finn."

p. 437, Karen Secrest, "The Wonderful World of Nils."

1

Understanding Writing as a Process

Good writing is not produced in a vacuum; it comes from thought. It is only after thinking, questioning, reflecting, and organizing that writing can take place. Writing is a process—a gradual progressive process—that begins with a search and ends with a discovery. No one understood this better than Michel Montaigne, who wrote the world's first essays; he worked on his first collection of essays for over eight years before he had them printed in 1580. You probably won't have quite so much time to spend on your essays, but you do have to be willing to resist the temptation to rush the process—skipping the research and settling for the first random idea that pops into your head—just to complete an assignment. The writing process will work for you, but only if you appreciate the value of *each* step in the process.

1. Getting Started
2. Choosing a Topic
3. Establishing a Purpose
4. Forming a Thesis Statement

5. Becoming Aware of Your Audience
6. Organizing Your Thoughts
7. Writing Your Paper
8. Choosing Effective Titles
9. Editing and Revising

GETTING STARTED

You do not have to go through the above steps in any particular order. In fact, many times you will start with establishing a purpose, since one of the best reasons for writing is that you want to say something. On the other hand, you might have a particular subject you want to write about; in that case, you would follow the original order. Whichever order you choose, spend time on these two steps. If these are weak, your work will be feeble no matter how much time you spend on the other steps.

CHOOSING A TOPIC

Students often overlook the importance of one of the first steps in the writing process—finding an *interesting* topic. Some students, especially those who have a hard time thinking of something to write about, are often so relieved to find a topic that they don't care how bland that topic might be. They use it anyway just to get their paper written. Unfortunately, the time they think they have saved by abandoning the search for an interesting topic is usually lost in the frustrating process of trying to formulate a decent thesis statement (controlling idea) about a vague, overworked topic. They don't seem to realize that dull topics produce dull thesis statements, and dull thesis statements produce dull papers. The sad thing is that by overlooking the value of this important step in the writing process, these students deprive themselves of the opportunity to experience the real pleasures of the writing process as a whole. They learn nothing, and they miss the joy of discovery. Instead, they just reinforce their negative feelings about writing: apprehension, confusion, frustration, and hostility. If you are one of those people who have a hard time getting started on a writing assignment, take heart. There are plenty of ways to find a good topic, and none of them are particularly difficult or time-consuming. Here are a few suggestions.

Brainstorming

Brainstorming is one of the most effective techniques for generating ideas. Whether you brainstorm by yourself or within a group, you can produce a surprising number of ideas in a short time. When you brainstorm within a group, one person throws out an idea and another responds with the first thought that comes to mind, and that thought generates another response, and so on. You just bounce ideas off each other until you think you have enough. Keep in mind that the ideas are not to be criticized; they don't have to be good. In brainstorming you are after quantity, not quality, and you never know when a trivial idea will inspire a great one.

Brainstorming by Yourself

Brainstorming by yourself involves the same process, but instead of bouncing ideas off others, you generate your own ideas by letting your mind wander from one thought to another. In both cases, it is important to say anything that comes into your head, no matter how crazy it sounds. You will be surprised at how quickly one idea generates another. For example:

marriage	lawsuits
divorce	malpractice
kids	incompetent doctors
child support	Dr. Davis
early	my mother's operation
late	outrageous hospital costs
never	outrageous boy/girlfriends

From a list of twenty-five or thirty ideas, you will be able to spot several interesting topics that could be narrowed down for an essay. Another way that you can brainstorm by yourself is to concentrate on one subject at a time. For example, if you picked a topic such as sports, you would jot down all of the sports-related topics you could think of. In a matter of minutes, you would have plenty of ideas.

Free Writing

Another method that often works quite well is free writing. You just start writing and keep writing for ten minutes. Whatever comes into your head you put down on paper, no matter how incoherent it sounds. You don't have to write in complete sentences, and you don't have to stop to correct grammar or punctuation. You just keep writing. Your aim is to get thoughts down on paper. The following is an example of free writing:

> standing in the unemployment line for two hours yesterday—that snippy little clerk—I'm so sick of being broke—wish I could win the lottery—wonder if Jim got back from Las Vegas yet—what a character he is—but a great friend—how true that old saying is about not knowing who your real friends are until you're down and out—couldn't have gotten along without him since I lost my job—it's cold in this blasted apartment—that landlord doesn't care if my kids get sick—he doesn't have to pay the doctor bills—poor Matthew—had to miss a whole week of school—how he loves school and Miss Mitch is such a good teacher—too bad nobody notices the good teachers—just the poor ones.

Most free writings, such as the one above, contain a number of unrelated ideas, but you can also do free writings that focus on only one idea. Both types can produce good topics for writing. Here is an example of free writing on one topic.

> standing in the unemployment line for two hours yesterday—it's disgusting—they treat you like you're some sort of bum—like I never worked and paid taxes—I helped pay the salaries of the people in that employment office for years—that snippy little clerk, couldn't have been more than 20, looked at me like I shouldn't have been taking up her time! Her time! Why do we have to take a whole morning or afternoon to file a simple form—incompetent creeps, the whole lot of them—I hope I get a job soon—I'd rather scrub floors than go through the humiliation of that dismal unemployment office.

Keeping a Journal

Some students are never at a loss for ideas, often because at the end of each day they record a few personal observations prompted by something that they saw or heard or experienced that day. If you decide to keep a journal, consider carrying a notebook with you throughout the day; you will then be able to record your impressions as soon as they occur to you. You don't have to wait for a traumatic event or an earth-shaking comment. As soon as a thought strikes you, write it down. The world can be fascinating if you just use your powers of observation.

Using the Library

When you are trying to think of a good topic for a writing assignment, don't forget libraries. A few minutes of browsing can produce any number of ideas. Book titles are always a good source of ideas, and titles of magazine articles can also provide food for thought. Consider the following examples:

Midwives: Portrait of a Timeless Profession
The First Deadly Sin
Does a Feminist Have the Right to Sing the Blues?
The Winds of War
Driven to Perfection
I Never Promised You a Rose Garden
The Passion to Provide
The Hero with a Thousand Faces
Custer Died for Your Sins
Voyage Around My Father

Do these titles interest you enough so that you would want to read the articles?

ESTABLISHING A PURPOSE

Once you have chosen a topic, you must think about why you want to write about that topic. Do you want to entertain your readers, to explain something to them, to persuade them to accept your viewpoint on an issue? Or do you have a combination of purposes— to both enlighten your readers and entertain them at the same time? Establishing a purpose gives you a sense of direction and helps you choose an appropriate method of development for your essay. For example, if your topic is public speaking, you might decide to entertain your reader by *classifying* the different types of orators in your speech class. You might, on the other hand, have a different purpose in mind. For example, if you want to help your readers overcome the fear of public speaking, you might choose to write a narrative essay relating an experience that taught you that an audience is nothing to be afraid of, or you might write a paper explaining the process of overcoming the fear of public speaking. If your topic is juvenile delinquency, you might want to find out why so many of America's youth fall into a life of crime. After going to the library and investigating the topic, you might then decide to write a *cause/effect* essay on juvenile crime in your state. If your topic is television, you might start thinking about how much you have learned from the programs on the public television station and decide that you want to convince your reader that television is not all bad. You would then be writing a *persuasive* essay. By establishing a clear purpose, then, you have taken a giant step in determining the focus of your paper. The next logical step is forming a specific thesis statement.

FORMING A THESIS STATEMENT

In addition to helping you determine what method of development to use, establishing a purpose also helps you arrive at a clear controlling idea for your essay. For instance, if the purpose is to entertain your readers by classifying the different types of orators in your speech class, it would not be difficult to come up with a thesis statement, once you decided how to label the categories. Your thesis statement might read something like this.

> Every time a student in my speech class approaches the podium, I wonder which type of orator I'm going to observe: Fearful Frieda, Patronizing Preacher, or Rigid Researcher.

By establishing a purpose, you are actually forming an attitude toward your topic, and that is the key to writing a good thesis statement. Asking yourself certain questions will help you narrow down your topic and form an attitude: "How do I feel about the topic?" "What do I want to say about the topic?" In other words,

Topic + Attitude = Controlling Idea
Controlling Idea = Thesis Statement

For example:

> Topic—public speaking
> Narrowed Topic—fear of public speaking
> Attitude—no need to fear public speaking
> Thesis Statement—I dreaded the last day of speech class, but what happened during my impromptu speech taught me an invaluable lesson: I will never again let an audience intimidate me.

A thesis statement, then, is just a clearly worded expression of your subject and attitude.

BECOMING AWARE OF YOUR AUDIENCE

No matter what your purpose is, it will be controlled, at least in part, by the audience for whom it is intended. No one would write the same for a kindergarten class and for a graduate school seminar. The obvious differences in age, education, and interests between these two audiences would require changes in tone, in organizational strategies, and in vocabulary level. Similarly, an essay directed at a specific audience, one that has already taken a definite stand on the issue you're discussing, should not be constructed in the same way as one directed toward a general, uncommitted audience. Different audiences respond to different persuasive techniques. In short, the better you know your audience, the more effective your writing will be. It is foolish to decide what kind of supporting details you're going to use in the body of your essay or how you're going to arrange them before you know exactly who your readers are.

Asking yourself specific questions such as the following should help you become aware of your audience:

1. Am I addressing a general audience or a specific audience?
2. What is the educational background of my readers?
3. Do they have any specific needs?
4. Do they have any specific interests?
5. Do they fall into any categories which might affect their perspective?
   a. Are they all engaged in a similar occupation?
   b. Have they all shared a similar experience?
6. Do they have any specific viewpoints about the topic I'm discussing?
7. How might their age, sex, and nationality affect their responses to my argument or to the way I have worded my argument?
8. Am I talking down to my audience, or have I maintained a respectful tone toward my readers throughout my essay?

ORGANIZING YOUR THOUGHTS

Your reader has a right to expect that you arrange your ideas according to some sensible pattern of organization, as effective writing normally is. Any writer, of course, is free to disregard traditional forms, but creating your own form may prove to be a monumental task, and you run the risk of leaving the reader confused altogether. Structure, then, is not an enemy; if fact, it can save you a great deal of groping and frustration, once you recognize that *form provides the means for carrying out your purpose.*

The most common overall form of the essay (like that of the paragraph) is the three-part structure of *introduction, body,* and *conclusion.*

Introduction

In the essay, the introduction is usually just a short lead-in to the thesis statement; the aim is to seize the reader's attention and direct it toward the subject of the essay and some specific attitude toward that subject.

The introductory paragraph—or paragraphs—usually *ends* with the thesis statement. A position almost as popular for the thesis statement is the first sentence of the body section. The thesis statement clearly identifies the subject of the essay and the writer's tone or attitude. Thus, it is the most important sentence of the essay, for it limits and controls the development of the entire essay.

Body

The body is the largest section of the essay, for it must provide the detailed support, the proof of your thesis statement. Everything in the body of the essay should relate, directly or indirectly, to the controlling idea expressed in the thesis statement, and there should be no unanswered questions or loose ends.

Conclusion

The conclusion of an essay functions much like its counterpart, the concluding sentence in the single paragraph. Like the concluding sentence, the concluding paragraph, though it may be brief, must leave no doubt that your discussion is ended; you don't raise some new issue or venture into some other area of discussion. Your conclusion should fulfill your readers' expectations and leave them satisfied that you have said what your thesis statement promised to say.

Outlining

One of the best ways to organize your thoughts is to make an outline before you start writing. The more detailed your outline, the more likely you are to end up with a unified, coherent essay; but even a rough outline is better than nothing. If you just start writing without any sense of where you are going, you will probably just create problems for yourself later. Through the process of outlining, you can eliminate serious problems such as inadequate development, imbalance, irrelevancies, or incorrect order that might otherwise appear in your first draft.

Once you have your controlling idea, you can start thinking about how to organize your paper: "How am I going to develop my thesis? What major supporting points (subtopics) am I going to use? How am I going to develop each subtopic?" For example, suppose that after investigating the effects on children of violence in TV and film, you arrive at the following thesis statement.

The amount of violence that American children have been exposed to, both on television and at the movies, has produced some damaging results.

Your rough outline might look something like this.

   I. Introduction
  II. Body
     A. Examples of violence on television and in films
     B. Cases of children imitating TV violence
     C. Cases of children imitating film violence
III. Conclusion

Once you have a basic outline, you can then work on a more specific outline of the body of your essay. Here is how one student organized her evidence on the same topic.

STUDENT EXAMPLE

   I. Introduction
     A. Definition of violence
     B. Statistics documenting problem
     C. Thesis statement
  II. Body
     A. Examples of violent scenes from television shows and movies
       1. Television
         a. Cartoon shows
         b. Weekly prime-time dramas
         c. Movies made for television
       2. Movies
         a. Serious dramas
         b. Cheap thrillers
         c. Comedies

B. Cases of children imitating violent scenes from television
    a. Superman cartoon
    b. Lizzie Borden TV movie
    c. Miami Vice
C. Cases of children imitating violent scenes from movies
    a. "Aliens"
    b. "Predator"
    c. "The Faces of Death"
III. Conclusion
  A. Summary
  B. Warning

Patti Wright (student)

WRITING YOUR PAPER

After you have decided on your controlling idea and written a clear thesis statement, you must decide on your organization.

1. How to introduce your topic
2. How to develop the body
3. How to conclude your paper
4. How to think of a good title

Introduction

Even after you have chosen a topic, your subject, and decided what you are going to say about the subject, your attitude, and tentatively phrased it in a thesis statement, the controlling idea, you still have to get started. In theory, that's easy. The introduction should attract your readers, lead them to the thesis statement—in short, lure them into reading the essay. But, of course, being interesting (not to mention exciting) does not come easily. There are, however, dozens of ways to introduce your essay. Here are a few traditional techniques.

Narrative

A brief, relevant anecdote or narrative that dramatizes your thesis gets attention and usually keeps it. Suppose, for instance, you are interested in becoming an environmentalist, in fact, a specialist in the protection of endangered species, and you want to write about that. You might begin with something like the following narrative:

Ever since they'd moved to the beach, Anne and her four-year-old son Charlie took an early morning walk, looking at the tiny mollusks burying themselves in the wet sand, at the sand pipers running at the very edge of the water, and, one lucky day, spotting a great sea turtle lumbering back into the water after laying her eggs. Now they had a special destination: under a jutting rock in a little cove they'd discovered a strange sea creature living in a large, convoluted, pink-streaked shell. Anne and Charlie greeted him every morning; Charlie sometimes brought him a piece of bacon which he grabbed with his translucent claws. But one morning as they approached his cove, they saw a large woman with a stick standing over it.

"Please don't", Anne shouted.

The woman waited 'til Anne and Charlie ran up.

"The ugly thing might have bit somebody," the woman said. The little waves rolled the lifeless shell back and forth.

You could then move to a thesis statement, saying ignorance and fear spur people to kill innocent creatures that should peacefully share the world with them.

Description or Setting

To describe where something takes place—its setting—is another good way to attract your reader's attention because most people have a lively sense of place and like to have it satisfied. Setting is especially valuable as an introduction to an essay developed by narration because when you tell a story, it is usually rooted in a place.

Suppose, for example, you were going to write an essay about the summer you spent on a farm, when you became convinced that you wanted to make a career of farming. You might want to describe the farm of that summer.

The two-lane, macadam road had for several miles followed the meanders of the small, brown river. Then, unexpectedly, an unpaved lane angled off to the right. Straight and steep it climbed the hill, a row of Indian Toby trees on each side of it. Beyond the trees, three buildings leaned slightly to the left. Neither the two sheds nor the barn had ever known a coat of paint; the wood had weathered to warm brown, lustrous where the sun shone on it. Over a half door, two elderly buckskin ponies gently gazed. At the top of the hill, the farmhouse, as innocent of paint as the barn and sheds, looked like a child's drawing of a house, tall and narrow. I grinned as I peered at it. But on this tumbledown farm, I found such serenity and satisfaction that I determined to be a farmer forever.

Then you go on to tell the story of your rural summer.

Statistics

Since most people are convinced by statistics, introducing your thesis statement by statistical evidence is usually provocative, especially if those figures are dramatic or controversial.

> Although the associate's degree is the Johnny-come-lately of academic achievement, it takes second place to no other college degree. During the decade of the seventies, over three and a half million students earned the associate's degree, an overall increase of 59.8 percent over the sixties. Students earning the bachelor's degree increased by only 10 percent.

You then go on to your thesis statement about the increasing importance of two-year colleges in American education.

Facts

Facts other than statistics can be effective in presenting background—those things your reader must know to understand your specific thesis. And facts can be used as vivid examples to lead to your thesis. Suppose, as a major in computer science, you wish to show how important the computer is in retrieving the ever-growing store of information. You might begin with facts that highlight this growth.

> About the time of the American Revolution, Dr. Samuel Johnson remarked that all the knowledge of the world could be contained in a thousand volumes; today several great university libraries have more than a thousand volumes about Dr. Johnson.

Then you go on to explain the importance of the computer in compiling and organizing vast amounts of data.

Quotations

A pertinent quotation that leads to your thesis statement is almost always successful because you have the help of another writer whose ideas and style already have authority.

You might decide to write on the psychological factors that cause Joe and Jane to fall in love. Your reading in psychology suggests that the real reason is proximity, but you know there is a romantic idea that love is an instantaneous recognition of soul mates "across a crowded room." You'll have to get this idea out of the way before you present your own, so you might begin with the quotation: "Who ever loved who loved not at first sight?"

Then you go on to explain that almost everybody did—except in romances. Or if you were writing about protecting endangered species, as discussed earlier, you might use Herman Melville's statement, "The most dangerous predator in the world is the white man."

Dispensing with the Opposition

If your thesis is controversial, you might begin by summing up the opposing arguments. Your thesis statement, then, would point out a fault or faults in your opponent's argument and go on to affirm your own point of view.

Contemporary Events

Because contemporary events concern, and perhaps trouble, most adults, referring to them is a fine introduction. You relate your specific thesis to a broader issue that already commands interest. If the issue is economic policy, for instance, anything worthwhile you have to say will gain attention because all your readers have something to say, too.

Justification

When you show the reader you are qualified to write on your subject—through your education, your interest, or your experience—you are employing justification. For example:

> Since I was a kid in junior high school, I've been a movie buff. In high school I got more serious about it; I was the only kid I knew who cared about who directed a movie. In college, I learned the joys of film festivals with critical analyses by academic critics. I also found the library had a sizable collection of serious movie criticism, which I devoured. I've never outgrown my delight in movies; I'm there for every good movie.

Then you can present your thesis statement—a firm opinion expressing your approval or disapproval of a movie or a movie topic.

Direct Statement

The most obvious, but often strongest, introduction is the direct statement of the idea you are going to support. It is strong because it gets to the point immediately; it does not try to lure the reader but assumes that the interest is intrinsic in the idea. For example, in another approach to the psychological basis of love, you might start out directly by saying

The romantics, as usual, are wrong about love; people don't fall in love, they grow into love.

The "Why Write" Approach

Perhaps the most persuasive introduction of all is the one that emphasizes the importance of the subject, the necessity of writing about it.

No household in America is not threatened by . . ., No member of the household is not endangered by . . . .

If you can make your threat, your remedy, your significance loom large, the "why write" approach is very successful.

Body

If you have enough details in the body of your essay, and they are arranged in a unified, coherent fashion, the value of your thesis statement should become clear to your reader.

Unity

The principal unifying device in your essay is the thesis statement since it states the controlling idea to which everything else must relate. Every sentence in your essay must support your thesis. Once you lose a reader with an irrelevant comment, you may never get him or her back. You have to make sure, therefore, that your thesis is sufficiently limited so that it can be adequately developed within the scope of an essay. The topic sentence of each body paragraph should clearly support the thesis statement and act like subtopics for it. Also, make sure that the sentences in each body paragraph refer to the right subtopic. The individual paragraphs themselves must be unified if your essay as a whole is to be unified.

Coherence

More than anything else, coherence is the result of an orderly plan. Successful writers don't flit from one thing to another; they provide an orderly progression of thought from *A* to *B* to *C*. There is purposeful movement from beginning to middle to end, and the logical connection between the parts is made clear to the reader. If you examine a well-written essay, you will find that it is usually easy to construct an outline clearly showing the logical relationship between one part and another. Using an outline can help you make your essay coherent, complete, and free from redundancies and irrelevancies.

The effective writer provides transitions that make it as easy as possible for the reader to follow the progression from one point to another.

Adequate Development

An essay is adequately developed when you have provided enough evidence to get the reader to accept your thesis. No matter how relevant your details are or how effectively they are arranged, if you don't have enough of them to prove your point, they all become meaningless. You can't measure adequate development in terms of a given number of words or sentences, but you can train yourself to see what the body of the essay needs in order to clarify the controlling idea. Look at the topic sentence in each body paragraph, and see if you have presented enough details to develop that topic sentence and answer any questions the reader might have. A well-developed essay will provide readers with a sense of wholeness and completeness and lead them naturally into the concluding paragraph.

Conclusion

Although a single sentence may sometimes suffice in concluding a brief essay, you usually need at least a short paragraph to tie up the loose ends and bring your essay to a conclusion. There are many effective methods of concluding an essay, but here are a few of the more common ones.

Summary

The summary highlights the main points of your essay and restates your controlling ideas. To avoid being boring and repetitious, you need to restate your points in fresh, vivid language.

The Clincher

The clincher adds a final dramatic example to drive home the main idea expressed in your thesis statement. The example needs to be one that will arrest your reader's attention and dramatize the main point of the essay.

The Challenge

Especially in an essay that makes a strong effort to persuade your reader, an effective method of concluding is to issue a challenge to your reader to take the steps necessary to solve the problem.

The Anecdote

Quite often, a little story that dramatizes your thesis can provide a very effective conclusion. In concluding an essay on the power of habit, for example, you might tell a little story about two elderly sisters, living in an old mansion, who habitually refused to discard anything, until at last, aged and enfeebled, they became trapped in their own heaps of refuse.

The Final Quotation

A carefully chosen quotation may provide a brief but fitting conclusion to your essay. For instance, an essay emphasizing the lasting value of education might conclude with the following quotation:

If your plan is for a year, plant rice:
If your plan is for ten years, plant a tree;
If your plan is for a hundred years, educate a man.

    or

Give me a fish, and I eat for a day;
teach me to fish, and I eat for a lifetime.

The Closing Metaphor

We might emphasize the quickness of the downfall of a dictator like Marcos of the Philippines or the Shah of Iran by ending the essay with the metaphor originally describing Tennyson's eagle.

He watches from his mountain walls,
And like a thunderbolt he falls.

Remember, your conclusion is important because it is the last thing you leave in the reader's mind.

CHOOSING EFFECTIVE TITLES

When you choose to write your title is up to you; many writers wait until they finish the last draft. This may be wise, since a final draft can be substantially different from a first rough draft.

But there is a danger in this practice. A title is more than a last-minute detail. Spend some time thinking about your title so that you can pique your readers' interest while telling them something specific about the content of the paper.

If you want to write effective titles, try to follow these guidelines.

1. Do more than state your topic.
2. Make sure that your title is informative. Give the reader some hint of your controlling idea. (*Why Johnny Can't Read*)
3. Make sure that you seize the reader's attention. Use a catchy title. Think of some interesting play on words (*Alice in Blunderland*) or use alliteration, two or more words beginning with the same sound, to catch the reader's attention (*Fit or Fat?*)
4. Be honest with your readers. Don't mislead them with your title just for the sake of winning their attention. An eye-catching headline that has little or nothing to do with what it introduces is simply a cheap journalistic trick.
5. Keep your title short. A brief, concise, easy-to-remember title is much more effective than a complete sentence.

EDITING AND REVISING

Once you have a completed first draft, you are ready for the last and very important step of rewriting. Rewriting breaks down into three parts: revising, editing, and proofreading. These steps are increasingly detailed.

There is no single, rigid formula you must follow in revising your paper, but you should set up some systematic procedure aimed at eliminating general weaknesses in structure and content, eliminating specific errors in wording and punctuation, and improving the overall readability of your essay. Asking yourself a series of questions is often the most effective way of revising, editing, and proofreading your paper. Below is one set of guidelines that might work for you. As you look at these guidelines, you will realize that some of them are unfamiliar to you. You need not worry about this because the purpose of this book is to explain such things; you are not expected to know all of them until you have completed the book. However, if you follow the guidelines that you do know and those you are learning week by week, your essays will improve.

Content

1. Do I have an effective title? Is it clever and informative?
2. Do I have an interesting introduction? Does it seize the reader's attention and provide a smooth lead-in to my controlling idea—my thesis statement?
3. Do I have a clearly stated thesis? Is it specific enough for the scope of my essay?
4. Do I have enough details to prove my point?
5. Do I have an effective conclusion? Does it leave the reader's mind focused on the controlling idea and provide a sense of completeness?
6. Have I followed sound, logical reasoning? Have I made any sweeping generalizations or invalid assumptions or other errors in judgment?
7. Is the tone of my essay consistent from beginning to end?
8. Have I omitted any important points or included any irrelevant details?
9. Does my essay say what I want it to say? Have I made my point?

Structure and Diction

1. Do I have a clear beginning, middle, and end?
2. Is my essay clear? Have I chosen the most effective method of development to illustrate my main idea?
3. Is my essay balanced? Is the introduction too long? Does each body paragraph lead logically to the next?
4. Do I have smooth transitions between paragraphs?
5. Do I have clearly stated subtopics at the beginning of each body paragraph? Is each body paragraph unified and coherent?
6. Have I arranged my details in a logical, effective order? Have I defined a concept before I've discussed it? Have I placed my most important point last?

Sentences

1. Do I have enough sentence variety to keep the reader interested?
2. Do I maintain a consistent point of view from one sentence to the next? Do I make any unnecessary shifts in tense? Do I shift from active to passive voice, from singular pronoun to plural pronoun, from third person to second person, and so on?
3. Have I used vivid, image-making language?
4. Do I have adequate transitions between sentences? Is each sentence connected clearly to the next?
5. Do any of my sentences contain errors in subject-verb agreement or pronoun-antecedent agreement?
6. Have I effectively positioned the ideas within my sentences? Are secondary ideas subordinated to main ideas? Are important ideas placed at the end of sentences or are they buried in the middle?
7. Have I used parallel wording to present a series of coordinate words, phrases, or clauses?
8. Have I clearly placed my modifiers next to the words they modify?
9. Have I made any incomplete, ambiguous, or illogical comparisons?
10. Does my essay read smoothly or do some of my paragraphs contain awkward sentence structure?

Words

1. Are my subjects, verbs, and modifiers clear and specific?
2. Are my verbs vague and boring or explicit and expressive?
3. Have I used an adjective where I should have used an adverb?
4. Have I used any clichés?
5. Did I include any slang expressions or glaring errors?
6. Does my essay contain any needless words? Have I used three or four words to indirectly express something that I could have directly stated in one well-chosen word?
7. Have I shown the reader that I know when to use general words and when to use specific words?
8. Have I shown the reader that I know when to use abstract words and when to use concrete words?
9. Have I considered both the denotative and connotative meaning of my words? (*Denotation*—literal meaning; *connotation*—implied meaning)
10. In general, have I used the right word in the right place?

Mechanics

1. Have I used punctuation to guide my reader from my introduction to my conclusion?
    a. Do I have any sentences separated with a comma instead of a stronger mark of punctuation?
    b. Have I placed commas indiscriminately throughout my essay?
    c. Have I checked every comma, semicolon, colon, and dash to see if I've used them correctly?
    d. Have I used quotation marks to give authors credit for their written or spoken words? Have I placed titles of magazine articles in quotation marks and underlined titles of books and newspapers?
2. Have I checked *carefully* for misspelled words?
    a. Have I taken any shortcuts in spelling, such as *thru* and *nite?*
    b. Have I misspelled look-alike or sound-alike words, such as *accept/except, affect/effect?*
    c. Have I checked a dictionary for the spelling of any word that I am the least bit unsure of?

EDITING

After you have revised your paper, you are ready to edit it— ideally after you have let some time pass. Now you are concentrating on the correlation between your writing and the expectations of your audience. Is the content going to be valuable to your readers? Or entertaining? Is the level of information suitable for your readers? Is your vocabulary appropriate for your subject and for your readers? Is your attitude consistent?

When you act as your own editor, you try to be as objective as possible about the suitability of your writing for your audience. You are evaluating your content, your tone, your taste, and your style.

PROOFREADING

Probably the last thing you will do before you turn your paper in is to proofread it. Remember that proofreading does not mean rewriting or editing but correcting mechanical errors in the presentation of your paper.

Check with your instructor to find his preference for proofreading. Some instructors will accept no proofreading corrections on papers; some will accept a few corrections if they are carefully done; some are willing to accept a sizable number. Confer with your instructor to find his preference. The most common changes made by proofreading are the following:

Delete—Take out unnecessary word—I want ~~want~~ to make this point.

Transpose—change position of two letters—tranpose

Insert—add a word or letter—I ^{want} to make a point

Spelling—delete ~~incorecte~~ ^{incorrect} spelling, put correct spelling above the deleted word.

Stet—write above an earlier correction to return copy to its original form—I recall his ^{stet} ~~first~~ plan.

Spell out—replace numerals, abbreviations, etc., with complete words—2 miles—Two miles

New Paragraph—place symbol before the first word in the new paragraph. ¶

No New Paragraph—write "no paragraph" at the beginning of paragraph to be combined with the preceding paragraph. no ¶

Punctuation—simply insert needed punctuation or delete unnecessary punctuation. Im going home. I'm going home.

OVERVIEW

Writing is, essentially, a series of choices. If you and twenty-five other students start out with the same general topic, *your* approach to that topic, *your* purpose, *your* thesis statement, *your* introductory techniques, *your* selection of evidence, *your* arrangement of details, *your* concluding thoughts, *your* word choice would differ from each of the twenty-five other papers because of the specific series of choices that you made.

What you regard as important or intriguing or entertaining depends on what you believe, what you need or desire, what you have experienced, and, perhaps most important, what you have read. Sharing other writers' experiences, thinking about their ideas and learning how they make their points can help you make your own writing effective. William Faulkner's advice to aspiring writers was very simple: "Read, read, read."

As you will learn in the subsequent chapters of this book, your writing skills can be affected not only by what you read but by *how* you read. As you examine the selections in the following chapters, think of them not as blueprints to imitate slavishly, but rather as effective writing models that you can learn something from. The authors of each of the readings that follow obviously spent time thinking before they began to write, and that is what you have to keep in mind throughout the writing process. If you want your ideas to have more impact then "dropping a rose petal into the Grand Canyon and waiting for the echo" (Nabokov), then, above all, THINK BEFORE YOU WRITE.

2

Narrating

ORGANIZATION

In Chaucer's *Canterbury Tales*, the rascally Pardoner gives the pilgrims a sample of his preaching with a sermon on "The love of money is the root of all evil." To drive home his theme, the Pardoner uses the tale of the three revelers as an *exemplum*, a story that illustrates a moral lesson. Although the stories in *The Canterbury Tales* were written before 1400—and the tale the Pardoner tells is far older than that—telling a story that illustrates your controlling idea is still one of the most effective ways of getting your point across to your reader.

One of the best sources for an illustrative narrative is your own experience. After all, what you know best is what you have seen, felt, and lived through, and your first-hand experience can provide convincing evidence to back up your opinions or claims. Often the best testimony in the world is that of one who can say, "I was there. I know from experience." Besides, writing from experience seems more real and genuine; even though others may have had similar experiences, no two people respond in the same way or attach the same significance to an incident.

Prewriting

To use your experience effectively, you must sift through your memory of people and events and choose an incident that has affected you, changed you, made you what you are. In other words, you must choose a *significant* incident, one that reveals some truth about you, about someone else, or about life.

Remember, however, that to have something significant to say does not mean that you must report a world-shaking event or present a profound idea. A revelation of your personality can make a delightful essay.

In an entrance examination, a student was given the following writing assignment: write about an experience you have had or imagined. She wrote the following paragraph, under the pressure of time and the tension of examinations, about the commonplace experience of desperation over what to write about. Probably every student has undergone this kind of despair; by recalling her own individual responses to this experience, she has written an amusing paragraph.

> As I sit hunched over this desk, elementary school size, racking my brain for something of interest while my legs fall asleep, I realize that I have never experienced anything. Ah, sure I've seen quite a few things during my short life, even heard some that would make your hair curl, but experienced? No, I can't honestly say I have; at least not in the sense of the word I envision, although my interpretation may be a little more extreme than most. When I hear experience, my mind instantly reverts to thoughts of kisses filled with fireworks and being trapped in an elevator with an escaped Nazi war criminal. The closest I've ever come is being kissed a little breathless and being stuck with my brother in an elevator (but that ended as soon as he let go of the DOOR HOLD button). So, as much as I hate to disappoint anyone, I can't write about an experience I've had until I've had one. If you don't mind waiting, you'll be the first person I'll tell.
>
> Betty A. Calafactor (student)

Not many of us have world-shaking experiences, but we all have our own interesting responses to the experiences that we all share. Choosing a subject and, more importantly, your attitude toward it are very important. You may well begin by examining your beliefs and feelings by asking yourself questions like these.

What do I feel that others do not seem to understand?

What made me feel this way?

Why do I do things that others do not do?

Why don't I do things that others do?

If I am different from other people, what made me that way?

Examine your memories; was there a specific event that altered your direction? Then think about incidents such as the following:

A childhood illness or accident

A move to new surroundings or a return to old ones

An event that revealed something about yourself

An event that changed your mind about some "rule to live by"

An event that changed your attitudes or your actions

Writing Your Thesis Statement

Once you have selected your topic, your next step is to write a clearly worded thesis sentence that presents both your subject (the experience) and your attitude (the significance of the experience). The thesis sentence is made up of these two elements—subject and attitude which form the *controlling idea.* You might start with just the subject and the attitude.

SUBJECT	ATTITUDE
Discovering reading	broadened my understanding
Telling the truth	doesn't always pay
Disobeying a rule	can be disastrous
Fulfilling a dream	can be disappointing
Being laughed at	is no laughing matter

Once you have your controlling idea, you have only to put it into a sentence, making it as interesting to the reader as possible.

> Since my family was then very poor, I was trapped in a miserable apartment in an even more miserable neighborhood with little chance of escape—until I discovered reading.
>
> Having been reared with stories of George Washington and the cherry tree and Honest Abe and his long walk to return a penny, I was convinced of the truth of the old adage "Honesty is the best policy" until I put it into practice at the age of ten.
>
> Although I believe in independence and in "being one's own

man," I learned last year that disobeying a rule, even a rule one doesn't believe in, can be disastrous.

They say "Getting there is half the fun," but sometimes "getting there" is all the fun there's going to be; this I discovered when, after years of saving, I set off to fulfill my life's dream.

It's fun to "poke fun," but being laughed at, I discovered too late, is no laughing matter.

Organizing Your Essay

To organize your essay, you need only remember the one/two/three form: introduction/body/conclusion. In the narrative essay, the retelling of the incident itself will make up the body. You must add an introduction that includes the thesis statement and a conclusion that reaffirms your thesis.

Writing the Introduction

To seize your readers' interest and to make them want to read your essay, your introduction should serve several purposes.

1. It should make clear the subject you are going to write about.
2. It should narrow that subject to a topic that can be discussed in an essay of the length you are planning to write.
3. It should set the tone of the essay; show whether the subject will be treated seriously, humorously, or persuasively.

An introduction to an essay on breaking rules, for example, could take several directions, each causing the reader to think differently about rules. Your introduction could lead the reader to think about the great rule breakers in history and the good they achieved by their actions.

Jesus Christ broke the rules of the Roman Empire. Martin Luther broke the rules of the Roman Catholic Church. Mahatma Gandhi broke the rules of the British Empire. Martin Luther King broke the rules of the segregated South. Heroes all, they broke the rules, and by doing so, brought good to large groups of people. But they paid dearly for breaking the rules.

Perhaps instead, you might want your reader to think of the terrible harm that can come from breaking the rules.

Man needs order, and little can be accomplished without it. A classroom without order becomes a place where no learning can take place. A football game without order would become chaos, and no game would take place. A country without order becomes a battleground, and the nation becomes powerless against its enemies. The basis of order lies in rules.

Or you may want to treat the matter lightly, to entertain your reader.

"Rules were made to be broken," so the old saying goes. "Do it now" said Jerry Rubin as he led the hippie rebellion of the sixties. Even the Declaration of Independence says that sometimes you have to break the rules. Well, I listened and I believed and I did it. But I won't do it again. Today I stop at all stop signs, throw my trash in the container, and don't walk on the grass.

Writing the Body

The body of your essay will consist of one or more paragraphs, each controlled by a topic sentence. The easiest and most logical order in the narrative essay is chronological, or time, order. You tell the story as it happened—first this, then this.

Most people find that it saves a lot of time to outline the essay first. Some people, however, try to avoid outlining; they write the essay and then revise and rewrite until some sort of order appears. This method may work well for some people, but it involves a lot of rewriting. If you do decide to outline first, the process of outlining your narrative is relatively simple. You jot down the major events as they happened, then divide them into logical categories. Each of these categories becomes a paragraph in the body of your essay. If you were writing the essay mentioned earlier on discovering reading, your rough outline might look like this.

1.	Living in a small country town.	the loneliness, the intellectual desert, the alienation
2.	Being assigned a report on *Winesburg, Ohio*	the annoyance at having to read more about a small town
3.	Reading the beginning of the novel	the awareness of the similarity of my life to George Richmond's
4.	Being swept into another world, another time	the recognition that George Richmond's experiences expanded my understanding of my own experiences

Once you have this list and have removed all irrelevant detail, you are ready to write topic sentences for the paragraphs in the body of your essay.

Topic Sentence, Paragraph 1
    A. Life in a small town is deadening.

Topic Sentence, Paragraph 2
    B. When the instructor gave the assignment, I thought it was pointless.

Topic Sentence, Paragraph 3
    C. Because I was so determined to succeed, I forced myself to start reading the novel.

Topic Sentence, Paragraph 4
    D. Suddenly, I wasn't frustrated; I was living in a larger world, expanding my experiences and better understanding them.

Writing the Conclusion

Your conclusion should leave the reader with a feeling of satisfaction, a sense of completeness. The conclusion should reaffirm your purpose in writing the essay.

A conclusion to the essay on reading might be persuasive.

Read! Read! Read! It's the answer to the loneliness; it's a way to survive the boredom; it can be a way out. For me, the step from reading to writing was not an insurmountable one. And I wrote my way out of the small town.

The conclusion might be psychological.

No longer did it matter to me that I had no friends who shared my interests and no activities that satisfied me. All of the boredom disappeared as I steered steamboats down the Mississippi with Twain, tested my courage in war with Crane, solved mysteries with Ellery Queen, and plotted murder with Macbeth. I rose above my environment.

The conclusion might be narrative.

I read everything I could borrow or steal, and it changed me. My language improved. My grades soared. I earned a scholarship and, later, a degree. I got a job, and I moved my mother and me uptown. I should kiss the teacher who assigned me that book report.

EXERCISE

Perhaps the earliest type of literature is the fable, in which animal characters represent types of human beings involved in a simple action to convey a message about human nature. The important element in a fable is not the story itself but the message it communicates. This is equally true of an essay developed by a narrative.

In the following fables, four from antiquity and attributed to Aesop and a modern one by James Thurber, the "morals,"* or thesis statements, have been omitted. For each, supply the moral you think best expresses the writer's purpose in telling the stories. Then, using animals as your characters, write an original fable that illustrates a moral that you believe in.

THE MICE AND THE WEASELS

There was war between the Mice and the Weasels in which the Mice always got the worst of it, numbers of them being killed and eaten by the Weasels. So they called a council of war, in which an old Mouse got up and said, "It's no wonder we are always beaten, for we have no generals to plan our battles and direct our movements in the field." Acting on his advice, they chose the biggest Mice to be their leaders, and these, in order to be distinguished from the rank and file, provided themselves with helmets bearing large plumes of straw. They then led out the Mice to battle, confident of victory; but they were defeated as usual and were soon scampering as fast as they could to their holes. All made their way to safety without difficulty except the leaders, who were so hampered by the badges of their rank that they could not get into their holes and fell easy victims to their pursuers.

MORAL: _____

THE CROW AND THE PITCHER

A thirsty Crow found a Pitcher with some water in it, but so little was there that, try as she might, she could not reach it with her beak, and it seemed as though she would die of thirst within sight of the remedy. At last, she hit upon a clever plan. She began dropping pebbles into

---

*   Since fables are a specific type of literature that includes a moral as the conclusion, *moral* is the correct term to use when discussing fables. With other writing, *moral* is an out-of-date term; preferable to *moral* is *theme* in discussing literary writing and *thesis statement* in expository prose.

the Pitcher, and with each pebble the water rose a little higher until at last it reached the brim, and the knowing bird was enabled to quench her thirst.

MORAL: _____

THE NORTH WIND AND THE SUN

A dispute arose between the North Wind and the Sun, each claiming that he was stronger than the other. At last they agreed to try their powers upon a traveller, to see which could soonest strip him of his cloak. The North Wind had the first try; and, gathering up all his force for the attack, he came whirling furiously down upon the man, and caught up his cloak as though he would wrest it from him by one single effort; but the harder he blew, the more closely the man wrapped it round himself. Then came the turn of the Sun. At first he beamed gently upon the traveller, who soon unclasped his cloak and walked on with it hanging loosely about his shoulders; then he shone forth in his full strength, and the man, before he had gone many steps was glad to throw his cloak right off and complete his journey more lightly clad.

MORAL: _____

THE GNAT AND THE BULL

A gnat alighted on one of the horns of a Bull and remained sitting there for a considerable time. When it had rested sufficiently and was about to fly away, it said to the Bull, "Do you mind if I go now?" the Bull merely raised his eyes and remarked, without interest, "It's all one to me; I didn't notice when you came, and I shan't know when you go away."

MORAL: _____

THE LITTLE GIRL AND THE WOLF

One afternoon a big wolf waited in a dark forest for a little girl to come along carrying a basket of food to her grandmother. Finally, a little girl did come along, and she was carrying a basket of food. "Are you carrying that basket to your grandmother?" asked the wolf. The little girl said yes, she was. So the wolf asked her where her grandmother lived, and the little girl told him, and he disappeared into the wood.

When the little girl opened the door of her grandmother's house, she saw that there was somebody in bed with a nightcap and nightgown on. She had approached no nearer than twenty-five feet from the bed when she saw that it was not her grandmother but the wolf, for even in a nightcap a wolf does not look any more like your grandmother than the Metro-Goldwyn lion looks like Calvin Coolidge. So the little girl took an automatic out of her basket and shot the wolf dead.

MORAL: _____

Night Watch

ROY POPKIN

Like fables, many narrative essays do not make the thesis statement until the end of the essay. In this sentimental little story, the author does not state his thesis until the final paragraph in which he ends his narrative and gives his purpose for telling it.

The story began on a downtown Brooklyn street corner. An elderly man had collapsed while crossing the street, and an ambulance rushed him to Kings County Hospital. There, during his few returns to consciousness, the man repeatedly called for his son.

From a smudged, oft-read letter, an emergency-room nurse learned that the son was a Marine stationed in North Carolina. Apparently, there were no other relatives.

Someone at the hospital called the Red Cross office in Brooklyn, and a request for the boy to rush to Brooklyn was relayed to the Red Cross director of the North Carolina Marine Corps camp. Because time was short—the patient was dying—the Red Cross man and officer set out in a jeep. They located the sought-after young man wading through marshy boondocks on maneuvers. He was rushed to the airport in time to catch the one plane that might enable him to reach his dying father.

It was mid-evening when the young Marine walked into the entrance lobby of Kings County Hospital. A nurse took the tired, anxious serviceman to the bedside.

"Your son is here," she said to the old man. She had to repeat the words several times before the patient's eyes opened. Heavily sedated because of the pain of his heart attack, he dimly saw the young man in the Marine Corps uniform standing outside the oxygen tent. He reached out his hand. The Marine wrapped his toughened fingers around the old man's limp ones, squeezing a message of love and encouragement. The nurse brought a chair, so the Marine could sit alongside the bed.

Nights are long in hospitals, but all through the night the

young Marine sat there in the poorly lighted ward, holding the old man's hand and offering words of hope and strength. Occasionally, the nurse suggested that the Marine move away and rest a while. He refused.

Whenever the nurse came into the ward, the Marine was there, oblivious of her and night noises of the hospital—the clanking of an oxygen tank, the laughter of night-staff members exchanging greetings, the cries and moans and snores of other patients. Now and then she heard him say a few gentle words. The dying man said nothing, only held tightly to his son through most of the night.

Along toward dawn, the patient died. The Marine placed on the bed the lifeless hand he had been holding, and went to tell the nurse. While she did what she had to do, he smoked a cigarette—his first since he got to the hospital.

Finally, she returned to the nurse's station, where he was waiting. She started to offer words of sympathy, but the Marine interrupted her. "Who was that man?" he asked.

"He was your father," she answered, startled.

"No, he wasn't," the Marine replied. "I never saw him before in my life."

"Why didn't you say something when I took you to him?" the nurse asked.

"I knew right off there'd been a mistake, but I also knew he needed his son, and his son just wasn't here. When I realized he was too sick to tell whether or not I was his son, I figured he really needed me. So I stayed."

With that, the Marine turned and left the hospital. Two days later a routine message came in from the North Carolina Marine Corps base informing the Brooklyn Red Cross that the real son was on his way to Brooklyn for his father's funeral. It turned out there had been two Marines with the same name and similar serial numbers in the camp. Someone in the personnel office had pulled out the wrong record.

But the wrong Marine had become the right son at the right time. And he proved, in a uniquely human way, that there are people who care what happens to their fellow man.

How Does the Author Make His Point?

1. What is the effect of saying that the Marine holds the dying man's hand all through the night? What is the emotional impact of stating

that the Marine smoked his first cigarette only after the death of the old man?

2. Why does holding back the thesis sentence until the end enforce the author's controlling idea? What would the reader's response be if the thesis statement came at the beginning of the essay?
3. From what point of view is this narrative told?
4. Do you think the opening paragraph is effective? Could you write a better one?
5. Do you think the author's use of direct dialogue is effective? Would you like to change it or write additional dialogue?

What Do You Think?

1. What is the tone of this essay? Why do you think the author made the young man a Marine?
2. From the relationship established between these two strangers, what is the implied relationship between the dying man and his real son? and between the Marine and his real father? What specific incidents or remarks support your answers?
3. Are the people in the story heroes or villains? Give examples to prove your point. Do you agree with him on this?
4. Have you heard of any similar occurrences where the "wrong" person became the right one?

Eddie Lovett, Polyhistor

BOB LANCASTER

This essay first appeared in a Philadelphia newspaper, a touching human interest story about a unique character in the backwaters of America.

Eddie Lovett is somebody you've almost certainly never heard of. He's a poor black unschooled man who has seldom strayed from the shack he built at the end of a dirt road in the remote backwoods of a rural county in Arkansas.

I looked him up a couple of years ago, when I was working in that area, because someone had told me that "a crazy black man on welfare has gone and built him a library out there in the middle of nowhere." It took me a long time to find his place, zigzagging through the endless piney woods of Bradley County, Arkansas, along a maze of little-used country roads, but finally I spotted a shabby tarpapered house with collard greens and cornstalks in the front yard, and a big corrugated-tin building next to it with a hand-lettered sign on top that said: "Eddie Lovett's Hobby Shop and Hippocrene Library—Eddie Lovett, Polyhistor." Beneath that was a smaller sign with the Latin inscription "Hic Habitat Felicitas"—Here Dwells Happiness.

A couple of adolescent boys were romping in the yard, and when I got out of the car they became silent and staring, unaccustomed to visitors, and, along with the inevitable couple of yapping mongrel farm dogs, they accompanied me to Eddie Lovett's front door, which was in such a state of decay that I thought it might crumble when I knocked on it. Eddie Lovett answered the door dressed in an old nightshirt and wearing a frazzled hairnet over what appeared to be crude homemade curlers in his long hair.

He was not very trustful and, frankly, not very friendly. He said he had work to do that day in his garden and his library, but I made an apppointment to come back at a later date—an appointment which Mr. Lovett figured I wouldn't keep because it was a hundred-mile drive back to my office. The dogs and the kids accompanied me back to my car, and as I drove away I looked back and saw the Polyhistor standing in the rotting doorway—an old and frightful and yet interesting figure. I resolved to come back, after all.

It was a beautiful Sunday afternoon when I returned to the Hippocrene Library in the piney woods. Eddie Lovett greeted me in his Sunday best this time—an overlarge sports jacket with age-worn pants and house slippers—and his long wavy hair was neatly combed, although it still looked astonishingly unusual. He explained the previous chilly reception by saying that I'd barged in on him unexpectedly when he was tired and looked a mess, and that he preferred to meet guests (and so far as I know I was the only one he'd ever had) like a gentleman.

With that, he unlocked the library and took me inside. Along the dark, unadorned walls there were about 2,000 books, which he said he'd bought mostly through book clubs and discount mail-order houses with what was left each month from his Army disability pension and welfare checks. They were a mixed bag— old textbooks, reference books, obscure histories, novels, classics— and virtually all of them had been scribbled with extensive underlinings and copious margin notes, evidence of the decades the Polyhistor had spent burning the midnight oil.

I spent the whole day and much of the night talking to him about his library, about his life and his books. His biography was not an uncommon one for a black growing up in the rural south in the Depression. He was the son of a sharecropper and spent most of his childhood working in the cotton fields, with little opportunity for formal education. Segregated schools for black children in that area were open only three or four motnhs a year, and the kids got to attend them only sporadically, stealing the time, more or less, from their duties in the field. Books (even textbooks) were a rarity in those "schools," but Eddie Lovett's father was a God-fearing man who first taught his children to read the Bible, then demanded that they continue to read it.

Eddie Lovett wanted to be an engineer when he grew up, but he knew that under the circumstances he couldn't. But he did what he could, spending (as a teen-ager) the first money he ever saved to buy by mail a book called *Ropp's Commercial Calculator*, from which he taught himself the rudiments of geometry and engineering.

He was drafted by the Army in 1942 and was allowed to

train as a general service engineer, which demanded that he search the base libraries for technical manuals. But he soon learned that those libraries were a gold mine. One day he picked up a copy of Hitler's *Mein Kampf* and read it through and suddenly realized that the war in which he was involved was being fought over ideas. He realized that Nazism was something that people had to contend with intellectually as well as physically, and he began to realize that it was just one of a whole panoply of ideas concerning which he was abysmally ignorant.

"After that," he told me, "the more I read, the more I learned, and the more I learned the more I understood how much I didn't know. I had an insatiable curiosity to go further, deeper." The lights were turned off early in the barracks during the war, but that didn't deter him. Listen to what he told me:

> The light burned in the latrine all night and I'd go down there at night and set there and read till two in the morning. I'd take a couple hours sleep then and I'd be ready to get up for reveille. I did that for years, years. . . . The first literature that attracted me was English—Shakespeare, Marlowe, Johnson, Jeffries, several others. I never was too fond of French literature. 'Course, it's deep. It's really an education. But I'm fond of French philosophy. Rene Descartes, he was my hero. Then I got on to Edgar Allen Poe. Got to reading one night at bedtime, got to reading "The Raven" and decided to learn it by memory. The boys said, you'll never do that, you're in the wrong place, you can't learn that in the Army. I said, I can learn it as good here in the Army as I could behind the plow. I said, I learned Lincoln's Gettysburg Address while plowing a mule. . . . Mathematics, world history, world geography, English literature, European history—those got to be my areas, and ancient history by all means. I got to reading about those great Carthaginians, that great battle, that 200-year battle between the Romans and the Carthaginians. . . . I got to dearly love reading about all that and the boys said, Lovett, you going to go crazy, and I said, I won't either.

He didn't go crazy, but he did have a lot of subsequent bad luck. After three tours of duty with the Army, he got out and started trying to find steady work to support his wife and family. But he suffered a stroke in Italy during the war, and was thereafter partially disabled by Bell's Palsy and had trouble holding down jobs, although he tried everything from carpentry in San Francisco to assembly line work at an auto plant in Detroit.

He moved back to the Arkansas woods to farm in 1958, and his wife died there a few years later, leaving him to raise their four children; the two oldest attended college on academic scholarships.

So Eddie Lovett raised kids and vegetables, reading Plato and Emerson, *Popular Mechanics* and *Plain Truth* magazine again from behind a plow. It was three years ago that he renovated an old shack near his house and christened it the Hippocrene Library and named himself its Polyhistor, a word of Greek derivation meaning one of encyclopedic knowledge.

All the time he's spent in his library had left its mark on Eddie Lovett. These are the kind of things he said during our long conversation:

> I've read Benjamin Franklin quite a bit and I notice that a lot of his *Poor Richard's Almanac* parallels the *Book of Proverbs*. He says, "Plow deep while the sluggard sleep, you shall have corn to sell and to keep." When I'm in here getting my mental gymnastics, well that's plowing, figuratively speaking. Now I know many people today older than I am, they can't sign their names. Some of them are kin to me. "Plow deep while the sluggards sleep." I sacrificed for everything you see here; that's plowing. Certain things I went without. Sometimes I'd need a pair of pants. I'd just say well I can do without the pants; I don't just have to go to town Saturday; I can wear these ragged pants around here but I can't wear them to town, so therefore I don't have to go to town. I'll just order me something from Roebuck and not have to go to town at all. That's plowing, figuratively speaking.

He got the chance in 1965 to practically apply the wisdom he's gleaned from his books. He desegregated the nearest white elementary school by enrolling his two youngest children there after having coached them carefully for two years on how to handle whatever turbulence or ugliness might develop in that area where school integration was unknown, feared, and reviled. Partly because of the way Eddie Lovett went about it—that is, quietly, without publicity or outside help, by preparing his own children for every exigency and by privately and eloquently convincing other parents and white leaders that his sole interest was giving his kids the educational opportunities he never got himself—there was no turbulence and no ugliness. It was one of the beautiful integration stories in the South that you never heard about, and it wasn't the only one.

After talking to Eddie Lovett, I made the long drive back to Little Rock and wrote a couple of articles about him for the *Arkansas*

Gazette. Among the readers of those articles was Charles Kuralt, who does feature stories for CBS News. Kuralt made the trip to the piney woods of Bradely County too, and the piece he did on Eddie Lovett turned the old guy into something of a national celebrity. Newspapers and magazines all over the country soon were sending reporters to the Hippocrene Library to talk to the Polyhistor. Hundreds of people made pilgrimages to the shack in the woods, bringing with them more books than Eddie Lovett knew what to do with.

There's a sequel to the story. Early this year, Eddie Lovett fell asleep in his library after spending most of the night reading there as was his habit. He was awakened by smoke and flames, and there was nothing he could do but stand outside in the darkness and cold and watch the library he'd built with such pride and sacrifice burn to the ground. Every book he owned burned, including the treasured copy of *Ropp's Commercial Calculator.*

But the story doesn't end there in ashes and disappointment. The wire services picked up the news reports of the fire, and pretty soon Eddie Lovett started receiving books and letters from all over the world. A convoy of well-wishers from Wisconsin drove down with 20,000 books, of which he took only 500. New York publishing houses sent crate after crate of books, and *Encyclopedia Britannica* sent him a new 30-volume set. Lady Bird Johnson sent a copy of her *White House Diary*, and grade-school kids from California and college kids from Harvard, Princeton, and Yale sent books and admiring letters. Some of the kids said they'd been thinking about dropping out of college but had reconsidered after reading his story. He received more than 8,000 books from 30 states and 5 foreign countries and 14 crates of library furniture for the Hippocrene Library II he hopes some day to be able to build.

Finally, the continuing largess got to be so overwhelming that a couple of weeks ago Eddie Lovett was obliged to make a public appeal. He said with gratitude that he had all the books he could handle for the moment and he urged contributors to give their unwanted volumes to people who needed them more.

He also said he wouldn't accept any of the offers of speaking engagements he'd received in the wake of the publicity, nor the offer of a free color TV set, nor the offer to install and pay for a telephone at his book-crowded shack. He said he appreciated those offers, but was afraid they'd just distract him from the business at hand—which was, of course, reading, studying, and thinking. Here is what he said, and the quotation is typical of him: "I am warring against my own ignorance and my battleground is here."

Hic Habitat Felicitas.

How Does the Author Make His Point?

1. Where is the thesis statement?
2. How does the author increase our interest in Eddie Lovett as the story progresses?
3. How does this differ from the usual straight news story?
4. What details does the author use to make Eddie Lovett appealing?
5. A good introduction attracts the reader's attention, tells the reader what the topic is about, and indicates the author's attitude toward his topic. How does Lancaster achieve these objectives in "Eddie Lovett, Polyhistor"?
6. How is this narrative strengthened by the author's descriptive details about who Eddie Lovett was and what kind of place he lived in?

What Do You Think?

1. Eddie Lovett, without a formal education, learned something that many college graduates fail to grasp—that the "real business at hand" is "reading, studying, and thinking." What else can you learn from the story of Eddie Lovett?
2. What is implicit in the notion that anyone who builds a library in "the middle of nowhere" is "crazy"?
3. What, in your opinion, was Eddie Lovett's greatest achievement?

University Days

JAMES THURBER

In this essay, the humorist James Thurber recalls some experiences of his college days at Ohio State. The essay is made up of five little narratives all on the subject of Thurber's career in the classroom. Notice that in all of these narratives he makes fun of himself. He portrays himself and the other students as inept and bumbling.

I passed all the other courses that I took at my university, but I could never pass botany. This was because all botany students had to spend several hours a week in a laboratory looking through a microscope at plant cells, and I could never see through a microscope. I never once saw a cell through a microscope. This used to enrage my instructor. He would wander around the laboratory pleased with the progress all the students were making in drawing the involved and, so I am told, interesting structure of flower cells, until he came to me. I would just be standing there. "I can't see anything," I would say. He would begin patiently enough, explaining how anybody can see through a microscope, but he would always end up in a fury, claiming that I could *too* see through a microscope but just pretended that I couldn't. "It takes away from the beauty of flowers anyway," I used to tell him. "We are not concerned with beauty in this course," he would say. "We are concerned solely with what I may call the *mechanics* of flars." "Well," I'd say, "I can't see anything." "Try it just once again," he'd say, and I would put my eye to the microscope and see nothing at all, except now and again a nebulous milky substance—a phenomenon of maladjustment. You were supposed to see a vivid, restless clockwork of sharply defined plant cells. "I see what looks like a lot of milk," I would tell him. This, he claimed, was the result of my not having adjusted the microscope properly, so he would readjust it for me, or rather, for himself. And I would look again and see milk.

I finally took a deferred pass, as they called it, and waited a year and tried again. (You had to pass one of the biological sciences or you couldn't graduate.) The professor had come back from vacation brown as a berry, bright-eyed, and eager to explain cell-structure again to his classes. "Well," he said to me, cheerily, when we met in the first laboratory hour of the semester, "we're going to see cells this time, aren't we?" "Yes, sir," I said. Students to right of me and to left of me and in front of me were seeing cells; what's more, they were quietly drawing pictures of them in their notebooks. Of course, I didn't see anything.

"We'll try it," the professor said to me, grimly, "with every adjustment of the microscope known to man. As God is my witness, I'll arrange this glass so that you see cells through it or I'll give up teaching. In twenty-two years of botany, I—" He cut off abruptly for he was beginning to quiver all over, like Lionel Barrymore, and he genuinely wished to hold onto his temper; his scenes with me had taken a great deal out of him.

So we tried it with every adjustment of the microscope known to man. With only one of them did I see anything but blackness or the familiar lacteal opacity, and that time I saw, to my pleasure and amazement, a variegated constellation of flecks, specks, and dots. These I hastily drew. The instructor, noting my activity, came back from an adjoining desk, a smile on his lips and his eyebrows high in hope. He looked at my cell drawing. "What's that?" he demanded, with a hint of a squeal in his voice. "That's what I saw," I said. "You didn't, you didn't, you *didn't*!" he screamed, losing control of his temper instantly, and he bent over and squinted into the microscope. His head snapped up. "That's your eye!" he shouted. "You've fixed the lens so that it reflects! You've drawn your eye!"

Another course that I didn't like, but somehow managed to pass, was economics. I went to that class straight from the botany class, which didn't help me any in understanding either subject. I used to get them mixed up. But not as mixed up as another student in my economics class who came there direct from a physics laboratory. He was a tackle on the football team, named Bolenciecwcz. At that time Ohio State University had one of the best football teams in the country, and Bolenciecwcz was one of its outstanding stars. In order to be eligible to play it was necessary for him to keep up in his studies, a very difficult matter, for while he was not dumber than an ox he was not any smarter. Most of his professors were lenient and helped him along. None gave him more hints in answering questions or asked him simpler ones than the economics professor, a thin, timid man named Bassum. One day when we were on the subject of transportation and distribution, it came Bolenciecwcz's turn to answer a question. "Name one means of transportation," the professor said to him. No light came into the big tackle's eyes. "Just any means of transportation," said the professor. Bolenciecwcz sat staring at him. "That is," pursued the professor, "any medium, agency, or method of going from one place to another." Bolenciecwcz had the look of a man who is being led into a trap. "You may choose among steam, horse-drawn, or electrically propelled vehicles," said the instructor. "I might suggest the one which we commonly take in making long journeys across land." There was a profound silence in which everybody stirred uneasily, including Bolenciecwcz and Mr. Bassum. Mr. Bassum abruptly broke this silence in an amazing manner, "Choo-choo-choo," he said, in a low voice, and turned instantly scarlet. He glanced appealingly around the room. All of us, of course, shared Mr. Bassum's desire that Bolenciecwcz should stay abreast of the class in economics, for the Illinois game, one of the hardest and most important of the season, was only a week off. "Toot, toot, tootooooooot!" some student with a deep voice moaned, and we all looked encouragingly at Bolenciecwcz. Somebody else gave a fine imitation of a locomotive letting off steam. Mr. Bassum himself rounded off the little show. "Ding, dong, ding, dong," he said, hopefully. Bolenciecwcz was staring at the floor now, trying to think, his great brow furrowed, his huge hands rubbing together, his face red.

"How did you come to college this year, Mr. Bolenciecwcz?" asked the professor. "*Chuffa* chuffa, *chuffa* chuffa."

"M'father sent me," said the football player.

"What on?" asked Bassum.

"I git an 'lowance," said the tackle, in a low, husky voice, obviously embarrassed.

"No, no," said Bassum. "Name a means of transportation. What did you *ride* here on?"

"Train," said Bolenciecwcz.

"Quite right," said the professor. "Now, Mr. Nugent, will you tell us—"

If I went through anguish in botany and economics—for different reasons—gymnasium work was even worse. I don't even like to think about it. They wouldn't let you play games or join in the exercises with your glasses on and I couldn't see with mine off. I bumped into professors, horizontal bars, agricultural students, and swinging iron rings. Not being able to see, I could take it but I couldn't dish it out. Also, in order to pass gymnasium (and you had to pass it to graduate) you had to learn to swim if you didn't know how. I didn't like the swimming pool, I didn't like swimming, and I didn't like the swimming instructor, and after all these years I still don't. I never swam but I passed my gym work anyway, by having another student give my gymnasium number (978) and swim across the pool in my place. He was a quiet, amiable blond youth, number 473, and he would have seen through a microscope for me if we could have got away with it, but we couldn't get away with it. Another thing I didn't like about gymnasium work was that they made you strip the day you registered. It is impossible for me to be happy when I am stripped and being asked a lot of questions. Still, I did better than a lanky agricultural student who was cross-examined just before I was. They asked each student what college he was in—that is, whether Arts, Engineering, Commerce, or Agriculture. "What college are you in?" the instructor snapped at the youth in front of me. "Ohio State University," he said promptly.

It wasn't that agricultural student but it was another a whole lot like him who decided to take up journalism, possibly on the ground that when farming went to hell he could fall back on newspaper work. He didn't realize, of course, that that would be very much like falling back full-length on a kit of carpenter's tools. Haskins didn't seem cut out for journalism, being too embarrassed to talk to anybody and unable to use a typewriter, but the editor of the college paper assigned him to the cow barns, the sheep house, the horse pavilion, and the animal husbandry department generally. This was a genuinely big "beat", for it took up five times as much ground and got ten times as great a legislative appropriation as the College of Liberal Arts. The agricultural student knew animals, but nevertheless his stories were dull and colorlessly written. He took all afternoon on each of them, on account of having to hunt for each letter on the typewriter. Once in a while he had to ask somebody to help him hunt. "C" and "L," in particular, were hard letters for him to find. His editor finally got pretty much annoyed at the farmer-journalist because his pieces were so uninteresting. "See here, Haskins," he snapped at him one day, "why is it we never have anything hot from you on the horse pavilion? Here we have two hundred head of horses on this campus—more than any other university in the Western Conference except Purdue—and yet you never get any real lowdown on them. Now shoot over to the horse barns and dig up something lively." Haskins shambled out and came back in about an hour; he said he had something. "Well, start it off snappily," said the editor, "Something people will read." Haskins set to work and in a couple of hours brought a sheet of typewritten paper to the desk; it was a two-hundred-word story about some disease that had broken out among the horses. Its opening sentence was simple but arresting. It read: "Who has noticed the sores on the tops of the horses in the animal husbandry building?"

Ohio State was a land grant university and therefore two years of military drill was compulsory. We drilled with old Springfield rifles and studied the tactics of the Civil War even though the World War was going on at the time. At 11 o'clock each morning thousands of freshmen and sophomores used to deploy over the campus, moodily creeping up on the old chemistry building. It was good training for the kind of warfare that was waged at Shiloh but it had no connection with what was going on in Europe. Some people used to think there was German money behind it, but they didn't dare say so or they would have been thrown in jail as German spies. It was a period of muddy thought and marked, I believe, the decline of higher education in the Middle West.

As a soldier I was never any good at all. Most of the cadets were glumly indifferent soldiers, but I was no good at all. Once General Littlefield, who was commandant of the cadet corps, popped up in front of me during regimental drill and snapped, "You are the main trouble with this university!" I think he meant that my type was the main trouble with the university but he may have meant me individually. I was mediocre at drill, certainly— that is, until my senior year. By that time I had drilled longer than anybody else in the Western Conference, having failed at military at the end of each preceding year so that I had to do it all over again. I was the only senior still in uniform. The uniform which, when new, had made me look like an interurban railway conductor, now that it had become faded and too tight made me look like Bert Williams in his bellboy act. This had a definitely bad effect on my morale. Even so, I had become by sheer practice little short of wonderful at squad maneuvers.

One day General Littlefield picked our company out of the whole regiment and tried to get it mixed up by putting it through one movement after another as fast as we could execute them: squads right, squads left, squads on right into line, squads right about, squads left front into line, etc. In about three minutes one hundred and nine men were marching in one direction and I was marching away from them at an angle of forty degrees, all alone. "Company, halt!" shouted General Littlefield. "That man is the only man who has it right!" I was made a corporal for my achievement.

The next day General Littlefield summoned me to his office. He was swatting flies when I went in. I was silent and he was silent too, for a long time. I don't think he remembered me or why he had sent for me, but he didn't want to admit it. He swatted some more flies, keeping his eyes on them narrowly before he let go with the swatter. "Button up your coat!" he snapped. Looking back on it now I can see that he meant me although he was looking at a fly, but I just stood there. Another fly came to rest on a paper in front of the general and began rubbing its hind legs together. The general lifted the swatter cautiously. I moved restlessly and the fly flew away. "You startled him!" barked General Littlefield, looking at me severely. I said I was sorry. "That won't help the situation!" snapped the General, with cold military logic. I didn't see what I could do except offer to chase some more flies toward his desk, but I didn't say anything. He stared out the window at the faraway figures of co-eds crossing the campus toward the library. Finally, he told me I could go. So I went. He either didn't know which cadet I was or else he forgot what he wanted to see me about. It may have been that he wished to apologize for having called me the main trouble with the university; or maybe he had decided to compliment me on my brilliant drilling of the day before and then at the last minute decided not to. I don't know. I don't think about it much any more.

How Does the Author Make His Point

1. In what ways does this essay differ in form from the rest of the essays in the book? What purpose does the title serve?
2. What would be a good thesis sentence for the essay?
3. This essay is really a series of five vignettes or anecdotes. Why do you think Thurber arranged them in the order he did? Would you have arranged them in a different order. How? Why?
4. How does the author achieve unity? What devices of coherence does he use?

What Do You Think?

1. Do any of the students or situations remind you of any classmate or courses that you took?
2. Is a teacher such as Bassum believable? Why or why not?
3. What should be done about the situation in botany class? What would you, as the teacher, do about Thurber's inability to see through a microscope? Have you ever had an experience in a class where everyone else seemed to be able to do something and you couldn't? Discuss your feelings and guess what the teacher's were.

A Woman Walks By

NEWMAN LEVY

This very brief essay presents a conflict, which is almost always the central portion of any narrative, in the divergent opinions of the husband and wife who observe a woman walking by. In this particular essay, the thesis statement is implied rather than overtly stated.

She walked swiftly by us, turned the corner sharply, and was gone. "That's an uncommonly good-looking girl," I said to my wife, who was deep in a crossword puzzle.

"Do you mean the one in that imitation blue taffeta dress with the green and red flowered design?"

"The girl that just walked by."

"Yes," said my wife, "with that dowdy rayon dress on. It's a copy of one I saw at Hattie Carnegie's, and a poor copy at that. You'd think, though, that she'd have better taste than to wear a chartreuse hat with it, especially with her bleached hair."

"Bleached? I didn't notice her hair was bleached."

"Good heavens, you could almost smell the peroxide. I don't mind a bit of make-up provided it looks fairly natural. But you could scrape that rouge off with a knife. They ought to add a course in make-up to the curriculum at Smith."

"Smith? Why Smith?"

"From her class pin, of course. You must have noticed it hanging from her charm bracelet."

"I wasn't looking at her wrist."

"I'll bet you weren't. Nor at those fat legs of hers, either. A woman with legs like that shouldn't wear high-heeled patent-leather shoes."

"I thought she was a very pretty girl," I said apologetically.

"Well, you may be right," said my wife. "I was busy with my puzzle and I didn't notice her particularly. What's the name of a President of the United States in six letters, beginning with T?"

How Does the Author Make His Point?

1. What is the author's point?
2. What are some of the derogatory adjectives that the author uses? What do these add to the story's interest.
3. Because the man speaks in general terms and the woman in specific terms, is the woman more convincing? If not, why not?
4. What is the tone of the essay? Is it humorous or hostile or both?

What Do You Think?

1. Do women have "a better eye" when looking at other women? Do they tend to "put down" members of their own sex?
2. Are women their own worst enemy? Explain.
3. What do you think about the last line? What is its purpose?

Cold Water on a Hot Shower

Tom Hritz

Tom Hritz, a columnist for the Pittsburgh Post Gazette, *has written a humorous essay narrating his experience and reaction to the attitude that everyday life is threatened by a multitude of dangers from commonplace things.*

I woke up yesterday morning feeling pretty bad. So I took a hot shower and I felt pretty good. Then I went downstairs to read the Post-Gazette over a cup of coffee and I started feeling pretty bad again.

"Uh-huh," you are probably thinking. "You started feeling pretty bad again because you read another story in the Post-Gazette about how drinking coffee, especially with sugar and cream, can kill you." Nope. That's not it. I started feeling pretty bad again because I read a story about how taking a hot shower can kill me.

Yes, according to this story, Julian Andelman, a water chemistry professor at Pitt's Graduate School of Public Health, said the vapor created by a hot shower may be filled with cancer-causing agents. Inhaling these vapors could eventually send you on a one-way trip down South, the report said.

And it gets worse. Julian Andelman also said that the vapor created in your bathtub, your kitchen sink and even your washing machine may contain these dangerous agents. The only good thing he had to say is that taking a bath is not as dangerous as taking a shower.

See, it probably works this way. Because these agents are more dangerous when inhaled than they are when drunk, taking a bath is safer than taking a shower because more people are inclined to drink their bath water than they are to inhale it.

At any rate, Julian Andelman admits that when people ask him if he still takes hot showers, he answers yes. "It's a risk-benefit analysis," he says, "and I still get a great benefit from a hot shower."

Given his devil-may-care bathing habits, I'd say that Julian Andelman's report on the dangers of taking a hot shower should be taken with a grain of salt. Of course, I hesitate to do that because we all know of the dangers of taking anything with a grain of salt. Or with an egg or a steak or a spoonful of sugar.

Risk-benefit analysis or not, I wish some of these scientists would keep their findings to themselves until they have more conclusive evidence of the dangers of all the things that are going to wipe out the human race. A lot of people may not be as brave as Julian Andelman—when it comes to defying death by taking a hot shower. Some of them are going to overreact to his report.

One fateful day, you'll walk into the office and some people will have these little signs taped to the walls and sitting on their desks. *Thank you for not taking a hot shower.* Or *Have you had your child dry-cleaned today?* The office will become a house divided, and a big fistfight will develop next summer at the office picnic between the showerers and the non-showerers.

Pressured by Passive Pollution from Taking Hot Showers groups, many people will immediately turn to taking cold showers. Although this will probably be roundly applauded by the Moral Majority who have been recommending it all along, the U.S. birth rate will plunge 92 percent during the first year. And of course, some people simply won't be able to stand the shock of a cold shower. So they'll start taking baths.

This could lead to real trouble with the water conservationists. Remember them? They are the people who were running around during the 1970s warning that the whole planet was going to dry up if we didn't quit squandering water.

They pretty much ordered everybody in the country to do two things to conserve water. 1) Put a sidewalk brick in their toilet tank so it would hold less water. 2) Take showers instead of baths because showers use less water than baths.

And we all did what we were told. We still have a brick in our toilet tank. And it worked, too. Maybe you haven't heard, but the level of Lake Erie is rising.

Well, Julian Andelman is going to get these water conservationists stirred up all over again. People will start taking baths recklessly again and the level of Lake Erie will start going down and the conservationists will start ordering us to put more sidewalk bricks in our toilet tanks.

And frankly, I'm not up for anymore sidewalk bricks in my toilet tank. Mainly because it will probably lead to the formation of a group that is trying to save the world's supply of sidewalk bricks.

How Does the Author Make His Point

1. How does Hritz get your attention in the first paragraph?
2. Hritz is a journalist, and this essay appeared in the *Pittsburgh Post Gazette*. What differences did you notice between the journalistic style shown here and the other essays in this unit?
3. What is the tone of the essay? To what audience is Hritz writing?
4. What *general* problem of the eighties is Hritz addressing?
5. Point out examples of satire in the piece.

What Do You Think?

1. Are we being bombarded by the results of studies saying that something is dangerous to our health? Give examples.
2. Do you think Hritz's examples of the results of such warnings (paragraphs 9, 10, 11, 14) are funny? true? exaggerated?
3. Do you intend to continue taking hot showers? Why or why not?

Very Cold and All Alone

GEORGETTE WALTON

This student recalls the personal experiences of her childhood in a poignant narrative.

Most people believe that childhood is a time of bliss and contentment in which a lack of knowledge and maturity keeps one safe from real suffering. This may be true in some cases; however, my childhood was a hideous nightmare from which I thought I'd never awaken. This situation existed not because of anything I'd done, nor because of my face; but, simply because I was different.

As a child, I was taller and bigger than any of the kids at my grade level. I was physically powerful for a child, but I grew up knowing that it was wrong to fight. As a result I was constantly ridiculed, made fun of, and degraded by my classmates who knew there would be no retaliation on my part.

I hated walking to school because the other kids would be there to taunt me, running behind me calling names and throwing things. So each school day I would awaken early and get to school as soon as possible. The doors were always opened early so I would go into the building and find a little used bathroom where I sat until first period. At one point, I became so frustrated that I would not go to school at all. I would contrive some sort of illness so that I could stay home, safe and secure with the only people I could really trust. Most of my free time was devoted to homework and reading, and since I had no social life at all, I became an "A" student. I found great comfort in reading. Through books I could escape from the living hell to which I had been condemned. I could go any place and become anyone I wanted to. I could be petite and pretty just like everyone else.

I do not remember doing any of the things that other children did. There were no parties or picnics with other children. I lived in an adult world. My family and my teachers were my only friends. Sometimes I felt as if I were not a child at all; I was simply living in a child's body trying to find some sense of identity in a world which I probably never would feel totally a part of. In order to survive, to remain sane, I encased myself in an invisible shell through which nothing could penetrate. The usual childhood tears could never escape from my eyes. I could not cry or show my feelings in any way, for that would reveal my weaknesses. So, I existed very cold and all alone.

Time passed and I met new people. Eventually, I went off to college. I could start over again and try to make my existence more pleasant. I grew at college, and along with my new found maturity came the realization that I could be that person I had always dreamed of by just being myself. I wonder if my torturing classmates remember me, and, if so, do they realize the effect they have had on my life. And often I wonder what life as a child would have been like without them.

How Does the Author Make Her Point?

1. What is the thesis sentence?
2. What type of introduction does the author use? In what way does it contribute to the poignancy of the essay?
3. Write an outline for the essay.

What Do You Think?

1. Becoming an "A" student is a goal for many students. This student's essay makes this attainment seem sad. Why? Do you know of any other examples of a goal reached through intense suffering?
2. The author could have solved some of her problems by using force. Should she have? Is using force ever acceptable? Explain your answer. (You might want to refer to "The Use of Force" in chapter 11.)
3. What is the saddest sentence in the essay? Defend your selection.
4. What techniques does the author use to make her situation real to you?

INTEGRATING READING AND WRITING SKILLS: HAVING A CLEAR PURPOSE

One of the first things you learn in a reading course is the importance of reading with a clear purpose in mind. What are you reading for: Facts? Explanations? Conclusions? Inspiration? For example, when a dairy farmer reads an FDA-survey on the number of farmers in his state who are selling nonpasteurized milk, he is reading for facts. When a steelworker employed in a plant that just laid off three hundred employees reads a letter from his director of personnel, he is reading to see if he still has a job. The worried steelworker might well skim over the introductory factual details about increased costs and declining profits and focus his eyes on that brief paragraph to see if he, too, has been laid off. A pediatrician who is reading the Surgeon General's latest report on "Women and Smoking" is reading for facts *and* conclusions. A research scientist examining a colleague's paper might be reading for the purpose of learning *how* the author arrived at his conclusions. A student who is studying a chapter in a textbook might be reading to absorb all of the facts, hypotheses, definitions, and examples he can.

When you read with a purpose in mind, you learn more in a shorter period of time. If you don't know what you are reading for, you won't know how to sort out what is important and what isn't. The problem is compounded when the material you are reading is vague and incoherent—in other words, when the writer had no clear purpose in mind before beginning to write. Having a clear purpose, then is important for both readers and writers—perhaps even more important for writers, for if readers lack a clear purpose, they are only wasting their own time, but if writers lack a clear purpose, they are wasting both their own time AND the readers'.

As you learned in the beginning of this chapter, a narrative essay without a clear purpose simply becomes a list of details arranged in chronological order. Now that you are aware of the importance of purpose in reading as well as writing, look at the following narrative from a reader's point of view. Suppose that you are personnel director at Toys International and you are reading a job applicant's response to the last question on the application form: "In a brief paragraph, tell us why you want to work at Toys International."

> One day last month, I was watching the neighbor's two little boys playing in my backyard. One had a tool box set, and the other had a doctor's kit. They took turns playing carpenter and doctor, and they seemed to be having a good time until both of them decided that they wanted to play with the hammer. Then all hell broke loose. A tug of war was on, and each little fighter was determined to win. At first, David, the older, seemed to be winning, but three-year-old Matthew soon got the best of him. He grabbed hold of the hammer and pulled so hard that the handle broke off. That's when I decided to apply for a job with Toys International.

Obviously, something is missing. The person in charge of hiring at Toys International will not be impressed. He or she is looking for a reason, an explanation, perhaps some indication of the applicant's personality or value system, but finds only a story about two little kids. The applicant apparently lost sight of his central purpose. He got so carried away talking about David and Matthew that he forgot *why* he was relating the story. If the applicant had been aware of his purpose, the personnel director might have found the answer that he or she was looking for. Suppose that the applicant had written this response instead.

One day last month, I was watching my neighbor's two little boys having a tug of war over a toy hammer. After a few minutes of yelling and tugging, three-year-old Matthew grabbed hold of the hammer and pulled so hard that the handle broke off. He fell back against the dogwood tree, and the sharp edge of the handle landed right above his left eye. The sight of the blood streaming down his face terrified the poor kid. It took his mother almost an hour to calm him down. The more I thought about it, the madder I got. First of all, the handle should never have broken off that easily. Toy hammers should not fall apart during a tug of war between pre-school children. Second, if the cheap plastic handle had not had such sharp, rough edges, Matthew would not have been hurt. When I thought about what could have happened to his eye, I just shuddered. I began to wonder if there was anybody in the toy business who cared about making good, safe toys for children, so I started to do a little research. That's when I learned of Toys International's almost spotless safety record, and after I talked to some parents who had purchased TI products, I also learned that your products are very durable. I have always wanted to use my talents in graphic design for a good purpose—not just to make money. That's why I'd like to work for Toys International. It would make me feel good to know that I am working for a company that cares about quality and safety—especially where children are concerned.

This response would answer the question clearly and would, undoubtedly, give the applicant a better chance of getting the job.

Exercise

The following suggestions were taken from a college textbook on writing. Read the material and then answer the following questions on the purpose of reading this passage.

1. **Learn to see beyond convenient generalizations.** Most people tend to see the objects around them in generic terms. Students, for example, can spend four years at a college and never notice what the major buildings on campus actually look like. Someone who develops good habits of observation will not merely see "buildings" but particular types of buildings—made out of various materials and designed according to specific architectural styles.

2. **Choose descriptive terms carefully.** A danger in descriptive writing is the careless adjective. In lazy writing there is often an abuse of synonyms, as though the writer assumed that closely related words mean more or less the same thing. Yet a careful writer who consults a dictionary will find a wealth of distinctions among words he or she might have used indiscriminately. For example, in describing the reflection of light, it is useful to know that "glittering," "glimmering," and "glistening" have different shades of meaning. A good dictionary, remember, is not merely a place to check spelling and isolated definitions; it can disclose a wide spectrum of important distinctions among seemingly similar words. Awareness of such distinctions will help give any writing clarity, accuracy, and force.

3. **Be aware of your own predispostions and expectations.** As social scientists consistently warn, what we see is frequently determined by what we expect to see. A careful observer takes such expectations into account. A sociologist, for example, fascinated by criminal subcultures (urban street gangs, for instance) might easily convey a distorted, romanticized view of the subculture's behavior. Journalists, too, may find their objectivity compromised by biases and preconceptions. If the writer, however, does not intend to adovcate a position, but intends to be intellectualy objective and neutral, then potentially distorting, preexisting attitudes toward the subject need to be carefully considered before writing.

4. **Consider your standpoint as observer.** Our perceptions are often determined by our particular position as observers. Where are you in location to an object or event? Are you close or far? Are you at the game or watching it on television? Are you a participant, an observer, or both? Whether writing in the arts or sciences, a consideration of our own physical point of view is extremely important.

5. **Be selective in the use of detail.** Though personal observations cannot exist without detail, some details are always more significant than others. We have all been bored by speakers who do not make distinctions between the significant and the trivial, who cannot tell us about a tour of Europe without dragging us through every airport along the way. Good observers, of course, do notice minutiae and small events. In "The Making of a Writer" Russell Baker describes in careful detail the manager of the grocery store where he worked as a boy. Yet Baker does not wallow in specificity; he makes each detail contribute to his portrayal of the manager's personality.

6. **Learn to see what is *not* there.** All good observers develop the habit of noticing missing details. A detective at the scene of a serious automobile accident might wonder why he finds no skid marks in sight. An ecologist may discover that the absence of a particular species signals a significant environmental change. Scientists especially learn to pay attention to the absence of phenomena, knowing that sometimes negative results can lead to positive discoveries. They know, too, that much valuable knowledge derives from inferring what is not seen from what is.

Robert Atwan and William Vesterman

What would be your purpose in reading this if you were

1. a student in a college English composition class?
2. an instructor reviewing the book from which it came to decide if he wanted it as a text for his college composition class?
3. a student preparing himself to take a placement exam in college composition?
4. a tutor in the tutorial lab who is seeking ways to help her students?

IMPROVING YOUR VOCABULARY: THE DICTIONARY AND THE THESAURUS

For both readers and writers, the most important reference tool is the dictionary, which performs the following tasks:

Lists the words in the language
Defines them
Gives the spelling or spellings
Indicates which part of speech a given word is
Provides standards of usage
Gives synonyms and antonyms
Gives the etymology, that is, the history and various meanings of the word

In subsequent chapters, the vocabulary sections discuss in detail some of the reference services a dictionary can give. But in a more general sense, the dictionary is valuable to you because it can increase your *awareness* of language. It is only by becoming aware of language, by becoming sensitive to it, that you can read and write with skill and pleasure.

The first important dictionary in English is usually considered to be Dr. Samuel Johnson's, published in 1755. Dr. Johnson had said that he hoped his dictionary would "refine and purify" the English language. But long before the end of the seven years it took him to make his dictionary, he realized that language was a living thing that could not be pinned down with rules. Since Johnson's time, dictionaries have tended to be descriptive rather than prescriptive. *Descriptive* means that dictionaries describe the language as writers and speakers use it; dictionaries are not *prescriptive* because they do not prescribe or lay down rules.

In the preface to his dictionary, Johnson made a statement that established the twofold purpose of any dictionary. He said, "Language is only the instrument of science [that is, knowledge] and words are but the signs [symbols] of ideas: I wish, however, that the instrument might be less apt to decay, and that the signs might be permanent, like the things which they denote."

Language is a living, changing thing in which two forces oppose each other—the force of change and the force of conservatism, which is hostile to change. The dictionary records the changes that occur in language in response to changes in living conditions and in the passing of events. But by describing the standard usage of educated speakers and writers, the dictionary slows down the process of change.

Without keeping in step with the life it records, language becomes rigid and ultimately "dead," like Latin. It grows remote from its users. On the other hand, if language changes too rapidly, it becomes only individualized self-expression. In either extreme, language loses its power as communication.

Types of Dictionaries

The greatest of all English dictionaries is *The Oxford English Dictionary* (O.E.D.), which most college libraries have. This scholarly, multivolume dictionary records the histories of over a million words. It illustrates in great detail the changes in meaning of many words over the many centuries that some form of English has existed.

Unabridged Dictionaries

Webster's Third New International Dictionary of the English Language, the best known of the unabridged dictionaries, offers complete definitions and many illustrations of the various uses of 450,000 words. Almost every college library owns a copy of this work, so you probably have it available when you need more information than a desk dictionary will give you.

Desk Dictionaries

Everyone who reads and writes needs a good, up-to-date desk dictionary. In choosing one of the many available, select one with 100,000 or more entries and a recent copyright date. Check also to see if one has any features you especially want, like *Webster's Ninth New Collegiate Dictionary*, in which illustrations of meanings are dated by their entrance into the language.

The following brief list includes some of the best desk dictionaires:

> *The American Heritage Dictionary of the English Language,* 2 ed. (Boston: Houghton Mifflin Company, 1982).
>
> *The Random House Dictionary of the English Language*, college ed., rev. (New York: Random House, 1982).
>
> *Webster's Ninth New Collegiate Dictionary* (Springfield, Mass.: Merriam-Webster, Inc., 1986).

The Thesaurus

If it is used with care, the thesaurus is another useful reference tool pertaining to vocabulary. The thesaurus is made up of groups of synonyms and antonyms. If you look up a general subject, the thesaurus will give you a wide choice of synonyms (or antonyms) for that subject or subtopics under it. However, the thesaurus does not discriminate among the various terms it suggests, so that the unwary reader is liable to choose a term far from his or her meaning.

Successful use of the thesaurus entails two steps: (1) look up your subject in the thesaurus to see what words may pertain to it; (2) then look up your selected synonym in the *dictionary*, which discriminates among various possibilities, so that you can choose the most precise word.

ASSIGNMENT

Examine the following morals from Aesop's fables and see if any of them make you think about something you've experienced. Choose one as a controlling idea and develop a narrative essay.

1. Appearances are deceptive—"The Wolf in Sheep's Clothing"
2. It is easy to despise what you cannot get—"The Fox and the Grapes"
3. Beware lest you lose the substance by grasping at the shadow—"The Dog and the Shadow"
4. Familiarity breeds contempt—"The Fox and the Lion"
5. Self-conceit may lead to self-destruction—"The Frog and the Ox"
6. There is always someone worse off than you—"The Hares and the Frogs"
7. Outside show is a poor substitute for inner worth—"The Fox and the Mask"
8. Better beans and bacon in peace than cakes and ale in fear—"The Town Mouse and the Country Mouse"
9. A little thing in hand is worth more than a great thing in prospect—"The Fisher and the Little Fish"
10. It is easy to be brave from a safe distance—"The Wolf and the Kid"

3

Describing

ORGANIZATION

To *describe* means "to picture verbally." A good description re-creates through words a sensory experience. In describing, you hope to share with your reader an impression you *received and responded to* because of something seen or heard or even smelled, tasted, or touched. To communicate this central impression, you recall the experience and select from it the specific details that make it up. The *end*, the purpose, of description is to convey this central impression; the *means* of description is to select and order details that lead to this central impression.

Prewriting

Observation

Good description begins with close observation. The person who does not notice things can form only a vague impression even for himself or herself and has no means to make that impression vivid to anyone else. Close observation depends on seeing and recording specific details. Your mind receives impressions so rapidly that you may not be aware that you are arriving at a central impression until you find yourself saying something like "My English instuctor's office is a mess!" This is adequate as a first step, but it is only a vague generalization. The person to whom you say it may accept it as your opinion, but he won't see what you see and feel what you feel.

Specific Detail

If you wish someone to see vividly with you and feel with you, you must go beyond the generalization. You must ask yourself *why* the office struck you as messy. You must recall specific details remembered from trips to that messy office. Remembering, you come up with items like the following:

A bookcase bulging with books, none standing upright

Piles of themes sliding sideways across the desk

No space left on the desk to work

Several dozen *New York Times* book review sections dumped in a corner

Three battered cartons overflowing with packets of yellowed, three-by-five note cards and dog-eared notebooks

Pertinent Detail

All the details should pertain to your central impression. In describing that office, you would not include details about the surrounding offices, whether neat or messy. Nor would you want to contradict the controlling impression of messiness by saying that the instructor is well dressed and tidy. Only details that refer to your subject and your response to your subject should be included.

Organization of Detail

Once you have a controlling impression in mind and a tentative list of pertinent and specific details, you need to decide what order or organization of details you consider most effective. There are many possiblities, but in description the usual order is spatial. You arrange your details according to some definite principle, usually following some normal pattern that the eye would follow. You might describe a place from right to left, from far to near, or a room from entry to back wall, or a person from head to foot. You might describe something from a fixed point or as you move toward it. The order you choose is up to you. You need only to be logical and consistent; you would not leap from a worm's-eye view to a bird's-eye view.

Writing the Descriptive Paper

Prepared with a central impression, a tentative list of specific details, and a tentative order for those details, you are ready to write. The overall organization of a descriptive essay is the same as that of any other essay—introduction, body, conclusion.

Introduction

The introductory paragraph should capture the attention of your reader by using any of the devices suggested in chapter 1. (In actual practice, you may not be writing your introduction until after you've writtten the rest of the paper.) Whatever type of introduction you write, its purpose is to lead your now-interested reader to your thesis statement. This usually is the last sentence in the introductory paragraph. It introduces your subject (what you are describing) and your response to it (your attitude). When the poet Wordsworth wrote, "My heart leaps up when I behold/A rainbow in the sky," he wrote a very good thesis statement for a brief description. His subject is the beauty of nature, to which his response is excited pleasure. He narrows his subject to one particular beauty and avoids a dull, generalized phrase like "the beauty of nature." Since everyone has seen a rainbow, his choice of that precise word creates an image the reader can see. In choosing an almost visceral phrase like "my heart leaps up," he makes the reader participate in his sensory experience.

The Body

As in other types of essays, the descriptive essay supplies the specific details that support the thesis statement. Nothing should appear in the body that does not go back directly to either subject or attitude. The body may be broken down into the various aspects of subject or attitude, with a paragraph or more devoted to each aspect. But the important thing is that all contribute to the central impression.

The word *select* has turned up a number of times in this discussion for the very good reason that selecting the best details from the wide range of possible details gives your essay clarity and effectiveness. Too many details create confusion; too few fail to give the picture; dull ones are boring. In selecting, you must develop your own judgment. What interested you? Do the details you selected create a complete picture without overcrowding? Do they all refer to the thesis statement? Answering these questions should steer you toward a good selection of details.

In the chapter called "Brute Neighbors" in *Walden*, Henry David Thoreau expresses his awareness of sharing his world with the wild, free, and secret animals of his woods. He and they live in amity and peace, but their world is not all peaceful, as he records in the excerpt called "The Battle of the Ants."

Since this excerpt is not the beginning of the essay, Thoreau uses no introductory material but plunges directly into his description.

I was witness to events of a less peaceful character. One day when I went out to my wood-pile, or rather my pile of stumps, I observed two large ants, the one red, the other much larger, nearly half an inch long, and black, fiercely contending with one another. Having once got hold they never let go, but struggled and wrestled and rolled on the chips incessantly. Looking farther, I was surprised to find that the chips were covered with such combatants, that it was not a *duellum*, but a *bellum*, a war between two races of ants, the red always pitted against the black, and frequently two red ones to one black. The legions of these Myrmidons covered all the hills and vales in my woodyard, and the ground was already strewn with the dead and dying, both red and black. It was the only battle-field I have ever witnessed, the only battle-field I ever trod while the battle was raging; internecine war; the red republicans on the one hand, and the black imperialists on the other. On every side they were engaged in deadly combat, yet without any noise that I could hear, and human soldiers never fought so resolutely. I watched a couple that were fast locked in each other's embraces, in a little sunny valley amid the chips, now at noon-day prepared to fight till the sun went down, or life went out. The smaller red champion had fastened himself like a vice to his adversary's front, and through all the tumblings on that field never for an instant ceased to gnaw at one of his feelers . . ., having already caused the other to go by the board; while the stronger black one dashed him from side to side, and as I saw on looking nearer, had already divested him of several of his members. They fought with more pertinacity than bulldogs. Neither manifested the least disposition to retreat. It was evident that their battle-cry was Conquer or Die. In the meanwhile there came along a single red ant on the hill-side of this valley, evidently full of excitement, who either had dispatched his foe, or had not yet taken part in the battle; probably the latter, for he had lost none of his limbs; whose mother had charged him to return with his shield or upon it. Or perchance he was some Achilles, who had nourished his wrath apart, and had now come to avenge or rescue his Patroclus. He saw this unequal combat from afar—for the blacks were nearly twice the size of the red,—he drew near with rapid pace till he stood on his guard within half an inch of the combatants; then, watching his opportunity, he sprang upon the black warrior and commenced his operations near the root of his right fore-leg, leaving the foe to select among his own members; and so there were three united for life, as if a new kind of attraction had been invented which put all other locks and cements to shame. I should not have wondered by this time to find that they had their respective musical bands stationed on some eminent chip, and playing their national airs the while, to excite the slow and cheer the dying combatants. I was myself excited somewhat even as if they had been men. The more you think of it, the less the difference. And certainly there is not the fight recorded in Concord history, at least, if in the history of America, that will bear a moment's comparison with this, whether for the numbers engaged in it, or for the patriotism and heroism displayed. For numbers and for carnage it was an Austerlitz or Dresden. Concord Fight! Two killed on the patriots' side, and Luther Blanchard wounded! Why here every ant was a Buttrick,—"Here! for God's sake, fire!"— and thousands shared the fate of Davis and Hosmer. There was not one hireling there. I have no doubt that it was a principle they fought for, as much as our ancestors, and not to avoid a three-penny tax on their tea, and the results of this battle will be as important and memorable to those whom it concerns as those of the battle of Bunker Hill at least.

I took up the chip on which the three I have particularly described were struggling, carried it into my house, and placed it under a tumbler on my window sill, in order to see the issue. Holding a microscope to the first mentioned red ant, I saw that, though we was assiduously gnawing at the near fore leg of his enemy, having severed his remaining feeler, his own breast was all torn away, exposing what vitals he had there to the jaws of the black warrior, whose breast-plate was apparently too thick for him to pierce; and the dark carbuncles at the sufferer's eyes shone with ferocity such as war only could excite. They struggled half an hour longer under the tumbler, and when I looked again the black soldier had severed the heads of his foes from their bodies, and the still living heads were hanging on either side of him like ghastly trophies at his saddlebow, still apparently as firmly fastened as ever, and he was endeavoring with feeble struggles, being without feelers and with only the remnant of a leg, and I know not how many other wounds, to divest himself of them, which at length, after half an hour more, he accomplished. I raised the glass, and he went off over the windowsill in that crippled state. Whether he finally survived that combat, and spent the remainder of his days in some Hotel des Invalides, I do not know; but I thought that his industry would not be worth much thereafter. I never learned which party was victorious, nor the cause of the war; but I felt for the rest of that day as if I had my feelings excited and harrowed by witnessing the struggle, the ferocity and carnage, of a human battle before my door.

Henry David Thoreau

The Conclusion

The conclusion sums up and restates the central impression. As the last thing you leave with your reader, the conclusion must emphasize the point you wish to make and the significance of your description, your reason for describing. Thoreau concludes the quoted section of his essay with an explicit statement of the idea implied throughout—that human beings and the rest of the natural world share much more of life than they realize.

Description as a Help to Other Writing

Although description is one of the four major types of writing (the others are narration, exposition, and argument/persuasion), only rarely does description stand alone in an entire essay. Usually description is provided to help convey the meaning of other types of writing. However, don't assume that because description is usually subsidiary, it is unimportant. In narration, for instance, description is vital in giving the setting. Action doesn't take place in a vacuum, so description is important in making vivid the place where action occurs.

In his novel *A European Education*, Romain Gary begins with a one-paragraph description that not only gives the setting but also establishes the tone of desperation and the will to survive.

The hideout was finished just as dawn began to glimmer. It was a wretched dawn in September, drizzling with rain. The pine trees floated in mist; the sky was lost somewhere out of sight. For a month they had been working secretly, by night; the Germans never risked leaving the main roads after dusk, but by day their patrols ranged the forest, hunting for the few remaining partisans whom hunger and despair had not yet forced to give up the fight. The den was twelve feet deep and fifteen feet wide. They had flung a mattress and some rugs into one corner; six sacks of potatoes, a hundred-weight each, were stacked along the earthen walls. In one of these walls, alongside the mattress, they had dug a hearth; the chimney flue came up to the surface a few yards from the hideout, in a coppice. The roof was solid. They had made good use of the door of an armored train which the partisans had derailed about a year ago, on the line from Wilno to Molodeczno.

Romain Gary

Description is also important in showing readers the characters and their actions. If readers can't visualize the characters, they are not going to care about what the characters do. Some well-selected details of description, usually given through another character, determine whom the reader will love or hate.

Charles Dickens, in *David Copperfield*, describes a Miss Murdstone, the hated sister of David's hated stepfather. (Notice that even Miss Murdstone's name acts against her, carrying, as it does, suggestions of *mur*der and grave*stone*.)

> It was Miss Murdstone who was arrived, and a gloomy-looking lady she was; dark, like her brother, whom she greatly resembled in face and voice, and with very heavy eyebrows, nearly meeting over her large nose, as if, being disabled by the wrongs of her sex from wearing whiskers, she had carried them to that account. She brought with her two uncompromising hard black boxes, with her initials on the lids in hard brass nails. When she paid the coachman she took her money out of a hard steel purse, and she kept the purse in a very jail of a bag which hung upon her arm by a heavy chain, and shut up like a bite. I had never, at that time, seen such a metallic lady altogether as Miss Murdstone was.

Although the depiction of Miss Murdstone gives the reader the impression of hardness and indomitability, the following description of a character, Reverend Starnes, describes an opposite type of person, a person ravaged by fear, advanced age, alcoholism, and, perhaps, psychosis.

> I was confronted by a wild bird of a man. In his late seventies, I guessed. He was actually a few inches taller than I, but his clothes seemed too big for him so he appeared to have shrunk, in weight and height, to a frail diminutiveness.
> His hair was an uncombed mess of gray feathers, and on his hollow cheeks was at least three days' growth of beard: a whitish plush. His temples were sunken, the skin on his brow so thin and

transparent that I could see the course of blood vessels. Rheumy eyes tried to stare at me, but the focus wavered. The nose was a bone.

He was wearing what had once been a stylish velvet smoking jacket, but now the nap was worn down to the backing, and the elbows shone greasily. Beneath the unbuttoned jacket was a soiled blue work-man's shirt, tieless, the collar open to reveal a scrawny chicken neck. His creaseless trousers were some black, glistening stuff, with darker stains and a tear in one knee. His fly was open. He was wearing threadbare carpet slippers, the heels broken and folded under. His bare ankles were not clean.

I was standing outside on the porch, he inside the house. Yet even at the distance I caught the odor: of him, his home, or both. It was the sour smell of unwashed age, of mustiness, spilled liquor, unmade beds and unaired linen, and a whiff of incense as rancid as all the rest.

Lawrence Sanders

While Miss Murdstone inspires fear, Reverend Starnes evokes pity or revulsion (depending on the reader). Both authors, however, give a clear picture of the sensations they experienced when confronted by the characters.

Through description, you recreate for your reader a sensory experience of a place or person you have experienced in life or in imagination. Your description lends reality to the story you're telling. In exposition, as well, you often rely on description to help you explain something. Particularly if you are trying to explain an abstraction, it is helpful to show your reader what your abstraction stands for. You can't *show* an abstraction, but you can describe the concrete examples of that abstraction. You can't make an image of anxiety, but you can describe the seventeen-year-old farm boy trying to work up the courage to ask the class beauty to the Junior Prom.

Look at the follwing example from James Clavell's best seller *Whirlwind*. When a strong, resourceful man suddenly discovers that he is powerless against the forces that threaten his wife, he feels terror. Clavell recreates this feeling for his reader.

Towering above the crowd, Erikki got out. Protectively, he put his arm around her, men, women, and some children crowding them, giving them little space. The stench of unwashed bodies was over-powering. He could feel her trembling, as much as she tried to hide it. Together they watched the squat man and others clambering into their spotless car, muddy boots on the seats. Others unlocked the rear door, carelessly removing and scattering their possessions, grubby hands reaching into pockets, opening everything—his bags and her bags. Then one of the men held up her filmy underclothes and night things to catcalls and jeers. The crones muttered their disapproval. One of them reached out and touched her hair. Azadeh backed away but those behind her would not give her room. At once Erikki moved his bulk to help but the mass of the crowd did not move though those nearby cried out, almost crushed by him, their cries infuriating the others who moved closer, threateningly, shouting at him.

Suddenly Erikki knew truly, for the first time, he could not protect Azadeh. He knew he could kill a dozen of them before they overpowered and killed him, but that would not protect her.

The realization shattered him.

His legs felt weak and he had an overpowering wish to urinate and the smell of his own fear choked him and he fought the panic that pervaded him. Dully he watched their possessions being defiled. Men were staggering away with their vital cans of gasoline without which he could never make Tehran as all gas stations were struck and closed. He tried to force his legs into motion but they would not work, nor would his mouth. Then one of the crones shouted at Azadeh who numbly shook her head and men took up the cry, jostling him and jostling her, men closing on him, their fetid smell filling his nostrils, his ears clogged with the Farsi.

His arm was still around her, and in the noise she looked up and he saw her terror but could not hear what she said. Again he tried to ease more room for the two of them but again he failed. Desperately he tried to contain the soaring, claustrophobic, panic-savagery and need to fight beginning to overwhelm him, knowing that once he began it would start the riot that would destroy her.

James Clavell

Can you feel the emotions Erikki is feeling—terror, frustration, revulsion—an almost paralyzing conflict between the urge to fight and the knowledge that to fight means death to both of them?

Description also plays an important part in persuasion. When the *New York Times* begins its annual Christmas drive to get its readers to contribute to a fund to buy Christmas presents for poor children, it describes the "hundred neediest cases" because the abstract concept of poor children is not nearly so persuasive as concrete descriptions of individual children—underfed, perhaps unloved, spending bleak holidays without a single present.

Description, the selection of a few vivid details to help the reader see what you see and feel what you feel, is of vital importance in most writing.

EXERCISE

The following paragraph was written by a student to fulfill an assignment in describing a place. Read the paragraph carefully and notice how the writer uses specific descriptive details to support his central impression of an unemployment office.

> I paused at the plate glass door, reluctant to enter this building of despair and depression, and then, feeling my shoulders drop a notch, I entered the unemployment office. It was crowded inside, but I quickly found the end of my assigned line, one of the many reaching out from the center—like spokes from the hub of a wheel. The people were all different, white, black, male, female, some tall and some short, but they all had one thing in common—unsmiling faces. And why not? There was nothing to smile about here. They blended in perfectly with the drab decor of the office. The floor, littered with cigarette butts, was scuffed thin from the thousands of pairs of feet that shuffled slowly through the years to the head of the line. Wood paneling, bleached at the bottom by the swishing of a mop, rises up to meet faded blue walls, which are decorated only on one end by a clock and a crooked picture. I wonder if it's a good picture. Who cares? It's too small to see from here. From an unseen corner, the clacking of a typewriter rises over the din of conversations. At least someone is working. "Next"—the word penetrates my thoughts, only to be quickly dismissed. Another glance at the clock shows that it has magically moved forty-five minutes. "NEXT"—this time, the word, more commanding, shakes my senses and I realize it's directed at me. Sheepishly, I move to the unsmiling face at the counter. The clerk's pencil flashes quickly across the papers, and then I am eagerly heading for the door, anxious to leave this building of despair and desperation.

> Robert Statti (student)

Did you notice how the writer projects his mood on the place he is describing; for example, he describes the building as a place of despair, but it is, of course, his despair. However, he also gives specific details that directly reveal his emotions. For instance, as he enters the unemployment office, his "shoulders drop a notch," and as he waits in line, "thousands of pairs of feet shuffled to the head of the line." He also indicated despair through the slowness of time: the forty-five minutes pass only by "magic" and the feet "shuffle through the years."

Suggest five specific details you might give if you were trying to communicate a central impression of

fright	surprise	love
anger	joy	disgust

The Scopes Trial

FREDERICK LEWIS ALLEN

In the following essay, you can see how carefully the author describes the town and people of Dayton, Tennessee, so that the reader visualizes the setting in which the trial takes place. Description thus makes the narrative vivid; we live for a moment in that hurly-burly and watch the action of the trial unfold.

It was a strange trial. Into the quiet town of Dayton flocked gaunt Tennessee farmers and their families in mule-drawn wagons and ramshackle Fords; quiet, godly people in overalls and gingham and black, ready to defend their faith against the "foreigners," yet curious to know what this new-fangled evolutionary theory might be. Revivalists of every sort flocked there, too, held their meetings on the outskirts of the town under the light of flares, and tacked up signs on the trees about the courthouse—"Read Your Bible Daily for One Week," and "Be Sure Your Sins Will Find You Out," and at the very courthouse gate:

THE KINGDOM OF GOD

The sweetheart love of Jesus Christ and Paradise Street is at hand. Do you want to be a sweet angel? Forty days of prayer. Itemize your sins and iniquities for eternal life. If you come clean, God will talk back to you in voice.

Yet the atmosphere of Dayton was not simply that of rural piety. Hotdog venders and lemonade venders set up their stalls along the streets as if it were circus day. Booksellers hawked volumes on biology. Over a hundred newspaper men poured into the town. The Western Union installed twenty-two telegraph operators in a room off a grocery store. In the courtroom itself, as the trial impended, reporters and camera men crowded alongside grimfaced Tennessee countrymen; there was a buzz of talk, a shuffle of feet, a ticking of telegraph instruments, an air of suspense like that of a first-night performance at the theater. Judge, defendant, and counsel were stripped to their shirt sleeves—Bryan in a pongee shirt turned in at the neck, Darrow with lavender suspenders, Judge Raulston with galluses of a more sober judicial hue—yet fashion was not wholly absent: the news was flashed over the wires to the whole country that the judge's daughters, as they entered the courtroom with him, wore rolled stockings like any metropolitan flappers. Court was opened with a pious prayer—and motion picture operators climbed upon tables and chairs to photograph the leading participants in the trial from every possible angle. The evidence ranged all the way from the admission of fourteen-year-old Howard Morgan that Scopes had told him about evolution and that it hadn't hurt him any, to the estimate of a zoölogist that life had begun something like six hundred million years ago (an assertion which caused gasps and titters of disbelief from the rustics in the audience). And meanwhile two million words were being telegraphed out of Dayton, the trial was being broadcast by the *Chicago Tribune's* station WGN, the Dreamland Circus at Coney Island offered "Zip" to the Scopes' defense as a "missing link," cable companies were reporting enormous increases in transatlantic cable tolls, and news agencies in London were being besieged with requests for more copy from Switzerland, Italy, Germany, Russia, China, and Japan. Ballyhoo had come to Dayton.

It was a bitter trial. Attorney-General Stewart of Tennessee cried out against the insidious doctrine which was "undermining the faith of Tennessee's children and robbing them of their chance of eternal life." Bryan charged Darrow with having only one purpose, "to slur at the Bible." Darrow spoke of Bryan's "fool religion." Yet again and again the scene verged on farce. The climax—both of bitterness and of farce—came on the afternoon of July 20th, when on the spur of the moment Hays asked that the defense be permitted to put Bryan on the stand as an expert on the Bible, and Bryan consented.

So great was the crowd that afternoon that the judge had decided to move the court outdoors, to a platform built against the courthouse under the maple trees. Benches were set out before it. The reporters sat on the benches, on the ground, anywhere, and scribbled their stories. On the outskirts of the seated crowd a throng stood in the hot sunlight which streamed down through the trees. And on the platform sat the shirt-sleeved Clarence Darrow, Bible on his knee, and put the Fundamentalist champion through one of the strangest examinations which ever took place in a court of law.

He asked Bryan about Jonah and the whale, Joshua and the sun, where Cain got his wife, the date of the Flood, the significance of the Tower of Babel. Bryan affirmed his belief that the world was created in 4004 B.C. and the flood occurred in or about 2348 B.C.; that Eve was literally made out of Adam's rib; that the Tower of Babel was responsible for the diversity of languages in the world; and that a "big fish" had swallowed Jonah. When Darrow asked him if he had ever discovered where Cain got his wife, Bryan answered: "No, sir; I leave the agnostics to hunt for her." When Darrow inquired, "Do you say you do not believe that there were any civilizations on this earth that reach back beyond five thousand years?" Bryan stoutly replied, "I am not satisfied by any evidence I have seen." Tempers were getting frazzled by the strain and the heat; once Darrow declared that his purpose in examining Bryan was "to show up Fundamentalism . . . to prevent bigots and ignoramuses from controlling the educational system of the United States," and Bryan jumped up, his face purple, and shook his fist at Darrow, crying, "To protect the word of God against the greatest atheist and agnostic in the United States!"

It was a savage encounter, and a tragic one for the ex-Secretary of State. He was defending what he held most dear. He was making—though he did not know it—his last appearance before the great American public which had once done him honor (he died scarcely a week later). And he was being covered with humiliation. The sort of religious faith which he represented could not take the witness stand and face reason as a prosecutor.

On the morning of July 21st Judge Raulston mercifully refused to let the ordeal of Bryan continue and expunged the testimony of the previous afternoon. Scopes's lawyers had been unable to get any of their scientific evidence before the jury, and now they saw that their only chance of making the sort of defense they had planned for lay in giving up the case and bringing it before the Tennessee Supreme Court on appeal. Scopes was promptly found guilty and fined one hundred dollars. The State Supreme Court later upheld the anti-evolution law but freed Scopes on a technicality, thus preventing further appeal.

Theoretically, fundamentalism had won, for the law stood. Yet really Fundamentalism had lost. Legislators might go on passing anti-evolution laws, and in the hinterlands the pious might still keep their religion locked in a science-proof compartment of their minds; but civilized opinion everywhere had regarded the Dayton trial with amazement and amusement, and the slow drift away from Fundamentalist certainty continued.

How Does the Author Make His Point?

1. What is the thesis statement?
2. In paragraph 2, Allen likens the situation in Dayton to a circus. What details support this comparison?
3. In paragraph 2, Allen juxtaposes (places together) several incongruous situations and people. Find and discuss these.
4. What is the turning point of the trial?
5. Why does the author mention the heat often?
6. Find the highly connotative words in sentence 1 of paragraph 7.
7. What do these words reveal about the author's feelings on Bryan's testimony?

What Do You Think?

1. In paragraph 3, Stewart, Darrow, and Bryan are quoted. Would you expect such statements in a court of law today? Give examples to support your answer.
2. What changes when the trial is moved outside? Discuss the effects that change of location might make.
3. Is Allen's conclusion accurate? Did the Scopes Trial end the battle between fundamentalism and science?
4. What feeling for Bryan did the essay evoke in you?

The Turtle

John Steinbeck

Notice the keen eye for detail and the strong appeal to the senses in the following passage from John Steinbeck's Grapes of Wrath:

. . . And over the grass at the roadside a land turtle crawled, turning aside for nothing, dragging his high-domed shell over the grass. His hard legs and yellow-nailed feet threshed slowly through the grass, not really walking, but boosting and dragging his shell along. The barley beards slid off his shell, and the clover burrs fell on him and rolled to the ground. His horny beak was partly open, and his fierce, humorous eyes, under brows like fingernails, stared straight ahead. He came over the grass leaving a beaten trail behind him, and the hill, which was the highway embankment, reared up ahead of him. For a moment he stopped, his head held high. He blinked and looked up and down. At last he started to climb the embankment. Front clawed feet reached forward but did not touch. The hind feet kicked his shell along, and it scraped on the grass, and on the gravel. As the embankment grew steeper and steeper, the more frantic were the efforts of the land turtle. Pushing hind legs strained and slipped, boosting the shell along, and the horny head protruded as far as the neck could stretch. Little by little the shell slid up the embankment until at last a parapet cut straight across its line of march, the shoulder of the road, a concrete wall four inches high. As though they worked independently the hind legs pushed the shell against the wall. The head upraised and peered over the wall to the broad smooth plain of cement. Now the hands, braced on top of the wall, strained and lifted, and the shell came slowly up and rested its front end on the wall. For a moment the turtle rested. A red ant ran into the shell, into the soft skin inside the shell, and suddenly head and legs snapped in, and the armored tail clamped in sideways. The red ant was crushed between body and legs. And one head of wild oats was clamped into the shell by a front leg. For a long moment the turtle lay still, and then the neck crept out and the old humorous frowning eyes looked about and the legs and tail came out. The back legs went to work, straining like elephant legs, and the shell tipped to an angle so that the front legs could not reach the level cement plain. But higher and higher the hind legs boosted it, until at last the center of balance was reached, the front tipped down, the front legs scratched at the pavement, and it was up. But the head of wild oats was held by its stem around the front legs.

Now the going was easy, and all the legs worked, and the shell boosted along, waggling from side to side. A sedan driven by a forty-year old woman approached. She saw the turtle and swung to the right, off the highway, the wheels screamed and a cloud of dust boiled up. Two wheels lifted for a moment and then settled. The car skidded back onto the road, and went on, but more slowly. The turtle had jerked into its shell, but now it hurried on, for the highway was burning hot.

And now a light truck approached, and as it came near the driver saw the turtle and swerved to hit it. His front wheel struck the edge of the shell, flipped the turtle like a tiddly-wink, spun it like a coin, and rolled it off the highway. The truck went back to its course along the right side. Lying on its back, the turtle was tight in its shell for a long time. But at last its legs waved in the air, reaching for something to pull it over. Its front foot caught a piece of quartz and little by little the shell pulled over and flopped upright. The wild oat fell out and three of the spearhead seeds stuck in the ground. And as the turtle crawled on down the embankment, its shell dragged dirt over the seeds. The turtle entered a dust road and jerked itself along, drawing a wavy shallow trench in the dust with its shell. The old humorous eyes looked ahead, and the horney beak opened a little. His yellow toe nails slipped a fraction in the dust.

How Does the Author Make His Point?

1. In this passage, the central impression is implied rather than directly stated. What do you think the central impression is?
2. Find examples of descriptive details made effective through parallel wording.

3. Underline every active verb that you can find in this passage. How much do these words contribute to the vivid picture that Steinbeck creates for his readers?

What Do You Think?

1. Was there any point in Steinbeck's description where you found yourself identifying with the turtle? Explain.
2. You can sometimes learn much about people simply by looking at their eyes. How do Steinbeck's descriptions of the turtle's eyes make you feel about the turtle?
3. Were you surprised when the truck driver deliberately swerved to hit the turtle? Why or why not? What, in your opinion, was Steinbeck's purpose in including this incident?

The Sounds of Manhattan

JAMES TUITE

In the first part of this chapter, you learned that good descriptive writing depends on keen observation, and that the writer of description must use all the senses to observe—not just the sense of sight. In the following example, notice how author James Tuite uses sounds to create a distinct mental image of New York.

New York is a city of sounds: muted sounds and shrill sounds: shattering sounds and soothing sounds: urgent sounds and aimless sounds. The cliff dwellers of Manhattan—who would be racked by the silence of the lonely woods—do not hear these sounds because they are constant and eternally urban.

The visitor to the city can hear them, though, just as some animals can hear a high-pitched whistle inaudible to humans. To the casual caller to Manhattan, lying restive and sleepless in a hotel twenty or thirty floors above the street, they tell a story as fascinating as life itself. And back of the sounds broods the silence.

Night in midtown is the noise of tinseled honky-tonk and violence. Thin strains of music, usually the firm beat of rock 'n' roll or the frenzied outbursts of the discotheque, rise from ground level. This is the cacophony, the discordance of youth, and it comes on strongest when nights are hot and young blood restless.

Somewhere in the canyons below there is shrill laughter or raucous shouting. A bottle shatters against concrete. The whine of a police siren slices through the night, moving ever closer, until an eerie Doppler effect brings it to a guttural halt.

There are few sounds so exciting in Manhattan as those of fire apparatus dashing through the night. At the outset there is the tentative hint of the first-due company bullying his way through midtown traffic. Now a first whistle from the opposite direction affirms that trouble is, indeed, afoot. In seconds, other sirens converging from other streets help the skytop listener focus on the scene of excitement.

But he can only hear and not see, and imagination takes flight. Are the flames and smoke gushing from windows not far away? Are victims trapped there, crying out for help? Is it a conflagration, or only a trash-basket fire? Or, perhaps, it is merely a false alarm.

The questions go unanswered and the urgency of the moment dissolves. Now the mind and the ear detect the snarling, arrogant bickering of automobile horns. People in a hurry. Taxicabs blaring, insisting on their checkered priority.

Even the taxi horns dwindle down to a precocious few in the gray and pink moments of dawn. Suddenly there is another sound, a morning sound that taunts the memory for recognition. The growl of a predatory monster? No, just garbage trucks that have begun a day of scavenging.

Trash cans rattle outside restaurants. Metallic jaws on sanitation trucks gulp and masticate the residue of daily living, then digest it with a satisfied groan of gears.

The sounds of the new day are businesslike. The growl of buses, so scattered and distant at night, becomes a demanding part of the traffic bedlam. An occasional jet or helicopter injects an exclamation point from an unexpected quarter. When the wind is right, the vibrant bellow of an ocean liner can be heard.

The sounds of the day are as jarring as the glare of a sun that outlines the canyons of midtown in drab relief. A pneumatic drill frays countless nerves with its rat-a-tat-tat, for dig they must to perpetuate the city's dizzy motion. After each screech of brakes there is a moment of suspension, of waiting for the thud or crash that never seems to follow.

The whistles of traffic policemen and hotel doormen chirp from all sides, like birds calling for their mates across a frenzied aviary. And all of these sounds are adult sounds, for childish laughter has no place in these canyons.

Night falls again, the cycle is complete, but there is no surcease from sound. For the beautiful dreamers, perhaps, the "sounds of the rude world heard in the day, lulled by the moonlight have all passed away," but this is not so in the city.

Too many New Yorkers accept the sounds about them as bland parts of everyday existence. They seldom stop to listen to the sounds, to think about them, to be appalled or enchanted by them. In the big city, sounds are life.

How Does the Author Make His Point?

1. What is the thesis sentence?
2. What words best describe the sounds the author describes?
3. Paragraphs 1, 2, 8, 9, and 12 contain comparisons—some literal, some figurative. Find them and discuss their effectiveness.
4. Without consulting a dictionary, see if you can guess the meanings of the following words by the context: *cacophony* (para.3), *raucous* (para. 4), *Doppler effect* (para. 4), *eerie* (para. 4), *conflagration* (para. 6), *scavenging* (para. 8), *masticate* (para. 9), *bedlam* (para. 10), *pneumatic* (para. 11), *aviary* (para. 12).
5. Personification, attributing human or animal characteristics to inanimate things, is used extensively by Mr. Tuite in this essay. Find six or eight examples of personification and tell how this technique contributes to the strength and vividness of this essay.
6. List the verbs in any one paragraph and discuss their effectiveness. Are they verbs you would have thought of or used?

What Do You Think?

1. After reading this essay, would you like to live in Manhattan? Does it sound exciting? Frightening? Disturbing?
2. Do you feel as Mr. Tuite does when you hear a fire siren? Describe your feelings.
3. Compare "The Sounds of Manhattan" with "The Scopes Trial." In what way do the settings seem similar and in what ways different?

The Death of the Moth

Virginia Woolf

Virginia Woolf, the distinguished novelist and critic, was also an essayist. As a novelist, she changed the course of the English novel by emphasizing the significance of the inner life of the mind and spirit. As an essayist, she gave not only psychological insight but a sense of the joy of life. The following essay is a good example of her celebration of life:

Moths that fly by day are not properly to be called moths; they do not excite that pleasant sense of dark autumn nights and ivy-blossom which the commonest yellow underwing asleep in the shadow of the curtain never fails to rouse in us. They are hybrid creatures, neither gay like butterflies nor sombre like their own species. Nevertheless the present specimen, with his narrow hay-coloured wings, fringed with a tassel of the same colour, seemed to be content with life. It was a pleasant morning, mid-September, mild, benignant, yet with a keener breath than that of the summer months. The plough was already scoring the field opposite the window, and where the share had been, the earth was pressed flat and gleamed with moisture. Such vigour came rolling in from the fields and the down beyond that it was difficult to keep the eyes strictly turned upon the book. The rooks too were keeping one of their annual festivities; soaring round the tree-tops until it looked as if a vast net with thousands of black knots in it has been cast up into the air; which, after a few moments sank slowly down upon the trees until every twig seemed to have a knot at the end of it. Then, suddenly, the net would be thrown into the air again in a wider circle this time, with the utmost clamour and vociferation, as though to be thrown into the air and settle slowly down upon the tree-tops were a tremendously exciting experience.

The same energy which inspired the rooks, the ploughmen, the horses, and even, it seemed, the lean bare-backed downs, sent the moth fluttering from side to side of his square of the window-pane. One could not help watching him. One was, indeed, conscious of a queer feeling of pity for him. The possibilities of pleasure seemed that morning so enormous and so various that to have only a moth's part in life, and a day moth's at that, appeared a hard fate, and his zest in enjoying his meagre opportunities to the full, pathetic. He flew vigorously to one corner of his compartment, and, after waiting there a second, flew across to the other. What remained for him but to fly to a third corner and then to a fourth? That was all he could do, in spite of the size of the downs, the width of the sky, the far-off smoke of houses, and the romantic voice, now and then, of a steamer out at sea. What he could do he did. Watching him, it seemed as if a fiber, very thin but pure, of the enormous energy of the world had been thrust into his frail and diminutive body. As often as he crossed the pane, I could fancy that a thread of vital light became visible. He was little or nothing but life.

Yet, because he was so small, and so simple a form of the energy that was rolling in at the open window and driving its way through so many narrow and intricate corridors in my own brain and in those of other human beings, there was something marvelous as well as pathetic about him. It was as if someone had taken a tiny bead of pure life and decking it as lightly as possible with down and feathers, had set it dancing and zigzagging to show us the true nature of life. Thus displayed one could not get over the strangeness of it. One is apt to forget all about life, seeing it humped and bossed and garnished and cumbered so that it has to move with the greatest circumspection and dignity. Again, the thought of all that life might have been had he been born in any other shape caused one to view his simple activities with a kind of pity.

After a time, tired by his dancing apparently, he settled on the window ledge in the sun, and the queer spectacle being at an end, I forgot about him. Then, looking up, my eye was caught by him. He was trying to resume his dancing, but seemed either so stiff or so awkward that he could only flutter to the bottom of the window-pane; and when he tried to fly across it he failed. Being intent on other matters I watched these futile attempts for a time without thinking, unconsciously waiting for him to resume his flight, as one waits for a machine, that has stopped momentarily, to start again without considering the reason for its failure. After perhaps a seventh attempt he slipped from the wooden ledge and fell, fluttering his wings, on to his back on the window-sill. The helplessness of his attitude roused me. It flashed upon me that he was in difficulties; he could no longer raise himself; his legs struggled vainly. But, as I stretched out a pencil, meaning to help him to right himself, it came over me that the failure and awkwardness were the approach of death. I laid the pencil down again.

The legs agitated themselves once more. I looked as if for the enemy against which he struggled. I looked out of doors. What had happened there? Presumably it was midday, and work in the fields had stopped. Stillness and quiet had replaced the previous animation. The birds had taken themselves off to feed in the brooks. The horses stood still. Yet the power was there all the same, massed outside indifferent, impersonal, not attending to anything in particular. Somehow it was opposed to the little hay-coloured moth. It was useless to try to do anything. One could only watch the extraordinary efforts made by those tiny legs against an oncoming doom which could, had it chosen, have submerged an entire city, not merely a city, but masses of human beings; nothing, I knew, had any chance against death. Nevertheless after a pause of exhaustion the legs fluttered again. It was superb this last protest, and so frantic that he succeeded at last in righting himself. One's sympathies, of course, were all on the side of life. Also, when there was nobody to care or to know, this gigantic effort on the part of an insignificant little moth, against a power of such magnitude, to retain what no one else valued or desired to keep, moved one strangely. Again, somehow, one saw life, a pure bead. I lifted the pencil again, useless though I knew it to be. But even as I did so, the unmistakable tokens of death showed themselves. The body relaxed, and instantly grew stiff. The struggle was over. The insignificant little creature now knew death. As I looked at the dead moth, this minute wayside triumph of so great a force over so mean an antagonist filled me with wonder. Just as life had been strange a few minutes before, so death was now as strange. The moth having righted himself now lay most decently and uncomplainingly composed. O yes, he seemed to say, death is stronger than I am.

How Does the Author Make Her Point?

1. In the last half of the first paragraph, the author gives us the setting; what purpose does this serve? What dominates the atmosphere in these lines?
2. Why does Woolf feel pity for the moth (paragraph 2)? What feeling for the moth replaces this pity at the end of the essay? Why?

3. Obviously, the author is describing more than just a moth here. What does the moth represent?
4. Would the essay have been more or less effective if the subject had been some higher life form such as a horse or a cat?
5. The struggle here is between what two forces? Can the moth win? Can any of us win?
6. Why does the author switch her point of view from I to one?

What Do You Think?

1. Should the writer have helped the moth to right itself? Why do you think she did not? Would you have done so? Why or why not?
2. Explain the dominant emotion that this essay evoked in you.
3. Have you ever observed an insect closely? What were your feelings about it and its endeavor?

Shake, Rattle, or Roll?

DANIEL SAMERIN
(student)

This student essay describes a day of dramatic contrasts.

During a field trip with a ninth grade class to McConnell's
Mill State Park one beautiful autumn day, I learned that when it
comes to survival, Mother Nature is a force to be reckoned with
by even the most civilized of societies.

The day started off full of excitement, for not only were we
students getting off a whole day of school, but we were going to a
place where we could let go of all our inhibitions.

Arriving at our destination, we left the bus and began
trekking down a hill through a path in the woods. Leaves were
falling all around us. The sun was shining in sudden bursts
through the foliage of the enormous trees that were visible as far
as the eye could see. Descending even further, I began to get an
eerie feeling. Huge boulders surrounded the passageway on both
sides, extending over it in some places, like a doorway welcoming
us into nature's hidden, secret home; while at the same time
warning us that if we were not careful or if we misbehaved, she
would crush us.

Entering nature's doorway, one could immediately hear the
faint sound of a waterfall in the distance. Excited and curious, we
ran down the path arriving at the bottom of a gully. It possessed
a rapidly flowing river, about a stone's throw wide, with beautiful
rushing cascades resembling steps made for a giant. The hills,
protecting the river on both sides, opened up the sky to let the
sun gleam in on her, making her ripples and white caps glisten
brighter than the world's biggest diamonds. The leaves on the
trees seemed to change colors right before our eyes as they
swayed from the brisk autumn breeze revealing their dark reds,
yellows, and golds. To our immediate left stood a log cabin which
was two stories high. To the left of that, a covered wooden bridge
crossed the waterway connecting its two banks. The architecture
of both buildings seemed to be over a hundred years old, yet they

looked recently built. Being overcome with awe, I wanted to get a better view of the whole area.

Separating from the group, I wandered farther down a path which ran parallel with the stream but which was set apart by heavy brush. Going farther, I noticed a location where large rocks separated the waterway from the path which seemed to provide easy access to the edge of the raging water. Daring, but cautiously, I began to tread the thirty or so feet of wet boulders. slipping occasionally, anxious to obtain a better field of vision. Upon arriving on a rock next to the water and standing straight up, I felt a sense of pride and achievement, rather like a mountain climber must feel when he reaches the crest of his challenge. I felt the spray of water that assaulted the rocks on which I stood and caught glimpses of tiny rainbows in the mist. The sweet scent of the fresh air would challenge the best perfume. Surely, I thought, this must be one of the most beautiful places in the world this time of year.

Then it happened: that strange, but all too familiar sound; a sound that I had never heard before, but recognized immediately, the sound of the rattler. Slowly turning toward shore, wishfully thinking that one of my friends had found a child's toy or a New Year's Eve noisemaker, I found the area deserted. A thousand different thoughts must have entered my mind during the next thirty seconds; however, what stood out the most were the three things that I knew about rattlesnakes: they make rattling noises; they are very deadly; and a person should be as still as possible if encountering one! Scanning the rocks, moving only my eyes, I was unable to see my adversary. Again, that terrifying sound penetrated the air; this time much closer and longer. Still, unable to see the serpent and expecting him to leap up at me from behind one of the rocks that separated me from the shore, I turned quickly toward the dangerously rapid, flowing water. Then I realized that what once I thought was an earthly paradise had suddenly turned into a death trap. Blaring that dreadful sound even closer, the reptile seemed to be giving me one last warning. Not hesitating another second, I bolted across the boulders with what must have been a look of terror on my face. Hurdling myself over the last rock and tumbling to the ground, I heard the cry of the rattler once again, this time at a safe, unthreatening distance.

Looking around, I was unable to envision the beauty experienced earlier within those same surroundings and cursed the snake for ruining my concept of paradise.

How Does the Author Make His Point?

1. Contrast the first and second halves of the essay.
2. One of the things that make this essay good is the student's use of figures of speech. Can you find several examples of metaphors, similes, personification (inanimate objects or animals taking on human characteristics), or other poetic language?
3. What specific details help you, the reader, to "see" McConnell's Mill State Park?
4. What unifies the essay?
5. Is the ending effective? Why or why not?

What Do You Think?

1. Have you ever had an experience such as this student, where one minute you were very happy and the next minute terrified or angry or devastated? Explain.
2. Was the author stupid to wander away from the others while in a strange place? or merely curious? adventurous? kidlike?
3. Would you recognize the sound of a rattler or other deadly warning signals? Discuss.

INTEGRATING READING WITH WRITING SKILLS: USING DETAILS TO FORM GENERALIZATIONS

One skill that both readers and writers need is the ability to derive generalizations from a group of details. A group of details that does not lead to a conclusion means little if anything. It must be related to a generalizing idea before the details are meaningful. The details lead to (or away from) a central impression.

In the following passage, see if you can determine the general impression that best describes the writer's father:

> My father is very skillful with small boats, whether they are sailboats, rowboats, or canoes. He utilizes his skill with these small craft to make himself a successful fisherman. However, he is equally skillful as a woodsman, and he is a very good shot. I have never known him to go fishing without bringing home a good catch, even when the other fishermen were doing nothing but losing their bait. The one time he came home from hunting with his game bag empty, my mother was frightened that he might be hurt or sick.

Which generalization best describes father?

1. My father is only happy when he captures what he's pursuing.
2. My father is an excellent hunter and fisherman.
3. My father makes my mother worry a lot.

Obviously, the right answer is that father is a good hunter and fisherman. The other two generalizations are not supported by the few details that are given. If you wished to be very emphatic about your father's capability in field and stream, you would probably add to these few details several more in order to make sure that you had sufficient evidence to support your generalization.

Not only must you have sufficient details for support of your generalization, but they must be specific details. Details about your mother worrying about your father in the hunting field or about his unhappiness if he has a bad day do not support your statement that he is an excellent sportsman. These three suggestions are really three different generalizations. If you read carefully, you will notice that good writers choose sufficient details to support specifically the generalization they wish to convey to their readers. You, as a writer, must follow their example.

Exercises

The following passage from Upton Sinclair's *The Jungle* describes conditions in Chicago's meatpacking plants in 1906. Let's hope things have changed! Actually, Sinclair's novel did lead to reform. What we have here is a combination of details, both factual and descriptive. However, there is no unifying statement, no controlling idea. Read the paragraph carefully and write a topic sentence that will unify the details.

There would be meat that had tumbled out on the floor, in the dirt and sawdust, where the workers had tramped and spit uncounted billions of consumption germs. There would be meat stored in great piles in rooms, and the water from leaky rooms would drip over it, and thousands of rats would race about on it. It was too dark in these storage places to see well but a man could run his hand over these piles of meat and sweep off handfuls of the dried dung of rats. These rats were nuisances, and the packers would put poisoned bread out for them, they would die, and then rats, bread, and meat would go into the hoppers together. This is no fairy story and no joke; the meat would be shoveled into carts, and the men who did the shoveling would not trouble to lift out a rat even when he saw one—there were things that went into the sausage in comparison with which a poisoned rat was a tidbit. There was no place for the men to wash their hands before they ate their dinner, and so they made a practice of washing them in the water that was to be ladled into the sausage. There were the butt-ends of smoked meat, and the scraps of corned beef, and all the odds and ends of the waste of the plants, that would be dumped into old barrels in the cellar and left there. Under the system of rigid economy which the packers enforced, there were some jobs that it only paid to do once in a long time, and among these was the cleaning out of the waste barrels. Every spring they did it; and in the barrels would be dirt and rust and old nails and stale water—and cart load after cart load of it would be taken and dumped into the hoppers with fresh meat, and sent out to the public's breakfast. Some of it they would make into "smoked" sausage—but as the smoking took time, and was therefore expensive, they would call upon their chemistry department, and preserve it with borax and color it with gelatine to make it brown. All of their sausage came out of the same bowl, but when they came to wrap it they would stamp some of it "special," and for this they would charge two cents more a pound.

Upton Sinclair

Based on the following facts widely reported in U.S. newspapers, write a general statement that makes the point the author wishes to convey.

> While working on a project involving the F-18 Hornet, two senior officers in the Navy Air Corps found that a diode cost $1,280. Since a diode is a device about the size of a grain of rice which is used to control electrical current, the officers decided the price was rather expensive and decided to see if they could find one equally effective that was cheaper. They did find one in a local hardware store, and it cost 34¢. In every minute of every day, the world spends $1.3 million on arms. During that minute, thirty children die because they lack the food and inexpensive vaccines that could save their lives. What's more, a single nuclear submarine costs as much as the annual education budget of twenty-three developing countries that have 160 million school-age children.

In the following paragraph, Alan Moorehead recalls his response upon first seeing a gorilla. From his details, construct a generalization that will unify his impressions.

> And the truth is he was wonderful. He was a huge shining male, half crouching, half standing, his mighty arms akimbo. I had not been

prepared for the blackness of him; he was a great craggy pillar of gleaming blackness, black crew-cut hair on his head, black deep-sunken eyes glaring toward us, huge rubbery black nostrils and a black beard. He shifted his posture a little, still glaring fixedly upon us, and he had the dignity and majesty of prophets. He was the most distinguished and splendid animal I ever saw and I had only one desire at that moment: to go forward towards him, to meet him and to know him: to communicate. This experience (and I am by no means the only one to feel it in the presence of a gorilla) is utterly at variance with one's reactions to all other large wild animals in Africa. If the lion roars, if you get too close to an elephant and he fans out his ears, if the rhinoceros lowers his head and turns in your direction, you have, if you are unarmed and even sometimes if you are, just one impulse and that is to run away. The beast you feel is savage, intrinsically hostile, basically a murderer. But with the gorilla there is an instant sense of recognition. You might be badly frightened, but in the end you feel you will be able to make some gesture, utter some sound, that the animal will recognize and understand. At all events you do not have the same instinct to turn and bolt.

Alan Moorehead

IMPROVING YOUR VOCABULARY: READING THE ENTIRE DICTIONARY ENTRY

No source of information is more important in building a good vocabulary than the dictionary. To get the most out of your dictionary, however, you should read the entire entry, that is, all the information given about that word as it is listed in the dictionary. Although the most frequent reason for looking up a word is to find out its present meaning or spelling, many entries give you a lot more information than this about a word. You spend most of your time looking up a word, finding it physically on the page; it is efficient, therefore, to spend an additional few seconds to learn all about that word. It is efficient, first, because the more you know about a subject, the better you remember it. Also, you have increased your store of knowledge.

In *The American Heritage Dictionary of the English Language*, the word *brand* has the following bits of information in the entry:

   I. Pronunciation—(brand)
  II. A Lowercase n—noun—part of speech
 III. Meanings
     1. a trade mark or distinctive name identifying a product or a manufacturer.
     2. the make of a product thus marked: a popular *brand* of soap

Describing   91

3. a mark indicating identity or ownership, burned on the hide of an animal with a hot iron
4. a mark formerly burned into the flesh of criminals
5. any mark of disgrace or notoriety; a stigma
6. an iron that is heated and used for branding
7. a piece of burning or charred wood
8. archaic (a term indicating the level of usage, i.e., no longer in common use)
    meaning a sword: "So flashed and fell the *brand* Excalibur." (Tennyson—an example of the archaic meaning)
IV. Second grammatical form—lowercase tr. v. (meaning a transitive verb); forms of the verb—branded, branding, brands.
V. Meanings of word as a verb—to mark with or as if with a *brand* or to mark with disgrace or infamy; stigmatize
VI. Etymology (Middle English *brand*, fire, torch, sword. Old English *brand*, piece of burning wood)
VII. Reference to further information—see *bhreu* in Appendix

By reading the entire entry, you have learned not just one word but several and how they should properly be used. In addition, you will probably have noticed a very similar word *brandish* which means to wave something, a weapon, perhaps, menacingly, as a sword.

Increased knowledge about a word leads us into some interesting byways that help us to remember the words as a part of our active vocabulary. Reading the entire entry of the word *Nike* would explain why there are Nike missile sites and Nike running shoes, for Nike was the Greek goddess of victory. If one Greek god leads to another, you might learn that Bacchus was the god of wine; from this, you could intelligently guess that a *bacchanal* is a celebration of this jolly god. Reading the entire entry for the verb *tantalize*, you would find a reference to the Greek character Tantalus who was punished by standing in water which drained away from him every time he bent to drink, and you would find that a *tantalus* is a piece of dining room equipment that keeps liquor locked away from every thirsty soul who does not have the key to unlock it and get to the bottles within it. Reading the dictionary would inform you that *witches' broom* has nothing to do with witch transportation but is an abnormal growth of small branches on a tree, that *John Dory* is not a man but a fish, and that you need not fear a puff adder because it's just a harmless North American snake.

Reading the entire entry of the word *idiot* would tell you that the ancient Greeks so admired men who went into public office that those who did not were known as *idiotes*, that is, private persons. From this comes our word *idiot*. Reading to the end of the entry for *gossamer*, meaning any sheer, gauzelike fabric and literally meaning *goose summer*, refers you to the late fall when cobwebs are thick and particularly visible because of the dew. Any fabric that looks like cobwebs is now referred to as gossamer, from *gos sommer*. The component parts of the word *trivia* are *tri*, meaning *three*, and *via*, meaning *ways or roads*. The origins of many words supply interesting or colorful information which helps you to retain those words and to perceive their exact meanings. Spending a little more time and attention on reading entire dictionary entries pays high dividends.

ASSIGNMENTS

A. The key to writing a good descriptive essay is conveying a clear central impression. If you are going to write a description of a person, ask yourself why this person is important enough to you to attract your attention. Why do you dislike him or love him? Does he or she remind you of anyone or anything? Why do you remember him?

Write a descriptive essay on one of the following topics or select one of your own which you will then support with sufficient specific details to create an interesting central impression:

A dirty, disheveled kid who evokes pity
A dirty, disheveled kid who evokes disgust
A plain girl who looks pretty
A pretty girl who looks dowdy
A handicapped person who evokes pity
A handicapped person who evokes admiration
The costume of a punk rocker
The hairstyle of a punk rocker
A tramp who hasn't lost his spirit
A playful puppy
A carefully cared for garden in a backyard
The body of a superb athlete like Arnold Schwarzenegger
A cozy kitchen
An elaborate hairdo
An exhausted football player
A favorite tree
A nontypical professor
A person who reminds you of some animal—a leopard, a fox, a rabbit, a lion, a rat, a mother hen, a sleek cat
A no-nonsense business woman

B. If you are writing to describe a place, you frequently make your description more telling if you indicate the time of day or the time of year that is being described. This frequently involves a contrast which projects different atmospheres suggested by the place. (It is frequently said that Shakespeare created a ninëword masterpiece when he described a tree in winter as having "Bare, ruined choirs/Where late the sweet birds sang." This description of the wintry tree recalls the happier times of summer.) For example, standing in an empty football stadium on a rainy morning in March projects a different atmosphere from standing in that stadium filled with cheering fans during a bright, blue October afternoon.

Choose from the following list of places or create one of your own to serve as a topic for a descriptive essay. Pay particular attention to the effect that the time of day or year has on what you are describing.

A high school auditorium on the opening night of the senior play

An abandoned steel mill on a cold, blustery December morning

A television studio five minutes before air time

A beachfront cottage on a soft, moonlit, midsummer evening

Your daughter's bedroom the morning after her slumber party

A hospital on a Sunday morning during breakfast

Your kitchen shortly after Thanksgiving dinner

A church on a hot, humid Sunday morning during the pastor's sermon

An operating room at 3:00 A.M. during emergency surgery

A waterfront at dawn

4

Explaining by Examples

RHETORIC

Traditionally, scholars have divided writing into four *modes of discourse,* that is, ways of speaking and writing.

Narration, which tells a story, almost always uses chronological (time) order.
Description, which recreates a sensory experience, uses spatial order.
Exposition, which explains a statement, uses various types of order.
Argument/Persuasion, which attempts to change a person's attitude or actions, uses one of the logical orders (induction or deduction).

The next few chapters offer some specific methods to develop essays using the expository order, the order used most often in business, politics, journalism, and, of course, education. Your aim in expository writing is to *explain* something to your reader.

Once you have decided what you want to explain and have put it into a sentence (your thesis statement), you must then decide how you can best develop your idea. There are many methods of development to choose from; you might divide and classify, compare or contrast, define, present facts, or give examples. Many authors use a combination of methods, choosing whichever method best suits the subtopic they are discussing. However, you cannot combine methods until you know what the methods are. Therefore, this chapter and the following four will discuss essays using a single method of development; the last three chapters will discuss combined methods.

One of the most common ways of illustrating a general theory or supporting an opinion on any subject is by using specific *examples*. In narration, as you have already seen, you use a single extended example or story—often an occurrence from personal experience—to illustrate your controlling idea. In *exemplification* (showing or illustrating by examples), however, a number of well-chosen examples offer specific support for your thesis. Used alone or in combination with other methods, examples can provide a powerful tool for clarifying, supporting, or proving your thesis statement.

Suppose you say that when interest rates are high, many young people are unable to buy a home. You have made a general statement with which many of your readers might agree, but without specific examples to show what you mean and to provide clear support for your statement, you offer only an opinion—your opinion, unsupported. If, however, you cite several typical examples in which young people have been prevented from buying a home because of the added cost of high interest on mortgages, then you give your reader some convincing reasons for accepting your opinion.

Choosing Good Examples

If an essay developed mainly by examples is going to be effective, then the examples themselves must be well chosen to provide clear and specific support for the thesis. To make sure they are clear and specific, you apply widely recognized standards: the examples should be *adequate, relevant, typical,* and *accurate.*

First, your thesis statement is a generalization, a theory or a point of view, and one or two examples are seldom adequate to support a generalization. If you don't want your reader to think you are jumping to a hasty conclusion, you need to provide enough specific examples to present convincing support for your opinion or point of view.

Then, too, your examples must be relevant. Keeping the purpose of your essay clearly in mind, select specific examples which do indeed illustrate, clarify, or prove your controlling idea.

For example, if your thesis statement claims that American students do not do as well as their foreign counterparts on achievement tests, you must present more accurate support than a few vague examples. Saying that "Asians do better on almost all tests," "students from the British Isles are better in science," "American students came in dead last on tests in most disciplines" will not convince the skeptic.

Specific and accurate factual examples are hard to ignore. If you want to prove your thesis statement, examples like the following are more likely to be accepted. "The results of the IEA Science Study done in 1987, which tested students from 24 countries, American students, even those taking advanced courses, scored below average in every category. On a test in which the average student should score 50, our first year biology and physics students averaged 34 percent, our beginning chemistry students 27 percent. Japanese students averaged 62 percent in chemistry, 71 percent in biology, and 58 percent in physics. Asian Americans make up 2 percent of our population, but there were '20 Asian-American students out of 70 among the scholarship winners in the Westinghouse Science Talent Search, the nation's oldest and most prestigious high school science competition' (*Time*, August 31, 1987). That's 2 percent of the population getting 28.5 percent of the prizes or almost 15 times what their numbers would win statistically." Of course, you would need more than two examples, but these illustrate the type of specific, accurate examples that will convince.

You must also guard against the temptation to use spectacular but nontypical examples, no matter how vivid they may be. No matter how many examples you could cite of Amish farmers in Pennsylvania who get along quite well without cars, you're not apt to convince your readers that they, the readers, don't need their own cars. To your readers, the examples of Amish farmers are neither relevant nor typical.

In the following excerpt from their essay "The Sounds of Silence," Mildred and Edward Hall carefully choose relevant, typical examples to support their thesis that people often communicate more through nonverbal signs than through language itself:

> Bob leaves his apartment at 8:15 A.M. and stops at the corner drugstore for breakfast. Before he can speak, the counterman says, "The usual?" Bob nods yes. While he savors his Danish, a fat man pushes onto the adjoining stool and overflows into his space. Bob scowls and the man pulls himself in as much as he can. Bob has sent two messages without speaking a syllable.

Henry has an appointment to meet Arthur at 11 o'clock; he arrives at 11:30. Their conversation is friendly, but Arthur retains a lingering hostility. Henry has unconsciously communicated that he doesn't think the appointment is very important or that Arthur is a person who needs to be treated with respect.

George is talking to Charley's wife at a party. Their conversation is entirely trivial, yet Charley glares at them suspiciously. Their physical proximity and the movements of their eyes reveal that they are powerfully attracted to each other.

Jose Ybarra and Sir Edmund Jones are at the same party and it is important for them to establish a cordial relationship for business reasons. Each is trying to be warm and friendly, yet they will part with mutual distrust and their business transactaion will probably fall through. Jose, in Latin fashion, moved closer and closer to Sir Edmund as they spoke, and this movement was miscommunicated as pushiness to Sir Edmund, who kept backing away from this intimacy, and this was miscommunicated to Jose as coldness. The silent languages of Latin and English are more difficult to learn than their spoken languages.

Mildred and Edward Hall

It may be difficult to make sure that your examples are accurate, but you need to use your best judgment to guard against biased opinions and distortions of fact. If you are to convince intelligent readers of the merits of your point of view, you need to demonstrate your willingness to look at the evidence fairly. Intelligent readers quickly become skeptical when they see that you are stacking the cards by presenting only examples that favor your thesis and ignoring obvious evidence to the contrary. You are not apt to convince them that the Arizona desert is a great place to live if the only examples you give concern a brief period when the desert blooms in the early spring. It is also important to recognize that not all sources are equally reliable: the *Treetop Tattler* is not on a par with the *New York Times* or the *Wall Street Journal*. A healthy sense of skepticism is indispensable, and whenever you are in doubt, try to verify your information through several sources that are as up-to-date and unbiased as possible.

ORGANIZATION

The essay developed through a series of examples is simple to organize. A brief introduction usually leads to your thesis statement. The topic sentence of each body paragraph will present a major supporting point for the thesis statement, and the paragraph will include whatever examples may be necessary to illustrate, explain, or prove that major point. The conclusion frequently provides a brief summary of what the examples illustrate and serves to reinforce the controlling idea of the essay.

The pattern of organization may be as simple as the following:

THESIS STATEMENT: A Generalization (Theory or Point of View)
TOPIC SENTENCE FOR BODY PARAGRAPH 1
  Specific Example 1
  Specific Example 2
  Specific Example 3
TOPIC SENTENCE FOR BODY PARAGRAPH 2
  Specific Example 1
  Extended Example
CONCLUSION: A brief summary of the main supporting points and examples, together with a restatement of the thesis in different words.

Climactic Order

Usually, the most effective method of arranging a series of supporting examples is *climactic order*—that is, the most telling example is placed *last*. Here are two outlines that illustrate climactic order.

Thesis Statement: Although I sometimes fear that my mother is too generous for her own good, her generosity seems to benefit her as well as all who come in contact with her.

A. She opens her house to all strays—animals and people.
B. She gives her money to anyone who she feels needs it more than she does.
C. She gives her time, which is really all any of us have, to those who need it.
D. But most of all, she gives her love, and all who receive it are a little better for it.

Conclusion: So though the house is crowded, the time and money a little short, the love is always there, and my mother blossoms.

Thesis Statement: Although we have an open class system in the United States, few people climb more than one step in their lifetimes.

A. Few people move upward since it involves changing their life-style—moving to a different area, dressing differently, learning a new language.
B. Also, people interested in raising their status must change their attitudes and habits; they must go to symphonies instead of hockey games, visit museums instead of bars, spend money for education instead of material things.
C. But, worse than all the rest, social climbers must give up the people closest to them; they find they have little in common with their family; friends are left behind with their "old" habits; everyone from their past will be gone.

Conclusion: Changing one's life style is tough, and learning to enjoy different pleasures is tougher, but giving up the people who have been the closest is the bitterest part of "moving up."

Transitions

The connection between your thesis statement and the specific examples must be clear to your reader. Placing your thesis statement at the end of your introduction makes it easier to move smoothly from your generalization to the supporting examples. Suppose that you wanted to convince your readers that "Living in the country is not necessarily dull and boring." The topic sentence of the first body paragraph might be linked to that thesis with a simple transitional phrase: "*For one thing,* there is always plenty to do, winter and summer."

Among the many transitional devices is the subordinate clause used to provide a clear link between the discussion in a previous paragraph and the topic sentence of the paragraph.

When we consider the many examples of waste in defense spending, . . . (new topic)

Although these freedoms are frequently taken for granted, . . . (new topic)

While many people assumed that such atrocities could never occur in the United States, . . . (new topic)

To provide smooth transition within and between the paragraphs of an essay, you will need to make use of all the various transitional devices at one time or another, including parallel wording, the use of synonyms, and the more obvious devices such as *enumeration* (first, second, third) and *addition* (in addition, also, likewise).

The Case Against Women

JAMES THURBER

Humorist James Thurber was a staff writer and illustrator for the New Yorker *for many years. Of his many sketches, comedies, and short stories, he is probably best known for* The Secret Life of Walter Mitty. *The examples he uses in the following essay are facetious.*

Introductory paragraph, consisting of a slight anecdote and one reason he hates women and concluding with his thesis statement

A bright-eyed woman, whose sparkle was more of eagerness than of intelligence, approached me at a party one afternoon and said, "Why do you hate women, Mr, Thurberg?" I quickly adjusted my fixed grin and denied that I hated women; I said I did not hate women at all. But the question remained with me, and I discovered when I went to bed that night that I had been subconsciously listing a number of reasons I do hate women. It might be interesting—at least it will help pass the time—to set down these reasons, just as they came up out of my subconscious.

First identified reason

In the first place, I hate women because they always know where things are. At first blush, you might think that a perverse and merely churlish reason for hating women, but it is not. Naturally, every man enjoys having a woman around the house who knows where his shirt studs and his briefcase are, and things like that, but he detests having a woman around who knows where everything is, even things that are of no importance at all, such as, say, the snapshots her husband took three years ago at Elbow Beach.

Example supporting reason

The husband has never known where these snapshots were since the day they were developed and printed; he hopes, in a vague way, if he thinks about them at all, that after three years they have been thrown out. But his wife knows where they are, and so do his mother, his grandmother, his great-grandmother, his daughter, and the maid. They could put their fingers on them in a moment, with that quiet air of superior knowledge which makes a man feel that he is out of touch with all the things that count in life. . . .

Second reason, pretending broad significance

Another reason I hate women (and I am speaking, I believe, for the American male generally) is that in almost every case where there is a sign reading "Please have exact change ready," a woman never has anything smaller than a ten-dollar bill. She gives ten-dollar bills to bus conductors and change men in subways and other such persons who deal in nickels and dimes and quarters. Recently, in Bermuda, I saw a woman hand the conductor on the little railway there a bill of such huge denomination that I was utterly unfamiliar with it.

Supporting narrative, example

I was sitting too far away to see exactly what it was, but I had the feeling that it was a five-hundred-dollar bill. The conductor merely ignored it and stood there waiting—the fare was just one shilling. Eventually, scrabbling around in her handbag, the woman found a shilling. All the men on the train who witnessed the transaction tightened up inside; that's what a woman with a ten-dollar bill or a twenty or a five-hundred does to a man in such situations—she tightens him up inside. The episode gives him the feeling that some monstrous triviality is threatening the whole structure of civilization. It is difficult to analyze this feeling, but there it is.

Third reason

Another spectacle that depresses the male and makes him fear women, and therefore hate them, is that of a woman looking another woman up and down, to see what she is wearing. The cold, flat look that comes into a woman's eyes when she does this, the swift coarsening of her countenance, and the immediate evaporation from it of all humane quality make the male shudder.

Effect of third reason

He is likely to go to his stateroom or his den or his private office and lock himself in for hours.

Example

I know one man who surprised that look in his wife's eyes and never afterward would let her come near him. If she started toward him, he would dodge behind a table or a sofa, as if he were engaging in some unholy game of tag. That look, I believe, is one reason men disappear, and turn up in Tahiti or the Arctic or the United States Navy.

Fourth reason

I (to quit hiding behind the generalization of "the male") hate women because they almost never get anything exactly right. They say, "I have been faithful to thee, Cynara, after my fashion" instead of "in my fashion."

Examples of fourth reasons

They will bet you that Alfred Smith's middle name is Aloysius, instead of Emanuel. They will tell you to take the 2:57 train, on a day that the 2:57 does not run, or if it does run, does not stop at the station where you are supposed to get off. Many men, separated from a woman by this particular form of imprecision, have never showed up in her life again. Nothing so embitters a man as to end up in Bridgeport when he was supposed to get off at Westport.

Fifth and sixth reasons

I hate women because they have brought into the currency of our language such expressions as "all righty" and "yes indeedy" and hundreds of others. I hate women because they throw baseballs (or plates or vases) with the wrong foot advanced. I marvel that more of them have not broken their backs. I marvel that women, who coordinate so well in languorous motion, look uglier and sillier than a goose-stepper when they attempt any form of violent activity.

Concluding and most important reason

I had a lot of other notes jotted down about why I hate women, but I seem to have lost them all, except one. That one is to the effect that I hate women because, while they never lose old snapshots or anything of that sort, they invariably lose one glove. I believe that I have never gone anywhere with any woman in my whole life who did not lose one glove. I have searched for single gloves under tables in crowded restaurants and under the feet of people in darkened movie theatres. I have spent some part of every day or night hunting for a woman's glove. If there were no other reason in the world for hating women, that one would be enough. In fact, you can leave all the others out.

I Led the Pigeons to the Flag

WILLIAM SAFIRE

Political columnist and word-watcher William Safire provides multiple examples to illustrate the various ways in which our language is mangled.

The most saluted man in America is Richard Stans. Legions of schoolchildren daily place their hands over their hearts to pledge allegiance to the flag, "and to the republic for Richard Stans." With all due patriotic fervor, the same kids salute "one nation, under guard." Some begin with "I pledge a legion to the flag," others with "I led the pigeons to the flag."

This is not a new phenomenon. When this generation comes to "One nation, indivisible," it is as likely to say, "One naked individual," as a previous generation was to murmur, "One nation is dirigible," or, "One nation and a vegetable." "The Stars Bangled Banger" is a great source for these creative mishearings: "the Donzerly light," "oh, the ramrods were washed," "grapefruit through the night" that our flag was still there.

Then there is the good Mrs. Shirley Murphy of the 23rd Psalm: "Shirley, good Mrs. Murphy, shall follow me all the days of my life." (Surely goodness and mercy would not lead us into Penn Station.)

Children make the sounds they hear fit the sense in their own heads. In "God Bless America," the misheard line, "Through the night with a light from a bulb" makes more practical sense than "a light from above." Writes David Thomas of Maine, "In Sunday school I used to sing, 'I will follow Henry Joyce,' as part of a hymn. Who Henry Joyce was didn't concern me. I was following him at the top of my lungs. When I learned to read, I found the words were, 'I will follow and rejoice.'"

Sometimes—even with the onset of adulthood—that awakening never takes place. In the song "Lucy in the Sky with Diamonds," the phrase "the girl with Kaleidoscope eyes" came across to one grandmother as "the girl with colitis goes by."

What is this mistaken hearing called? In each of the

following categories, childlike translation can lead to semantic change.

The "Guylum Bardo" syndrome. The simple misdivision of words—as in the name of bandleader Guy Lombardo—is called metanalysis (for "wrong cutting"). Many of the words we use today are mistaken divisions of the past: a "napron" in Middle English became an "apron"—the "n" slid over to the left; an "eke-name" of six centuries ago became a "nickname"—the "n" slid to the right.

Oft-heard names and phrases may undergo instant changes. Thus we hear of crooner Victor Moan, actress Sophie Aloran, musician "Big Spider" Beck, pro-football back Frank O'Harris, novelist Gorvey Doll. Some runners, poised at the starting line, hear, "On your market-set-go!" Millions of children consider the letter of the alphabet between "k" and "p" to be "ellemeno"—just as the more creative of their parents understand the TV meteorologist's mention of "a patchy fog" as "Apache fog." Danny Boy, hero of "The Londonderry Air," casts a backward glance at what is often thought of as "The London Derriere." Future historians may wonder why chicken-hearted jounalists coveted "the Pullet Surprise."

The "Jose, can you see?" syndrome. The transmutation of words when they pass through different cultures or languages is known to linguists as the Law of Hobson-Jobson. British soldiers in India heard the Mohammedan cry, "Ya-Hasan, ya-Husain!" and called it "hobsonjobson." American soldiers in Japan transmuted a popular Japanese song, "Shina no Yoru," into "She Ain't Got No Yo-Yo." Similarly, "O Tannenbaum" is sometimes rendered "Oh, atom bomb."

Malapropisms. The humorous misuse of similar-sounding words is named after Mrs. Malaprop, a character in *The Rivals*, a 1775 play by Richard Sheridan. More people than you suspect read and pronounce "misled" as "mizzled." Others hum what they call "the bronze lullaby," though it must spin Brahms in his grave. One fascinating malapropism is "to hold in escarole," which combines the escrow function with the slang metaphor of money as lettuce.

Folk etymology involves the creation of new words by mistake, misunderstanding or mispronunciation. "Tawdry," for example, comes from Saint Audrey's, a place in England where cheap merchandise was sold. The slurred "and" is one of the prolific changers of phrases. When "hard and fast" is spoken quickly, it becomes "hard 'n' fast," which sometimes gets transformed to "harden-fast rules." In the same way, the old "whole kin 'n' caboodle" is occasionally written as "kitten caboodle," a good name for a satchel in which to carry a cat.

In a 1954 *Harper's Magazine* article, "The Death of Lady Mondegreen," author Sylvia Wright recalled a Scottish ballad, "The Bonny Earl of Murray" from Thomas Percy's *Reliques of Ancient English Poetry,* which sounded to her like this:

> Ye Highlands and Ye Lowlands,
>   Oh, Where Hae Ye Been?
> They Hae Slain The Earl Amurray,
>   And Lady Mondegreen.

She envisioned the bonny Earl holding the beautiful Lady Mondegreen's hand, both bleeding profusely, but faithful unto death. "By now," Miss Wright wrote, "several of you more alert readers are jumping up and down in your impatience to point out that according to the poem, after they killed the Earl of Murray, they LAID HIM ON THE GREEN. I know, but I won't give in to it. Leaving him to die all alone without even anyone to hold his hand—I won't have it."

I have several other expressions that also shouldn't be taken for granite. But a nuff, I suppose, is a nuff.

How Does the Author Make His Point?

1. What is the thesis statement?
2. What is the purpose of the rather long introduction?
3. Choose one paragraph and break it down into topic sentence, main detail, and supporting detail.
4. What are the major points of the essay that the examples support?
5. Discuss the effectiveness of the conclusion. Why does this two-sentence conclusion make the point here?

What Do You Think?

1. If you were a teacher, what valuable lessons could you learn from Safire's essay?
2. In his essay, the author noted that "Children make the sounds they hear fit the sense in their own heads." Do you remember any examples of this phenomenon from your own childhood?
3. Can you give any other examples in any of Safire's categories? (Look up *bedlam*, for example.)

Death in the Open

LEWIS THOMAS

Biologist and physician Lewis Thomas is one of those fine scientist-writers who can share his knowledge and perception with simplicity and precision. As "Death in the Open" illustrates, he sees more deeply into ordinary events than most of us and shares that vision with all without the slightest pretense.

Most of the dead animals you see on highways near the cities are dogs, a few cats. Out in the countryside, the forms and coloring of the dead are strange; these are the wild creatures. Seen from a car window they appear as fragments, evoking memories of woodchucks, badgers, skunks, voles, snakes, sometimes the mysterious wreckage of a deer.

It is always a queer shock, part of a sudden upwelling of grief, part unaccountable amazement. It is simply astounding to see an animal dead on a highway. The outrage is more than just the location; it is the impropriety of such visible death, anywhere. You do not expect to see dead animals in the open. It is the nature of animals to die alone, off somewhere, hidden. It is wrong to see them lying out on the highway; it is wrong to see them anywhere.

Everything in the world dies, but we only know about it as a king of abstraction. If you stand in a meadow, at the edge of a hillside, and look around carefully, almost everything you catch sight of is in the process of dying, and most things will be dead long before you are. If it were not for the constant renewal and replacement going on before your eyes, the whole place would turn to stone and sand under your feet.

There are some creatures that do not seem to die at all; they simply vanish totally into their own progeny. Single cells do this. The cell becomes two, then four, and so on, and after a while the last trace is gone. It cannot be seen as death; barring mutation, the descendants are simply the first cell, living all over again. The cycles of the slime mold have episodes that seem as conclusive as death, but the withered slug, with its stalk and fruiting body, is plainly the transient tissue of a developing animal; the free-swimming amebocytes use this organ collectively in order to produce more of themselves.

There are said to be a billion billion insects on the earth at any moment, most of them with very short life expectancies by our standards. Someone has estimated that there are 25 million assorted insects hanging in the air over every temperate square mile, in a column extending upward for thousands of feet, drifting through the layers of the atmosphere like plankton. They are dying steadily, some by being eaten, some just dropping in their tracks, tons of them around the earth, disintegrating as they die, invisibly.

Who ever sees dead birds, in anything like the huge numbers stipulated by the certainty of the death of all birds? A dead bird is an incongruity, more startling than an unexpected live bird, sure evidence to the human mind that something has gone wrong. Birds do their dying off somewhere, behind things, under things, never on the wing.

Animals seem to have an instinct for performing death alone, hidden. Even the largest, most conspicuous ones find ways to conceal themselves in time. If an elephant missteps and dies in an open place, the herd will not leave him there; the others will pick him up and carry the body from place to place, finally putting it down in some inexplicably suitable location. When elephants encounter the skeleton of an elephant out in the open, they methodically take up each of the bones and distribute them, in a ponderous ceremony, over neighboring acres.

It is a natural marvel. All of the life of the earth dies, all of the time, in the same volume as the new life that dazzles us each morning, each spring. All we see of this is the odd stump, the fly struggling on the porch floor of the summer house in October, the fragment on the highway. I have lived all my life with an embarrassment of squirrels in my backyard, they are all over the place, all year long, and I have never seen, anywhere, a dead squirrel.

I suppose it is just as well. If the earth were otherwise, and all the dying were done in the open, with the dead there to be looked at, we would never have it out of our minds. We can forget about it much of the time, or think of it as an accident to be avoided, somehow. But it does make the process of dying seem more exceptional than it really is, and harder to engage in at the times when we must ourselves engage.

In our way, we conform as best we can to the rest of nature. The obituary pages tell us of the news that we are dying away, while the birth announcements in finer print, off at the side of the page, inform us of our replacements, but we get no grasp from this of the enormity of scale. There are 3 billion of us on the earth, and all 3 billion must be dead, on a schedule, within this lifetime. The vast mortality, involving something over 50 million of us each year, takes place in relative secrecy. We can only really know of the deaths in our households, or among our friends. These, detached in our minds from all the rest, we take to be unnatural events, anomalies, outrages. We speak of our own dead in low voices; struck down, we say, as though visible death can only occur for cause, by disease or violence, avoidably. We send off for flowers, grieve, make ceremonies, scatter bones, unaware of the rest of the 3 billion on the same schedule. All of that immense mass of flesh and bone and consciousness will disappear by absorption into the earth, without recognition by the transient survivors.

Less than a half century from now, our replacements will have more than doubled the numbers. It is hard to see how we can continue to keep the secret, with such multitudes doing the dying. We will have to give up the notion that death is catastrophe, or detestable, or avoidable, or even strange. We will need to learn more about the cycling of life in the rest of the system, and about our connection to the process. Everything that comes alive seems to be in trade for something that dies, cell for cell. There might be some comfort in the recognition of synchrony, in the information that we all go down together, in the best of company.

How Does the Author Make His Point?

1. What is the thesis statement?
2. In paragraph 2, the author uses two words in an unusual fashion. What are the words? What effect does this usage have on you as a reader?
3. Paragraphs 4 and 5 discuss what could be rather dry, biological facts. How does the author make them interesting?
4. Paragraphs 6, 7, and 8 prove what point?

5. The author uses large numbers several times: billion billion, 25 million, 3 billion, 50 million. What is his purpose?
6. How does the conclusion bring the essay to a logical and purposeful end?
7. What are the main ideas in the essay (as opposed to supporting detail)?

What Do You Think?

1. Do you agree with what the author says—in the first part of paragraph 2—about the "upswelling of grief" . . . the "unaccountable amazement"?
2. What did you learn from this article? What did you already know but gained new insights into?
3. What is the author's attitude toward death? What is yours? Did the article change your attitude in any way?
4. Would you say that the message here is pessimistic, optimistic, matter-of-fact?

One Season Fits All

ELLEN GOODMAN

Ellen Goodman is a widely read newspaper columnist who comments good-humoredly on the social changes in our lives that she deplores. In this essay, she is objecting to the commercialism that rushes the natural seasons and dislocates our holidays.

I have just been invited to an end-of-season sale. That, in itself, is not surprising. After all, spring ended on Thursday.

But the season that has gone on sale in my local department store is not spring. It is summer. I have been invited to an end-of-summer sale.

Now here I am, a woman who has not yet burned a strap mark onto her shoulder, and they are selling out the last sundresses. A woman who has not been in the water, but is warned to get my red-hot bathing suit before they're all gone. A woman who has barely turned on an air conditioner and is told that "summer must go" to make room for fall. The fall, mind you.

My personal dismay at this invitation (it does not require an R.S.V.P.) is not the result of some profound desire to rush out to the nearest dressing room, stand in front of a three-way mirror basking in blue fluorescent light, and buy a bikini. Frankly, I prefer candlelight and hand mirrors and hand-me-downs.

But it seemed to me that this end-of-season sale was the ultimate markdown of the entire concept of seasons. Today, seasons have themselves gone entirely out of season.

It's bad enough that we uprooted assorted holidays from their rightful place on the calendar and dropped them onto Monday. Imagine what Mother Washington would say if she knew she had given birth to George on a third Monday. But we now manipulate whole seasons out of their sequence without even a thought of Mother Nature.

The most blatant example of this is in sports, where the schedules are about as natural as Astroturf. The Boys of Summer start playing with the snow and end in the frost. Hockey teams were still skating after the ice had melted in northern Manitoba.

As for football, I suppose that it's become the tomato of sports. You can get it all year round now, but it's lost its flavor.

In fact, it is food that has been altered the most by our unseasonable way of life. When I was a kid, we used to wait for the strawberries to ripen. Now we wait for the plane to arrive. It's possible to get almost anything at any time of year. But it's impossible to get it to taste like anything.

I have a Vermont friend who flunked a blind tasting of berries one January. They were not blue or black, she maintained; they were a species known as "Made in California."

Not only do we alter seasons, we invent some. Tell me, for example, what our ancestors would make of the "cruise season"? Or the holiday season as we have come to know and love it. The Plastic Man of the modern commercial world can stretch its arms into the most distant calendars and pocketbooks.

Once I read that Eleanor Roosevelt had all her Christmas shopping done by Thanksgiving. Today she'd be running late. The Christmas catalogs have all arrived by Columbus Day. They are all decking the commercial halls with imported holly before Halloween. The 12 days of Christmas have extended to 120.

Where did all the seasons go? What happened to the dictionary definition of season as "one of the four natural divisions of the year"? It seems that the more we are divided from nature, the less the seasons are divided from each other.

Nature plays a much smaller role in the life of the average urban American that it once did. Fewer and fewer of us actually work outdoors. From Monday to Friday we may only encounter the outdoors between the car and the door. Weather has become a weekend event.

Increasingly, the air we breath and the water we use is heated and cooled to a monolithic comfort zone. If you don't love winter, you can leave it on the next super-saver. If you can't stand the heat, you can get out of the kitchen and into an air-conditioned movie theater.

It's hard to know whether the ability to protect ourselves from nature is worth the price of alienation. But it's part of the Western desire to master nature instead of living with it. We consider it progress that when we get up in the morning we have to turn on the radio to know what the temperature is.

Indeed, if the Bible were written today, it wouldn't say, "To everything there is a season." The psalm of modern life reads: "One season fits all."

How Does the Author Make Her Point?

1. What is Goodman's thesis statement? Is the placement of the thesis statement effective? Why or why not?
2. What examples does Goodman use to show that we have abandoned seasons? Are they effective? Which one is the most effective? Why?
3. What is the tone of the essay? Does it change? Note the paragraphs that are light, serious, sarcastic, satirical, or those that combine tones.
4. Why does the author quote the Bible in the final paragraph?
5. Goodman suggests a reason for our extending sports and shopping seasons and inventing cruise and holiday seasons. Where does she state the reason openly and where must you deduce the reason behind the changes?

What Do You Think?

1. Have you ever been annoyed by department stores rushing the seasons? Are you able to shop for a warm jacket in July?
2. Do you think we lose something when we divorce ourselves from natural seasons? (Goodman calls it alienation.)
3. Would you like to go back to the "good old days" or do you prefer society as it is today?
4. Have we discarded the seasons? Why? Do you disagree with Goodman's essay?

The Monster

DEEMS TAYLOR

Deems Taylor was a war correspondent, a magazine editor, and an eminent music critic as well as a composer of symphonic and choral works. In "The Monster," he presents a composer who was anything but lovable but who, according to Taylor, deserves our love and respect anyway.

He was an undersized little man, with a head too big for his body—a sickly little man. His nerves were bad. He had skin trouble. It was agony for him to wear anything next to his skin coarser than silk. And he had delusions of grandeur.

He was a monster of conceit. Never for one minute did he look at the world or at people, except in relation to himself. He was not only the most important person in the world, to himself; in his own eyes he was the only person who existed. He believed himself to be one of the greatest dramatists in the world, one of the greatest thinkers, and one of the greatest composers. To hear him talk, he was Shakespeare, and Beethoven, and Plato, rolled into one. And you would have had no difficulty in hearing him talk. He was one of the most exhausting conversationalists that ever lived. An evening with him was an evening spent in listening to a monologue. Sometimes he was brilliant; sometimes he was maddeningly tiresome. But whether he was being brilliant or dull, he had one sole topic of conversation: himself. What *he* thought and what *he* did.

He had a mania for being in the right. The slightest hint of disagreement, from anyone, on the most trivial point, was enough to set him off on a harangue that might last for hours, in which he proved himself right in so many ways, and with such exhausting volubility, that in the end his hearer, stunned and deafened, would agree with him, for the sake of peace.

It never occurred to him that he and his doing were not of the most intense and fascinating interest to anyone with whom he came in contact. He had theories about almost any subject under the sun, including vegetarianism, the drama, politics, and music; and in support of these theories he wrote pamphlets, letters, books . . . thousands upon thousands of words, hundreds and hundreds of pages. He not only wrote these things, and published them—usually at somebody else's expense—but he would sit and read them aloud, for hours, to his friends and his family.

He wrote operas; and no sooner did he have the synopsis of a story, but he would invite—or rather summon—a crowd of his friends to his house and read it aloud to them. Not for criticism. For applause. When the complete poem was written, the friends had to come again, and hear *that* read aloud. Then he would publish the poem, sometimes years before the music that went with it was written. He played the piano like a composer, in the worst sense of what that implies, and he would sit down at the piano before parties that included some of the finest pianists of his time, and play for them, by the hour, his own music, needless to say. He had a composer's voice. And he would invite eminent vocalists to his house, and sing them his operas, taking all the parts.

He had the emotional stability of a six-year-old child. When he felt out of sorts, he would rave and stamp, or sink into suicidal gloom and talk darkly of going to the East to end his days as a Buddhist monk. Ten minutes later, when something pleased him, he would rush out of doors and run around the garden, or jump up and down on the sofa, or stand on his head. He could be grief-stricken over the death of a pet dog, and he could be callous and heartless to a degree that would have made a Roman emperor shudder.

He was almost innocent of any sense of responsibility. Not only did he seem incapable of supporting himself, but it never occurred to him that he was under any obligation to do so. He was convinced that the world owed him a living. In support of this belief, he borrowed money from everybody who was good for a loan—men, women, friends, or strangers. He wrote begging letters by the score, sometimes groveling without shame, at others loftily offering his intended benefactor the privilege of contributing to his support, and being mortally offended if the recipient declined the honor. I have found no record of his ever paying or repaying money to anyone who did not have a legal claim upon it.

What money he could lay his hands on he spent like an Indian rajah. The mere prospect of a performance of one of his operas was enough to set him to running up bills amounting to ten times the amount of his prospective royalties. On an income that would reduce a more scrupulous man to doing his own laundry, he would keep two servants. Without enough money in his pocket to pay his rent, he would have the walls and ceiling of his study lined with pink silk. No one will ever know—certainly he never knew—how much money he owed. We do know that his greatest benefactor gave him $6,000 to pay the most pressing of his debts in one city, and a year later had to give him $16,000 to enable him to live in another city without being thrown into jail for debt.

He was equally unscrupulous in other ways. An endless procession of women marched through his life. His first wife spent twenty years enduring and forgiving his infidelities. His second wife had been the wife of his most devoted friend and admirer, from whom he stole her. And even while he was trying to persuade her to leave her first husband he was writing to a friend to inquire whether he could suggest some wealthy woman—*any* wealthy woman—whom he could marry for her money.

He was completely selfish in his other personal relationships. His liking for his friends was measured solely by the completeness of their devotion to him, or by their usefulness to him, whether financial or artistic. The minute they failed him—even by so much as refusing a dinner invitation—or began to lessen in usefulness, he cast them off without a second thought. At the end of his life he had exactly one friend left whom he had known even in middle age.

He had a genius for making enemies. He would insult a man who disagreed with him about the weather. He would pull endless wires in order to meet some man who admired his work, and was able and anxious to be of use to him—and would proceed to make a mortal enemy of him with some idiotic and wholly uncalled-for exhibition of arrogance and bad manners. A character in one of his operas was a caricature of one of the most powerful music critics of his day. Not content with burlesquing him, he invited the critic to his house and read him the libretto aloud in front of his friends.

The name of this monster was Richard Wagner. Everything that I have said about him you can find on record—in newspapers, in police reports, in the testimony of people who knew him, in his own letters, between the lines of his autobiography. And the curious thing about this record is that it doesn't matter in the least.

Because this undersized, sickly, disagreeable, fascinating little man was right all the time. The joke was on us. He *was* one of the world's greatest dramatists; he *was* a great thinker; he *was* one of the most stupendous musical geniuses that, up to now, the world has ever seen. The world did owe him a living. People couldn't know those things at the time, I suppose; and yet to us, who know his music, it does seem as though they should have known. What if he did talk about himself all the time? If he had talked about himself for twenty-four hours every day for the span of his life he would not have uttered half the number of words that other men have spoken and written about him since his death.

When you consider what he wrote—thirteen operas and music dramas, eleven of them still holding the stage, eight of them unquestionably worth ranking among the world's great musico-dramatic masterpieces—when you listen to what he wrote, the debts and heartaches that people had to endure from him don't seem much of a price. Eduard Hanslick, the critic whom he caricatured in *Die Meistersinger* and who hated him ever after, now lives only because he was caricatured in *Die Meistersinger*. The women whose hearts he broke are long since dead; and the man who could never love anyone but himself has made them deathless atonement, I think, with *Tristan und Isolde*. Think of the luxury with which for a time, at least, fate rewarded Napoleon, the man who ruined France and looted Europe; and then perhaps you will agree that a few thousand dollars' worth of debts were not too heavy a price to pay for the *Ring* trilogy.

What if he was faithless to his friends and to his wives? He had one mistress to whom he was faithful to the day of his death: Music. Not for a single moment did he ever compromise with what he believed, with what he dreamed. There is not a line of his music that could have been conceived by a little mind. Even when he is dull, or downright bad, he is dull in the grand manner. There is greatness about his worst mistakes. Listening to his music, one does not forgive him for what he may or may not have been. It is not a matter of forgiveness. It is a matter of being dumb with wonder that his poor brain and body didn't burst under the torment of the demon of creative energy that lived inside him, struggling, clawing, scratching to be released; tearing, shrieking at him to write the music that was in him. The miracle is that what he did in the little space of seventy years could have been done at all, even by a great genius. Is it any wonder that he had no time to be a man?

How Does the Author Make His Point?

1. Why does the author withhold the name of the man he is describing until the last quater of the essay? With the identification, the direction of the essay changes. In one sentence, identify the author's purpose in the first eleven paragraphs and his new purpose in the final four paragraphs.

2. Why is there no thesis statement at the beginning? In what two sentences in the essay does Taylor give his controlling idea?

3. How are the paragraphs in the essay constructed? Can you pick out each of the topic sentences? Are the paragraphs adequately developed—enough details supplied to prove the controlling idea?

4. Is "The Monster" a good title? Is it a good title for the final paragraphs as well as the first?

5. Discuss the conclusion. What does each of the last three sentences contribute to the essay?

What Do You Think?

1. Do you agree that the world owes geniuses a living?

2. How would you react to an evening with Wagner? Discuss your probable reactions to the evenings described in paragraphs 2 through 5.

3. Does Wagner's genius excuse his faults? All of them? Some of them? Which would you excuse?

Honeymoon Hints

MARK PLESHENKO
(student)

This essay uses some bizarre examples to poke fun at the traditional honeymoon trip.

Remember when marriage was a beginning? Now it's a last resort. All over America, couples who have lived together successfully for years are rushing like lemmings to get married, leaving like starry-eyed teenagers on honeymoons, and, within a few short months, pleading for a divorce. If you ask what went wrong, all they will say is that there's a big difference between living together and being married—a big difference which they can't quite explain but which managed, in the space of a two-week honeymoon, to destroy their relationship. After lengthy research, it has become clear that the problem is not so much what happened on the honeymoon as *where* it happened. Couples who have lived together for years before getting married and going on honeymoons are very different from those who have not. The problem is they don't realize it. So they pick a spot recommended for honeymooners, and they go there all bright and dewey-eyed, and the whole thing falls apart. Why? Because they chose a place where they should never have gone. For example . . .

RED CHINA—It is often true that when established couples marry, they get overly ambitious. They want to go on a big honeymoon and explore a place where few couples have ventured. Lately, that place has been Red China. But here's the rub. There are no double beds in Red China. None—not a one! Also, the People's Republic is openly anti-snuggles. Now at first, admittedly, twin beds are rather sweet—reminds one of the fifties. But add to this the open transom on your hotel room door and the dirty looks you'll receive if you dare to hold hands in the street, and you've got a situation that spells trouble.

THE CARRIBBEAN—specifically BOREmuda, where the sun rises and sets every day. The beaches are so tranquil even the gulls doze off in flight. It's just twenty-one miles long and a yawn wide. Get the picture? This is no place for a new beginning.

ETHIOPIA—A lot of established couples feel that a country in a state of change will be the perfect thing to complement their own transitional situation and that the accompanying sense of danger will definitely be a turn-on. And it will be, if machine guns and snipers are your bag. Or an openly hostile hotel management. Or the dismal shantytown that now dominates the view from your suite. The question then becomes, is there love after battle fatigue?

HAWAII—Research has indicated that there is nothing more depressing to a newly married, previously established couple than a ruined island paradise. The first time they get mugged on Waikiki, they realize that nothing is truly lasting. Like a carefully nurtured tan that fades in but a few days of the island's incredibly frequent rains, their love seems doomed—so doomed, in fact, that neither a pre-mixed pina colada nor an evening with Don Ho could possibly revive it.

You might not think that the four spots listed could actually destroy a relationship in so short a time as the length of a honeymoon, but it happens every day. These spots should certainly be avoided because they only increase one's sense of failure. The best advice for newlyweds is not to honeymoon at all and risk destroying their relationship.

How Does the Author Make His Point?

1. Why is the author's introduction effective?
2. Do you think that the author arranged his examples effectively? Can you think of a good reason for placing Hawaii last?
3. Do you think that all of the author's examples are equally effective, or do you feel that one is more effective than another?
4. How would you characterize the tone of this essay?

What Do You Think?

1. Do you think that the author's view of marriage as "a last resort" is justified?
2. Do you agree with author's implication that Americans often place too much emphasis on the traditional honeymoon trip?
3. Can you think of any additional honeymoon spots that would provide good examples for this essay?

INTEGRATING READING WITH WRITING SKILLS: IDENTIFYING MAIN IDEAS AND SUPPORTING IDEAS

Reading and writing skills supplement each other. The techniques you learn to be a good reader can be applied to make you a good writer; the techniques you learn to be a good writer can be applied to heighten your reading skills. In no place is this more obvious than in identifying the main idea and then determining what are the supporting details for that idea. For one thing, the main idea is frequently the first sentence in a paragraph or in a group of paragraphs.

In the following brief quotation from *Huckleberry Finn*, Mark Twain makes a clear, simple statement of a main idea. "It was a mighty nice family, and a mighty nice house too." Then he narrows this main idea with a second sentence. "I hadn't seen no house out in the country before that was so nice and had so much style." He follows this more specific sentence with a number of supporting details.

> It didn't have an iron latch on the front door, nor a wooden one with a buckskin string, but a brass knob to turn, the same as houses in a town. There warn't no bed in the parlor, not a sign of a bed; but heaps of parlors in towns has beds in them. There was a big fireplace that was bricked on the bottom, and the bricks was kept clean and red by pouring water on them and scrubbing them with another brick; sometimes they washed them over with red water-paint that they call Spanish-brown, same as they do in town. They had big brass dog-irons that could hold up a saw-log. There was a clock on the middle of the mantel-piece with a picture of a town painted on the bottom half of the glass front and a round place in the middle of it for the sun, and you could see the pendulum swing behind it. It was beautiful to hear that clock tick; and sometimes when one of these peddlers had been along and scoured her up and got her in good shape, she would start in and strike a hundred and fifty before she got tuckered out. They wouldn't took any money for her.

These details of doorknobs and tidy fireplaces and ornaments on the mantelpiece all relate to the first sentence, the topic sentence about the nice house in the country. The next three pages are made up of further details about the nice family in their nice house—about their books, the poems they write, the paintings on the walls. Even if you can't visualize all the details in this paragraph (such as the brass dog irons), we know from the statement of the main idea and the context (the surrounding writing) that the house and family are nice. From the time Twain introduces this nice family of the Grangerfords, he has said admiring things about them. The summarizing effect of this approval is to make us recognize even more completely that Mark Twain wants us to be well aware that this family is nice. Even the fact that their clock strikes 150 times brings approval from Huck. Everything surrounding, that is, the entire context of their introduction, supports the main idea of their niceness.

Sometimes details are given within a sentence. Even within a single complex sentence, it is easy to identify the main idea. The main idea is always expressed in the independent clause; a subsidiary idea is expressed in a dependent clause. For example, note the differences in meaning between the following two sentences:

> Although I laughed at the movie, it was sad.
> Although it was sad, I laughed at the movie.

In addition, the transitional phrases that link sentences and paragraphs also establish the relationship of main idea and subsidiary idea. These words or phrases also shift the emphasis in a sentence.

> He loved the children, *but* he disciplined them carefully.
> He loved his children; *nevertheless*, he disciplined them carefully.
> He loved his children; *so* he disciplined them carefully.

It is sometimes possible to gain a general understanding of a chapter in a textbook simply by reading the chapter heading, the introductory paragraph, and the first sentences of each body paragraph. Look at the following example from a history textbook on the American West:

WESTWARD MIGRATION DURING THE GREAT DEPRESSION

To the poverty-stricken migrants of the thirties, the West was still the land of opportunity, even if only in their minds. For during these desperate years, many had little to live for but a vision, a hope, which, real or imagined, gave them courage to go on. The West thus performed a dual function for Americans. It represented a real extension of their opportunities, and it continued to serve as a mystic symbol.

This dual function of the West was particularly noticeable in California. . . .

Californians were not happy to see the newcomers because they arrived with little funds. . . .

Not surprisingly, the influx of Dust Bowl refugees created many tensions in California. . . .

Such labor unrest brought a reaction from employers. . . .

The living conditions of many of these new migrants were wretched. . . .

Under such circumstances the education of children was all but forgotten. . . .

In this case, the author's good writing habits help the student develop good reading comprehension skills. Major points are clearly stated in topic sentences at the beginning of each paragraph. The student then expects specific details to follow about the tensions in California, the wretched living conditions of the migrants, their poor education. In the paragraph about the migrants' living conditions, for instance, the student will see a body of specific examples used as supporting details.

The living conditions of many of these new migrants were wretched. One investigator in 1935 reported that he found a two-room cabin in which 41 persons from southeast Oklahoma lived. Another described a one-room shack in which fifteen men, women, and children were huddled, living in unimaginable filth. On December 3, 1937, the California State Immigration and Housing Commission ordered thirty shanties near Visalia condemned as unfit for human habitation. Most camps had no baths, no showers or plumbing, and workers bathed in and drank from the same water supply found in nearby irrigation ditches. Near Kingsburg eighteen families were found living under a bridge. Other workers lived in cardboard cartons, or in tents improvised from gunny sacks, with coffee cans serving for chimneys. In such an environment health conditions were appalling. Six thousand cases of influenza were reported in one county during February, 1937. Scores of babies died of diarrhea and enteritis. Social worker Tessie Williams in 1937 reported the case of one woman who, upon leaving the county hospital, returned with her baby to live under a tree. A family of seven was reported to have eaten little more than bread and potatoes over a period of several months. Some ate nothing but beans and fried dough and oatmeal; one family of eight lived on dandelions and boiled potatoes. "I'm getting mighty tired of just beans and water," one woman moaned, "but even that may run out any day now."

John A. Garrity

These examples in the body of the paragraph all refer to ideas more specific than the general idea of "living conditions." Notice, however, that some are more specific than others. A detail referring to "a one-room shack in which fifteen men, women, and children were huddled in unimaginable filth" is very specific. The detail explaining that "Most camps had no baths, no showers or plumbing . . ." is a little less specific because it refers to the migrant camps in general, not to a specific home in a migrant camp. Both sentences, however, are more specific than the first sentence, referring to "wretched living conditions," and thus they act as supporting details.

It is important to see the basic distinction between a general idea and its specific supports and details, but it is also important to see the relationships among these supporting details. In many paragraphs, the sentences form a kind of inverted pyramid: the first sentence or two is the general idea; there may then follow a relatively broad support for the generalization, and that may be followed by increasingly narrowed supports. That is, the organization runs from generalization to broad support to narrowed support or supports. For example, in the last part of the paragraph above, you can see three distinct patterns of main idea and subordinate ideas.

> Wretched Living Conditions
> > Health Conditions Were Appalling
> > > Six thousand cases of influenza . . .
> > > Scores of babies died of diarrhea . . .
> > > Social worker Tessie Williams in 1937 reported . . .
> > > A family of seven was reported to have eaten little . . .
> > > > Some ate nothing but beans and fried dough . . .
> > > > "I'm getting mighty tired of just beans and water . . .

"Health conditions" is a subtopic of "living conditions" because it refers to a specific kind of living condition. The diseases and poor nutrition mentioned in the next five sentences are specific examples of appalling health conditions, and the last sentence, the quotation, refers directly to the preceding detail about poor nutrition.

Remember that supporting details only have real significance when they are related to something else—a main idea, a subtopic, or another detail. So to read with intelligence and to write with clarity, you must consider the details as they relate to each other and to the main idea that you are trying to convey.

EXERCISE

The following paragraph—altered to fit outline form—is an eyewitness account of a man walking to Galway during the Great Famine in Ireland in 1847. It illustrates how main supporting details (subtopics) and more specific details referring to the subtopics can be included effectively in the same sentence. Notice how the picture formed in your mind becomes more vivid with every additional detail.

We saw sights that will never wholly leave the eyes, cowering wretches
1. almost naked in the savage weather
2. prowling in turnip fields, and endeavoring to grub up roots which had been left
3. but running to hide as the mailcoach rolled by groups and families
1. sitting or wandering on the highroad
2. with failing steps, and dim patient eyes
3. gazing hopelessly into infinite darkness and despair parties of tall, brawny men
1. once the flower of Meath and Galway
2. stalking by with a fierce but vacant scowl
3. as if they realised that all this ought not to be, he knew not whom to blame, saw none whom they could rend in their wrath

Sometimes, I could see, in front of the cottages, little children
1. leaning against a fence when the sun shone out—for they could not stand—
2. their limbs fleshless, their bodies half-naked,
3. their faces bloated yet wrinkled, and of a pale greenish hue—
4. children who would never, it was too plain, grow up to be men and women.

Devin Adair, *The Story of the Irish Race*

Write two more specific details for each of the main supporting details provided in each of the following:

A. Controlling Idea: The energy of your high school football coach is limitless.
1. He never stands still.
2. He constantly talks with his hands.
3. His eyes are never at rest.
4. He always fires up his players with team spirit.
B. Controlling Idea: The atmosphere of your doctor's office is cold and impersonal.
1. The grim, unsmiling receptionist
2. The modern, functional furniture
3. The antiseptic smells
4. The people in the waiting room
C. Controlling Idea: Television commercials insult a woman's intelligence.

1. Those that portray women as dutiful, domestic servants
2. Those that portray women as vain, materialistic conformists
3. Those that portray women as brainless, sexual objects
4. Those that portray women as passive, obedient wives

IMPROVING YOUR VOCABULARY: THE RIGHT WORD

One of the great American stylists is Mark Twain, who, appropriately enough, has many wise things to say about style, many of them pertaining to the right word. He once said the difference between the right word and the almost right word is the difference between the lightning and the lightning bug. In a somewhat more formal statement, he expressed the same idea. He said, "A powerful agent is the right word. Whenever we come upon one of those intensely right words in a book or newspaper, the resulting effect is physical as well as spiritual, and electrically prompt."

The bemused student writer is certainly willing to grant power to the "right word" but is at something of a loss to find that right word. The dictionary, the thesaurus, the speech of his friends and acquaintances all contribute help in finding the right word.

Some basic rules can help him. One of the most important of these rules is to choose the simple word over the "big" word, assuming always that the simple word does carry the meaning the writer wants. In a famous book called *Modern English Usage*, the scholar H.W. Fowler had this to say about "big" words and right words.

It need hardly be said that shortness is a merit in words: there are often reasons why shortness is not possible; much less often there are occasions when length, not shortness, is desirable: but it is a general truth that the short words are not only handier to use, but more powerful in effect: extra syllables reduce, not increase, vigor. . . . There are many good reasons, however, against any attempt to avoid, because it is a polysyllable, the word that will give our meaning best. What is here deprecated is the tendency among the ignorant to choose, because it is a polysyllable, the word that gives their meaning no better or even worse.

Fowler is not the only person to comment on the vigor of short words. In the following excerpt, Gelett Burgess says that "short words are words of might." You will notice that in this article there are no words longer than one syllable.

Except ye utter by the tongue words easy to be understood, how shall it be known what is spoken? for ye shall speak into the air.

I COR. 14:2

This is a plea for the use of more short words in our talk and in what we write. Through the lack of them in our speech is apt to grow stale and weak, and, it may be, hold more sham than true thought. For long words at times tend to hide or blur what one says.

What I mean is this: If we use long words too much, we are apt to talk in ruts and use the same old, worn ways of speech. This tends to make what we say dull, with no force or sting. But if we use short words, we have to say real things, things we know; and say them in a fresh way. We find it hard to hint or dodge or hide or half say things.

For short words are bold. They say just what they mean. They do not leave you in doubt. They are clear and sharp, like signs cut in a rock.

And so, if you should learn to use words with force and skill, it is well first to use short words as much as you can. It will make your speech crisp and give zest and tang to what you say or write.

To prove that this is true, let us see what can be done here and now with short words. If I tell what I have to say in this plain way—that is, with naught but short words—you may think of it as but an odd freak of mine. But I hope it is more than a mere stunt. I shall try to show that one can say much that is true and live and with good strong meat of thought in it, in a way that does not come from books; that does not, as the phrase goes, "smell of the lamp."

Of course I need not be quite so strict and hold to a hard and fast rule. Some long words might be used and I could, I think, still prove my point. But I have thought that one might learn more and feel more sure that I am right from a talk which shows by its own form just what I would teach. And to do that I have made that form just as pure as it can be.

Well then, first let us see just what place short words have in our tongue.

Short words must have been our first words when the world was young. The minds of men were raw, like a child's. Men's needs were few and so their thoughts were crude. Life for a man was in the main but a hunt for food, a fight with foes, a quest for a mate and a search for a place to rest safe from the storm and wild beasts. And for his mate there was thought but of their brat, the pot on the fire, the skins with which to make clothes.

Their first words, no doubt, were mere grunts or growls, barks, whines, squeals like those of the beasts. These rough strange sounds were made to show how they felt. They meant joy or pain or doubt or rage or fear—things like that. But these sounds came, in time, to grow more and more plain as real words. They were short words, strong and clear. And these first short words, used by our sires, way, way, back in the dark of time, still have strength and truth. They are bred in our flesh and bone. We may well call such words the life blood of our speech.

And so when we feel, we still use short words. If we know joy we say, "I love you more than all the world! Kiss me!" In our pride we cry, "I have got it! I have won!" With glee we shout, "Good for you! That is right!" And if we fear, we use short words. We yell, "The house is on fire! Come quick!" We moan in our woe, "Oh, why have you done this!" or weep, "She is gone. She has left me!" We wail, "I am sick. I feel bad." All fierce moods, too, use short words. We snarl, "I hate you!" We growl, "I will kill you!"

Most words we call bad are short words, too. A curse or an oath is bound to be made of short words or it does not sting. That is why such **terms** as damn and hell and worse words that stink of filth seem full of force to one who has the mind of a child—or beast.

And words which to most seem still more vile, coarse sex words, they are short as well. They must needs be since they tell of the stark, raw facts and acts of life. But at least they are not pale and weak. They do not slide off the truth. Nor do they gild dirt or mask low thoughts by sly tricks of speech as do some long words. What they mean they say right out and you know where you are with them.

Short words, you see, come from down deep in us—from our hearts or guts, not from the brain. For they deal for the most part with things that move and sway us, that make us act. And so they are said with not much heed of their use. We think out loud, that is all; and the words come to our lips as do smiles or scowls. At times we do not quite know how we use them—just as we do not know, much of the time, that we breathe; just as we walk, too, at times, with no care for our steps. That, I think, is why short words tend to make our thoughts more live and true.

Gelett Burgess

To return to Mark Twain, he gave some further principles of good writing when he had once volunteered to read the essays in a writing contest by the young women at the Buffalo Female Academy. He awarded the first prize to an essay that

relates a very simple little incident in unpretentious language. It has the very rare merit of stopping when it is finished. It shows a freedom from adjectives and superlatives, which is attractive, not to say seductive—and let us remark in passing that one can seldom run his pen through an adjective without improving his manuscript. We can say further that there is a singular aptness of language noticeable in it—denoting a shrewd facility of selecting just the right word for the service needed, as a general thing. It is a high gift. It is the talent which gives accuracy, grace, and vividness in descriptive writing.

Although there is no question of the value of the short, strong word, you do not want to ignore any resource of vocabulary for all words *under the right circumstances* can lend effect to your writing. Long words, unfamiliar words, specialized words also have proper places in your writing.

Since simple words, through frequent usage, often demand little explanation or thought, they can lend to inaccuracy or over-simplification. For example, *dumped,* as applied to a candidate for office, suggests speed and violence of a removal which may actually have been considerate and orderly. In this case, *substitute* might be a better choice. Short words also tend to be highly connotative, that is, emotionally charged. This is fine unless you are trying for objectivity; then you might choose the less familiar word—for example, *infant* rather than *baby, reside* rather than *live.*

Long, learned words are many times more concise and precise than the short, familiar word with its numerous meanings, its simple conception, and its emotional connotation. This is particularly true when you are writing about academic or scientific subjects. Consider such words as *ontogeny* from biology or *amortization* from finance, and you will realize that the most precise and concise way to refer to these complicated concepts is with long, unfamiliar words. Another reason for deciding upon the less familiar word is that it is unfamiliar and sends you to the dictionary where, if you read the whole entry, you often get a rich flavor from the little-known word. For example, take the adjective *ancillary,* meaning subordinate, but which derives from *ancilla,* meaning a little handmaid in a Latin household. The history of this word lends emphasis to it. In all cases the basis on which you choose your words is determined solely by their appropriateness to your subject and your audience.

However, no matter how much good advice a beginning writer receives, nothing is as valuable in helping him to choose the right word as the habit of reading and reading and reading. It is the acquaintanceship with words well used by other careful writers that makes our writing effective. It is only when good writing is familiar to us through broad reading that we can discover the right words for ourselves.

ASSIGNMENTS

A. Almost everyone has experienced the classic frustration embodied in what is known as "Murphy's Law" (If anything can go wrong, it will). Since the inception of Captain Murphy's famous dictum in 1949,

American pundits have formulated numerous corollaries to the "law." Below you will find some of the corollaries catalogued by Arthur Block in *Murphy's Law and Other Reasons Why Things Go Wrong*. Choose one which you can readily identify with—one which suggests a truth which you can clearly illustrate from your own experiences. Then, using that "truth" as your controlling idea, develop an illustrative essay by providing *examples* of your experiences.

1. Nothing is as easy as it looks.
2. When any mechanical contrivance fails, it will do so at the most inconvenient time.
3. You can fool all of the people some of the time, and some of the people all of the time, but you can't fool Mom.
4. No one is listening until you make a mistake.
5. Any child who chatters nonstop at home will adamantly refuse to utter a word when requested to demonstrate for an audience.
6. To err is human—to blame it on someone else is even more human.
7. Experience is something you don't get until just after you need it.
8. No books are lost by lending except those you particularly wanted to keep.
9. Opportunity always knocks at the least opportune moment.
10. Computers are unreliable, but humans are even more unreliable.

B. Think of an adjective which characterizes one of your most interesting friends, relatives, or coworkers. Then write an essay in which you provide examples of the personality trait exemplified by that person. For example, you might immediately think of someone who is particularly witty or temperamental or absent-minded. You can use your dictionary to help you with this assignment and perhaps learn some new words in the process. If you skim through your dictionary, you might find that an adjective you've never used before actually provides you with a perfect characterization of someone that you see almost every day—a "fatuous" boss, an "obstreperous" neighbor, an "audacious" child, or a "pedantic" friend.

C. Use the library to help you choose an interesting topic. With a little diligent research, you can find some fascinating information which would provide good examples for an illustrative essay. You might, for instance, find examples of

1. diseases that changed the course of history
2. shocking instances of book banning in twentieth-century America
3. well-known leaders who never made good grades in school
4. unusual word origins
5. important scientific truths discovered accidentally
6. landmark decisions determined by one person's vote
7. remarkable achievements of the severely handicapped
8. obscure women who were the driving force behind famous men
9. gems of real medical wisdom in old wives' tales

In writing your paper, make sure that your thesis statement expresses a controlling idea. It should not be a mere statement of fact, and it should not be a repetition of the title of a source you have used. For instance, if you used John Train's book about *Remarkable Occurrences* as a source of examples, then don't write a thesis statement such as

Here are some examples of remarkable occurrences.

Think about what the examples illustrate. Then, after checking other sources, you might come up with a thesis statement like this.

Since some things that have actually happened are so incredible, writers of fiction would reject them.

Then examples such as the story of Alfred Packer or the traffic problem in Ohio will take on more meaning. (Packer ate five prospectors in Colorado, and the judge sentencing Packer to hang "indignantly pointed out that 'There was only six Democrats in all of Hinsdale County and you ate five of them!'") The traffic problem in Ohio would provide a less bizarre but nonetheless humorous example of fact being stranger than fiction. "In 1895 there were only two cars in the whole state of Ohio. They collided.")

5

Explaining a Process

Explaining a process is a basic form of exposition. Like narration, process frequently takes place in time; that is, it might follow a chronological order. Like division and classification, this order requires that the subject be divided into a series of steps, logically arranged from first to last. Whether the process being explained is a natural one, such as the development of a storm, or a technological one, such as beer making, the controlling purpose is to inform, to show how something occurs or how to do something.

The process to be explained may range from simple instructions on how to assemble a set of bookshelves to an explanation of the complex process whereby brain cells transmit information. Regardless of its simplicity or complexity, the process follows definite steps arranged according to a logical sequence. First this is done or takes place, and then something else is done or takes place—always with some end-point or result in mind.

The following article illustrates a process that results in a change of attitude and action for one student:

PROBLEM STUDENT GETS LAST LAUGH

HIGH POINT, N.C. (AP)—He was once every teacher's nightmare, defiant and angry. Now Chris LaFortuna is a dream student, scoring a perfect 800 on the Scholastic Aptitude Test's verbal section months after getting straight F's.

"Until recently I thought of school as a very hostile place," LaFortuna said. "I had this attitude that school was something I didn't want to dirty myself with."

LaFortuna, who failed ninth grade, couldn't even see the point of staying in school all day. But instead of dropping out of his junior year at Andrews High School, he made another decision. No longer a minor at age 18, he accepted an offer to move into the home of Micki McCall, her husband and their three children.

Mrs. McCall, who works in the school cafeteria, says she is a firm believer in using positive reinforcement and celebrating small successes.

"We had parties when Chris stayed in school all day," she said. "When he had been in school all week, we just walked on air."

LaFortuna's diet had been a major part of his problem, with certain foods causing allergic reactions, she said.

"Some of my F's were because of absences," LaFortuna said. "I felt too listless and discouraged to come to school some days. Some of the foods put me to sleep."

LaFortuna learned last week that his total score from the May SAT, counting the verbal and math sections, was 1370 of a possible 1600. His last report card had two A's, two B's and one C.

"None of us should get much credit," Heatherly said of the teachers and administrators who helped LaFortuna. "Most of the credit goes to that young man. He really has done a remarkable job of getting his head screwed on right."

"I had the foolish attitude that anybody who was a principal was automatically on the other side," LaFortuna said. "I didn't know the other side of what."

Beaver County Times, June 11, 1987

As you can see, the process here involves the following four steps:

1. Remove the student from the environment.
2. Use positive reinforcement; celebrate even minor successes.
3. Check for physical or allergic causes.
4. Get appropriate medical attention and follow doctors' suggestions.

"How To" Instructions

Scores of "how-to" books and videos vie for space on bookstore shelves and crowd drugstore racks—telling you how to grow your own vegetables, how to have a better sex life, how to retire as a millionaire at age forty-seven. But beyond the "how to" of giving instructions, writing to explain a process may take many forms and serve many purposes. In explaining how social unrest can turn to violence, for instance, the sociologist can explain the stages of a riot. The pediatrician or child psychologist might explain the process of growing up by tracing the successive stages in child development. The historian might endeavor to explain an institution such as parliamentary government by tracing its development throughout various historical periods.

Five Key Steps in Explaining a Process

Whatever process you wish to explain, these five key steps will clarify it.

1. Formulate a clear thesis statement that indicates the subject you intend to deal with and the purpose of your explanation.
2. Determine the main steps of the process and state each one clearly in the correct, logical sequence. (Thus, you build a carefully constructed outline to serve as a guide for testing the structure of your explanation.)
3. Take care to present every necessary detail as exactly as possible in the simplest wording.
4. Write with a specific audience in mind and use clear transitions to guide your reader from one step to the next.
5. Warn your reader against common errors or sources of trouble. Sometimes it may even be necessary to point out the results of performing a particular step in the wrong way. After all, you don't want your reader to have the cake fall flat or the car stall in traffic.

All of us have suffered because someone's instructions were unclear. Indeed, it is frequently considered an indication of intelligence to be able to give precise instructions. Can you tell somebody how to get to the nearest interstate highway or the closest airport without confusing him? Can you write the recipe and technique for making your prize upside-down cake or how to change a tire? All too often we forget a step in the process or obscure it with unnecessary steps.

One thing that will help you to explain your process well is to know your audience. How much basic information does your reader need to be given? Does he have to have any specialized knowledge? The writer must determine how much information the reader needs and then supply it in order to make the explanation clear. Instructions that would be comprehensible to an experienced technician might baffle the average do-it-yourself mechanic.

In the following passage, S.J. Perelman, American humorist and scriptwriter for the Marx Brothers, epitomizes the frustrations of the unhandy when confronted with routine instructions:

> One stifling summer afternoon last August, in the attic of a tiny stone house in Pennsylvania, I made a most interesting discovery: the shortest, cheapest method of inducing a nervous breakdown ever perfected. In this technique (eventually adopted by the psychology department of Duke University, which will adopt anything), the subject is placed in a sharply sloping attic heated to 340°F. and given a mothproof closet known as the Jiffy-Cloz to assemble. The Jiffy-Cloz, procurable at any department store or neighborhood insane asylum, consists of half a dozen gigantic sheets of red cardboard, two plywood doors, a clothes rack, and a packet of staples. With these is included a set of instructions mimeographed in pale-violet ink, fruity with phrases like "Pass Section F through Slot AA, taking care not to fold tabs behind washers (see Fig.9)." The cardboard is so processed that as the subject struggles convulsively to force the staple through, it suddenly buckles, plunging the staple deep into his thumb. He thereupon springs up with a dolorous cry and smites his knob (Section K) on the rafters (RR). As a final demonic touch, the Jiffy-Cloz people cunningly omit four of the staples necessary to finish the job, so that after indescribable purgatory, the best the subject can possibly achieve is a sleazy, capricious structure which would reduce any self-respecting moth to helpless laughter. The cumulative frustration, the tropical heat, and the ghostly chuckling of the moths are calculated to unseat the strongest mentality.

> S.J. Perelman

ORGANIZATION

Whether your purpose is to give direct instructions on how to do something or to explain how something occurs or operates, the same pattern of organization prevails. In effect, you put one foot in front of the other and explain the process *step by step* from first to last.

The introduction usually needs to be no more than one brief paragraph directing the readers' attention to the process and the purpose for describing it. The thesis statement most commonly comes at the end of the first paragraph or at the beginning of the second—at least in shorter essays.

The arrangement of the body of the essay will be largely determined by the process itself and by the degree of detail needed. The stages of a process have a necessary sequence, and that sequence must be followed step by step. In some instances, each body paragraph might deal with a single stage; in others, several paragraphs might be devoted to a more detailed examination of an individual stage. But each step must be carefully covered in sufficient detail so that there are no loose ends and no unanswered questions.

Writing a clear and thorough description of a process calls for careful thought, not only about the process itself, but about the reader. Thoughtful writers try to put themselves in the position of the reader and then to anticipate what the reader will want and need to know. Certainly, the reader has a right to expect that the steps will be presented in proper sequence from a single, consistent point of view. Furthermore, the reader expects the connection between one step and another to be clearly shown. Though the use of "first" . . . "second" . . . "third" . . . "fourth" is not necessarily faulty, it can quicky become stale and boring. You should take note of how skillful writers use a variety of transitional words and phrases to provide flexibility and interest.

If, as in most essays, the introduction with its thesis statement has set forth the general purpose in describing the specific process, the conclusion is the logical place to emphasize the significance or practical value of the information and to make readers feel that, indeed, they have learned something worthwhile.

How Dictionaries Are Made

S. I. Hayakawa

In the following essay, which forms a part of the fourth chapter of Language in Thought and Action, *S.I. Hayakawa examines the process in making a dictionary:*

> *The first paragraph, including the anecdote with a bit of dialogue, leads into the more specific point stated at the beginning of the second paragraph.*

It is widely believed that every word has a correct meaning, that we learn these meanings principally from teachers and grammarians (except that most of the time we don't bother to, so that we ordinarily speak "sloppy English"), and that dictionaries and grammars are the supreme authority in matters of meaning and usage. Few people ask by what authority the writers of dictionaries and grammars say what they say. I once got into a dispute with an Englishwoman over the pronunciation of a word and offered to look it up in the dictionary. The Englishwoman said firmly, "What for? I am English. I was born and brought up in England. The way I speak is English." Such self-assurance about one's own language is not uncommon among the English. In the United States, however, anyone who is willing to quarrel with the dictionary is regarded as either eccentric or mad.

> *Here the author states his purpose clearly and directly. Here the first and second steps of the process are explained.*

Let us see how dictionaries are made and how the editors arrive at definitions. What follows applies, incidentally, only to those dictionary offices where firsthand, original research goes on—not those in which editors simply copy existing dictionaries. The task of writing a dictionary begins with reading vast amounts of the literature of the period or subject that the dictionary is to cover. As the editors read, they copy on cards every interesting or rare word, every unusual or peculiar occurrence of a common word, a large number of common words in their ordinary uses, and also the sentences in which each of these words appears, thus:

pail
The dairy *pails* bring home increase of milk.

Keats, Endymion
1, 44–45

Here is the third step in the process.

That is to say, the context of each word is collected, along with the word itself. For a really big job of dictionary-writing, such as the *Oxford English Dictionary* (usually bound in about twenty-five volumes), millions of such cards are collected, and the task of editing occupies decades. As the cards are collected, they are alphabetized and sorted. When the sorting is completed, there will be for each word anywhere from two or three to several hundred illustrative quotations, each on its card.

The fourth, fifth, and sixth steps are explained.

To define a word, then, the dictionary-editor places before him the stack of cards illustrating that word; each of the cards represents an actual use of the word by a writer of some literary or historical importance. He reads the cards carefully, discards some, rereads the rest, and divides up the stack according to what he thinks are the several senses of the word. Finally, he writes his definitions, following the hard-and-fast rule that each definition *must* be based on what the quotations in front of him reveal about the meaning of the word. The editor cannot be influenced by what *he* thinks a given word *ought* to mean. He must work according to the cards or not at all.

Here the author explains the larger purpose behind his explanation of the process. The sentence in italics states his purpose, and he concludes with two examples to illustrate his point.

The writing of a dictionary, therefore, is not a task of setting up authoritative statements about the "true meanings" of words, but a task of *recording,* to the best of one's ability, what various words *have meant* to authors in the distant or immediate past. *The writer of a dictionary is a historian, not a lawgiver.* If, for example, we had been writing a dictionary in 1890, or even as late as 1919, we could have said that the word "broadcast" means "to scatter" (seed, for example), but we could not have decreed that from 1921 on, the most common meaning of the word should become "to disseminate audible messages, etc., by radio transmission." To regard the dictionary as an "authority," therefore, is to credit the dictionary-writer with gifts of prophecy which neither he nor anyone else possesses. In choosing our words when we speak or write, we can be *guided* by the historical record afforded us by the dictionary, but we cannot be *bound* by it, because new situations, new feelings are always compelling us to give new uses to old words. Looking under a "hood," we should ordinarily have found, five hundred years ago, a monk; today, we find a motorcar engine.

How to Say Nothing in Five Hundred Words

PAUL ROBERTS

As a faculty member at Cornell University, Paul Roberts must have had hundreds of themes that resembled the one he describes here. And reading them, he must have felt frustration, fatigue, and despair. Perhaps he hopes to alleviate some of this frustration for both student and professor with this essay.

It's Friday afternoon, and you have almost survived another week of classes. You are just looking forward dreamily to the week end when the English instructor says: "For Monday you will turn in a five-hundred-word composition on college football."

Well, that puts a good big hole in the week end. You don't have any strong views on college football one way or the other. You get rather excited during the season and go to all the home games and find it rather more fun than not. On the other hand, the class has been reading Robert Hutchins in the anthology and perhaps Shaw's "Eighty-Yard Run," and from the class discussion you have got the idea that the instructor thinks college football is for the birds. You are no fool. You can figure out what side to take.

After dinner you get out the portable typewriter that you got for high school graduation. You might as well get it over with and enjoy Saturday and Sunday. Five hundred words is about two double-spaced pages with normal margins. You put in a sheet of paper, think up a title, and you're off:

Why College Football Should Be Abolished

College football should be abolished because it's bad for the school and also bad for the players. The players are so busy practicing that they don't have any time for their studies.

This, you feel, is a mighty good start. The only trouble is that it's only thirty-two words. You still have four hundred and sixty-eight to go, and you've pretty well exhausted the subject. It comes to you that you do your best thinking in the morning, so you put away the typewriter and go to the movies. But the next morning you have to do your washing and some math problems, and in the afternoon you go to the game. The English instructor turns up too, and you wonder if you've taken the right side after all. Saturday night you have a date and Sunday morning you have to go to church. (You can't let English assignments interfere with your religion.) What with one thing and another it's ten o'clock Sunday night before you get out the typewriter again. You make a pot of coffee and start to fill out your views on college football. Put a little meat on the bones.

Why College Football Should Be Abolished

In my opinion, it seems to me that college football should be abolished. The reason why I think this to be true is because I feel that football is bad for the colleges in nearly every respect. As Robert Hutchins says in his article in our anthology in which he discusses college football, it would be better if the colleges had race horses and had races with one another, because then the horses would not have to attend classes. I firmly agree with Mr. Hutchins on this point, and I am sure that many other students would agree too.

One reason why it seems to me that college football is bad is that it has become too commercial. In the olden times when people played football just for the fun of it, maybe college football was all right, but they do not play football just for the fun of it now as they used to in the old days. Nowadays college football is what you might call a big business. Maybe this is not true at all schools, and I don't think it is especially true here at State, but certainly this is the case at most colleges and universities in America nowadays, as Mr. Hutchins points out in his very interesting article. Actually the coaches and alumni go around to the high schools and offer the high school stars large salaries to come to their colleges and play football for them. There was one case where a high school star was offered a convertible if he would play football for a certain college.

Another reason for abolishing college football is that it is bad for the players. They do not have time to get a college education, because they are so busy playing football. A football player has to practice every afternoon from three to six and then he is so tired that he can't concentrate on his studies. He just feels like dropping off to sleep after dinner, and then the next day he goes to his classes without having studied and maybe he fails the test.

(Good ripe stuff so far, but you're still a hundred and fifty-one words from home. One more push.)

Also I think college football is bad for the colleges and the universities because not very many students get to participate in it. Out of a college of ten thousand students only seventy-five or a hundred play football, if that many. Football is what you might call a spectator sport. That means that most people go to watch it but do not play it themselves.

(Four hundred and fifteen. Well, you still have the conclusion, and when you retype it, you can make the margins a little wider.)

These are the reasons why I agree with Mr. Hutchins that college football should be abolished in American colleges and universities.

On Monday you turn it in, moderately hopeful, and on Friday it comes back marked "weak in content" and sporting a big "D."

This essay is exaggerated a little, not much. The English instructor will recognize it as reasonably typical of what an assignment on college football will bring in. He knows that nearly half of the class will contrive in five hundred words to say that college football is too commercial and bad for the players. Most of the other half will inform him that college football builds character and prepares one for life and brings prestige to the school. As he reads paper after paper all saying the same thing in almost the same words, all bloodless, five hundred words dripping out of nothing, he wonders how he allowed himself to get trapped into teaching English when he might have had a happy and interesting life as an electrician or a confidence man.

Well, you may ask, what can you do about it? The subject is one on which you have few convictions and little information. Can you be expected to make a dull subject interesting? As a matter of fact, this is precisely what you are expected to do. This is the writer's essential task. All subjects, except sex, are dull until somebody makes them interesting. The writer's job is to find the argument, the approach, the angle, the wording that will take the reader with him. This is seldom easy, and it is particularly hard in subjects that have been much discussed: College Football, Fraternities, Popular Music, Is Chivalry Dead?, and the like. You will feel that there is nothing you can do with such subjects except repeat the old bromides. But there are some things you can do which will make your papers, if not throbbingly alive, at least less insufferably tedious than they might otherwise be.

Avoid the Obvious Content   Say the assignment is college football. Say you've decided to be against it. Begin by putting down the arguments that come to your mind: it is too commercial, it takes the students' minds off their studies, it is hard on the players, it makes the university a kind of circus instead of an intellectual center, for most schools it is financially ruinous. Can you think of any more arguments, just off hand? All right. Now when you write your paper, *make sure that you don't use any of the material on this list.* If these are the points that leap to your mind, they will leap to everyone else's too, and whether you get a "C" or a "D" may depend on whether the instructor reads your paper early when he is fresh and tolerant or late, when the sentence "In my opinion, college football has become too commercial," inexorably repeated, has brought him to the brink of lunacy.

Be against college football for some reason or reasons of your own. If they are keen and perceptive ones, that's splendid. But even if they are trivial or foolish or indefensible, you are still ahead so long as they are not everybody else's reasons too. Be against it because the colleges don't spend enough money on it to make it worthwhile, because it is bad for the characters of the spectators, because the players are forced to attend classes, because the football stars hog all the beautiful women, because it competes with baseball and is therefore un-American and possibly Communist inspired. There are lots of more or less unused reasons for being against college football.

Sometimes it is a good idea to sum up and dispose of the trite and conventional points before going on to your own. This has the advantage of indicating to the reader that you are going to be neither trite nor conventional. Something like this:

> We are often told that college football should be abolished because it has become too commercial or because it is bad for the players. These arguments are no doubt very cogent, but they don't really go to the heart of the matter.

Then you go to the heart of the matter.

Take the Less Usual Side   One rather simple way of getting into your paper is to take the side of the argument that most of the citizens will want to avoid. If the assignment is an essay on dogs, you can, if you choose, explain that dogs are faithful and lovable companions, intelligent, useful as guardians of the house and protectors of children, indispensable in police work—in short, when all is said and done, man's best friends. Or you can suggest that those big brown eyes conceal, more often than not, a vacuity of mind and an inconstancy of purpose; that the dogs you have known most intimately have been mangy, ill-tempered brutes, incapable of instruction; and that only your nobility of mind and fear of arrest prevent you from kicking the flea-ridden animals when you pass them on the street.

Naturally personal convictions will sometimes dictate your approach. If the assigned subject is "Is Methodism Rewarding to the Individual?" and you are a pious Methodist, you have really no choice. But few assigned subjects, if any, will fall in this category. Most of them will lie in broad areas of discussion with much to be said on both sides. They are intellectual exercises, and it is legitimate to argue now one way and now another, as debaters do in similar circumstances. Always take the side that looks to you hardest, least defensible. It will almost always turn out to be easier to write interestingly on that side.

This general advice applies where you have a choice of subjects. If you are to choose among "The Value of Fraternities" and "My Favorite High School Teacher" and "What I Think About Beetles," by all means plump for the beetles. By the time the instructor gets to your paper, he will be up to his ears in tedious tales about the French teacher at Bloombury High and assertions about how fraternities build character and prepare one for life. Your views on beetles, whatever they are, are bound to be a refreshing change.

Don't worry too much about figuring out what the instructor thinks about the subject so that you can cuddle up with him. Chances are his views are no stronger than yours. If he does have convictions and you oppose him, his problem is to keep from grading you higher than you deserve in order to show he is not biased. This doesn't mean that you should always cantankerously dissent from what the instructor says; that gets tiresome too. And if the subject assigned is "My Pet Peeve," do not begin, "My pet peeve is the English instructor who assigns papers on 'my pet peeve.'" This was still funny during the War of 1812, but it has sort of lost its edge since then. It is in general good manners to avoid personalities.

Slip Out of Abstraction If you will study the essay on college football [near the beginning of this essay], you will perceive that one reason for its appalling dullness is that it never gets down to particulars. It is just a series of not very glittering generalities: "football is bad for colleges," "it has become too commerical," "football is a big business," "it is bad for the players," and so on. Such round phrases thudding against the reader's brain are unlikely to convince him, though they may well render him unconscious.

If you want the reader to believe that college football is bad for the players, you have to do more than say so. You have to display the evil. Take your roommate, Alfred Simkins, the second-string center. Picture poor old Alfy coming home from football practice every evening, bruised and aching, agonizingly tired, scarcely able to shovel the mashed potatoes into his mouth. Let us see him staggering up to the room, getting out his econ textbook, peering desperately at it with his good eye, falling asleep and failing the test in the morning. Let us share his unbearable tension as Saturday draws near. Will he fail, be demoted, lose his monthly allowance, be forced to return to the coal mines? And if he succeeds, what will be his reward? Perhaps a slight ripple of applause when the third-string center replaces him, a moment of elation in the locker room if the team wins, of despair if it loses. What will he look back on when he graduates from college? Toil and torn ligaments. And what will be his future? He is not good enough for pro football, and he is too obscure and weak in econ to succeed in stocks and bonds. College football is tearing the heart from Alfy Simkins and, when it finishes with him, will callously toss aside the shattered hulk.

This is no doubt a weak enough argument for the abolition of college football, but it is a sight better than saying, in three or four variations, that college football (in your opinion) is bad for the players.

Look at the work of any professional writer and notice how constantly he is moving from the generality, the abstract statement, to the concrete example, the facts and figures, the illustration. If he is writing on juvenile delinquency, he does not just tell you that juveniles are (it seems to him) delinquent and that (in his opinion) something should be done about it. He shows you juveniles being delinquent, tearing up movie theatres in Buffalo, stabbing high school principals in Dallas, smoking marijuana in Palo Alto. And more than likely he is moving toward some specific remedy, not just a general wringing of the hands.

It is no doubt possible to be too concrete, too illustrative or anecdotal, but few inexperienced writers err this way. For most the soundest advice is to be seeking always for the picture, to be always turning general remarks into seeable examples. Don't say "Sororities teach girls the social graces." Say, "Sorority life teaches a girl how to carry on a conversation while pouring tea, without sloshing the tea into the saucer." Don't say, "I like certain kinds of popular music very much." Say, "Whenever I hear Gerber Sprinklittle play 'Mississippi Man' on the trombone, my socks creep up my ankles."

Get Rid of Obvious Padding   The student toiling away at his weekly English theme is too often tormented by a figure: five hundred words. How, he asks himself, is he to achieve this staggering total? Obviously by never using one word when he can somehow work in ten.

He is therefore seldom content with a plain statement like "Fast driving is dangerous." This has only four words in it. He takes thought, and the sentence becomes:

> In my opinion, fast driving is dangerous.

Better, but he can do better still:

> In my opinion, fast driving would seem to be rather dangerous.

If he is really adept, it may come out:

> In my humble opinion, though I do not claim to be an expert on this complicated subject, fast driving, in most circumstances, would seem to be rather dangerous in many respects, or at least so it would seem to me.

Thus four words have been turned into forty, and not an iota of content has been added.

Now this is a way to go about reaching five hundred words, and if you are content with a "D" grade, it is as good a way as any. But if you aim higher, you must work differently. Instead of stuffing your sentences with straw, you must try steadily to get rid of the padding, to make your sentences lean and tough. If you are really working at it, your first draft will greatly exceed the required total, and then you will work it down, thus:

> It is thought in some quarters that fraternities do not contribute as much as might be expected to campus life.

Some people think that fraternities contribute little to campus life.

The average doctor who practices in small towns or in the country must toil night and day to heal the sick.

Most country doctors work long hours.

When I was a little girl, I suffered from shyness and embarrassment in the presence of others.

I was a shy little girl.

It is absolutely necessary for the person employed as a marine fireman to give the matter of steam pressure his undivided attention at all times.

The fireman has to keep his eye on the steam gauge.

You may ask how you can arrive at five hundred words at this rate. Simple. You dig up more real content. Instead of taking a couple of obvious points off the surface of the topic and then circling warily around them for six paragraphs, you work in and explore, figure out the details. You illustrate. You say that fast driving is dangerous, and then you prove it. How long does it take to stop a car at forty and at eighty? How far can you see at night? What happens when a tire blows? What happens in a head-on collision at fifty miles an hour? Pretty soon your paper will be full of broken glass and blood and headless torsos, and reaching five hundred words will not really be a problem.

Call a Fool a Fool   Some of the padding in freshman themes is to be blamed not on anxiety about the word minimum but on excessive timidity. The student writes, "In my opinion, the principal of my high school acted in ways that I believe every unbiased person would have to call foolish." This isn't exactly what he means. What he means is, "My high school principal was a fool." If he was a fool, call him a fool. Hedging the thing about with "in-my-opinion's" and "it-seems-to-me's" and "as-I-see-it's" and "at-least-from-my-point-of-view's" gains you nothing. Delete these phrases whenever they creep into your paper.

The student's tendency to hedge stems from a modesty that in other circumstances would be commendable. He is, he realizes, young and inexperienced, and he half suspects that he is dopey and fuzzy-minded beyond the average. Probably only too true. But it doesn't help to announce your incompetence six times in every paragraph. Decide what you want to say and say it as vigorously as possible, without apology and in plain words.

Linguistic diffidence can take various forms. One is what we call *euphemism*. This is the tendency to call a spade "a certain garden implement" or women's underwear "unmentionables." It is stronger in some eras than others and in some people than others but it always operates more or less in subjects that are touchy or taboo: death, sex, madness, and so on. Thus we shrink from saying "He died last night" but say instead "passed away," "left us," "joined his Maker," "went to his reward." Or we try to take off the tension with a lighter cliché: "kicked the bucket," "cashed in his chips," "handed in his dinner pail." We have found all sorts of ways to avoid saying *mad*: "mentally ill," "touched," "not quite right upstairs," "feeble-minded," "innocent," "simple," "off his trolley," "not in his right mind." Even such a now plain word as *insane* began as a euphemism with the meaning "not healthy."

Modern science, particularly psychology, contributes many polysyllables in which we can wrap our thoughts and blunt their force. To many writers there is no such thing as a bad schoolboy. Schoolboys are maladjusted or unoriented or misunderstood or in the need of guidance or lacking in continued success toward satisfactory integration of the personality as a social unit, but they are never bad. Psychology no doubt makes us better men and women, more sympathetic and tolerant, but it doesn't make writing any easier. Had Shakespeare been confronted with psychology, "To be or not to be" might have come out, "To continue as a social unit or not to do so. That is the personality problem. Whether 'tis a better sign of integration at the conscious level to display a psychic tolerance toward the maladjustments and repressions induced by one's lack of orientation in one's environment or—" But Hamlet would never have finished the soliloquy.

Writing in the modern world, you cannot altogether avoid modern jargon. Nor, in an effort to get away from euphemism, should you salt your paper with four-letter words. But you can do much if you will mount guard against those roundabout phrases, those echoing polysyllables that tend to slip into your writing to rob it of its crispness and force.

Beware of Pat Expressions   Other things being equal, avoid phrases like "other things being equal." Those sentences that come to you whole, or in two or three doughy lumps, are sure to be bad sentences. They are no creation of yours but pieces of common thought floating in the community soup.

Pat expressions are hard, often impossible, to avoid, because they come too easily to be noticed and seem too necessary to be dispensed with. No writer avoids them altogether, but good writers avoid them more often than poor writers.

By "pat expressions" we mean such tags as "to all practical intents and purposes," "the pure and simple truth," "from where I sit," "the time of his life," "to the ends of the earth," "in the twinkling of an eye," "as sure as you're born," "over my dead body," "under cover of darkness," "took the easy way out," "when all is said and done," "told him time and time again," "parted the best of friends," "stand up and be counted," "gave him the best years of her life," "worked her fingers to the bone." Like other clichés, these expressions were once forceful. Now we should use them only when we can't possibly think of anything else.

Some pat expressions stand like a wall between the writer and thought. Such a one is "the American way of life." Many student writers feel that when they have said that something accords with the American way of life or does not they have exhausted the subject. Actually, they have stopped at the highest level of abstraction. The American way of life is the complicated set of bonds between a hundred and eighty million ways. All of us know this when we think about it, but the tag phrase too often keeps us from thinking about it.

So with many another phrase dear to the politician: "this great land of ours," "the man in the street," "our national heritage." These may prove our patriotism or give a clue to our political beliefs, but otherwise they add nothing to the paper except words.

Colorful Words   The writer builds with words, and no builder uses a raw material more slippery and elusive and treacherous. A writer's work is a constant struggle to get the right word in the right place, to find that particular word that will convey his meaning exactly, that will persuade the reader or soothe him or startle or amuse him. He never succeeds altogether—sometimes he feels that he scarcely succeeds at all—but such successes as he has are what make the thing worth doing.

There is no book of rules for this game. One progresses through everlasting experiment on the basis of ever-widening experience. There are few useful generalizations that one can make about words as words, but there are perhaps a few.

Some words are what we call "colorful." By this we mean that they are calculated to produce a picture or induce an emotion. They are dressy instead of plain, specific instead of general, loud instead of soft. Thus, in place of "Her heart beat," we may write, "Her heart *pounded, throbbed, fluttered, danced.*" Instead of "He sat in his chair," we may say, "He *lounged, sprawled, coiled.*" Instead of "It was hot," we may say, "It was *blistering, sultry, muggy, suffocating, steamy, wilting.*"

However, it should not be supposed that the fancy word is always better. Often it is as well to write "Her heart beat" or "It was hot" if that is all it did or all it was. Ages differ in how they like their prose. The nineteenth century liked it rich and smoky. The twentieth has usually preferred it lean and cool. The twentieth century writer, like all writers, is forever seeking the exact word, but he is wary of sounding feverish. He tends to pitch it low, to understate it, to throw it away. He knows that if he gets too colorful, the audience is likely to giggle.

See how this strikes you: "As the rich, golden glow of the sunset died away along the eternal western hills, Angela's limpid blue eyes looked softly and trustingly into Montague's flashing brown ones, and her heart pounded like a drum in time with the joyous song surging in her soul." Some people like that sort of thing, but most modern readers would say, "Good grief," and turn on the television.

Colored Words   Some words we would call not so much colorful as colored—that is, loaded with associations, good or bad. All words—except perhaps structure words—have associations of some sort. We have said that the meaning of a word is the sum of the contexts in which it occurs. When we hear a word, we hear with it an echo of all the situations in which we have heard it before.

In some words, these echoes are obvious and discussable. The word *mother*, for example, has, for most people, aggreeable associations. When you hear *mother* you probably think of home, safety, love, food, and various other pleasant things. If one writes, "She was like a mother to me," he gets an effect which he would not get in "She was like an aunt to me." The advertiser makes use of the associations of *mother* by working it in when he talks about his product. The politician works it in when he talks about himself.

So also with such words as *home, liberty, fireside, contentment, patriot, tenderness, sacrifice, childlike, manly, bluff, limpid.* All of these words are loaded with associations that would be rather hard to indicate in a straightforward definition. There is more than a literal difference between "They sat around the fireside" and "They sat around the stove." They might have been equally warm and happy around the stove, but *fireside* suggests leisure, grace, quiet tradition, congenial company, and *stove* does not.

Conversely, some words have bad associations. *Mother* suggests pleasant things, but *mother-in-law* does not. Many mothers-in-law are heroically lovable and some mothers drink gin all day and beat their children insensible, but these facts of life are beside the point. The point is that *mother* sounds good and *mother-in-law* does not.

Or consider the word *intellectual*. This would seem to be a complimentary term, but in point of fact it is not, for it has picked up aoosications of impracticality and ineffectuality and general dopiness. So also such words as *liberal, reactionary, Communist, socialist, capitalist, radical, schoolteacher, truck driver, undertaker, operator, salesman, huckster, speculator.* These convey meaning on the literal level, but beyond that—sometimes, in some places—they convey contempt on the part of the speaker.

The question of whether to use loaded words or not depends on what is being written. The scientist, the scholar, try to avoid them, for the poet, the advertising writer, the public speaker, they are standard equipment. But every writer should take care that they do not substitute for thought. If you write, "Anyone who thinks that is nothing but a Socialist (or Communist or capitalist)" you have said nothing except that you don't like people who think that, and such remarks are effective only with the most naive readers. It is always a bad mistake to think your readers more naive than they really are.

Colorless Words But probably most student writers come to grief not with words that are colorful or those that are colored but with those that have no color at all. A pet example is *nice*, a word we would find it hard to dispense with in casual conversation but which is no longer capable of adding much to a description. Colorless words are those of such general meaning that in a particular sentence they mean nothing. Slang adjectives like *cool* ("That's real cool") tend to explode all over the language. They are applied to everything, lose their original force, and quickly die.

Beware also of nouns of very general meaning, like *circumstances, cases, instances, aspects, factors, relationships, attitudes, eventualities,* etc. In most circumstances you will find that those cases of writing which contain too many instances of words like these will in this and other aspects have factors leading to unsatisfactory relationships with the reader resulting in unfavorable attitudes on his part and perhaps other eventualities, like a grade of "D." Notice also what "etc." means. It means "I'd like to make this list longer, but I can't think of any more examples."

How Does the Author Make His Point?

1. The author spends eleven paragraphs on an introduction. Is this much content necessary? Effective?
2. Of all the essays written on this subject, this one has survived the test of time. Why is this one so effective?
3. What is the tone of the essay?
4. What are the seven steps in the process Roberts outlines for improving your writing? Which do you believe is the most important?
5. Roberts uses examples to prove his point. What, in your opinion, is the *best* example he uses?

What Do You Think?

1. Do the topics English professors assign make writing more difficult?
2. Would you prefer an assignment based on method of development rather than on topic? Why or why not?
3. Have you ever done any of the things Roberts suggests in the first eleven paragraphs in order to get a theme in on time? Explain.

The Spider and the Wasp

Alexander
Petrunkevitch

Alexander Petrunkevitch, a longtime faculty member at Yale, was a world-renowned zoologist. Although he was a man of broad learning (writing on such things as free will in German, translating the poems of Byron into Russian and of Pushkin from Russian into English), he was also a scholar of deep knowledge. He spent more than fifty years of his life studying spiders. In this essay, he analyzes the natural process of life-out-of-death.

To hold its own in the struggle for existence, every species of animal must have a regular source of food, and if it happens to live on other animals, its survival may be very delicately balanced. The hunter cannot exist without the hunted; if the latter should perish from the earth, the former would, too. When the hunted also prey on some of the hunters, the matter may become complicated.

This is nowhere better illustrated than in the insect world. Think of the complexity of a situation such as the following: There is a certain wasp, *Pimpla inquisitor*, whose larvae feed on the larvae of the tussock moth. *Pimpla* larvae in turn serve as food for the larvae of a second wasp, and the latter in their turn nourish still a third wasp. What subtle balance between fertility and mortality must exist in the case of each of these four species to prevent the extinction of all of them! An excess of mortality over fertility in a single member of the group would ultimately wipe out all four.

This is not a unique case. The two great orders of insects, Hymenoptera and Diptera, are full of such examples of interrelationship. And the spiders (which are not insects but members of a separate order of arthropods) also are killers and victims of insects.

The picture is complicated by the fact that those species which are carnivorous in the larval stage have to be provided with animal food by a vegetarian mother. The survival of the young depends on the mother's correct choice of a food which she does not eat herself.

In the feeding and safeguarding of their progeny the insects and spiders exhibit some interesting analogies to reasoning and some crass examples of blind instinct. The case I propose to describe here is that of the tarantula spiders and their arch-enemy, the digger wasps of the genus Pepsis. It is a classic example of what looks like intelligence pitted against instinct—a strange situation in which the victim, though fully able to defend itself, submits unwittingly to its destruction.

Most tarantulas live in the Tropics, but several species occur in the temperate zone and a few are common in the southern U.S. Some varieties are large and have powerful fangs with which they can inflict a deep wound. These formidable looking spiders do not, however, attack man; you can hold one in your hand, if you are gentle, without being bitten. Their bite is dangerous only to insects and small mammals such as mice; for a man it is no worse than a hornet's sting.

Tarantulas customarily live in deep cylindrical burrows, from which they emerge at dusk and into which they retire at dawn. Mature males wander about after dark in search of females and occasionally stray into houses. After mating, the male dies in a few weeks, but a female lives much longer and can mate several years in succession. In a Paris museum is a tropical specimen which is said to have been living in captivity for 25 years.

A fertilized female tarantula lays from 200 to 400 eggs at a time; thus it is possible for a single tarantula to produce several thousand young. She takes no care of them beyond weaving a cocoon of silk to enclose the eggs. After they hatch, the young walk away, find convenient places in which to dig their burrows and spend the rest of their lives in solitude. Tarantulas feed mostly on insects and millepedes. Once their appetite is appeased, they digest the food for several days before eating again. Their sight is poor, being limited to sensing a change in the intensity of light and to the perception of moving objects. They apparently have little or no sense of hearing, for a hungry tarantula will pay no attention to a loudly chirping cricket placed in its cage unless the insect happens to touch one of its legs.

But all spiders, and especially hairy ones, have an extremely delicate sense of touch. Laboratory experiments prove that tarantulas can distinguish three types of touch: pressure against the body wall, stroking of the body hair and riffling of certain very fine hairs on the legs called trichobothria. Pressure against the body, by a finger or the end of a pencil, causes the tarantula to move off slowly for a short distance. The touch excites no defensive response unless the approach is from above where the spider can see the motion, in which case it rises on its hind legs, lifts its front legs, opens its fangs and holds this threatening posture as long as the object continues to move. When the motion stops, the spider drops back to the ground, remains quiet for a few seconds and then moves slowly away.

The entire body of a tarantula, especially its legs, is thickly clothed with hair. Some of it is short and woolly, some long and stiff. Touching this body hair produces one of two distinct reactions. When the spider is hungry, it responds with an immediate and swift attack. At the touch of a cricket's antennae the tarantula seizes the insect so swiftly that a motion picture taken at the rate of 64 frames per second shows only the result and not the process of capture. But when the spider is not hungry, the stimulation of its hairs merely causes it to shake the touched limb. An insect can walk under its hairy belly unharmed.

The trichobothria, very fine hairs growing from disklike membranes on the legs, were once thought to be the spider's hearing organs, but we now know that they have nothing to do with sound. They are sensitive only to air movement. A light breeze makes them vibrate slowly without disturbing the common hair. When one blows gently on the trichobothria, the tarantula reacts with a quick jerk of its four front legs. If the front and hind legs are stimulated at the same time, the spider makes a sudden jump. This reaction is quite independent of the state of its appetite.

These three tactile responses—to pressure on the body wall, to moving of the common hair and to flexing of the trichobothria—are so different from one another that there is no possibility of confusing them. They serve the tarantula adequately for most of its needs and enable it to avoid most annoyances and dangers. But they fail the spider completely when it meets its deadly enemy, the digger wasp Pepsis.

These solitary wasps are beautiful and formidable creatures. Most species are either a deep shiny blue all over, or deep blue with rusty wings. The largest have a wing span of about four inches. They live on nectar. When excited, they give off a pungent odor—a warning that they are ready to attack. The sting is much worse than that of a bee or common wasp, and the pain and swelling last longer. In the adult stage the wasp lives only a few months. The female produces but a few eggs, one at a time at intervals of two or three days. For each egg the mother must provide one adult tarantula, alive but paralyzed. The tarantula must be of the correct species to nourish the larva. The mother wasp attaches the egg to the paralyzed spider's abdomen. Upon hatching from the egg, the larva is many hundreds of times smaller than its living but helpless victim. It eats no other food and drinks no water. By the time it has finished its single gargantuan meal and become ready for wasphood, nothing remains of the tarantula but its indigestible chitinous skeleton.

The mother wasp goes tarantula-hunting when the egg in her ovary is almost ready to be laid. Flying low over the ground late on a sunny afternoon, the wasp looks for its victim or for the mouth of a tarantula burrow, a round hole edged by a bit of silk. The sex of the spider makes no difference, but the mother is highly discriminating as to species. Each species of Pepsis requires a certain species of tarantula, and the wasp will not attack the wrong species. In a cage with a tarantula which is not its normal prey the wasp avoids the spider, and is usually killed by it in the night.

Yet when a wasp finds the correct species, it is the other way about. To identify the species the wasp apparently must explore the spider with her antennae. The tarantula shows an amazing tolerance to this exploration. The wasp crawls under it and walks over it without evoking any hostile response. The molestation is so great and so persistent that the tarantula often rises on all eight legs, as if it were on stilts. It may stand this way for several minutes. Meanwhile the wasp, having satisfied itself that the victim is of the right species, moves off a few inches to dig the spider's grave. Working vigorously with legs and jaws, it excavates a hole 8 to 10 inches deep with a diameter slightly larger than the spider's girth. Now and again the wasp pops out of the hole to make sure that the spider is still there.

When the grave is finished, the wasp returns to the tarantula to complete her ghastly enterprise. First she feels it all over once more with her antennae. Then her behavior becomes more aggressive. She bends her abdomen, protruding her sting, and searches for the soft membrane at the point where the spider's leg joins its body—the only spot where she can penetrate the horny skeleton. From time to time, as the exasperated spider slowly shifts ground, the wasp turns on her back and slides along with the aid of her wings, trying to get under the tarantula for a shot at the vital spot. During all this maneuvering, which can last for several minutes, the tarantula makes no move to save itself. Finally the wasp corners it against some obstruction and grasps one of its legs in her powerful jaws. Now at last the harassed spider tries a desperate but vain defense. The two contestants roll over and over on the ground. It is a terrifying sight and the outcome is always the same. The wasp finally manages to thrust her sting into the soft spot and holds it there for a few seconds while she pumps in the poison. Almost immediately the tarantula falls paralyzed on its back. Its legs stop twitching; its heart stops beating. Yet it is not dead, as is shown by the fact that if taken from the wasp it can be restored to some sensitivity by being kept in a moist chamber for several months.

After paralyzing the tarantula, the wasp cleans herself by dragging her body along the ground and rubbing her feet, sucks the drop of blood oozing from the wound in the spider's abdomen, then grabs a leg of the flabby, helpless animal in her jaws and drags it down to the bottom of the grave. She stays there for many minutes, sometimes for several hours, and what she does all that time in the dark we do not know. Eventually she lays her egg and attaches it to the side of the spider's abdomen with a sticky secretion. Then she emerges, fills the grave with soil carried bit by bit in her jaws, and finally tramples the ground all around to hide any trace of the grave from prowlers. Then she flies away, leaving her descendant safely started in life.

In all this the behavior of the wasp evidently is qualitatively different from that of the spider. The wasp acts like an intelligent animal. This is not to say that instinct plays no part or that she reasons as man does. But her actions are to the point; they are not automatic and can be modified to fit the situation. We do not know for certain how she identifies the tarantula—probably it is by some olfactory or chemo-tactile sense—but she does it purposefully and does not blindly tackle a wrong species.

On the other hand, the tarantula's behavior shows only confusion. Evidently the wasp's pawing gives it no pleasure, for it tries to move away. That the wasp is not simulating sexual stimulation is certain, because male and female tarantulas react in the same way to its advances. That the spider is not anesthetized by some odorless secretion is easily shown by blowing lightly at the tarantula and making it jump suddenly. What, then, makes the tarantula behave as stupidly as it does?

No clear, simple answer is available. Possibly the stimulation by the wasp's antennae is masked by a heavier pressure on the spider's body, so that it reacts as when prodded by a pencil. But the explanation may be much more complex. Initiative in attack is not in the nature of tarantulas; most species fight only when cornered so that escape is impossible. Their inherited patterns of behavior apparently prompt them to avoid problems rather than attack them. For example, spiders always weave their webs in three dimensions, and when a spider finds that there is insufficient space to attach certain threads in the third dimension, it leaves the place and seeks another, instead of finishing the web in a single plane. This urge to escape seems to arise under all circumstances, in all phases of life and to take the place of reasoning. For a spider to change the pattern of its web is as impossible as for an inexperienced man to build a bridge across a chasm obstructing his way.

In a way the instinctive urge to escape is not only easier but more efficient than reasoning. The tarantula does exactly what is most efficient in all cases except in an encounter with a ruthless and determined attacker dependent for the existence of her own species on killing as many tarantulas as she can lay eggs. Perhaps in this case the spider follows its usual pattern of trying to escape, instead of seizing and killing the wasp, because it is not aware of its danger. In any case, the survival of the tarantula species as a whole is protected by the fact that the spider is much more fertile than the wasp.

How Does the Author Make His Point?

1. What is the purpose of the rather long introduction? Do the scientific terms add to or detract from its interest? Why do you think the author included these terms?
2. What is the thesis statement?
3. Why do you think the author gives the result of the struggle first (in paragraph 8) and then goes to the beginning of the process—the wasp going tarantula-hunting—in the next paragraph?
4. Outline the steps of the process of the wasp defeating the spider. Use parallel form in your steps such as the following:

complete sentences:	The wasp first searches for her victim
	The wasp next . . . etc.
or	
participial phrases:	Searching for the tarantula
	Identifying the tarantula . . . etc.
or	
words:	The search
	The identification . . . etc.

5. If what the author says in the first paragraph is true, how is it that the species of tarantula spiders does not become extinct and, in turn, cause the extinction of the digger wasps?

What Do You Think?

1. In the last two paragraphs, the author uses intelligent guesses to explain why the spider acts as he does. Which do you accept, or do you have a better explanation?
2. What is the effect of the scientific descriptions of the insects and their habits on you?
3. Did you find the essay interesting? Why or why not?

Coming to an Awareness of Language

MALCOLM X with
ALEX HALEY

*Malcolm X was a leader of the Black Muslim movement. He died at
age thirty-nine, shot to death as he spoke at a rally in Harlem in 1965.
He had grown up in a ghetto where his life was made up of drugs and
drug pushing, prostitution and pimping and thieving, but he became one
of the most powerful blacks of the sixties.*

This selection is from The Autobiography of Malcolm X, *which
was written with the help of Alex Haley, who later wrote* Roots. *A large
part of Malcolm X's power came from his ability to persuade people of the
values of his ideas. In this brief essay, he tells how, while he was in
prison, he first learned of the power of language.*

I've never been one for inaction. Everything I've ever felt
strongly about, I've done something about. I guess that's why,
unable to do anything else, I soon began writing to people I had
known in the hustling world, such as Sammy the Pimp, John
Hughes, the gambling house owner, the thief Jumpsteady, and
several dope peddlers.

I never got a single reply. The average hustler and criminal
was too uneducated to write a letter. I have known many slick,
sharp-looking hustlers, who would have you think they had an
interest in Wall Street; privately, they would get someone else to
read a letter if they received one. Besides, neither would I have
replied to anyone writing me something as wild as "the white man
is the devil."

But at that time, I felt that the real reason was that the white
man knew he was the devil.

Later on, I even wrote to the Mayor of Boston, to the
Governor of Massachusetts, and to Harry S. Truman. They never
answered; they probably never even saw my letters. I
handscratched to them how the white man's society was
responsible for the black man's condition in this wilderness of
North America.

It was because of my letters that I happened to stumble upon
starting to acquire some kind of a homemade education.

I became increasingly frustrated at not being able to express what I wanted to convey in letters that I wrote. In the street, I had been the most articulate hustler out there—I had commanded attention when I said something. But now, trying to write simple English, I not only wasn't articulate, I wasn't even functional. How would I sound writing in slang, the way I would say it, something such as, "Look daddy, let me pull your coat about a cat."

Many who today hear me somewhere in person, or on television, or those who read something I've said, will think I went to school far beyond the eighth grade. This impression is due entirely to my prison studies.

It had really begun back in the Charlestown Prison, when Bimbi first made me feel envy of his stock of knowledge. Bimbi had always taken charge of any conversation he was in, and I had tried to emulate him. But every book I picked up had few sentences which didn't contain anywhere from one to nearly all of the words that might as well have been in Chinese. When I just skipped those words, of course, I really ended up with little idea of what the book said. So I had come to the Norfolk Prison Colony still going through only book-reading motions. Pretty soon, I would have quit even these motions, unless I had received the motivation that I did.

I saw that the best thing I could do was get hold of a dictionary—to study, to learn some words. I was lucky enough to reason also that I should try to improve my penmanship. It was sad. I couldn't even write in a straight line. It was both ideas together that moved me to request a dictionary along with some tablets and pencils from the Norfolk Prison Colony School.

I spent two days just riffling uncertainly through the dictionary's pages. I'd never realized so many words existed! I didn't know *which* word I needed to learn. Finally, just to start some kind of action, I began copying.

In my slow, painstaking, ragged handwriting, I copied into my tablet everything printed on that first page, down to the punctuation marks.

I believe it took me a day. Then aloud, I read back, to myself, everything I'd written on the tablet. Over and over, aloud, to myself, I read my own handwriting.

I woke up the next morning, thinking about those words— immensely proud to realize that not only had I written so much at one time, but I'd written words that I never knew were in the world. Moreover, with a little effort, I also could remember what many of these words meant. I reviewed the words whose meanings I didn't remember. Funny thing, from the dictionary's first page right now, that "aardvark" springs to my mind. The dictionary had a picture of it, a long-tailed, long-eared, burrowing African mammal, which lives off termites caught by sticking out its tongue as an anteater does for ants.

I was so fascinated that I went on—I copied the dictionary's next page. And the same experience came when I studied that. With every succeeding page, I also learned of people and places and events from history. Actually the dictionary is like a miniature encyclopedia. Finally the dictionary's A section had filled a whole tablet—and I went on into the B's. That was the way I started copying what eventually became the entire dictionary. It went a lot faster after so much practice helped me to pick up handwriting speed. Between what I wrote in my tablet, and writing letters, during the rest of my time in prison I would guess I wrote a million words.

I suppose it was *inevitable* that as my word-base broadened, I could for the first time pick up a book and read and now begin to understand what the book was saying. Anyone who has read a great deal can imagine the new world that opened. Let me tell you something: from then until I left that prison, in every free moment I had, if I was not reading in the library, I was reading on my bunk. You couldn't have gotten me out of books with a wedge. Between . . . my correspondence, my visitors . . . and my reading of books, months passed without my even thinking about being imprisoned. In fact, up to then, I never had been so truly free in my life.

How Does the Author Make His Point?

1. How does the introduction seize the reader's attention?
2. How does this essay exhibit some of the strengths of autobiography?
3. How does the author make what might ordinarily be a dull process interesting?

What Do You Think?

1. How did the author's frustration ultimately contribute to his education?
2. Malcolm X says that he had never been "so truly free" as when he opened up his world through reading. Has reading opened up any new worlds for you?
3. What are the implications about education as a way out of crime?

How to Live to Be 200

STEPHEN LEACOCK

Before World War I, Stephen Leacock became Canada's best-loved humorist, and he has warmed Canadian hearts (and many others) ever since. For the past decade, an important prize has been awarded every year in his honor to the best contemporary humorist.

Some people have suggested that he was driven into comedy by his occupation as a professor of economics ("the dismal science," as Thomas Carlyle called it) at McGill University. Be that as it may, his essays reflect his personal, derisive attitude toward the foibles and manners of his time. And his topic may strike you as surprisingly timely; there are many people today "going out in silly little suits and running Marathon heats before breakfast."

Twenty years aago I knew a man called Jiggins, who had the Health Habit. He used to take a cold plunge every morning. He said it opened his pores. After it he took a hot sponge. He said it closed the pores. He got so that he could open and shut his pores at will . . .

After he had got his undershirt on, Jiggins used to hitch himself up like a dog in harness and do Sandow exercises. He did them forwards, backwards, and hind-side up.

He could have got a job as a dog anywhere. He spent all his time at this kind of thing. In his spare time at the office, he used to lie on his stomach on the floor and see if he could lift himself up with his knuckles. If he could, then he tried some other way until he found one that he couldn't do. Then he would spend the rest of his lunch hour on his stomach, perfectly happy.

In the evenings in his room he used to lift iron bars, cannon-balls, heave dumb-bells, and haul himself up to the ceiling with his teeth. You could hear the thumps half a mile.

He liked it . . .

Jiggins is dead. He was, of course, a pioneer, but the fact that he dumb-belled himself to death at an early age does not prevent a whole generation of young men from following in his path.

They are ridden by the Health Mania.

They makes themselves a nuisance.

They get up at impossible hours. They go out in silly little suits and run Marathon heats before breakfast. They chase around barefoot to get the dew on their feet. They hunt for ozone. They bother about pepsin. They won't eat meat because it has too much nitrogen. They won't eat fruit because it hasn't any. They prefer albumen and starch and nitrogen to huckleberry pie and doughnuts. They won't drink water out of a tap. They won't eat sardines out of a can. They won't use oysters out of a pail. They won't drink milk out of a glass. They are afraid of alcohol in any shape. Yes, sir, afraid. "Cowards."

And after all their fuss they presently incur some simple old-fashioned illness and die like anybody else.

Now people of this sort have no chance to attain any great age. They are on the wrong track.

Listen. Do you want to live to be really old, to enjoy a grand, green, exuberant, boastful old age and to make yourself a nuisance to your whole neighborhood with your reminiscences?

Then cut out all this nonsense. Cut it out. Get up in the morning at a sensible hour. The time to get up is when you have to, not before. If your office opens at eleven, get up at ten-thirty. Take your chance on ozone. There isn't any such thing anyway. Or, if there is, you can buy a Thermos bottle full for five cents, and put it on a shelf in your cupboard. If your work begins at seven in the morning, get up at ten minutes to, but don't be liar enough to say that you like it. It isn't exhilarating, and you know it.

Also, drop all that cold-bath business. You never did it when you were a boy. Don't be a fool now. If you must take a bath (you don't really need to), take it warm. The pleasure of getting out of a cold bed and creeping into a hot bath beats a cold plunge to death. In any case, stop gassing about your tub and your "shower," as if you were the only man who ever washed.

So much for that point . . .

Understand that it is only a fad of modern medicine to say that cholera and typhoid and diphtheria are caused by bacilli and germs; nonsense. Cholera is caused by a frightful pain in the stomach, and diphtheria is caused by trying to cure a sore throat.

Now take the question of food.

Eat what you want. Eat lots of it. Yes, eat too much of it. Eat till you can just stagger across the room with it and prop it up against a sofa cushion. Eat everything that you like until you can't eat any more. The only test is, can you pay for it? If you can't pay for it, don't eat it. And listen—don't worry as to whether your food contains starch, or albumen, or gluten, or nitrogen, If you are a damn fool enough to want these things, go and buy them and eat all you want of them. Go to a laundry and get a bag of starch, and eat your fill of it. Eat it, and take a good long drink of glue after it, and a spoonful of Portland cement. That will gluten you, good and solid.

If you like nitrogen, go and get a druggist to give you a canful of it at the soda counter, and let you sip it with a straw. Only don't think that you can mix all these things up with your food. There isn't any nitrogen or phosphorus or albumen in ordinary things to eat. In any decent household all that sort of stuff is washed out in the kitchen sink before the food is put on the table.

And just one word about fresh air and exercise. Don't bother with either of them. Get your room full of good air, then shut up the windows and keep it. It will keep for years. Anyway, don't keep using your lungs all the time. Let them rest. As for exercise, if you have to take it, take it and put up with it. But as long as you have the price of a hack and can hire other people to play baseball for you and run races and do gymnastics when you sit in the shade and smoke and watch them—great heavens, what more do you want?

How Does the Author Make His Point?

1. What is the thesis statement? What words in it clearly indicate the writer's attitude toward his subject?
2. The title "How to—" indicates that this is a process essay. Where is it first made clear that the intent of the author is comedy? Where does the introduction end and the process begin?
3. Among the many devices to achieve comedy, two of the most frequent are overstatement and understatement. Which of these two devices does Leacock use? Give a couple of specific examples.

What Do You Think?

1. Are there people today who are health fanatics?
2. What is the author's purpose in writing this essay? Is he just trying to be amusing, or does he have a point to make beyond that?

When You Camp Out, Do It Right

ERNEST HEMINGWAY

Ernest Hemingway was one of America's great writers, winning both the Pulitzer and Nobel prizes for literature. His most famous novels include The Sun Also Rises, A Farewell to Arms, For Whom the Bell Tolls, and The Old Man and the Sea. *Noted for his stories on war and sport, Hemingway was an avid hunter and fisherman and, therefore, as those of you who have read his Nick Adams stories know, an expert on camping.*

Thousands of people will go into the bush this summer to cut the high cost of living. A man who gets his two week's salary while he is on vacation should be able to put those two weeks in fishing and camping and be able to save one week's salary clear. He ought to be able to sleep comfortably every night, to eat well every day and to return to the city rested and in good condition.

But if he goes into the woods with a frying pan, an ignorance of black flies and mosquitoes, and a great and abiding lack of knowledge about cookery, the chances are that his return will be very different. He will come back with enough mosquito bites to make the back of his neck look like a relief map of the Caucasus. His digestion will be wrecked after a valiant battle to assimilate half-cooked or charred grub. And he won't have had a decent night's sleep while he has been gone.

He will solemnly raise his right hand and inform you that he has joined the grand army of never-agains. The call of the wild may be all right, but it's a dog's life. He's heard the call of the tame with both ears. Waiter, bring him an order of milk toast.

In the first place he overlooked the insects. Black flies, no-see-ums, deer flies, gnats and mosquitoes were instituted by the devil to force people to live in cities where he could get at them better. If it weren't for them everybody would live in the bush and he would be out of work. It was a rather successful invention.

But there are lots of dopes that will counteract the pests. The simplest perhaps is oil of citronella. Two bits' worth of this purchased at any pharmacist's will be enough to last for two weeks in the worst fly and mosquito-ridden country.

Rub a little on the back of your neck, your forehead and your wrists before you start fishing, and the blacks and skeeters will shun you. The odor of citronella is not offensive to people. It smells like gun oil. But the bugs do hate it.

Oil of pennyroyal and eucalyptol are also much hated by mosquitoes, and with citronella they form the basis for many proprietary preparations. But it is cheaper and better to buy the straight citronella. Put a little on the mosquito netting that covers the front of your pup tent or canoe tent at night, and you won't be bothered.

To be really rested and get any benefit out of a vacation a man must get a good night's sleep every night. The first requisite for this is to have plenty of cover. It is twice as cold as you expect it will be in the bush four nights out of five, and a good plan is to take just double the bedding that you think you will need. An old quilt that you can wrap up is as warm as two blankets.

Nearly all outdoor writers rhapsodize over the browse bed. It is all right for the man who knows how to make one and has plenty of time. But in a succession of one-night camps on a canoe trip all you need is level ground for your tent floor and you will sleep all right if you have plenty of covers under you. Take twice as much cover as you think that you will need, and then put two-thirds of it under you. You will sleep warm and get your rest.

When it is clear weather you don't need to pitch your tent if you are only stopping for the night. Drive four stakes at the head of your made-up bed and drape your mosquito bar over that, then you can sleep like a log and laugh at the mosquitoes.

Outside of insects and bum sleeping the rock that wrecks most camping trips is cooking. The average tyro's idea of cooking is to fry everything and fry it good and plenty. Now, a frying pan is a most necessary thing to any trip, but you also need the old stew kettle and the folding reflector baker.

A pan of fried trout can't be bettered and they don't cost any more than ever. But there is a good and bad way of frying them. The beginner puts his trout and his bacon in, and over a brightly burning fire the bacon curls up and dries into a dry tasteless cinder and the trout is burned outside while it is still raw inside. He eats them and it is all right if he is only out for the day and going home to a good meal at night. But if he is going to face more trout and bacon the next morning and other equally well-cooked dishes for the remainder of two weeks he is on the pathway to nervous dyspepsia.

The proper way is to cook over coals. Have several cans of Crisco or Cotosuet or one of the vegetable shortenings along that are as good as lard and excellent for all kinds of shortening. Put the bacon in and when it is about half cooked lay the trout in the hot grease, dipping them in cornmeal first. Then put the bacon on top of the trout and it will baste them as it slowly cooks.

The coffee can be boiling at the same time and in a smaller skillet pancakes being made that are satisfying the other campers while they are waiting for the trout.

With the prepared pancake flours you take a cupful of pancake flour and add a cup of water. Mix the water and flour and as soon as the lumps are out it is ready for cooking. Have the skillet hot and keep it well greased. Drop the batter in and as soon as it is done on one side loosen it in the skillet and flip it over. Apple butter, syrup or cinnamon and sugar go well with the cakes.

While the crowd have taken the edge from their appetites with flapjacks the trout have been cooked and they and the bacon are ready to serve. The trout are crisp outside and firm and pink inside and the bacon is well done—but not too done. If there is anything better than that combination the writer has yet to taste it in a lifetime devoted largely and studiously to eating.

The stew kettle will cook you dried apricots when they have resumed their predried plumpness after a night of soaking, it will serve to concoct a mulligan in, and it will cook macaroni. When you are not using it, it should be boiling water for the dishes.

In the baker, mere man comes into his own, for he can make a pie that to his bush appetite will have it all over the product that mother used to make, like a tent. Men have always believed that there was something mysterious and difficult about making a pie. Here is a great secret. There is nothing to it. We've been kidded for years. Any man of average office intelligence can make at least as good a pie as his wife.

All there is to a pie is a cup and a half of flour, one-half teaspoonful of salt, one-half cup of lard and cold water. That will make pie crust that will bring tears of joy into your camping partner's eyes.

Mix the salt with the flour, work the lard into the flour, make it up into a good workmanlike dough with cold water. Spread some flour on the back of a box or something flat, and pat the dough around a while. Then roll it out with whatever kind of round bottle you prefer. Put a little more lard on the surface of the sheet of dough and then slosh a little flour on and roll it up and then roll it out again with the bottle.

Cut out a piece of the rolled out dough big enough to line a pie tin. I like the kind with holes in the bottom. Then put in your dried apples that have soaked all night and been sweetened, or your apricots, or your blueberries, and then take another sheet of the dough and drape it gracefully over the top, soldering it down at the edges with your fingers. Cut a couple of slits in the top dough sheet and prick it a few times with a fork in an artistic manner.

Put it in the baker with a good slow fire for forty-five minutes and then take it out and if your pals are Frenchmen they will kiss you. The penalty for knowing how to cook is that the others will make you do all the cooking.

It is all right to talk about roughing it in the woods. But the real woodsman is the man who can be really comfortable in the bush.

How Does the Author Make His Point?

1. What are the three purposes of a camping vacation according to Hemingway's first paragraph?
2. What are the three things that make people give up camping? Is the answer to this the thesis statement of the essay? State the thesis in a sentence.
3. What are the two things you need for a good night's sleep in the wild? Why does Hemingway stress these?
4. What cooking utensils should you take with you on a camping trip? Why?
5. How many processes does Hemingway explain in this short essay? Be careful, some are not so easy to spot.
6. Why is the very short conclusion effective?

What Do You Think?

1. Camping equipment has changed a lot since the author wrote this essay in the twenties. Would you do things differently today? Do some things remain the same?
2. To what group of people is Hemingway addressing his advice? Support your answer.
3. Why do you think people choose camping for their vacations? Is it always to save money?

How to Design a Haunted House

ROBERTSON DAVIES

Robertson Davies, dramatist, actor, novelist, and distinguished academic, is also renowned for his speeches, which are collected in One Half of Robertson Davies. The following excerpt is taken from one of those speeches made to the Ontario Association of Architects. After having discussed architecture for the theater, he turned his attention to architecture in the novel.

Now let us turn to Architecture and the Novel. Modern novelists have turned their backs on architecture—except in detective stories, where it is absolutely essential to prove that nobody could have entered the room where the beautiful blonde was murdered. But the great novelists of the past leaned very heavily on architectural devices, usually of a kind not found in modern building. You know the kind of thing I mean. In countless novels written fifty years ago the heroine, having discovered that her husband was deceiving her with the beautiful brunette, crept away to the *nursery* to weep over her beloved children.

How is she expected to do that in a house which hasn't any nursery? No woman of ordinary sensibility can creep away to weep in the *rumpus-room.* The thing is a psychological absurdity, and by making it so you have contributed to the break-up of the modern home.

And the *study*—how many modern houses have a study? Yet every man needs a study. Not to study in, of course, but to retire to when the pressure of domestic life is too great. He summons the other members of the family to meet him there. "George, I should like to see you in my study," he says to his son, when he wants to tell him to stop spending so much money. "Mary, come to my study," he says when he wants to tell his daughter to break off her affair with that beatnik she has been meeting on the sly. "My dear, will you come into my study," he says, when he wants to tell his wife that he knows what she has been up to with that handsome Mexican dentist. But most of all he needs his study to *sulk* in. Every man must have a private sulking-place, and as his wife always wants the bedroom for that purpose, he must have a study, or bottle up his sulks. And if he bottles his sulks, it won't be long before he has to be taken away in a strait-jacket. How can he sulk in the living area, which his children are using as the play-area, while his wife is right beside him in the kitchen-area, without so much as a screen to divide them? By forgetting the study you have struck an underhand blow at the mental health of the nation.

His wife, as I have said, sulks in the bedroom. I wish I could call it a *boudoir* but those wretched little boxes in modern houses cannot rise to the dignity of such a term. You know what a boudoir is. It's a bedroom that you can pace in. Consider this passage, from a very fine novel, written not quite a century ago by Mrs. Henry Wood:

> Scarce able to see through the mist of tears that clouded her violet eyes, Lady Maude sought her boudoir. There, among the treasures she had brought from her childhood home, she paced the floor, lost in sombre reverie. Had I but known, she mused as she walked toward the window, had I but known when I gave my trust, my hand—yea, all that a woman holds in store of love and tenderness—to Cyril, that a day might come when I should wish, nay, implore Almighty God, for the power to recall every gift, I should have ended my life rather than yield to his suit. Yes, all of this, these broad acres, this stately mansion, yes, and—O God, be merciful!—even my children, I should have wished undone . . . She turned at the window and continued her weary pacing.

Do you see what I am getting at? She said all of that while making one trip from the door to the window. The book tells us that Lady Maude was tall—say five foot eight—and therefore one of her paces might be estimated at twenty-five inches. Everybody knows that when you are pacing and regretting at the same time, you take a step to every word. Therefore Lady Maude took 85 paces of 25 inches apiece, which is 2,125 inches or 177 feet from door to window. Assuming that the room was a double cube, and that she was walking the long way of it, that means that the dimensions of her boudoir were 177 by 88, giving her a floor space of 15,576 square feet. No wonder she was able to keep the treasures of her old home in it. If they had included a couple of racehorses she could have kept them in it, without serious inconvenience.

I would like to urge upon you the convenience and charm of an amenity which was to be found in virtually every house described by Sir Walter Scott. I refer, of course, to the Secret Passage. Time and again in Scott's novels somebody reveals that a secret passage leads from the castle to the shepherd's hut, and as it inevitably led also from the shepherd's hut to the castle, it meant that both the shepherd and the lord of the manor had the good of it. It made life much simpler at all kinds of junctures when simplicity was needed. You could escape from the castle in a hurry, and you could also get into the castle unseen. In cases of murder or abduction this was invaluable. In ordinary domestic crises it meant that somebody could slip down to the hut and borrow a bottle of whisky if guests came unexpectedly. Still more often, it meant that the shepherd could sneak up to the castle and steal a bottle of whisky when he wanted one. It provided that element of surprise, of the unexpected, which modern domestic architecture so noticeably lacks.

How long is it since any of you included a Secret Passage in a new house? Of course I realize the difficulties you work under. Modern contractors don't know how to keep a secret. The union would certainly object to the old custom of cutting out the tongues of all the men who had worked on the job. The building inspector—they never have any imagination—would insist that it be equipped with electric light, drainage, and an air-changing system, because he would not realize that the essence of a secret passage is darkness, dampness, and a seepage of natural gas.

I have spoken of Drama and Fiction as they relate to architecture, and I hope that I have reminded you of the fact that you, gentlemen, are the designers of the scenery against which we act out the drama of our personal lives. What our personal lives are you know only too well, and I really think that you must bear some measure of blame. If we are dull, who knows what a livelier setting might not do to improve our performances? If we lack splendour, is it because we live in circumstances where a single splendid gesture might knock the place down? Don't suppose that I blame you entirely. You are what we have made you, fully as much as we are what you have made us. But would it not be possible for some of us—a few of your architects, and a handful of us ordinary people—to conspire to bring a whisper of magnificence, a shade of lightheartedness, and a savour of drama into the settings of our daily lives? I think it would. Anyhow, I think we should try.

How Does the Author Make His Point?

1. What is the thesis statement?
2. The thesis appears to be just a joke. If you consider it in terms of the conclusion, however, you will see that he has a point far more significant than joking. What is it?
3. How does the audience influence this essay?
4. What tone does Davies adopt in this essay?
5. Why is his description of Lady Maude's boudoir funny?

What Do You Think?

1. Is most comedy written for a serious purpose or just for the pleasure it gives?
2. Does Davies have a realistic idea of people, or are his characters so exaggerated they don't seem real at all?
3. Davies says that his quotation about Lady Maude comes from a "very fine novel." Is this sarcastic or a straightforward evaluation?
4. What is the significance of his title?

INTEGRATING READING SKILLS WITH WRITING SKILLS: EXPLAINING FOR CLARITY/READING FOR COMPREHENSION

Open any textbook on reading, and somewhere within it, the author will call your attention to the importance of reading "actively"—that is, reading for meaning. The best readers are those who have developed the skill of reading to answer questions. Good students, for example, are not passive readers. When they study, they do not simply read words on a page; they pose questions to themselves as they read. Then, whatever they are reading takes on more meaning because they see more than just words and sentences on a page; they see *answers* to questions.

For example, if you were reading an explanation of the parole process in this country, you would get more out of your reading if you considered some of the following questions:

1. What is the purpose of this process?
2. How many steps are involved in the process?
3. What is the relationship between one step and another?
4. Is one step more important than another?

5. Are there any common misconceptions about this process which this article clarifies?
6. Do I understand this process or do I need more background information?

Anticipating the questions that might come to a reader's mind can also help writers organize their material effectively and develop their points adequately. Before writing a final draft, for example, writers should ask themselves questions such as the following:

1. Have I clearly established the purpose of this process?
2. Have I adequately explained each step and shown the reader how one step relates to the next?
3. Have I ignored the significance of any particular step?
4. Have I cleared up any common misconceptions about the process?
5. Have I used any jargon that the reader would not understand?
6. Have I shown the reader the importance of understanding this process?
7. Have I explained special key words?

EXERCISE

Examine the following explanation of the scientific method as seen from the perspective of a motorcycle mechanic. Keeping in mind the goal of reading for meaning, actively question as you read and see how much you can learn about the scientific method.

Solution of problems too complicated for common sense to solve is achieved by long strings of mixed inductive and deductive inferences that weave back and forth between the observed machine and the mental hierarchy of the machine found in the manuals. The correct program for this interweaving is formalized as scientific method.

The real purpose of scientific method is to make sure Nature hasn't misled you into thinking you know something you don't actually know. There's not a mechanic or scientist or technician alive who hasn't suffered from that one so much that he's not instinctively on guard. That's the main reason why so much scientific and mechanical information sounds so dull and so cautious. If you get careless or go romanticizing scientific information, giving it a flourish here and there, Nature will soon make a complete fool out of you. It does it often enough anyway even when you don't give it opportunities. One must be extremely careful and rigidly logical when dealing with

Nature; one logical slip and an entire scientific edifice comes tumbling down. One false deduction about the machine and you can get hung up indefinitely.

In Part One of formal scientific method, which is the statement of the problem, the main skill is in stating absolutely no more than you are positive you know. It is much better to enter a statement "Solve Problem: Why doesn't cycle work?" which sounds dumb but is correct, than it is to enter a statement "Solve Problem: What is wrong with the electrical system?" when you don't absolutely *know* the trouble is *in* the electrical system. What you should state is "Solve Problem: What is wrong with cycle?" and *then* state as the first entry of Part Two: "Hypothesis Number One: The trouble is in the electrical system. "You think of as many hypotheses as you can, then you design experiments to test them to see which are true and which are false.

This careful approach to the beginning questions keeps you from taking a major wrong turn which might cause you weeks of extra work or can even hang you up completely. Scientific questions often have a surface appearance of dumbness for this reason. They are asked in order to prevent dumb mistakes later on.

Part Three, that part of formal scientific method called experimentation, is sometimes thought of by romantics as all of science itself because that's the only part with much visual surface. They see lots of test tubes and bizarre equipment and people running around making discoveries. They do not see the experiment as part of a larger intellectual process and so they often confuse experiments with demonstrations, which look the same. A man conducting a gee-whiz science show with fifty thousand dollars' worth of Frankenstein equipment is not doing anything scientific if he knows beforehand what the results of his efforts are going to be. A motorcycle mechanic, on the other hand, who honks the horn to see if the battery works is informally conducting a true scientific experiment. He is testing a hypothesis by putting the question to nature. The TV scientist who mutters sadly, "The experiment is a failure; we have failed to achieve what we had hoped for," is suffering mainly from a bad scriptwriter. An experiment is never a failure solely because it fails to achieve predicted results. An experiment is a failure only when it also fails adequately to test the hypothesis in question, when the data it produces don't prove anything one way or another.

Skill at this point consists of using experiments that test only the hypothesis in question, nothing less, nothing more. If the horn honks, and the mechanic concludes that the whole electrical system is working, he is in deep trouble. He has reached an illogical conclusion. The honking horn only tells him that the battery and horn are working. To design an experiment properly he has to think very rigidly in terms of what directly causes what. This you know from the hierarchy. The horn doesn't make the cycle go. Neither does the battery, except in a very indirect way. The point at which the electrical system *directly* causes the engine to fire is at the spark plugs, and if you don't test here, at the output of the electrical system, you will never really know whether the failure is electrical or not.

To test properly the mechanic removes the plug and lays it against the engine so that the base around the plug is electrically grounded, kicks the starter lever and watches the spark-plug gap for a blue spark. If there isn't any he can conclude one of two things: (a) there is an electrical failure or (b) his experiment is sloppy. If he is experienced he will try it a few more times, checking connections, trying every way he can think of to get that plug to fire. Then, if he can't get it to fire, he finally concludes that *a* is correct, there's an electrical failure, and the experiment is over. He has proved that his hypothesis is correct.

In the final category, conclusions, skill comes in stating no more than the experiment has proved. It hasn't proved that when he fixes the electrical system the motorcycle will start. There may be other things wrong. But he does know that the motorcycle isn't going to run until the electrical system is working and he sets up the next formal question: "Solve problem: what is wrong with the electrical system?"

He then sets up hypotheses for these and tests them. By asking the right questions and choosing the right tests and drawing the right conclusions the mechanic works his way down the echelons of the motorcycle hierarchy until he has found the exact specific cause or causes of the engine failure, and then he changes them so that they no longer cause the failure.

An untrained observer will see only physical labor and often get the idea that physical labor is mainly what the mechanic does. Actually the physical labor is the smallest and easiest part of what the mechanic does. By far the greatest part of his work is careful observation and precise thinking. That is why mechanics somethimes seem so taciturn and withdrawn when performing tests. They don't like it when you talk to them because they are concentrating on mental images, hierarchies, and not really looking at you or the physical motorcycle at all. They are using the experiment as part of a program to expand their hierarchy of knowledge of the faulty motorcycle and compare it to the correct hierarchy in their mind. They are looking at underlying form.

IMPROVING YOUR VOCABULARY: LEVELS OF USAGE

Even though you were told as a child, "Don't say that. That's a bad word," now that your are grown-up, there are no "bad" words. There are only words that are misused. Choosing the right word is an important part of your writing. There are ugly words, there are coarse words, there are words that refer to indecent or disgusting actions or conditions, but the words themselves are only referents to the distasteful situation. If the word is appropriately used to make such a reference and that is the concept the writer wishes to make, the word is not a "bad" word. Of course, use of vile or indecent words as a commonplace of conversation or an expression of mild annoyance is bad usage. The words, like computers, make no mistakes; it is only the usage that is bad.

There are certain standards of usage generally recognized by educated people. The key word concerning usage is *appropriateness.* A word's appropriateness is determined by its level of usage. The level of usage is comparable to a neighborhood. A word that is acceptable at one level of usage, or in one neighborhood—one context or situation—may be unacceptable in another. For example the language you use in casual lunchroom conversation is not the same language you use in a job interview. And the wording used in writing a humorous anecdote would differ from the wording used in a serious study on arms control. A good desk dictionary is your best practical guide to the choice of words to be used in a particular context.

For practical purposes, usage can be divided into three broad areas that overlap to some extent: formal, informal, and nonstandard. *Formal English* is appropriate for lectures and sermons, serious discussions, legal and scientific writing, literary criticism, and other serious and carefully written works. *Informal English* (sometimes referred to as *general English*) is the language of most everyday affairs: normal everyday conversation, the ordinary news of the day, the less formal writing of most newspaper columns, and familiar essays, such as narratives of personal experience. Able speakers and writers move freely from the formal to the informal and blend the two in varying degrees to suit the audience and the circumstances. *Nonstandard English,* however, is rarely appropriate. On occasion—in humorous narrative or dialogue, for example—it may suit your purpose, but nonstandard English tends to brand its users as being uneducated or at least careless in their use of language. It is generally assumed that educated people don't need nonstandard English to express their ideas, and if they do use it, they use it deliberately to achieve a desired effect.

ASSIGNMENTS

A. The word *process* implies change (*"process*—a continuing development involving many changes"). Some processes involve a change in form or appearance (the growth process, the healing process). Other processes involve a change in both appearance and value (the manufacturing process, the artistic process), and still others involve less visible types of changes—in status or point of view or self-esteem (the election process, the educational process, the divorce process). Finally, some processes involve changes in the environment in general (the acculturation process, the legislative process, the research process, the creative process).

Look at each of the changes listed below and think about the type of process that might have brought about that change. Then explain one of the processes in a logical, coherent essay. Explain the process of going from

a social drinker to an alcoholic
a rookie to a pro
a wife to a mother
single life to married life
marriage to divorce
boyhood to manhood
an idealist to a cynic
a rough idea to a finished "A" paper
an outsider to an insider
a conforming viewpoint to a nonconforming viewpoint
independent wage earner to dependent job seeker
imprisonment through ignorance to liberation through knowledge
a poor to a good student
a wallflower to a belle of the ball
fat to thin
poor to rich (rags to riches)
a mamma's boy to an independent man
a slob to a neatnik
lazy to vital
depression to optimism
radical to conservative
boredom in a class to excitement

B. Write an essay in which you explain one of the following processes:

How to overcome a phobia
How to learn from failure
How to tune out distractions

How to make a subject challenging
How to win over an enemy
How to look at yourself objectively
How to quit smoking
How to balance a budget
How to cope with unemployment
How to get tough with your doctor
How to enjoy a vacation no matter what goes wrong
How to live with a pet
How to decorate a room
How to choose a wardrobe on a budget
How to improve your appearance, public image, public speaking

C. Write an essay in which you explain a specific example of one of the following:

A growth process
A testing process
A judicial process
A bureaucratic process
A learning process
An inspection process
A manufacturing process
A political process
A medical process
A creative process
A healing process
A destructive process
A legislative process
An acculturation process
A financial process
A socialization process
A refurbishing process
An aging process
A humiliating process
A frustrating process

6

Comparing and Contrasting

RHETORIC

Comparing and contrasting is something you do often in your everyday life. Every time you say something like "Jimmy looks like a young Abe Lincoln" or "My boss makes J.R. Ewing look like a Santa Claus," you are comparing or contrasting.

Very often you learn something new by comparing it to something you already know. If you asked your friend what she meant when she said *ethnocentrism*, for example, she might explain it to you by comparing it to a word you already know. "You know what egotism is? Well, ethnocentrism is the same feeling of superiority, pride, and boastfulness, but it's held by a group—a race, a nationality, or a religion—instead of an individual." Speaking to an economist, an English teacher might clarify his point on the widespread misuse of language by saying, "We have devaluated the currency of communication." A playwright might emphasize the traits of one character by including another character with the opposite traits. Tiny Tim's father (Bob Cratchit) and Scrooge are examples of such character foils. In short, comparing and contrasting is a good way to make a point in an essay.

PREWRITING

Choosing a Topic

Perhaps the most difficult part of writing the comparison (pointing out similarities) or contrast (pointing out differences) is choosing a worthy subject. Your essay must make a point; merely pointing out numerous likenesses and differences is not enough. As in all essays, you must have a central purpose, a reason for writing the essay, that you make clear by using either comparison or contrast.

Also, you must avoid the obvious. Pointing out the similarities between like things (high school football and college football) or the differences between unlike things (going to high school and going to college) proves nothing. Usually, the first topics that come to you— "My mother and father are complete opposites," "College is quite different from high school," "My dog and cat are just alike"—are poor topics because they are trite, obvious, and too general. Give some thought to your topic.

Perhaps you already have a topic, some similarities or differences between two things that other people seem not to have noticed. If so, you need read no further in this section. On the other hand, if you have no ready subject at hand, you might try brainstorming, alone or with a group. Just write down every word that someone says as quickly as possible or, if alone, write down every word that comes to your mind. Then see of any of the words could be matched for a good comparison or contrast essay.

Suppose you come up with the following list:

fish	eagles
fish soup	American eagle
dinner	emblems
dinner date	flag
Le Monte	patriotism
McDonald's	nationalism
hamburgers	war
french fries	warrior
French people	peace
Europe	peace talks
Asia	nuclear weapons
Asian flu	nuclear power
flying	women power
birds	E.R.A.

As you look over your list, a little thought will give you quite a few possible topics for a comparison or contrast.

> Contrast two dinner dates with the same person at the same restaurant that turned out to be quite different.
> Compare or contrast wedding customs in two different cultures.
> Contrast the American eagle as a national emblem and the wild turkey, which Benjamin Franklin wanted as our national bird.
> Contrast nationalism and partriotism.
> Contrast warriors of old with our present-day soldiers.
> Contrast the subtle power of women over men with the powerlessness of women to get the E.R.A. passed.

Any list will probably give you ten or twelve possible topics. Choose one that interests you and think about possible points of similarity (comparison) or difference (contrast). If you don't have enough material, do a little research.

Establishing the Bases for Comparison or Contrast

Once you have decided on a good topic and obtained sufficient information to prove your point, you are ready to work on an outline. You must compare or contrast the subjects on the same bases. For example, if you are writing about two cars, you would not make a very clear point if you explained the cost of one and the comfort of the other. The outline will help you to make the comparison or contrast clear.

Suppose you had recently run across an article on teachers in the 1880s and decided to contrast the teachers of today with the teachers of one hundred years ago. After some research, you might choose as the bases of contrast the following:

1. Duties demanded
2. Activities restricted
3. Subject matter taught
4. Educational background required
5. Prestige awarded
6. Pay received
7. Personal appearance
8. Power held

Once you have established a list—the principles on which you will base your contrast—you must organize your material.

ORGANIZATION

The comparison or contrast essay follows the same one-two-three pattern of introduction, body, and conclusion that many other essays follow.

Introduction and Thesis Statement

Your introduction states your purpose, tells the reader why you are writing about this subject. It could be light and personal.

> After listening to my brother-in-law complain for three hours about how hard he works at his job—he teaches high school history—I got disgusted. Maybe I rebelled because he wouldn't listen to how hard I worked at my job; I'm a research chemist. Anyway, I decided to use my research skills to determine whether he had it better or worse than his predecessors in the field. Boy, am I ready for him next time!

It could be factual and serious.

> Teachers get paid far less than any other professional with similar training. Their responsibilities are great. The stress of the job is unquestioned. Teachers rank second only to doctors in suicides. Thousands of teachers are assaulted by students every year. Burnouts are common. Yet compared to an earlier group, teachers of today are doing very well indeed.

Once you have your introduction, you must write a carefully worded thesis statement, one that clearly states the purpose of your essay. The thesis statement for the comparison or contrast essay *differs* from those of other essays in that it has two subjects—the two items that are being compared or contrasted (in this case, teachers of today and teachers of the 1880s.)

The thesis statement must also establish the *basis* for the comparison or contrast and indicate what you are trying to demonstrate or prove. It would not be sufficient to say that teachers of today are different from teachers of the 1880s or that their jobs are different. Possible thesis statements would include

> If the teachers of today were sent back one hundred years, they would not recognize the profession; other than having children in front of them, nothing would be the same.

The advancements made by those in the teaching profession may seem to them to be few—until the duties and compensations of the teacher of today are contrasted with those of the teacher of one hundred years ago.

Body

In organizing the body of your comparison or contrast paragraph, you have three choices: the point-by-point method, the block method, or the combination method.

1. *Point-by-point method*: In this method, you compare or contrast the two subjects feature for feature. Every time you say something about one subject, you immediately say something on the same point about the other. In discussing the duties of the teachers of the 1880s and the 1980s, you might begin like this.

   Today's teacher walks into a warm classroom and flips a switch to turn on the lights. His counterpart of the 1880s was expected to arrive an hour before the children, bringing with him a scuttle of coal. With paper and kindling, he would start a fire in the classroom stove, so that the room would be warm when the students came. While the stove heated, the teacher filled the kerosene lamps and cleaned their chimneys.

2. *Block method*: In this method, you tell everything about one subject and then, in the next paragraph, tell everything about the second. In contrasting the two teachers, you might first describe a typical day in the life of today's teacher and then go on to a typical day in the life of the teacher of the 1880s.

3. *Combination method*: In this method, you may discuss similarities (or differences) point by point and differences (or similarities) in the block method or vice versa. The combination method adds variety to longer essays.

Often, your subject will determine which method is best. If you wanted to give a picture or an impression of something, be it a city or a car, you would probably use the block method. You would not want to interrupt your contrast of the sleepy old town you grew up in with details of the busy metropolis it has now become. If you were comparing or contrasting the appearance of two cars, you would again probably choose the block method. On the other hand, if you were contrasting the mechanical characteristics of two cars, you could make your points clearer by using the point-by-point method, thereby discussing the transmission of car A with the transmission of car B before the reader forgets the specifics. In a longer example or when your supports are varied, you may want to combine methods. For example, you might want to give an overall picture to begin with and so would use the block method. You might want to follow that with details of specific comparisons or contrasts in which case you would use the point-by-point method.

The outline will be organized differently according to the method you choose. If you decide to use the point-by-point method, your outline might be organized like this.

A. Duties demanded
   1. Teachers today
   2. Teachers in the 1880s
B. Activities restricted
   1. Teachers today
   2. Teachers in the 1880s
C. Subject matter taught
   1. Teachers today
   2. Teachers in the 1880s
D. Educational background required
   1. Teachers today
   2. Teachers in the 1880s
E. Prestige awarded
   1. Teachers today
   2. Teachers in the 1880s
F. Pay received
   1. Teachers today
   2. Teachers in the 1880s
G. Personal appearance
   1. Teachers today
   2. Teachers in the 1880s
H. Power held
   1. Teachers today
   2. Teachers in the 1880s

If you use the block method, you would use the same details, but they would be arranged like this.

A. The teacher of today
   1. Duties demanded
   2. Activities restricted
   3. Subject matter taught
   4. Educational background required
   5. Prestige awarded
   6. Pay received
   7. Personal appearance
   8. Power held

B. The teacher of the 1880s
  1. Duties demanded
  2. Activities restricted (same as above list)

If you use a combination of methods, your outline might look like this.

A. Describing a typical day. (block method)
  1. A typical day for a teacher in the 1880s
    a. Duties demanded
    b. Subject matter taught
  2. A typical day for a teacher today.
    a. Duties demanded
    b. Subject matter taught
B. Analyzing the specifics of those typical days.(point-by-point method)
  1. Duties demanded
  2. Activities restricted
  3. Subject matter taught
  4. Educational background required
  5. Prestige awarded
  6. Pay received
  7. Personal appearance
  8. Power held

Writing the Essay

Once you have your outline, writing the essay should be relatively easy. As in all essays, you must be unified, coherent, specific, and provide adequate transitions. The last two requirements are particularly important.

Be specific. It is particularly important in a comparison or contrast to use specific detail because you will not be convincing unless you are specific. Consider the following examples used to contrast the pay of the teachers of today with teachers of the 1880s:

Vague: Teachers today get a good pension paid for in part by themselves, but teachers in the past had to save for their old age from their meager salaries.
Specific: Teachers today can receive a pension of one-half their average yearly salary after thirty years of service. In 1880, the teacher was admonished to save money from each paycheck for his old age.
Vague: Teachers today can depend upon a salary increase every year, but for their 1880 counterpart, increases were rare.

Specific: Teachers today can depend upon an increment of several hundred to several thousand dollars per year depending upon the state they teach in and their years of service. In 1880, the teacher might, if he had performed "his labor faithfully and without fault for five years . . . be given an increase of twenty-five cents per week in his pay, providing the Board of Education approved."

Provide adequate transitions. Transitions are particularly important in comparison and contrast because they highlight the movement of thought within the essay. With the point-by-point method, you must use transitions every time you switch from one aspect of a subject to a similar aspect of the other. For example,"car A . . .; on the other hand, car B . . ." or "the sociology class . . .; likewise, the psychology class . . . ."

With the block method, you have only one major shift, approximately in the middle of the essay. But since there is only one major shift, you must be sure to make clear to the reader exactly when you move to the other subject of your essay. You may need to use an entire sentence or two of transition. For example, "But the dusty, friendly old town of my youth has changed." This sentence implies that the town is no longer so dusty nor so friendly and, depending upon the transitional *but*, implies that you are moving into the second half—the second subject—of your essay where you will describe the cold, new town.

Obviously, you must select transitions that reflect the relationship between your ideas. If you are comparing, use transitions such as *likewise, similarly,* and *also* to show a switch in subject. If you are contrasting, use words or phrases like *on the other hand, however, yet, in contrast* and *on the contrary*. With the combination method, you must make certain that the shifts between blocks are clear, the shift between block and point-by-point is clearly marked, and within the point-by-point you have identified each shift.

Concluding the Essay

Writing the conclusion to the comparison or contrast essay takes a bit of care. Since you have two subjects, you must include *both* in your conclusion, along with reiterating your purpose in writing the essay. A common error, especially with the block method, is to include only the second subject in your conclusion. Another common error is to conclude with a feeble, unconvincing statement, such as, "So you see that *A* is quite similar to (or different from) *B*."

Your conclusion should re-emphasize your purpose in writing the essay, tie up all loose ends, and leave the reader with a feeling of completeness.

The essay on the teachers might conclude in this way.

> The teacher of today has a difficult job; he or she works long hours, has enormous responsibilities, and receives, at times, little respect and much abuse. However, the teacher of a hundred years ago had many disadvantages and few of the advantages of the teacher of today. Teaching is, and always has been, a trying job, but, in comparison, today's teacher has some compensations, mainly in salary and freedom.

Analogy

Analogy is a method of explaining an unfamiliar thing by comparing it with something more familiar; however, the comparison is of a special kind. The analogy does not, as straightforward comparison does, compare things on a common basis. Analogy does not make a full comparison; it compares only certain, limited characteristics.

Analogies vary in type. One type is just a phrase. For example, if you say, "Harry has a sharp mind," or even just "Harry's sharp," you are making an implied analogy between Harry's intelligence and a tool keen enough to cut easily. Another type is a brief description. For example, an eye doctor might explain to a patient that the patient's detached retina looks like "old wallpaper sagging off a wall." Victor Hugo described the battlefield at Waterloo as a huge letter A. Still another kind of analogy can be a fully developed essay, as in "The Deacon's Masterpiece".

In the following paragraph, Thomas H. Huxley describes life as a game of chess:

> It is a game which has been played for untold ages, every man and woman of us being one of the two players in a game of his or her own. The chessboard is the world, the pieces are the phenomena of the universe, the rules of the game are what we call the laws of Nature. The player on the other side is hidden from us. We know that his play is always fair, just and patient. But also we know, to our cost, that he never overlooks a mistake, or makes the smallest allowance for ignorance. To the man who plays well, the highest stakes are paid, with that sort of overflowing generosity with which the strong shows delight in strength. And one who plays ill is checkmated—without

haste, but without remorse. My metaphor will remind some of you of the famous picture in which Retzsch has depicted Satan playing at chess with man for his soul. Substitute for the mocking fiend in that picture a calm, strong angel who is playing for love, as we say, and would rather lose than win—and I shall accept it as an image of human life.

Thomas H. Huxley

Not all analogies are verbal or wholly verbal. For example, a globe is a useful teaching tool because of its analogy to the earth. In a more complicated example, scientists compare the vast stretch of geologic time (six billion years) with a single calendar year. In a diagram of a single year, they show the earth as being formed on January 1; the first microscopic life appearing on March 29; the first fish on November 29; the first dinosaurs on December 15 (they lived 40 to 45 million years and died out on December 26); ape-man showing up at seventeen minutes after six on December 31; and Christ being born comes at fourteen seconds before midnight. When the purpose of analogy is to give information, it can be very instructive.

When the purpose of analogy is to communicate emotional or imaginative ideas, it can be highly effective if vivid and fresh. The poet William Butler Yeats wrote a fine analogy to explain the abstract idea he put in his title, "The Coming of Wisdom with Time."

> Though leaves are many, the root is one;
> Through all the lying days of my youth
> I swayed leaves and flowers in the sun;
> Now I may wither into the truth.

William Butler Yeats

However, when the purpose of analogy is to present a convincing cause-and-effect argument, you must be aware that you can prove nothing by analogy. Comparisons like Yeats's, known as *figurative analogies*, can only *suggest*, not prove. A good figurative analogy can enlarge your readers' understanding of your point without being either complete or literally true. But to support sound cause-and-effect reasoning, an analogy must, first, have a number of important likenesses that are relevant to your comparison and, second, have no important differences that are relevant. Even then, your analogy will only suggest (though perhaps powerfully) but not prove your argument.

Created Equal?

PAUL B. HORTON and
CHESTER L. HUNT

The belief that free and compulsory education gives everyone an equal chance at success is questioned in the following essay by Paul B. Horton and Chester L. Hunt, two professors of sociology at Western Michigan University. By contrasting the experiences of a lower-class child and a middle-class child on the first day of school, the authors show that by the time children start school many of the attitudes, values, and goals that have been shaped by their experiences may hinder efforts to reach them.

Thesis statement

Each social class is a system of behavior, a set of values, and a way of life. While some overlapping and some exceptions occur, it remains true that the average middle-class child has a socialization vastly different from that of the average lower-class child. Let us take just one aspect of socialization—those experiences which shape ambition, education, and work habits—and see how they differ between two social-class worlds.

Introduction to first part of contrast (background information)

The typical upper-middle-class child lives in a class subculture where he is surrounded by educated, cultivated persons who speak the English language correctly most of the time, enjoy classical music, buy and read books, travel, and entertain graciously. He is surrounded by people who are ambitious, who go to work even when they don't feel like it, and who struggle to make their mark in the world. He is acquainted with the successes of ancestors, relatives, and friends, and it is normal for him simply to assume that, like them, he is going to amount to something in the world.

Topic sentence

When he goes to school, scrubbed and expectant, he finds a teacher whose dress, speech, manner, and conduct norms are much like those he already knows. He is met by a series of familiar objects—picture books, chalkboard, and others—and introduced into a series of activities which are already familiar. The teacher finds him an appealing and responsive child, while he finds school a comfortable and exciting place. When the teacher says, "Study hard so you can do well and become a success some day," her exhortation makes sense to him. His parents echo these words, meanwhile he sees people like him—older brothers, relatives, family acquaintances—who actually *are* completing educations and moving on into promising careers. For him, to grow up means to complete an advanced education and get himself launched into a career.

Introduction to second part of contrast (background information)

The lower-lower-class child lives in a class subculture where scarcely anybody has a steady job for very long. To be laid off and go on relief is a normal experience, carrying no sense of shame or failure. He lives in a world where one can spend his weekends in drinking, gambling, and sexual exploration and miss work on Monday without sacrificing the respect of his friends or neighbors. In his world, meals are haphazard and irregular: many people sleep three or four to a bed; and a well-modulated speaking voice would be lost amid the neighborhood clatter.

Topic sentence

He goes to school often unwashed and unfed, and meets a woman, unlike anyone in his social world. Her speech and manner are unfamiliar, and when he acts in ways that are acceptable and useful in his social world, she punishes him. The classroom materials and activities are unfamiliar. The teacher, who usually comes from a sheltered middle-class world, is likely to decide that he is a sullen, unresponsive child, while he soon concludes that school is an unhappy prison. He learns little. The school soon abandons any serious effort to teach him, defines him as a "discipline problem," and concentrates upon keeping him quiet so that the other children can learn. When the teacher says, "Study hard so you can do well and become a success some day," her words make no sense to him. They receive no reinforcement from his parents, who are apt to be hostile and uncooperative toward the school. More important, he sees almost nobody *like* him, nobody in his world, who actually is using school as a stepping-stone to a career. In his world, the flashy cars and flashy women are possessed by those who picked a lucky number, or got into the rackets, or found an "angle." Thus the school fails to motivate him. For him, "growing up" means to drop out of school, get a car, and escape from the supervision of teachers and parents. His horizon of ambition seldom extends beyond the next weekend. His work habits are casual and irregular. Soon he marries and provides for his children a life which duplicates the experiences of his own socialization. Thus the class system operates to prepare most children for a class status similar to that of their parents.

Concluding paragraphs

Such differences in class behavior are found in virtually every activity of life—food habits, personal care, discipline and child care, reading tastes, conversational interests, vocabulary and diction, religious behavior, sleeping arrangements, sex life. Even the procedures followed in making love, according to Kinsey (1948, pp. 355–357), show important class differences.

Concluding sentence reaffirms thesis statement.

This is what we mean in speaking of class subcultures—that a great many of the normal life experiences of people in one class differ from those of people in another class.

Grant and Lee: A Study in Contrasts

BRUCE CATTON

Bruce Catton is one of America's most widely read Civil War historians. He combines an acute sense of detail with an exhaustive body of research to recreate for his readers the most tragic period in American history. In the following essay, Catton presents a perceptive analysis of two of the Civil War's greatest figures, Grant and Lee—"very different, yet under everything very much alike."

When Ulysses S. Grant and Robert E. Lee met in the parlor of a modest house at Appomattox Court House, Virginia, on April 9, 1865, to work out the terms for the surrender of Lee's Army of Northern Virginia, a great chapter in American life came to a close, and a great new chapter began.

These men were bringing the Civil War to its virtual finish. To be sure, other armies had yet to surrender, and for a few days the fugitive Confederate government would struggle desperately and vainly, trying to find some way to go on living now that its chief support was gone. But in effect it was all over when Grant and Lee signed the papers. And the little room where they wrote out the terms was the scene of one of the poignant, dramatic contrasts in American history.

They were two strong men, these oddly different generals, and they represented the strengths of two conflicting currents that, through them, had come into final collision.

Back of Robert E. Lee was the notion that the old aristocratic concept might somehow survive and be dominant in American life.

Lee was tidewater Virginia, and in his background were family, culture, and tradition . . . the age of chivalry transplanted to a New World which was making its own legends and its own myths. He embodied a way of life that had come down through the age of knighthood and the English country squire. America was a land that was beginning all over again, dedicated to nothing much more complicated than the rather hazy belief that all men had equal rights, and should have an equal chance in the world. In such a land Lee stood for the feeling that it was somehow of advantage to human society to have a pronounced inequality in the social structure. There should be a leisure class, backed by ownership of land; in turn, society itself should be keyed to the land as the chief source of wealth and influence. It would bring forth (according to this ideal) a class of men with a strong sense of obligation to the community; men who lived not to gain advantage for themselves, but to meet the solemn obligations which had been laid on them by the very fact that they were privileged. From them the country would get its leadership; to them it could look for the higher values—of thought, of conduct, of personal deportment—to give it strength and virtue.

Lee embodied the noblest elements of this aristocratic ideal. Through him, the landed nobility justified itself. For four years, the Southern states had fought a desperate war to uphold the ideals for which Lee stood. In the end, it almost seemed as if the Confederacy fought for Lee; as if he himself was the Confederacy . . . the best thing that the way of life for which the Confederacy stood could ever have to offer. He had passed into legend before Appomattox. Thousands of tired, underfed, poorly clothed Confederate soldiers, long-since past the simple enthusiasm of the early days of the struggle, somehow considered Lee the symbol of everything for which they had been willing to die. But they could not quite put this feeling into words. If the Lost Cause, sanctified by so much heroism and so many deaths, had a living justification, its justification was General Lee.

Grant, the son of a tanner on the Western frontier, was everything Lee was not. He had come up the hard way, and embodied nothing in particular except the eternal toughness and sinewy fiber of the men who grew up beyond the mountains. He was one of a body of men who owed reverence and obeisance to no one, who were self-reliant to a fault, who cared hardly anything for the past but who had a sharp eye for the future.

These frontier men were the precise opposites of the tidewater aristocrats. Back of them, in the great surge that had taken people over the Alleghenies and into the opening Western country, there was a deep, implicit dissatisfaction with a past that had settled into grooves. They stood for democracy, not from any reasoned conclusion about the proper ordering of human society, but simply because they had grown up in the middle of democracy, and knew how it worked. Their society might have privileges, but they would be privileges each man had won for himself. Forms and patterns meant nothing. No man was born to anything, except perhaps to a chance to show how far he could rise. Life was competition.

Yet along with this feeling had come a deep sense of belonging to a national community. The Westerner who developed a farm, opened a shop, or set up in business as a trader could hope to prosper only as his own community prospered—and his community ran from the Atlantic to the Pacific and from Canada down to Mexico. If the land was settled, with towns and highways and accessible markets, he could better himself. He saw his fate in terms of the nation's own destiny. As its horizons expanded, so did his. He had, in other words, an acute dollars-and-cents stake in the continued growth and development of his country.

And that, perhaps, is where the contrast between Grant and Lee becomes striking. The Virginia aristocrat, inevitably, saw himself in relation to his own region. He lived in a static society which could endure almost anything except change. Instinctively, his first loyalty would go to the locality in which that society existed. He would fight to the limit of endurance to defend it, because in defending it he was defending everything that gave his own life its deepest meaning.

The Westerner, on the other hand, would fight with an equal tenacity for the broader concept of society. He fought so because everything he lived by was tied to growth, expansion, and a constantly widening horizon. What he lived by would survive or fall with the nation itself. He could not possibly stand by unmoved in the face of an attempt to destroy the Union. He would combat it with everything he had, because he could only see it as an effort to cut the ground out from under his feet.

So Grant and Lee were in complete contrast, representing two diametrically opposed elements in American life. Grant was the modern man emerging; beyond him, ready to come on the stage, was the great age of steel and machinery, of crowded cities and a restless, burgeoning vitality. Lee might have ridden down from the old age of chivalry, lance in hand, silken banner fluttering over his head. Each man was the perfect champion of his cause, drawing both his strengths and his weaknesses from the people he led.

Yet it was not all contrast, after all. Different as they were— in background, in personality, in underlying aspiration—these two great soldiers had much in common. Under everything else, they were marvelous fighters. Furthermore, their fighting qualities were really very much alike.

Each man had, to begin with, the great virtue of utter tenacity and fidelity. Grant fought his way down the Mississippi Valley in spite of acute personal discouragement and profound military handicaps. Lee hung on in the trenches at Petersburg after hope itself had died. In each man there was an indomitable quality . . . the born fighter's refusal to give up as long as he can still remain on his feet and lift his two fists.

Daring and resourcefulness they had, too: the ability to think faster and move faster than the enemy. These were the qualities which gave Lee the dazzling campaigns of Second Manasses and Chancellorsville and won Vicksburg for Grant.

Lastly, and perhaps greatest of all, there was the ability, at the end, to turn quickly from war to peace once the fighting was over. Out of the way these two men behaved at Appomattox came the possibility of a peace of reconciliation. It was a possibility not wholly realized, in the years to come, but which did, in the end, help the two sections to become one nation again . . . after a war whose bitterness might have seemed to make such a reunion wholly impossible. No part of either man's life became him more than the part he played in their brief meeting in the McLean House at Appomattox. Their behavior there put all succeeding generations of Americans in their debt. Two great Americans, Grant and Lee—very different, yet under everything very much alike. Their encounter at Appomattox was one of the great moments of American history.

How Does the Author Make His Point?

1. Where does the author state his thesis?
2. How effective is the introduction? In this essay, the author combines two types of introduction. Name them.
3. What method of comparison/contrast (point-by-point, block or combination) does the author use in the first part of his essay? Where does he switch to the other method? Why does he change?
4. Discuss the purpose of paragraph 12.
5. What is the purpose of switching from contrast to comparison? Does this change weaken or strengthen the essay? Explain.
6. In what way does the conclusion add to the unity of the essay?

What Do You Think?

1. What are your feelings on the two ways of life embodied by the two men? Which better typifies the way you believe is right? Explain.
2. See how many differences in the two men you can state in single words. For example: Grant—future; Lee—past.
3. Suppose the South had won the war. What kind of society would we have in America now? Could the nation Lee envisioned have lasted?

Marriage East and West

DAVID and
VERA MACE

In this excerpt from the book Marriage East and West, *the Indian women interviewed by David and Vera Mace suggest some potential problems with American courtship practices.*

"Tell us," said Kusima, "about the young people in the West. We want to know how *they* get married."

Night was falling at the close of a sultry Indian day. A cool, refreshing breeze playfully caressed the glittering black tresses of the girls' hair and set their gay saris fluttering. All teenagers, they had been invited along by our host because we had expressed a desire to know what Indian young people thought about love and marriage. The girls, ten of them, were squatting on the veranda floor in a wide circle. Being awkward Westerners who couldn't sit comfortably on folded legs, we had been provided with low stools.

We gave as good an account as we could of how our young people are free to meet each other and have dates; how a boy and girl will fall in love; and how, after a period of going steady, they become engaged and then get married. We knew that young people in the East live a very restricted life and have their marriages arranged for them by their parents, so we felt a little relieved that they had chosen to question us about our delightful romantic traditions. We didn't want to make them *too* envious, but we naturally were glad to demonstrate our superiority in this matter of finding a mate.

When we had finished, there was a meditative silence. Concluding that they had been impressed, we decided to start a discussion.

"Wouldn't you like to be free to choose your own marriage partners, like the young people do in the West?"

"Oh, no!" several voices replied in chorus.

Taken aback, we searched their faces.

"Why not?"

"For one thing," said one of them, "doesn't it put the girl in a very humiliating position?"

"Humiliating? In what way?"

"Well, doesn't it mean that she has to try to look pretty, and call attention to herself, and attract a boy, to be sure she'll get married?"

"Well, perhaps so."

"And if she doesn't want to do that, or if she feels it's undignified, wouldn't that mean she mightn't get a husband?"

"Yes, that's possible."

"So a girl who is shy and doesn't push herself forward might not be able to get married. Does that happen?"

"Sometimes it does."

"Well, surely that's humiliating. It makes getting married a sort of competition in which the girls are fighting each other for the boys. And it encourages a girl to pretend she's better than she really is. She can't relax and be herself. She has to make a good impression to get a boy, and then she has to go on making a good impression to get him to marry her."

Before we could think of an answer to this unexpected line of argument, another girl broke in.

"In our system, you see," she explained, "we girls don't have to worry at all. We *know* we'll get married. When we are old enough, our parents will find a suitable boy, and everything will be arranged. We don't have to go into competition with each other."

"Besides," said a third girl, "how would we be able to judge the character of a boy we met and got friendly with? We are young and inexperienced. Our parents are older and wiser, and they aren't as easily deceived as we would be. I'd far rather have my parents choose for me. It's so important that the man I marry should be the right one. I could so easily make a mistake if I had to find him for myself."

Another girl had her hand stretched out eagerly.

"But *does* the girl really have any choice in the West?" she said. "From what I've read, it seems that the boy does all the choosing. All the girl can do is to say yes or no. She can't go up to a boy and say 'I like you. Will you marry me? can she?"

We admitted that this was not the done thing.

"So," she went on eagerly, "when you talk about men and women being equal in the West, it isn't true. When our parents are looking for a husband for us, they don't have to wait until some boy takes it into his head to ask for us. They just find out what families are looking for wives for their sons, and see whether one of the boys would be suitable. Then, if his family agrees that it would be a good match, they arrange it together."

How Do the Authors Make Their Point?

1. Actually, this short essay contains two contrasts. Name them.
2. The bulk of the essay is made up of conversation. Why is this more effective than just relating what had taken place?
3. What assumptions do the authors make in paragraph 3?
4. Do you see some merit in the arguments of the Indian girls? Outline their arguments.

What Do You Think?

1. Is it common for every culture to think its customs and ways of doing things are best?
2. Which of the arguments given by the Indian girls do you agree with? With which do you disagree?
3. Do you think we could adopt any of these customs into our courtship practices? Why or why not?
4. This interview was held in the fifties. Have the courtship practices in the United States changed since then? How?

In Praise of Reticence

MELVIN MADDOCKS

Reticence *is a disinclination to speak; a reticent person is habitually silent. At one time, reticence was admired, and the stereotype of the strong, silent man was the hero of many movies, particularly westerns.*

Today some think that the reticent person has nothing to say or, worse, has something to hide. In this essay, Maddocks gives his views on reticence and its opposite, garrulity.

The DC-9 has climbed to 30,000 ft. You have that serene, floating, god-above-gravity feeling—the small miracle of flying. Your fellow god, the one in the cockpit, is mumbling the usual comforting inaudibles over the P.A. ("Off to the leftmmmmmzzz . . ."). You give the other passengers a quick scan; apparently not a hijacker in sight. A small prayer of thanks might be in order.

But then there is a minor throat-clearing on your right. Your seatmate is about to speak. You are about to suffer a disaster that neither man nor computer can guard against: Instant Intimacy. Relentlessly, he tells you all about his business, his childhood, his sex life. Why do the airlines spend their money eliminating the middle seat? Why don't they put up confessional grilles instead?

Let's call your seatmate Charlie O. (for Oral). He is not just a minor nuisance, but the personification of a major menace. People today tell complete strangers things they once wouldn't have confessed to a priest, a doctor or a close friend: their cruelest fears; their most shameful inadequacies; their maddest fantasies. We are witnessing something like the death of reticence.

Inspect the bestseller list. Charlie O. has it cornered. He is the tattletale from whom we learn *Everything We Always Wanted to Know About Sex*—and a lot we didn't really want to know, thanks all the same. *Charlie O.'s Complaint* is not that he can't help doing it but that he can't help talking about it. In the theater, Charlie O. is the playwright shouting the most four-letter words the loudest. He is also the journalist who will share with 7,000,000 readers a 20-year history of his drinking problem. The short version, or the long one if he can find an editor to pay. Not even his loved ones are safe. He will describe in detail his wife's change of life, his daughter's ordeal with drugs, or his son's battle against not-so-latent homosexuality.

Self-disclosure has become an art form—indeed, it threatens to become the only art form. The Charlie O. who shows-and-tells not only earns an automatic reputation for honesty but for talent. Johnny, Merv and Dick fight to get him, and then he tells even more. Hang a mike boom above his big mouth and stand back. Let lesser men insert the bleeps. If he isn't already a celebrity, Instant Intimacy practiced with a closeup camera on a Nielsen audience of 7.2 will make him one. Instantly.

You call it exhibitionism? He calls it Moral Courage and Mental Health. *Talking is good.* This is the center and the circumference of Charlie O.'s credo. The more talking, the better.

Open your well-dinned ears to the talk show that is life. Charlie O.'s credo has carried the day. The reticent man, even as he mutters "Crashing bore!" in the direction of the nearest Charlie O., is bullied into feeling that he suffers from constipation of the heart ("What are you holding back? Don't you care?"). The old values—talk is cheap, "strong" goes with "silent"—have been reversed. *Articulate and outspoken*: does praise come higher? *He can't communicate*: this is the kiss of death from kindergarten on.

Talking It All Out supposedly helps cure everything from bad marriages to war. But your old seatmate Charlie O. is not the pink-cheeked life-giver he pretends to be. He is a monologist whose unstinting offer of himself is the purest self-indulgence. One ear is as good as another for him—or even no ear at all. Like Samuel Beckett's Krapp, he might as well be sitting in an empty room droning into a tape recorder: Narcissus with a microphone instead of a mirror.

In his life, in his art, Charlie O. wants to be Me. But he has no time to develop a self, he's so busy giving it away. For all his I-witnessing, one is left with remarkably little presence. Charlie O. wears his openness like the ultimate mask. The whine of his voice, the color of his pubic hair—what else is there to remember really? As Psychiatrist Leslie Farber puts it, he has taken the fig leaf off his genitals only to cover up his face.

There is a mischief, a self-destructiveness built into garrulity. A little-known law of psychology called the Lombard Effect states that a talker raises the level of his voice in reflex response to an increase in environmental noise (including other voices), but at the cost of intelligibility. The talker puts things less accurately and, furthermore, he is less accurately understood by his equally harassed listeners. The Lombard Effect is a fair metaphor for the distracted life, 1970.

The fact that people "can no longer carry on authentic dialogue with one another," Philosopher Martin Buber has warned, is "the most acute symptom of the pathology of our time." It is as if in our loneliness, in our anxiety to communicate, we have produced a modern Tower of Babel. Everybody talking at once, but without quite facing one another. Speech, the most social impulse of all, has turned into an act of aggression—against others and finally against ourselves.

One of the things talked most shrilly about these days is the need for privacy—for what a friend writing about Painter Paul Klee called "creative quiet." Klee's face, he explained, "was that of a man who knows about day and night, sky and sea and air. He did not speak about these things. He had no tongue to tell of them." Our cursed explicitness, our compulsion to tell all, has sacrificed this sense of the ineffable. Perhaps no more severe penalty can be exacted on the gift of speech.

What is the alternative? Like Charlie O., the reticent man has his credo. He believes that rests are as much a part of music as the notes, that a man's silences are as much a part of what he means as what he says. The reticent man would not reject the argument: "How do I know what I think until I hear what I say?" But he would add: "How do I know what I *believe* until I hear what I *don't* say?" He would certainly insist that the deepest feelings, as well as the deepest meanings, thrive on understatement—that the ultimate intimacy is shared silence. The reticent man may well be a Romantic at silence, but he tries to be a Classicist at speech. He believes that reticence is the art of knowing what can be said and what cannot be said, and he is prepared to stake civilization on this art.

There is a small, very private organization known as Fighters for the Freedom of Silence. They are not necessarily opposed to freedom of speech. In fact, they regard themselves as its truest friends, since they insist through their silence that words are not to be taken lightly. Guidance counselors, bartenders, lay analysts—the career listeners—make the most avid members. The FFFOS have not yet purchased their own airline, on which Trappist flight rules can be enforced. But they do have their own underground soundproof club. Numbed by the unsolicited revelations life daily forces upon them, they retreat there one evening a week to recuperate from fellow man's confessional excesses. Over the door—gold leaf and Old English on fumed oak—reads this inscription: PLEASE SHUT UP.

Are you listening—are you for once listening, Charlie O.?

How Does the Author Make His Point?

1. Why does the author use an airplane as the setting in his introduction?
2. What two qualities is Maddocks contrasting in this essay?
3. What strategies does the author use to support his claim that garrulity and not reticence has become the way of life in the United States?
4. How does society feel about the Charlie O's? How does the author see them?
5. How does the author characterize the reticent man? Why does he withhold this description until so late in the essay?
6. What is the implication about Charlie O. in the conclusion? In what way does this strengthen the argument?

What Do You Think?

1. Is what the author saying true? (Look particularly at paragraph 3) Have you ever had a similar experience with a Charlie O? Have you ever acted like Charlie O?
2. Did you recognize the allusions in the essay—*Charlie O's complaint*; Johnny, Merv, and Dick; Samuel Beckett's *Krapp*; Narcissus; Tower of Babel? How do they help to get the message across?
3. In paragraph 7, the author contrasts the old and new values. Which do you feel are the best? Explain your attitudes about openness and reticence.

The Deacon's Masterpiece

LEWIS THOMAS

During the Age of Enlightenment, the eighteenth century, scholars believed that man could achieve perfection in himself, in his environment, and in his society. Even recently, people believed this; Cary Grant, the famed movie star who died in 1987 said that in his youth he believed he would live forever—he thought that before he reached old age, medicine would have advanced to the point where all illnesses could be cured and all deficiencies eliminated. Perhaps today, with organ transplants and miracle drugs, we are approaching that threshold. But if we can't avoid death, wouldn't it be great if we could go quickly and easily. In this essay, Lewis Thomas uses analogy—the comparison of two wildly disparate things—to explore this possibility.

The brightest and most optimistic of my presentiments about the future of human health always seem to arouse a curious mixture of resentment and dismay among some very intelligent listeners. It is as though I'd said something bad about the future. Actually, all I claim, partly on faith and partly from spotty but unmistakable bits of evidence out of the past century of biomedical science, is that mankind will someday be able to think his way around the finite list of major diseases that now close off life prematurely or cause prolonged incapacitation and pain. In short, we will someday be a disease-free species.

Except for gaining a precise insight into the nature of human consciousness (which may elude us for a very long time, perhaps forever), I cannot imagine any other limits to the profundity of our understanding of living things. It may happen within the next few centuries, maybe longer, but when it does it will bring along, inevitably, the most detailed sorts of explanations for human disease mechanisms. It is an article of faith with me that we will then know how to intervene directly, to turn them around or prevent them.

Something like this has already happened for most of the major infections. Even though we are still in a primitive, earliest stage in the emergence of biology, as compared, say, to physics, we have accomplished enough basic science to permit the development of specific antimicrobial antiserums and an impressive list of safe, rational viral vaccines. Within fifty years after the recognition of bacteria as pathogens we had classified them and learned enough of their metabolic intricacies so that the field was ready for antibiotics. In the years since the late 1940s the first great revolution in technology in all the long history of medicine has occurred, and infectious diseases that used to devastate whole families have now been almost forgotten.

Events moved rapidly in the field of infection, and this may have represented abnormally good luck. For some of the others—heart disease, cancer, stroke, the senile psychoses, diabetes, schizophrenia, emphysema, hypertension, arthritis, tropical parasitism, and the like—we may be in for a longer, more difficult pull, but maybe not. With the pace of research having increased so rapidly in the last two decades, and the remarkable new young brains enlisted for the work of biology, we could be in for surprises at almost any time. Anyway, sooner or later, they will all become nonmysteries, accountable and controllable.

These prospects seem to me exciting and heartening, and it is hard to face the mute, sidelong glances of disapproval that remarks along these lines usually generate. You'd think I'd announced an ultimate calamity.

The trouble comes from the automatic question, "Then what?" It is the general belief that we need our diseases—that they are natural parts of the human condition. It goes against nature to tamper and manipulate them out of existence, as I propose. "Then what?" What on earth will we die of? Are we to go on forever, disease-free, with nothing to occupy our minds but the passage of time? What are the biologists doing to us? How can you finish life honorably, and die honestly, without a disease?

This last is a very hard question, almost too hard to face, and therefore just the sort of question you should look around for a poem to answer, and there is one. It is "The Deacon's Masterpiece, or, The Wonderful 'One-Hoss Shay,'" by Oliver Wendell Holmes. On the surface, this piece of rather dreadful nineteenth-century doggerel seems to concern the disintegration of a well-made carriage, but inside the verse, giving it the staying power to hold on to our minds for over a full century, is a myth about the human death.

Moreover, it is a myth for the modern mind. It used to be the common wisdom that the living body was a vulnerable, essentially ramshackle affair, always at risk of giving way at one point or another, too complicated to stay in one piece. These days, with what is being learned about cellular biology, especially the form and function of subcellular structures and their macromolecular components, and the absolutely flawless arrangements for drawing on solar energy for the needs of all kinds of cells, the most impressive aspect of life is its sheer, tough power. With this near view, it becomes a kind of horrifying surprise to realize that things can go wrong—that a disorder of one part can bring down the whole amazing system. Looked at this way, disease seems a violation of nature, an appalling mistake. There must be a better way to go.

Thus, a detailed anatomy of Holmes's carriage can be read as a metaphor for a live organism—or, for that matter, a cell:

> Now in building of chaises, I tell you what,
> There is always *somewhere* a weakest spot—
> In hub, tire, felloe, in spring or thill,
> In panel, or crossbar, or floor, or sill,
> In screw, bolt, thoroughbrace—lurking still. . . .
> And that's the reason, beyond a doubt,
> That a chaise *breaks down*, but doesn't *wear out*.

This was the nineteenth-century view of disease, and the source of our trouble today. It assumes that there is always, somewhere, a weakest part, as though foreordained. Without fundamental, localized flaws in the system, it might simply age away. As it is, it is doomed to break down prematurely, unless you can figure out how to find and fix the flawed item. Dr. Holmes, in the science of his day, saw little likelihood of this, but he did see, in his imagination, the possibility of sustained perfection. The Deacon is his central, Olympian Creator, symbolizing Nature, incapable of fumbling. What he designs is the perfect organism.

> . . . so built that it *couldn'* break down . . .
> . . . "the weakes' place mus' stan' the strain;
> 'N' he way t' fix it, uz I maintain,
> Is only jest
> T' make that place uz strong uz the rest."

Then, the successive acts of creation, collectively miraculous, scriptural in tone.

. . . the strongest oak,
That couldn't be split nor bent nor broke . .
He sent for lancewood to make the thills;
The crossbars were ash, from the straightest trees,
The panels of white-wood, that cuts like cheese,
But lasts like iron for things like these. . . .
Step and prop-iron, bolt and screw,
Spring, tire, axle, and linchpin too,
Steel of the finest, bright and blue;
Thoroughbrace bison-skin, thick and wide;
Boot, top, dasher, from tough old hide . . .
That was the way he "put her through."
"There!" said the Deacon, "naow she'll dew!"

And dew she did. The chaise lived, in fact, for a full, unblemished hundred years of undiseased life, each perfect part surrounded by all the rest. It was born from the Deacon's hands in 1755, the year of the great Lisbon earthquake, and it died on the earthquake centenary, to the hour, in 1855.

The death was the greatest marvel of all. Up to the last minute, the final turn of the splendid wheels, the thing worked perfectly. There was aging, of course, and Holmes conceded this in his myth, but it was a respectable, decent, proper sort of aging:

A general flavor of mild decay,
But nothing local, as one may say.
There couldn't be—for the Deacon's art
Had made it so like in every part
That there wasn't a chance for one to start.

And then, the hour of death:

. . . The wheels were just as strong as the thills,
And the floor was just as strong as the sills,
And the panels just as strong as the floor. . . .
And the back crossbar as strong as the fore . . .
And yet, as a *whole*, it is past a doubt
In another hour it will be *worn out*!

What a way to go!

First of November, 'Fifty-five!
This morning the parson takes a drive.
Now, small boys, get out of the way!

Here comes the wonderful one-hoss shay,
Drawn by a rat-tailed, ewe-necked bay.
"Huddup!" said the parson. Off went they.

And the death scene itself. No tears, no complaints, no
listening closely for last words. No grief. Just, in the way of the
world, total fulfillment. Listen:

All at once the horse stood still
Close by the meet'n'-house on the hill.
First a shiver, and then a thrill,
Then something decidedly like a spill—
And the parson was sitting upon a rock,
At half past nine by the meet'n'-house clock—

And, finally, the view of the remains:

What do you think the parson found,
When he got up and stared around?
The poor old chaise in a heap or mound
As if it had been to the mill and ground!. . .
. . . it went to pieces all at once—
All at once, and nothing first—
Just as bubbles do when they burst.

My favorite line in all this is one packed with the most
abundant meaning, promising aging as an orderly, drying-up
process, terminated by the most natural of events: "As if it had
been to the mill and ground!"

This is, in high metaphor, what happens when a healthy old
creature, old man or old mayfly, dies. There is no outside evil
force, nor any central flaw. The dying is built into the system so
that it can occur at once, at the end of a preclocked, genetically
determined allotment of living. Centralization ceases, the forces
that used to hold cells together are disrupted, the cells lose
recognition of each other, chemical signaling between cells comes
to an end, vessels become plugged by thrombi and disrupt their
walls, bacteria are allowed free access to tissues normally
forbidden, organelles inside cells begin to break apart; nothing
holds together; it is the bursting of billions of bubbles, all at once.

What a way to go!

How Does the Author Make His Point?

1. What is the purpose of paragraphs 2, 3, and 4?
2. What is the thesis statement? Why does it come so late in the essay?
3. Pick out the specific bases of comparison the author uses: that is, *carriage* equals *human being*.
4. Discuss the effectiveness of the author's five-word conclusion.

What Do You Think?

1. What do you think of the author's suggestion that when you have a very hard question, you should look for a poem for an answer? Have you found any poems that give you comfort, solace, joy, understanding?
2. Do you think medical science will ever advance to the point where all diseases are conquered?
3. If death did come to humans as destruction came to the carriage, would there be "no tears, no complaints . . ." as Thomas suggests in paragraph 4?

From Courtship to Dating

Patti Wright
(student)

The following student essay draws a sharp contrast between colonial courtship customs and today's dating.

A famous Greek philosopher believed that the only permanent reality is the reality of change. Although courtship of some nature has almost always existed, the customs associated with it have undergone numerous changes. When noting the vast differences between colonial day courtship and modern-day romance, the reality of change becomes quite obvious.

Colonial courtship was short in duration, with marriage always being the end result. Because of poor transportation, the suitor always lived near his girl, and friendship between the two families was usually well established. Since colonial rules required parental consent before the courtship could begin, the girl had little choice in mate selection. Chaperones always accompanied the courting couples since they were not permitted to be alone. For that matter, most Puritan New England couples married not because of love but for the potential of love. Also, colonial couples engaged in a peculiar practice called bundling. This involved the courting couple going to bed fully dressed or, in some cases, placing the girl in a bundling bag or placing a bundling board between the couple. While some historians believe this custom aided in conserving firewood and candles, other historians reasoned that it allowed the courting couple time to get to know each other since hard work dominated the daylight hours. Then, after establishing moderate wedding plans, the couple presented written parental consent to the town clerk. Also, banns, a public notice of intent to wed, were posted. The wedding took place at the bride's home, and the newly married couple quickly began adjusting to the rugged day-to-day living of colonial times.

On the other hand, the twentieth century refers to courting merely as dating, and the rituals involved appear quite permissive when compared to those of yesteryear. Not only do couples rarely marry the first person they date, but society in general also encourages individuals to date several potential spouses before deciding on a marriage partner. Due to modern transit, worldwide universities, numerous military bases, and so on, the prospective mate can live far or near, and the families, in some instances, meet for the first time just prior to the wedding. Also, in contrast to colonial times, individuals generally select their own mate. Furthermore, today's couples rarely ask parental consent prior to marriage let alone consent to date. Again, unlike colonial couples, modern twosomes spend numerous hours completely unchaperoned, and, except in unusual circumstances, today's couples are normally in love before the marriage proposal. Although the custom of bundling is unheard of in modern times, couples do go to bed together, in some instances, before marriage, but definitely not for the purpose of conserving firewood and candles. In addition, even though most states require couples contemplating marriage to purchase a marriage license, only a few religious sects still practice banns. Furthermore, expensive, festive weddings, seldom held in the bride's home, dominate today's fashion. Long, leisurely honeymoons normally follow the gala celebration before routine day-to-day living begins.

To some, the courting practices of years gone by hold a certain flicker of romance even in such a strict society while others prefer the permissiveness of the space age. However, when looking closely at the differences, all would agree that courting has definitely endured several distinct changes.

How Does the Author Make Her Point?

1. Is the author's introduction effective?
2. Does the author use adequate transitions both within the body paragraphs and between the body paragraphs?
3. Are the body paragraphs adequately developed?

What Do You Think?

1. Do you think that there might be many couples today who, like colonial couples, marry "not because of love but for the potential of love"?
2. Do you think any of the colonial courtship customs hold a certain "flicker of romance"?

3. In what ways do you think courting practices have changed for the better? In what ways have they changed for the worse?

INTEGRATING READING WITH WRITING SKILLS: PREWRITING/PREREADING

It is almost universally believed that reading and writing skills go hand in hand, that as a student learns to read well, his writing skills almost automatically improve. Basic to this belief are the two underlying concepts of prewriting and prereading. Several chapters in this book discuss the value of prewriting before the actual writing takes place. The main points of prewriting include the choice of a good topic, the establishment of a clear purpose, the statement of that purpose in a thesis, the selection of an appropriate method of development, and, finally and also important, a coherent outline of the idea as it is to be presented. In the outline, writers first establish their central purpose, then set forth the main idea, organize the supporting ideas, determine whether there is enough material to prove their point, and eliminate excessive or irrelevant material.

In comparison with prewriting, the objective of prereading is to heighten the readers' understanding. In prereading, the reader determines the central purpose, locates the main idea, and looks to see what points support it. The reader will probably also determine the method of organization. Both writer and reader need to emphasize the understanding of a clear purpose, of logical organization, of good transitions, and adequate development.

EXERCISE

In the following passage, Hans Küng compares and contrasts two great philosophers. Although philosophical discussion is frequently difficult to understand, the clarity of Küng's writing is such that his thought is easily understood even when it is analyzed only by prereading. Notice how much can be learned by applying the following questions to Küng's excerpt:

1. What topic does the title suggest?
2. If there are subheads, what do they suggest?
3. Do the first sentences of each body paragraph go together to make a consistent whole?
4. As Küng moves from point to point, can you follow him because he has paragraphs or phrases or words of transition?

5. Does his method of development lead to efficient presentation of his idea?
6. Does the concluding paragraph restate and summarize his main idea?

Write out the answers to these six questions, doing only the suggested reading before you answer each question. For example, read only the title and explain what you think it means before going on to the subheadings.

Convergences and Divergences

Among the great men of seventeenth-century France, it would be impossible to find two men who were at once so similar and so dissimilar as Descartes and Pascal. It may throw light on problems that are still pressing today if we briefly outline these resemblances and differences.

Like Descartes, Pascal was a genius as a mathematician, as a physicist, and as an engineer. Like Descartes also, he was a modern man of the world, a brilliant man of letters, and a profound thinker.

He was a mathematician of genius. His father and tutor wanted to keep him away from mathematics, so that he could concentrate first on Latin and Greek. But his elder sister Gilberte gives a detailed account of the twelve-year-old boy drawing triangles and circles in charcoal on the tiles in his spare time thus working out independently the basic laws of geometry. . . . At the age of sixteen he was recognized as one of the leading mathematicians of his time. . . . At a later stage, prompted by observation of dice playing . . ., he contributed in a variety of works to the foundation of the calculus of probabilities. . . . He conceived his *Histoire du roulette* during a night when he was kept awake with a raging toothache, reflecting on the problem of the cycloid (the curve described by a point on the rim of a wheel as it moves forward) and coming close to the discovery of infinitesimal calculus. . . .

He was a physicist of genius. It was, again, at the age of twelve that Pascal wrote his essay on acoustics . . . after noting that the sound emitted by a pewter plate when struck by a spoon stopped as soon as he touched the plate with his finger. Over ten years later, . . . he produced an irrefutable proof of the existence of empty space (a fact previously disputed on account of nature's supposed abhorrence of a vacuum). . . .

He was an engineer of genius. He invented not only the hydraulic press but—at the age of nineteen—also the first calculating machine to function in order to help his father, a very busy tax commissioner in Richelieu's service. He obtained a patent for the model, the prototype of our computer, which he had produced in more than fifty variations in the course of two years of intensive work.

He was a modern man of the world. Like Descartes, he came from a wealthy family, managing his father's property shrewdly to the end, and he had access in Paris to exclusive social circles. . . . Like Decartes, Pascal was regarded as a man of wit and taste, skeptical in regard to customs and prejudices.

He was a brilliant man of letters. . . . Pascal together with Descartes did more than anyone else at the time to contribute to the renown of French prose, particularly academic prose, which is distinguished by its simplicity and elegance, from the complicated and obscure style too often adopted by scholars elsewhere even today. The works of Descartes and Pascal—who both also wrote good Latin—became classics of the French language. . . .

He was a profound thinker. Like Descartes, Pascal produced few books and, after his very private education by his father, he enjoyed the utmost freedom and was not tied to any particular calling or mission. Like Descartes, he possessed an extraordinary gift for analytic discrimination, which was made even more effective by his brilliant use of language. Like Descartes, he had a positive passion for thinking. "Man is only a reed, . . . but he is a thinking reed." . . . Like Descartes, Pascal also despised scholasticism, considering that the Bible had no more authority than Aristotle's physics. . . . And like Descartes, he had a flair for tracking down the problems of man, and in this respect he advanced perhaps farther than the former the ultimate ground of human existence.

It is at this very point that divergences appear. They bring out clearly the difference between these contemporaries, despite all their similarities.

When geniuses meet, it is not always the signal for displays of mental lightning: human sympathy is one of the conditions for understanding. When the great "geometer" (Descartes) in Holland, Pascal's elder by a generation, heard of the "mystic hexagram" of the infant prodigy in France, he remarked somewhat cooly that the father must have discovered it. . . . He was distrustful, and Pascal remained cautious. They were not enemies, but neither did they become friends. . . . Was the older man jealous of the very successful, spoiled young man? Certainly this played a part. At any rate, Descartes claimed in the following year that he had anticipated the great barometer experiment. . . . The question of who was first became an occasion for continual disputes at that time among aspiring scholars. . . .

Was it then a question of jealousy? Certainly not merely that. Here were two men who belonged to the same period, the same country, working in the same fields of knowledge, whose lives admittedly did not run parallel with each other but converged, drew toward each other and then—not finding a point of intersection—diverged again, drew away from each other. Why? What were the essential reasons for these divergences?

In mathematics, physics, and philosophy, Decartes is the man of method. He had been educated methodically and systematically in the Jesuit College and he remained methodical throughout his life. He followed a daily rhythm in his life which was always the same, maintaining imperturbably a balance between the claims of mind and body. He investigated methodically first the world and then his own self. He devoted his first publications to the question of method. . . . He left nothing to chance. He avoided difficulties. He needed to be undisturbed, to lead a life without conflict. He proceeded step by step from problem to problem, always resolutely keeping the whole scheme in mind, and thus developed his method into a system. He crowned his work in philosophy and natural science with a comprehensive synthesis.

Pascal, coming between two sisters (their mother died three years after his birth), educated entirely at home, was in both life and learning a man of deep feeling: feeling in the best and broadest sense, of profound experience, sensitivity, endurance, of suffering and passion. From youth onward he was frail and, after his hectic two years' work on his calculating machine, he scarcely spent a single day free from pain. A complex genius . . ., he not only did not refuse suffering but accepted it and even heightened it, finally almost pathologically bringing on his own suffering. Far from frightening him, difficulties only spurred him on to deeper involvement. . . . He could work on arithmetical or geometrical problems or at his own calculating machine like someone possessed. This man, who never attended school or university . . . was interested only in great, difficult, "insoluble" problems; he rushed from one question to another without working out a total plan, even in mathematics and experimentation relying independently on the inspiration of the moment. Given more to aphorisms than to systems, he scarcely bothered about a comprehensive synthesis. . .

The world itself therefore seemed different to Descartes and Pascal, for each looked at it differently. . . . It was a question of human cognition as such, human consciousness as a whole. Descartes had identified the soul with consciousness and reduced all its functions to thinking. Pascal was too fine an observer, not only of nature but also of the human psyche, to agree to such a reduction, despite his insistence on the importance of thought. At first he had nothing against Descarte's emphasis on reason. He was himself too rational for that: as a mathematician, physicist, and engineer, he could hardly fail to be. Nevertheless, reason alone is not sufficient. . . . "We know the truth not only through our reason but also through our heart. . . ."

Pascal thought that all "geometricians," all mathematicians, ought also to have intuitive minds. . . . But the reasons why mathematicians are not intuitive is that they cannot see what is in front of them; for being accustomed to the clear-cut, obvious principles of mathematics and to draw no conclusions until they have clearly seen and handled their principles, they become lost in matters requiring intuition, whose principles cannot be handled in this way. . . . "Mathematicians who are merely mathematicians therefore reason soundly as long as everything is explained to them by definitions and principles; otherwise they are unsound and intolerable, because they reason soundly only from clearly defined principles."

Against this background we can perhaps understand why Pascal had planned in his greatest work to write a highly critical chapter against the most outstanding representative of the *esprit de geometre*. This seems to be the meaning of the note: "Write against those who probe science too deeply. Descartes."

Hans Küng

IMPROVING YOUR VOCABULARY: DENOTATION AND CONNOTATION

The *denotation* of a word is its *literal* meaning, a meaning without emotional and subjective overtones. It has no sense of approval or disapproval built into it. It simply points (refers) to what it means (its *referent*). For example, if you use the word *peacock*, you are just indicating a particular kind of large bird; you are not implying that you *approve* of the peacock for its beauty or *disapprove* of its bad temper and ugly voice. The word *peacock* is a *neutral* term, for its sole function is to indicate what bird it is, to point out its referent. *All words have a denotative meaning.*

In most dictionaries, the first meaning given is the oldest and, so, the primary or basic meaning. Primary meanings are always denotative. At their simplest, denotative words point out things or actions, like *my desk* or *the shouting in the hall*. At a higher level, they denote things or actions that are not actually present, like *the white cliffs of Dover* or *the songs of the minstrels*. At a still higher level, they denote things that never really were, like a *mermaid* or *Cloud Nine*. You can denote a whole class, like *student body*, or an abstraction, like *ambition*. At all these levels, you are referring to the primary, the denotative, meaning.

The *connotation* of a word suggests an *attitude* toward the referent. Connotation relies on the associations and emotions words are capable of arousing. Connotative words may be thought of as carrying an emotional charge. Some are positively charged (peace, sweetness, truth, faith, efficient); others are negatively charged (viciousness, hate, bigotry, brutality). Not only the advertiser, the politician, and the poet, but all effective writers choose their words carefully for their connotative value.

Quite frequently, you must choose one word from among many having the same denotation; *man, guy, fellow, chap, jock, gentleman* denote an adult human male; but each has a different connotation. The connotative word or words chosen reflect the writer's attitude; one person's *statesman* is another person's *politician*; one person's *castle* is another person's *cottage*—and so it goes.

The important thing always is this: Do the words do what you want them to do in a given situation? The right word must have not only the right denotation but the right connotation; it must convey not only an accurate reference but the exact attitude you wish to convey. Sensitivity to connotation comes not only from looking in the dictionary but also from paying attention to words in context. Words have sound, shape, and feel. Some are puny, others husky; some are soft and feminine, others masculine and macho. The feeling for words is vital to both the poet and the persuader, and it is something you need to cultivate through careful reading and constant effort to find not just any word that will do but the *right word,,* right for you and for your reader. Some words have only neutral terms. Usually, these words are highly specific. Technical and scientific terms tend to have only denotations. Some words have only favorable connotations (home, hearth, fireside). Some words have only unfavorable connotations (evil, stupidity, fat). Usually, there are more of these than of favorable connotations.

In the following list, supply all the connotations you can think of:

	NEUTRAL TERM	FAVORABLE TERM	UNFAVORABLE TERM
Example:	Dog	Purebred	Mutt, Mongrell, Cur
1.	Horse		
2.	Child		
3.	Woman		
4.	Wife		
5.	Doctor		

6. Thin _____ _____ _____
7. Serious _____ _____ _____
8. Flexible _____ _____ _____
9. To talk _____ _____ _____
10. To walk _____ _____ _____

ASSIGNMENT

Otto L. Bettmann, founder of one of the world's greatest picture libraries, has been chronicling America's past for over forty years. One of his most fascinating works deals with the period from the end of the Civil War to the early 1900s. In his book, *The Good Old Days—They Were Terrible*, Bettmann argues that the current nostalgia about "the good old days" is totally unfounded—a "benevolent haze" obscuring the fact that for the average breadwinner, "life was an unremitting hardship."

Each of the following passages from Bettmann's book provides a brief glimpse of another era. Read them carefully and see if you can draw any interesting comparisons or contrasts between "the good old days" and the present or perhaps from just a few years ago and today. For example, you might discern some striking differences in people's attitudes toward children or education, or you might discover some surprising similarities where you would expect to find differences.

After you get a good idea, narrow it down to a thesis statement from which you can develop an essay of comparison or contrast. For example, some of the comments might have you think about the changing role of women in American society. You might then think of the differences between your mother and your grandmother. Focusing on a specific idea, you might decide to write an essay contrasting your mother's conception of marriage with your grandmother's.

Doctors: The old-time country doctor, dedicated and compassionate, was by today's standards a medical ignoramus.

Drinking: Child alcoholics were not uncommon, having developed an early taste for drink as the result of constant trips to the bar to have a pitcher filled with "beer for Father."

Teaching: Teaching was an occupation of minimal prestige, with low pay, low standards, and a high turnover rate. A man who had failed at everything bought himself a birch rod and became a teacher.

Children: If recreational facilities for adults were limited, they were totally absent for children: in the scheme of things during the 1860s through the nineties, children simply did not count.

Football: Violence as a leisure activity was not a monopoly of the prize ring. It was the only ingredient of college football, which seasonally transformed intelligent young men into grunting Neanderthalers.

Hospitals: Patient care was a common occupation for drunken women, who were permitted to work in a hospital in lieu of serving a prison sentence.

Loneliness: There was no place lonelier than the frontier. . . . At least the city dweller is in touch with humanity. . . . The settlers of the frontier, for months at a time, did not have even that little comfort.

Pollution: The smoke that billowed over the landscape was seen as a good omen; it meant prosperity.

Hunting: Although hunting as a leisure activity did not have the widespread following it does today, the devastation of wildlife was far greater. Hunters engaged in outright butchery. . . .

Drug addiction: More from ignorance than greed, doctors abetted, and often created, the sinister craving by their careless prescribing of opiates, which occupied about 75 percent of their medical bags.

Policemen: The policeman's hatred of the public was reciprocated. Most people thought of them as ruffians who constantly guzzled free beer.

Classroom discipline: The teacher was more warden than instructor, his routine more physical than intellectual.

Working conditions: Whether a worker was mutilated by a buzz saw, crushed by a beam, interred in a mine, or fell down a shaft, it was always "his own bad luck." Companies disclaimed responsibility.

The law: Judges—merciless on the poor defendant with no friends—would never convict a rich man. . . . The rich could and did, literally, get away with murder.

Farm life: As a rule the young hated the farm, its demoralizing hardships, its idiot monotony, its isolation, and as soon as they grew to independence . . . thousands broke away from the land and settled in cities large and small.

Strikes: The attitude of the authorities toward strikers . . . was exclusively punitive, and the public at large agreed with this approach.

Mental Illness: Families hid a demented member as if he were evidence of sin. The poor creatures were kept in attics, in cellars; on Staten Island a lunatic was confined to an outhouse.

Traffic accidents: The engine of city mayhem was the horse . . .
Runaways were common. According to the National Safety Council,
the horse-associated fatality rate was ten times the car-associated rate
of modern times.

City schools: The New York Commissioner of Education
frankly admitted in 1871 that "thousands of children leave school
without being able to read and write".

Leisure: For the working masses, vacations did not exist. For
those above subsistence level, ideology got in the way, their imperative
of success producing a tireless rhythm of life where relaxation was
tantamount to laziness.

Otto Bettmann

7

Dividing and Classifying

RHETORIC

Dividing and classifying is a method of organizing a subject which is done in two essential steps. First, you break down a subject into logical divisions, just as you might begin to arrange the items you bought at the supermarket into canned goods, frozen food, fresh fruit and vegetables, and household products like soap and furniture polish. Second, you discuss each of the divisions by identifying the similarities of items within the division and differences from items in the other divisions. As a principle of organization, dividing and classifying has almost universal application; automobiles, drivers, students, teachers, and almost all aspects of your everyday life can be divided and classified in different ways.

To take one simple example, the *Consumer's Guide to Car Buying,* put out by the National Highway Traffic Safety Administration, divides cars into four main divisions based on weight: large, intermediate, compact, and subcompact. Using these basic divisions, the guide then classifies all of the common makes on the basis of various characteristics: safety, fuel economy, maintenance, and insurance. These divisions can be subdivided and classified to show further things within each main division. Such a system of division and classification is helpful in clarifying a great deal of information useful to the potential car buyer.

In writing a theme developed by division and classification, the most important principle to remember is that this kind of development aims at providing useful and informative groupings of things. To be useful and informative, the divisions and classifications must rest on a consistent and sensible basis. For instance, it would be useful information to divide voters into groups classified as Republicans, Democrats, and Independents. To divide them into blue-eyed, brown-eyed, or green-eyed would serve no obvious, useful purpose.

The purposes of division and classification are to bring order out of chaos or to make a complex subject intelligible. If division and classification is to serve these purposes, there are certain guidelines to follow.

1. Choose a subject that can logically be divided. (This is easy to do; almost anything or any idea can be broken down into its component parts. For example, something existing in time always has a beginning, a middle, and an end; something that exists in space always has a top and a bottom, a front and a back.)

2. Choose a consistent and logical basis on which to divide your subject. If you are classifying the kinds of science courses that are offered at your school, you might logically classify them as social sciences, physical sciences, biological sciences, and mathematics. It would not be logical to include noncredit courses in this list.

3. Once you have established an appropriate principle for dividing, do not shift it without reason. You might, of course, investigate your subject from one point of view and then shift to a different point of view using a different principle, but you must be consistent in applying one principle at a time.

4. If your classification is to be complete, it should account for all members of a group or class. Sometimes, when you know that you cannot possibly deal with every member of a group, it may be best to entitle them "main divisions" or "major types." Sometimes, you may need to set up an artificial category such as "others" or "undecided" to make the classification logically complete.

5. You should establish divisions or classes which do not overlap and put each item in only one category. It would not be logical, for instance, to classify meats as pork, beef, lamb, and cold cuts.

6. Avoid either/or classifications for either/or is more properly contrast.

Any sensible analysis of a group of students, for instance, will yield more categories than just good students and bad students. Even if you wish to make only two categories, you will find yourself not using division and classification but using contrast.

EXERCISE

To check your understanding of the guidelines, point out any errors or inconsistencies in the following classifications:

Stores: department stores, specialty shops, national retailers, catalog stores, maternity stores

Climates: tropical, subtropical, temperate, arctic, coastal

College degrees: associate degree, bachelor's degree, master's degree, M.D.

Mammals: wild mustangs, coyotes, prairie dogs, land turtles

ORGANIZATION

The organization of a division and classification essay requires two steps. If these steps are clear and precise, the essay *is* organized.

Having chosen a subject that lends itself to division, the first step is determining and following the divisions, that is, separating your subject into comprehensible parts. For example, the students in any one of your classes could be classified in a number of ways—by I.Q., by the section of the country they come from, by age, by socioeconomic level, by ethnic background, by location in the classroom, or by career goals. The choice is yours, but you must be consistent, and your classification must make your point.

The second step is to explain each classification in order to advance your purpose, to convince your reader. Depending upon the relative difficulty of your subject, each classification may be developed by one or more paragraphs. Unless there is some real reason not to, you should develop each classification to relatively equal lengths; that is, your essay should be balanced.

Suppose that you have given some thought to the different kinds of students you have met. From your observations, you might decide that many of the students fall into a nontraditional group that appears to consist of three fairly distinct categories.

1. People retraining for an occupation
2. Mature adults seeking enrichment
3. High school students seeking advanced placement

These main divisions would provide your main blocks of development, and you could expand them as far as you wish to or need to, whether you devote a single paragraph to each or provide half a dozen paragraphs of detailed analysis of each.

As with other methods of writing, the division and classification essay uses the customary organization—introduction, thesis statement, body, and conclusion. An effective introduction attracts and focuses your reader's attention on the central idea of your essay as stated in your thesis. The wording of your thesis statement is of paramount importance, for it not only expresses the main point you want to make but provides direction for the development of your essay. Though it may be placed elsewhere in the essay—even at the end—one of the most prominent places for the thesis statement is at the end of a fairly brief introductory paragraph.

Some writers may find it easier to write the introduction after they have the essay fairly well fleshed out. Once they have the thesis statement down on paper, they proceed to write the body of the essay and come back to the introduction after the first or second draft is completed. You might at least consider that method, especially if you find yourself having trouble with the introduction.

More conventionally, starting from a rough outline, you might introduce an essay on the new group of students in this way.

> *At the community college I attend and at most other colleges, I suspect, a new and different group of students is swelling the enrollment and gradually changing some popular notions about college students. From my observations, these nontraditional students seem to fall mainly into three different categories.*

A thesis sentence such as the one given here points the direction for the development of the body of the essay. In a short essay, each of the three main divisions might be dealt with in a single paragraph; in a longer essay, these main divisions could be broken down in various ways. For example, one group of nontraditional students are people who must retrain for an occupation.

1. People who have become handicapped and can no longer perform tasks required in their former jobs
2. People who have lost their previous jobs because of technological changes or shifts in demands for consumer goods.
3. People who have advanced to a higher position in their jobs and now must acquire new skills necessary for their new positions.

Each of these three could become the subject for a paragraph of development.

While a clear and specific thesis statement and good organization are key elements in unifying the essay, you still need to carry your reader along smoothly from point to point and from paragraph to paragraph in the body of your essay. Here are some samples of *subordinate clause transitions* that might work well in an essay such as the one on the different groups of students.

> *When these new students discover that they have an advantage in life experience,* they are far less likely to see themselves as being disadvantaged.
>
> *Having seen a clear need to change the direction of their lives,* these students plunge into their studies and demand to know everything possible.
>
> *Since they are not driven in the same way as career changers,* the mature adults seeking enrichment are usually able to accept the whole routine of lectures and tests and grades more philosophically.

The subordinate clause transition is just one of many techniques, but you do need to give some attention to taking your readers with you through the various steps of development. Remember, your readers don't have your classifications before them, and, most of all, they don't necessarily share your patterns of thinking. It is up to you as a writer to make your ideas clear and easy to follow. Other techniques that will help your reader are (1) enumeration, (as is done in this sentence) (2) repetition of key terms, (use of the same word rather than a synonym) (3) parallel structure (similar ideas in similar grammatical form—"I came, I saw, I conquered").

Your purpose, your audience, and your development all should point to the conclusion, the thought you want to leave in your reader's mind. Among the many ways of concluding an essay, probably the most common provides a conclusion that balances the introduction and reasserts the thesis. A conclusion such as this might serve quite well for the essay on nontraditional students.

> These three groups, which together make up a substantial portion of the enrollment at community colleges, have led the way in the changes we see taking place on our campuses today. These nontraditional learners are now very much a part of the college scene, and their numbers are growing every year.

Effective Legal Writing and Speaking

GEORGE D. GIBSON

English is not just for English class. Even students who succeed in English classes sometimes forget they are learning to write not just for English classes but for all the classes they are going to take—and for all their vocational and social lives.

In the following essay, George Gibson, a distinguished member of the Washington and Virginia bars, points out the fundamentals of good English for lawyers. He's right, of course, but the fundamentals he stresses are not restricted to lawyers alone. The English language is one of the greatest languages of the world, capable of clarity, precision, poignancy, and eloquence. But to achieve these, students must take their English skills out of the English classroom and use them in all they do.

Notice how Gibson's points apply to lawyers and to all other writers.

A. Introduction   The most common difficulty in speaking or writing clearly lies in not knowing clearly what one wishes to say. . . .

* * *

Yet one of the most persistent criticisms of the lawyer in action is that his writing is so poor, wordy, vague, uncertain. This criticism comes from the Bench, from leading members of the Bar, from assessment committees in law firms.

So it is a sobering fact, especially because the spoken or written word is the key to our livelihood and the survival of our profession. True enough, we are employed to think. But that is not enough. The result of our thinking must be communicated with effect. Clients want results. Our thinking is useful, in short, only if we can make use of it to explain or persuade. That is true in all cases, whatever the subject or forum.

* * *

B. The Word   The basic element of communication is the word. We may say it corresponds to a point in the language of geometry.

As a point is exact, so also the word must be precise. By all means use the word that most precisely identifies your chosen concept . . .

But do not overdo your reverence for words. If one word states the idea, two words will only blur it. A common compliment is that a speaker has "great command of the English language." That is a basic error. It is not the *use* of the English language that wins the compliment. It is the *restraint* in the use of the English language. If unnecessary words are eliminated, the ideas will prevail. The compliment really means that the speaker has such command of the English language that he is able to forgo all words except the one that fits precisely. The idea then comes through most clearly. Brevity is not only the soul of wit, it is also the source of power. Indeed it is the chief vehicle of power . . .

If you are going to use few words, choose the simple ones. Fancy words do not remain in fashion long. Foreign words may mystify rather than inform.

Use strong words. This does not mean strong language. Winged words are best. Tame words do no good. Vague words put your audience to sleep. Outworn phrases may send them out the door. Among honest strong words, the nouns and verbs are packed with meaning, far more so than adjectives and adverbs. Indeed, the perfect choice of a noun or verb has such pungency that it is diluted by adding any adjective or adverb. The active voice is always more striking than the passive, for that tends toward the impersonal and vague.

* * *

C. The Sentence   If we refer to a word as a point in the language of geometry, the sentence is a line in the language of geometry. It embodies movement through successive points and thus has structure.

Nothing can replace a healthy respect for the structure of our ancient English sentence. It has a subject. It has a verb. It has an object or a predicate.

That means a pattern of words that respects the pattern of thought and moves arm in arm with it to a common conclusion. We might call it coherence or congruity. This habit of coherence is the most valuable single virtue a writer or speaker can acquire. If these remarks succeed only in emphasizing its urgency, they will have been worthwhile.

The simplest material of togetherness is space. Judicious use of it will be rewarding. The best use is to keep related words together and to keep unrelated words apart. The reader does not then have to disentangle on his own, but can follow without effort.

An elemental instance is to keep modifiers next to the word they modify. Instead of saying "He only corrected two mistakes"—which leaves open the possibility that there were many more that he did not correct—say "He corrected only two mistakes." That is unambiguous . . .

A closely related rule is to be sure that any relative pronoun you use follows closely after its antecedent, so that its reference is immediately apparent. Notorious violaters of this rule are "They," "it," and the like, which, without any identifiable antecedent, often make it so difficult for a lawyer to follow the statements of a witness. Having properly used a pronoun, get the full benefit of it by continuing to use it as long as the antecedent reasonably persists in the reader's mind. To shove the full antecedent down his throat unnecessarily accuses him of not having even average intelligence.

As the relative pronoun must follow closely to be intelligible, so a participle phrase at the start of a sentence must refer only to the subject of the sentence. Thus, "arriving at the airport, he was met by friends," rather than "Arriving at the airport, friends were there to meet him." Violations of this rule lead often to absurdity. Thus, "Being old and dingy, I was able to buy the house cheap."

Going back to our elemental design of the sentence as hanging principally on the subject and the verb, it is helpful to the reader if you avoid inserting any phrase or clause between the subject and the verb. If the phrase can be transferred to the beginning of the sentence, the thought will flow more swiftly from subject to verb and make a more vigorous communication . . .

The most important place in a sentence is the end. The end is what the reader remembers most vividly and perhaps with the greatest pleasure. It thus receives the greatest prominence and attention. "In short order the Third Fleet suffered serious reverses" makes a stronger impression than if we say "In short order serious reverses were suffered by the Third Fleet." The end receives the greatest prominence not only because of its position, but also because it is usually the logical predicate, that is, the new element that the sentence is designed to communicate. For much the same reason, special importance attaches to the last sentence of a paragraph and to the last paragraph of a composition.

Conversely, the other prominent position in a sentence is its beginning. The power of that position is increased if the first word is anything other than the subject. Thus "Home is the sailor" is far more exciting than "The sailor is home." The thought of "homeness" can be made still more vivid by repetition with contrasting order. Thus, "Home is the sailor, home from the sea and the hunter home from the hill." But that may be venturing a little further than the sober statements expected of a lawyer . . .

D. The Paragraph   The paragraph is the flexible unit with which compositions of every nature can be devised . . . It may be long if justified by order. Or it may be as short as a single word. The only requirement is that it obey the central law of togetherness by visibly hanging together both in topic and in mood. These are not really very rigid limitations . . .

Again keeping in mind that our reader is a wary animal who will escape if any opportunity is allowed, it is helpful to begin each new paragraph with a disclosure of its new topic. The mere indentation alerts the reader to a coming novelty and he is gratified if he is told soon rather than kept in impatient suspense. For much the same reason it is helpful if the paragraph is restricted to a single topic, because that is the easiest to take home.

Howsoever adaptable and fluid the paragraph structure is, remember that as in the case of the sentence, the most important place is at the end. That is the place where the object sought can be most usefully stated and most easily remembered. In short, emphasis is at the end.

E. The Larger Text   When you move beyond a paragraph and develop a larger text, it must be shaped, even more than those smaller elements, by the audience you are addressing. What sort of person are you talking to? What are his interests? What are his vocabulary and his method of speaking? Your appeal must be expressed in words that are familiar to him if he is to be informed or persuaded. You may remember the enthusiastic traveler who landed in the 42 boxes of clothes he had bought for the trip because he had failed in boarding ship to make himself understood by the crew:

> I said it in Hebrew—I said it in Dutch—
> I said it in German and Greek
> But I wholly forgot (and it vexes me much)
> That English is what you speak!

With your audience identified, what is your main point? Drive straight to it, without any alarms or excursions. Every word should bring you closer to the target. Cheap decorations will only delay your arrival. Shopworn similes will blunt your aim. Now that you have been graduated to the larger text, you speak in three-dimensional values. That means you must not only have length and breadth, but also depth. The audience expects that you will make commensurate use of your resources.

You will, of course, prepare a careful outline first of all. Sharpened by this outline, develop the whole thing as simply and naturally as you can. Follow it scrupulously in writing, approximately in speaking.

Never forget the ancient maxim to say what you are going to say, then to say what you are saying and finally to say what you have said. When you reach the second stage in that development, your audience will recognize the point as one already mentioned and receive it as a welcome friend, instead of a disturbing stranger. When you conclude with a further repetition of that statement, they are likely to share your view that this is the only conclusion that could possibly be reached. And be sure to use the same term on each of the three occasions, without elegant variations.

Friends, Good Friends—and Such Good Friends

JUDITH VIORST

Judith Viorst is an essayist with a wide following among the readers of the numerous popular magazines for which she writes. In this essay, she classifies the types of friends women may have, distinguishing among a broad variety of relationships.

Women are friends, I once would have said, when they totally love and support and trust each other, and bare to each other the secrets of their souls, and run—no questions asked—to help each other, and tell harsh truths to each other (no, you can't wear that dress unless you lose ten pounds first) when harsh truths must be told.

Women are friends, I once would have said, when they share the same affection for Ingmar Bergman, plus train rides, cats, warm rain, charades, Camus, and hate with equal ardor Newark and Brussels sprouts and Lawrence Welk and camping.

In other words, I once would have said that a friend is a friend all the way, but now I believe that's a narrow point of view. For the friendships I have and the friendships I see are conducted at many levels of intensity, serve many different functions, meet different needs and range from those as all-the-way as the friendship of the soul sisters mentioned above to that of the most nonchalant and casual playmates.

Consider these varieties of friendship:

Convenience friends. These are the women with whom, if our paths weren't crossing all the time, we'd have no particular reason to be friends: a next-door neighbor, a woman in our car pool, the mother of one of our children's closest friends or maybe some mommy with whom we serve juice and cookies each week at the Glenwood Co-op Nursery.

Convenience friends are convenient indeed. They'll lend us their cups and silverware for a party. They'll drive our kids to soccer when we're sick. They'll take us to pick up our car when we need a lift to the garage. They'll even take our cats when we go on vacation. As we will for them.

But we don't, with convenience friends, ever come too close or tell too much; we maintain our public face and emotional distance. "Which means,"says Elaine, "that I'll talk about being overweight but not about being depressed. Which means I'll admit being mad but not blind with rage. Which means I might say that we're pinched this month but never that I'm worried sick over money."

But which doesn't mean that there isn't sufficient value to be found in these friendships of mutual aid, in convenience friends.

Special-interest friends. These friendships aren't intimate, and they needn't involve kids or silverware or cats. Their value lies in some interest jointly shared. And so we may have an office friend or a yoga friend or a tennis friend or a friend from the Women's Democratic Club.

"I've got one woman friend," says Joyce, "who likes, as I do, to take psychology courses. Which makes it nice for me—and nice for her. It's fun to go with someone you know and it's fun to discuss what you've learned, driving back from the classes." And for the most part, she says, that's all they discuss.

"I'd say that what we're doing is doing together, not being together," Suzanne says of her Tuesday-doubles friends. "It's mainly a tennis relationship, but we play together well. And I guess we all need to have a couple of playmates."

I agree.

My playmate is a shopping friend, a woman of marvelous taste, a woman who knows exactly *where* to buy *what*, and furthermore is a woman who always knows beyond a doubt what one ought to be buying. I don't have the time to keep up with what's new in eyeshadow, hemlines and shoes and whether the smock look is in or finished already. But since (oh, shame!) I care a lot about eyeshadow, hemlines and shoes, and since I don't *want* to wear smocks if the smock look is finished, I'm very glad to have a shopping friend.

Historical friends. We all have a friend who knew us when . . . maybe way back in Miss Meltzer's second grade, when our family lived in that three-room flat in Brooklyn, when our dad was out of work for seven months, when our brother Allie got in that fight where they had to call the police, when our sister married the endodontist from Yonkers and when, the morning after we lost our virginity, she was the first, the only, friend we told.

The years have gone by and we've gone separate ways and we've little in common now, but we're still an intimate part of each other's past. And so whenever we go to Detroit we always go to visit this friend of our girlhood. Who knows how we looked before our teeth were straightened. Who knows how we talked before our voice got unBrooklyned. Who knows what we ate before we learned about artichokes. And who, by her presence, puts us in touch with an earlier part of ourself, a part of ourself it's important never to lose.

"What this friend means to me and what I mean to her," says Grace, "is having a sister without sibling rivalry. We know the texture of each other's lives. She remembers my grandmother's cabbage soup. I remember the way her uncle played the piano. There's simply no other friend who remembers those things."

Crossroads friends. Like historical friends, our crossroads friends are important for *what was*—for the friendship we shared at a crucial, now past, time of life. A time, perhaps, when we roomed in college together; or worked as eager young singles in the Big City together; or went together, as my friend Elizabeth and I did through pregnancy, birth and that scary first year of new motherhood.

Crossroads friends forge powerful links, links strong enough to endure with not much more contact than once-a-year letters at Christmas. And out of respect for those crossroads years, for those dramas and dreams we once shared, we will always be friends.

Cross-generational friends. Historical friends and crossroads seem to maintain a special kind of intimacy—dormant but always ready to be revived—and though we may rarely meet, whenever we do connect, it's personal and intense. Another kind of intimacy exists in the friendships that form across generations in what one woman calls her daughter-mother and her mother-daughter relationships.

Evelyn's friend is her mother's age—"but I share much more than I ever could with my mother"—a woman she talks to of music, of books, and of life. "What I get from her is the benefit of her experience. What she gets—and enjoys—from me is a youthful perspective. It's a pleasure for both of us."

I have in my own life a precious friend, a woman of 65 who has lived very hard, who is wise, who listens well; who has been where I am and can help me understand it; and who represents not only an ultimate ideal mother to me but also the person I'd like to be when I grow up.

In our daughter role we tend to do more than our share of self-revelation; in our mother role we tend to receive what's revealed. It's another kind of pleasure—playing wise mother to a questing younger person. It's another very lovely kind of friendship.

Part-of-a-couple friends. Some of the women we call our friends we never see alone—we see them as part of a couple at couples' parties. And though we share interests in many things and respect each other's views, we aren't moved to deepen the relationship. Whatever the reason, a lack of time or—and this is more likely—a lack of chemistry, our friendship remains in the context of a group. But the fact that our feeling on seeing each other is always, "I'm *so* glad she's here" and the fact that we spend half the evening talking together says that this too, in its own way, counts as a friendship.

(Other part-of-a-couple friends are the friends that came with the marriage, and some of these are friends we could live without. But sometimes, alas, she married our husband's best friend; and sometimes, alas, she *is* our husband's best friend. And so we find ourself dealing with her, somewhat against our will, in a spirit of what I'll call *reluctant* friendship.)

Men who are friends. I wanted to write just of women friends, but the women I've talked to won't let me—they say I must mention man-woman friendships too. For these friendships can be just as close and as dear as those that we form with women. Listen to Lucy's description of one such friendship:

"We've found we have things to talk about that are different from what he talks about with my husband and different from what I talk about with his wife. So sometimes we call on the phone or meet for lunch. There are similar intellectual interests—we always pass on to each other the books that we love—but there's also something tender and caring too."

In a couple of crises, Lucy says "He offered himself, for talking and for helping. And when someone died in his family he wanted me there. The sexual, flirty part of our friendship is very small, but *some*—just enough to make it fun and different." She thinks—and I agree—that the sexual part, though small is always *some*, is always there when a man and a woman are friends.

It's only in the past few years that I've made friends with men, in the sense of a friendship that's *mine*, not just part of two couples. And achieving with them the ease and the trust I've found with women friends has value indeed. Under the dryer at home last week, putting on mascara and rouge, I comfortably sat and talked with a fellow named Peter. Peter, I finally decided, could handle the shock of me minus mascara under the dryer. Because we are for each other. Because we're friends.

There are medium friends, and pretty good friends, and very good friends indeed, and these friendships are defined by their level of intimacy. And what we'll reveal at each of these levels of intimacy is calibrated with care. We might tell a medium friend, for example, that yesterday we had a fight with our husband. And we might tell a pretty good friend that this fight with our husband made us so mad that we slept on the couch. And we might tell a very good friend that the reason we got so mad in that fight that we slept on the couch had something to do with that girl who works in his office. But it's only to our very best friends that we're willing to tell all, to tell what's going on with that girl in his office.

The best of friends, I still believe, totally love and support and trust each other, and bare to each other the secrets of their souls, and run—no questions asked—to help each other, and tell harsh truths to each other when they must be told.

But we needn't agree about everything (only 12-year-old girl friends agree about *everything*) to tolerate each other's point of view. To accept without judgment. To give and to take without ever keeping score. And to *be* there, as I am for them and as they are for me, to comfort our sorrows, to celebrate our joys.

How Does the Author Make Her Point?

1. What is Viorst's thesis statement?
2. What tone does she set in her introduction?
3. Why is her tone particularly well suited to popular magazines?
4. What is the effect of Viorst's saying, "I wanted to write just of women friends, but. . . ." Why doesn't she make up her mind before she begins to write?

What Do You Think?

1. Do you find this classification useful or merely mildly interesting?
2. Would you consider the classification of part-of-a-couple friends (division) as friends or acquaintances?
3. Does Viorst's analysis of self-revelation under point 5 strike you as psychologically sound?

What Do You Call a Platypus?

ISAAC ASIMOV

Isaac Asimov is best known for his science fiction writing; he is, indeed, one of the giants in this field. However, he has written hundreds of books on an amazing number of subjects, including mathematics, physics, astronomy, the Bible, mythology, linguistics, and Shakespeare. He has also taught biochemistry at the Boston University School of Medicine. In "What Do You Call a Platypus," Asimov discusses taxonomy, the science of classification in an essay developed by division and classification.

In 1800, a stuffed animal arrived in England from the newly discovered continent of Australia.

The continent had already been the source of plants and animals never seen before—but this one was ridiculous. It was nearly two feet long, and had a dense coating of hair. It also had a flat rubbery bill, webbed feet, a broad flat tail, and a spur on each hind ankle that was clearly intended to secrete poison. What's more, under the tail was a single opening.

Zoologists stared at the thing in disbelief. Hair like a mammal! Bill and feet like an aquatic bird! Poison spurs like a snake! A single opening in the rear as though it laid eggs!

There was an explosion of anger. The thing was a hoax. Some unfunny jokester in Australia, taking advantage of the distance and strangeness of the continent, had stitched together parts of widely different creatures and was intent on making fools of innocent zoologists in England.

Yet the skin seemed to hang together. There were no signs of artificial joining. Was it or was it not a hoax? And if it wasn't a hoax, was it a mammal with reptilian characteristics, or a reptile with mammalian characteristics, or was it partly bird, or *what*?

The discussion went on heatedly for decades. Even the name emphasized the ways in which it didn't seem like a mammal despite its hair. One early name was *Platypus anatinus* which is Graeco-Latin for "Flat-foot, ducklike." Unfortunately, the term, platypus, had already been applied to a type of beetle and there must be no duplication in scientific names. It therefore received another name, *Ornithorhynchus paradoxus,* which means "Bird-beak, paradoxical."

Slowly, however, zoologists had to fall into line and admit that the creature was real and not a hoax, however upsetting it might be to zoological notions. For one thing, there were increasingly reliable reports from people in Australia who caught glimpses of the creature alive. The *paradoxus* was dropped and the scientific name is now *Ornithorhynchus anatinus.*

To the general public, however, it is the "duckbill platypus," or even just the duckbill, the queerest mammal (assuming it is a mammal) in the world.

When specimens were received in such condition as to make it possible to study the internal organs, it appeared that the heart was just like those of mammals and not at all like those of reptiles. The egg-forming machinery in the female, however, was not at all like those of mammals, but like those of birds or reptiles. It seemed really and truly to be an egg-layer.

It wasn't till 1884, however, that the actual eggs laid by a creature with hair were found. Such creatures included not only the platypus, but another Australian species, the spiny anteater. That was worth an excited announcement. A group of British scientists were meeting in Montreal at the time, and the egg-discoverer, W. H. Caldwell, sent them a cable to announce the finding.

It wasn't till the twentieth century that the intimate life of the duckbill came to be known. It is an aquatic animal, living in Australian fresh water at a wide variety of temperatures—from tropical streams at sea level to cold lakes at an elevation of a mile.

The duckbill is well adapted to aquatic life, with its dense fur, its flat tail, and its webbed feet. Its bill has nothing really in common with that of the duck, however. The nostrils are differently located and the platypus bill is different in structure, rubbery rather than duckishly horny. It serves the same function as the duck's bill, however, so it has been shaped similarly by the pressures of natural selection.

The water in which the duckbill lives is invariably muddy at the bottom and it is in this mud that the duckbill roots for its food supply. The bill, ridged with horny plates, is used as a sieve, dredging about sensitively in the mud, filtering out the shrimps, earthworms, tadpoles and other small creatures that serve it as food.

When the time comes for the female platypus to produce young, she builds a special burrow, which she lines with grass and carefully plugs. She then lays two eggs, each about three quarters of an inch in diameter and surrounded by a translucent, horny shell.

These the mother platypus places between her tail and abdomen and curls up about them. It takes two weeks for the young to hatch out. The new-born duckbills have teeth and very short bills, so that they are much less "birdlike" than the adults. They feed on milk. The mother has no nipples, but milk oozes out of pore openings in the abdomen and the young lick the area and are nourished in this way. As they grow, the bills become larger and the teeth fall out.

Yet despite everything zoologists learned about the duckbills, they never seemed entirely certain as to where to place them in the table of animal classification. On the whole, the decision was made because of hair and milk. In all the world, only mammals have true hair and only mammals produce true milk. The duckbill and spiny anteater have hair and produce milk, so they have been classified as mammals.

Just the same, they are placed in a very special position. All the mammals are divided into two subclasses. In one of these subclasses ("Prototheria" or "first-beasts") are the duckbill and five species of the spiny anteater. In the other ("Theria" or just "beast") are all the other 4,231 known species of mammals.

How Does The Author Make His Point?

1. Why did the author choose to introduce his subject as he did?
2. Why does the author include so much precise, scientific description of the animal and its life in his essay?
3. What did you learn about scientific classification by reading this essay?
4. Why was the platypus so hard to classify? Why do scientists *not* call it "platypus"?

What Do You Think?

1. How do you distinguish a bird from a mammal?
2. At first, the British scientists thought the platypus was a hoax. Do you know of any scientific hoaxes—that fooled people for a long time?
3. Why do you think scientists must classify everything?

Fans

PAUL GALLICO

Paul Gallico wrote sports, plays for movies and television (remember Pride of the Yankees) *and novels. Most of his best writing was done in the twenties when sport was in its Golden Age. In this essay, he classifies sports fans. Have they changed much?*

> *Crowd: A large number of persons congregated or collected into a close body without order; a great number of persons; especially, the great body of people; the populace; the masses; the multitude. . . .*
> —Webster's New International Dictionary

The fight crowd is a beast that lurks in the darkness behind the fringe of white light shed over the first six rows by the incandescents atop the ring, and is not to be trusted with pop bottles or other hardware. The tennis crowd is the pansy of all the great sports mobs and is always preening and shushing itself. The golf crowd is the most unwieldy and most sympathetic, and is the only horde given to mass production of that absurd noise written generally as "tsk tsk tsk tsk," and made between tongue and teeth with head-waggings to denote extreme commiseration. The baseball crowd is the most hysterical, the football crowd the best-natured and the polo crowd the most aristocratic. Racing crowds are the most restless, wrestling crowds are the most tolerant, and soccer crowds the most easily incitable to riot and disorder. Every sports crowd takes on the characteristics of the individuals who compose it. Each has its particular note of hysteria, its own little cruelties, mannerisms, and bad mannerisms, its own code of sportsmanship and its own method of expressing its emotions.

For instance, people who go to horse races want to win money. People who follow golf matches are bad golfers. People who go to tennis matches are pleased with rhythm and beauty. People who go to baseball games are all grandstand experts and thoroughly familiar with the game. People who attend the polo matches are either somebody or trying to be. The spectators at big college football games are the most wholesome people in the world, but they know nothing about the game and care less.

People who go to prize fights are sadistic.

When two prominent pugilists are scheduled to pummel one another in public on a summer's evening, men and women file into the stadium in the guise of human beings, and thereafter become a part of a gray thing that squats in the dark until, at the conclusion of the bloodletting, they may be seen leaving the arena in the same guise they wore when they entered.

As a rule, the mob that gathers to see men fight is unjust, vindictive, swept by intense, unreasoning hatreds, vain of its swift recognition of what it believes to be sportsmanship. It is quick to greet the purely phony move of the boxer who extends his gloves to his rival, who has slipped or been pushed to the floor, and to reward this stimulating but still baloney *beau geste* with a pattering of hands which indicates the following: "You are a good sport. We recognize that you are a good sport, and we know a sporting gesture when we see one. Therefore we are all good sports, too. Hurrah for us!"

The same crowd doesn't see the same boxer stick his thumb in his opponent's eye or try to cut him with the laces of his glove, butt him or dig him a low one when the referee isn't in a position to see. It roots consistently for the smaller man, and never for a moment considers the desperate psychological dilemma of the larger of the two. It howls with glee at a good finisher making his kill. The Roman hordes were more civilized. Their gladiators asked them whether the *coup de grâce* should be administered or not. The *pièce de résistance* at the modern prize fight is the spectacle of a man clubbing a helpless and vanquished opponent into complete insensibility. The referee who stops a bout to save a slugged and punch-drunken man from the final ignominy is hissed by the assembled sportsmen. . . .

The golf gallery is the Punchinello of the great sports mob, the clown crowd, an uncontrollable, galloping, galumphing horde, that wanders hysterically over manicured pasture acreage of an afternoon, clucking to itself, trying to keep quiet, making funny noises, sweating, thundering over hills ten thousand strong, and gathering, mousey-still, around a little hole in the ground to see a man push a little ball into the bottom of it with a crooked iron stick. If the ball goes in they raise a great shout and clap their hands and sometimes slap one another on the back, crying "Oh, boy!" and "Beautiful, beautiful, magnificent!" And when the white pellet just sneaks past the rim of the orifice or twists out of it, or goes up and looks in and sticks on the edge, a great mass murmur of pity runs through the group and they sound their "Oh's" like a Greek chorus greeting the arrival of a new set of catastrophes. Then it is that they make their absurd clucking noises and shake their heads, some in unison, some in anti-unison, like mechanical dolls all set off at once.

The golf gallery is closest of any to the game that is being played. Every individual in the stampede is familiar with the implements used and the problems that arise from tee to green. They are really vicarious players, and the crass outsider who rattles a toy movie camera at one of the artists just as he is about to apply a delicate brush of his poker against the side of the quiescent ball is given the hissing and glaring-at of his life.

The tennis audiences were always my favorites, preening themselves, bestowing refined approval in well-bred and well-repressed little outbursts, beaming upon the contestants and on one another, glaring at someone rustling a piece of paper, expressing righteous indignation at the unwelcome intrusion of an ordinary spectator who vulgarly screams, "Come on, you Johnny, sock it again!"

They are experts at registering shocked and delighted approval when an erring player cries "Nuts," or "Damn," to let them know that they feel he has been a muggins, but withal a virile and manly one. They, too, hum with smug sympathy when a player pouts or makes a move at a missed ball, pat-a-caking their hands to indicate recognition of the fine points of the game, and rooting for the player with the most slickum on his hair.

Baseball and football crowds are happiest when they feel that they have become a part of the game that is being played for them. The solidly packed football stands begin to chant, "We want a touchdown," or "Hold that line!" And when the touchdown is scored or the line holds, the crowd takes part credit. In baseball, sections of the rooters set out deliberately to rattle a pitcher with rhythmic or anti-rhythmic hand-clappings, whichever they think will annoy him the most, or by setting up a bedlam of sound, or by waving somewhat cloudy pocket-handkerchiefs at him. Most rooting, as a matter of fact, grows out of the individual spectator's desire to identify himself with the proceedings on the field, to shake himself free of the anonymity of the crowd and become an active participant in a sport for which nature happens not to have fitted him.

The loveliest girls in the world sit in the football crowds, their fresh faces framed in fur. The toughest babies in town seem to collect at the ball games, idle sisters sitting in pairs chewing gum, fanning themselves with their score cards and adding their harsh screams to the hullabaloo that accompanies a sharply hit ball or the race between ball and man for the base. The baseball crowd is cosmopolitan. It contains representatives from every walk in life and from every profession. It is the most expert gathering in the world, and the most appreciative of skill. The crowd of sixty thousand that sits in the Yankee Stadium on a Sunday afternoon in midsummer, and the World Series crowd of the same number that watches the inter-league play-off in the fall, are as different as black and white, although both are looking at the same game. World Series spectators aren't regular baseball fans. Most of them have never seen a game before. They are drawn by the ballyhoo, the publicity and the higher prices. They sit on their hands and refuse to warm up to the rising and falling tides of battle. The bleacher crowd gets a better view of the game than the snootier patrons in the stands and boxes. They see the game the way the players see it.

Horse-racing crowds are nervous, greedy, fortune-hunting, always milling and moving about, whispering, circulating, muttering until the wheeling ponies suddenly freeze them into a temporary immobility, feverish in its intensity, the same pregnant calm that falls upon the onlookers when the little pill is hippity-skipping on the whirling wheel, between *rouge et noir*.

How Does the Author Make His Point?

1. What is the thesis statement? Is it a good one? Why or why not? Could you construct a better one?
2. Which fans does Gallico seem most contemptuous of? Support your answer.
3. What is the major difference in the actions of fans at football and baseball games?
4. According to Gallico, different sports attract different people. Explain this classification.

What Do You Think?

1. Have spectators changed since Gallico wrote this article in 1931? How? Give specific examples.

2. Do you yourself behave differently depending upon which sport you're watching? Why?

3. Why do you think the author does not discuss wrestling crowds and soccer crowds? Does this detract from the essay?

4. What statements does Gallico make that you disagree with? Explain why you believe these are not true.

Pink and Brown People

THOMAS SOWELL

Thomas Sowell is an economist, a graduate of Harvard, Columbia, and the University of Chicago, and a firm believer in the traditional values of hard work, perseverance, and finding a helping hand at the end of one's own arm.

A man who says we should really "tell it like it is" refers to whites and blacks as "pink people" and "brown people." These jarring phrases are of course more accurate, but that may be why they are jarring. Race is not an area especially noted for accuracy—or for rationality or candor. More often it is an area of symbolism, stereotype, and euphemism. The plain truth sounds off-key and even suspicious. Gross exaggerations like *white* and *black* are more like the kind of polarization that we are used to. Racial classifications have always been a problem, but in the United States such attempts at neat pigeonholing become a farce, in view of the facts of history.

Less than a fourth of the "black" population of the United States is of unmixed African ancestry. And a noted social historian estimates that tens of millions of whites have at least one black ancestor somewhere in generations past. Even in the old South, where "one drop of Negro blood" was supposed to make you socially black, the actual laws required some stated fraction of black ancestry, to avoid "embarassing" some of the "best" white families.

What all this boils down to is a wide spectrum of racial mixtures with an arbitrary dividing line and boldly contrasting labels applied to people on either side of the line. The human desire for classification is not going to be defeated by any biological facts. Those who cannot swallow pseudobiology can turn to pseudohistory as the basis for classification. Unique cultural characteristics are now supposed to neatly divide the population.

In this more modern version, the ghetto today is a unique social phenomenon—a unique problem calling for a unique solution. Many of those who talk this way just happen to have this solution with them and will make it available for a suitable combination of money and power.

Ghettos today certainly differ from white middle-class neighborhoods. But past ghettos always differed from past middle-class neighborhoods, even when both were white. Indeed, the very word *ghetto* came historically from a white minority community of people, classified by the fact that they held religious services one day earlier than the others. People will classify on any basis. With today's recreation-oriented weekends, religious classifications are often based on what service you *would have* attended.

American ghettos have always had crime, violence, overcrowding, filth, drunkenness, bad school teaching, and worse learning. Nor are blacks historically unique even in the degree of these things. Crime and violence were much worse in the nineteenth-century slums, which were almost all white. The murder rate in Boston in the middle of the nineteenth century was about three times what it was in the middle of the twentieth century. All the black riots of the 1960s put together did not kill half as many people as were killed in one white riot in 1863.

The meaning of the term *race riot* has been watered down in recent times to include general hell raising (and posing for television) in the hell-raisers' own neighborhood. In the nineteenth century it was much uglier. Thousands of members of one "race" invaded the neighborhood of another "race"—both, typically, European—to maim, murder, and burn. Today's disorders are not in the same league, whether measured in blood or buildings.

Squalor, dirt, disease? Historically, blacks are neither first nor last in any of these categories. There were far more immigrants packed into the slums (per room or per square mile) than is the case with blacks today—not to mention the ten thousand to thirty thousand children with no home at all in nineteenth-century New York. They slept under bridges, huddled against buildings or wherever they could find some semblance of shelter from the elements.

Even in the area where many people get emotional—educational and I.Q. test results—blacks are doing nothing that various European minorities did not do before them. As of about 1920, any number of European ethnic groups had I.Q.'s the same as or lower than the I.Q.'s of blacks today. As recently as the 1940s, there were schools on the Lower East Side of New York with academic performances lower than those of schools in Harlem.

Much of the paranoia that we talk ourselves into about race (and other things) is a result of provincialism about our own time as compared to other periods of history. Violence, poverty, and destroyed lives should never be accepted. But there is little chance of solving any problem unless we see it for what it is, not what it appears to be in the framework of reckless rhetoric.

How Does the Author Make His Point?

1. What is the thesis statement?
2. Would Sowell really prefer that races be referred to as "pink and brown"? Explain your answer.
3. Why does the author use the terms *pseudobiology* and *pseudohistory* in paragraph 3? Which of the two does he discuss in the remaining paragraphs of this essay?
4. Why does the author include a history of American ghettos and "race" riots? How do these support his main point?
5. Discuss the author's tone. Does Sowell's tone seem emotional or detached, prejudiced or objective? Are his words colored, colorful, or colorless? (Refer to Paul Roberts's article in the process chapter.)
6. How effective is the conclusion?

What Do You Think?

1. What does Sowell mean in paragraph 2 when he refers to "some stated fraction of black ancestry" and in paragraph 5 when he writes of citizens "classified by the fact that they held religious services one day earlier than the others"? Why do you think he refrains from giving the specific fraction and naming the group?
2. Is there such a thing as "the human desire for classification" mentioned in the third paragraph?
3. Are we paranoid about "race (and other things)" as Sowell states in his conclusion? What "other things" are we paranoid about?

On Reading Trash

BOB SWIFT

Bob Swift is a syndicated newspaper columnist whose interests are as varied as books on the shelves in his children's rooms. Here he gives some advice to parents.

If you want kids to become omnivorous readers, let them read trash. That's my philosophy, and I speak from experience.

I don't disagree with The National Endowment for the Humanities, which says every high school graduate should have read 30 great works of literature, including the Bible, Plato, Shakespeare, Hawthorne, the Declaration of Independence, "Catcher in the Rye," "Crime and Punishment" and "Moby Dick."

It's a fine list. Kids should read them all, and more. But they'll better readers if they start off on trash. Trash? What I mean is what some might call "popular" fiction. My theory is, if you get kids interested in reading books—no matter what sort— they will eventually go on to the grander literature all by themselves.

In the third grade I read my first novel, a mystic adventure set in India. I still recall the sheer excitement at discovering how much fun reading could be.

When we moved within walking distance of the public library, a whole new world opened. In the library I found that wonder of wonders, the series. What a thrill, to find a favorite author had written a dozen or more other titles.

I read a series about frontiersmen, learning about Indian tribes, beef jerky and tepees. A Civil War series alternated young heroes from the Blue and the Gray, and I learned about Grant and Lee and the Rock of Chickamauga.

One summer, in Grandpa Barrow's attic, I discovered the Mother Lode, scores of dusty books detailing the adventures of Tom Swift, The Rover Boys, The Submarine Boys, The Motorcycle Boys and Bomba the Jungle Boy. It didn't matter that some were written in 1919; any book you haven't read is brand new.

Another summer I discovered Edgar Rice Burroughs. I swung through jungles with Tarzan, fought green Martians with John Carter, explored Pellucidar at the Earth's core, flew through the steamy air of Venus with Carson Napier. Then I came across Sax Rohmer and, for book after book, prowled opium dens with Nayland Smith, in pursuit of the insidious Fu Manchu.

In the seventh grade, I ran across Booth Tarkington's hilarious Penrod books and read them over and over.

My cousin went off to war in 1942 and gave me his pulp magazines. I became hooked on Doc Savage, The Shadow, G8 and His Battle Aces, The Spider, Amazing Stories. My folks wisely did not object to them as trash. I began to look in second-hand book shops for past issues, and found a Blue Book Magazine, with an adventure story by Talbot Mundy. It led me back to the library, for more of Mundy's Far East thrillers. From Mundy, my path led to A. Conan Doyle's "The Lost World," Rudyard Kipling's "Kim," Jules Verne, H.G. Wells and Jack London.

Before long I was whaling with Herman Melville, affixing scarlet letters with Hawthorne and descending into the maelstrom with Poe. In due course came Hemingway, Dos Passos, "Hamlet," "The Odyssey," "The Iliad," "Crime and Punishment." I had discovered "real" literature by following the trail of popular fiction.

When our kids were small, we read aloud to them from Doctor Dolittle and Winnie the Pooh. Soon they learned to read, and favored the "Frog and Toad" and "Freddie the Pig" series.

When the old Doc Savage and Conan the Barbarian pulps were reissued as paperbacks, I brought them home. The kids devoured them, sometimes hiding them behind textbooks at school, just as I had. They read my old Tarzan and Penrod books along with Nancy Drew and The Black Stallion.

Now they're big kids. Each kid's room is lined with bookshelves, on which are stacked, in an eclectic mix, Doc Savage, Plato, Louis L'Amour westerns, Thomas Mann, Gothic romances, Agatha Christie, Sartre, Edgar Allen Poe, science-fiction, Saul Bellow, Shakespeare, Pogo, Greek tragedies, Hemingway, Kipling, Tarzan, "Zen and the Art of Motorcycle Maintenance," F. Scott Fitzgerald, "Bomba the Jungle Boy," Nietzsche, The Iliad, "Dr. Dolittle," Joseph Conrad, Fu Manchu, Hawthorne, Penrod, Dostoevsky, Ray Bradbury, Herman Melville, Fitzgerald, "Conan the Barbarian" . . . more. Some great literature, some trash, but all good reading.

How Does the Author Make His Point?

1. How does the author classify books?
2. What is the purpose of the second and third paragraphs? Is this a good technique to use in persuasion?
3. Swift uses various methods of development in this short essay. Find examples of persuasion, examples, narrative.
4. What is the tone of the essay?
5. How does the final sentence of the essay emphasize and summarize Swift's philosophy of reading?

What Do You Think?

1. Do you agree that every high school student should read the works listed in paragraph 2? How many have you read? How many led you on to read other books?
2. What were the first books you read or had read to you? What do you remember about them?
3. Why do you think the author mixes titles, authors, characters, and types of literature into his list in the last paragraph?
4. How many of the books mentioned in the essay have you read? How many titles do you recognize? Did the essay make you want to read any of the works?

The TV as Teacher

DEBBIE LUCCI (student)

The following student essay classifies children's programs on public television according to various methods of instruction.

Many parents are quick to agree that television, for the most part, is a bad influence on children. All of the violence, bloodshed, murders, illicit sex, and profane language give television programs a dreadful name. After all, parents don't want their children to learn negative values and horrible behavior, but the public television station offers three programs for toddlers that just might change parents' attitudes toward TV. Pre-school children are taught to count, to cooperate, to read, and to value themselves as individuals. "Mister Rogers' Neighborhood," "Electric Company," and "Sesame Street" are designed to educate the preschooler, but the teaching methods employed by each program can be divided into distinctive styles.

The first method of teaching involves a one-on-one relationship between the teacher, Mr. Rogers, and the toddler. He treats the children like adults, asking them questions as if he were talking to his peers. At the beginning of the show, Mr. Rogers comes in singing, "Won't you be my neighbor." Then he changes his shoes and sweater. He follows the same simple routine every day which includes conversing with Mr. McFeely and Chef Brockett and taking a ride on the trolley to visit "The Land of Make Believe." After calling on Lady Elaine, King Friday, Henrietta, Handyman Negri, and Prince Tuesday, the trolley returns the intent pupil to Mr. Rogers where, in a very soft-spoken voice, he tells the children, "I like you just the way you are." He is the children's friend; he has a way of making each child feel important; he has the children's trust and that is how he teaches them so effectively.

A second method of instructing tots is employed by "The Electric Company." This program deals with teaching preschoolers how to read words and simple sentences, spelling, and word recognition. At the beginning of the program, a lady screams, "Hey you guys!" This starts off a series of silly animations which include a singing and dancing nose used to illustrate the letter "n." The method of teaching sometimes borders on the ridiculous. For example, one of the characters, Letterman, changes the letters on various words. The story being told might center around a snake. Letterman zooms in adorned with a helmet, goggles, and a red flowing cape and changes the "sn" in snake to a "c" creating the word cake. The cake then becomes a part of the story. This show uses an immense amount of action, yelling, and a variety of characters including Spiderman, Letterman, Supergirl, and Roadrunner to illustrate a point. Since the program is so exciting and fast-moving, it can hold the interest of most pre-schoolers, and, as a method of teaching, it is extremely effective.

A third method of educating toddlers is used by "Sesame Street." This program teaches children to count, to recite the alphabet, and to cooperate with others by employing strange and funny creatures to become the children's friends. Every preschooler knows that the big, yellow-feathered creature is Big Bird, that Oscar the Grouch is fuzzy and green and lives in a steel-gray garbage can, that the big-eyed royal blue character is the Cookie Monster, that Bert is tall, thin, and extremely neat whereas Ernie is short, stocky, and a mess. "Sesame Street" depends on the children's fascination with the lovable creatures to make learning a game. The Count, a purple Dracula with an emerald green cape, delights in counting everything. Whenever he appears on the show, he automatically starts to count regardless of what is going on around him. So the minute the child spies the Count, he too begins to enumerate. This program also relies on repetition and employs several adults which include Mr. Hooper, Maria, Olivia, John, and Bob to repeat and reinforce the letters, numbers and simple words introduced by Big Bird and his friends. This method of teaching is quite effective because the children believe these creatures to be their friends, and preschoolers listen to what peers say.

In conclusion, all three methods of teaching provide an excellent approach to making the learning process fun for the preschooler. The public television station gives parents a chance to let their youngsters view some television, and at the same time, provides three good sources of education.

How Does the Author Make Her Point?

1. Does the essay have an effective introduction?
2. Are the body paragraphs arranged effectively? Should the body paragraphs in this essay be arranged in any particular order?
3. How does the author make effective use of examples?

What Do You Think?

1. Do you feel that one of the teaching methods referred to in the essay is more effective than another?
2. The essay refers only to the strengths of shows like "Mr. Rogers' Neighborhood," "The Electric Company," and "Sesame Street." Do you see any weaknesses in the teaching methods employed by any of the children's programs mentioned?
3. Do you think that the author has provided enough evidence to justify her conclusion?

INTEGRATING READING WITH WRITING SKILLS: RECOGNIZING DIFFERENT PATTERNS OF ORGANIZATION

One of the things you learn by dividing and classifying is the importance of organization. You learn how to bring order out of confusion by breaking down general information into more specific information and then categorizing it in some sort of logical order. It is a process that is so pervasive in everyday life that you might have a tendency to take it for granted and thus minimize its importance. Imagine, for example, trying to find Mark Twain's autobiography in a library where the books were simply piled randomly on the shelves. When you walk into a library, you just assume that the books will be arranged in an orderly fashion. You rarely think of the hours and hours of dividing and classifying that went into the systematic arrangement so that you could know exactly where to find what you're looking for.

In both reading and writing, however, organization is not something that you can take for granted. The writer's organization is crucial—not just for the writer, but for the reader as well. One of the best ways to improve reading comprehension consists of learning how to recognize the writer's method of organization. As reading authority Horace Johnson explains, "If you can discover in detail how the work is put together, you will find it easier and faster to take apart." Intelligent readers thus use their writing skills to sharpen their reading skills (improving both comprehension and speed by recognizing different methods of organization). Conversely, intelligent writers recognize the relationship between the writer's organization and the reader's ability to comprehend, and they make that organizational pattern clearly visible to the reader. For example, look at a short passage from Robert M. Pirsig's best seller, *Zen and the Art of Motorcycle Maintenance*. After introducing his subject (logic), he goes on to write one of the best brief explanations of inductive and deductive reasoning that the average reader is likely to come across. Using the motorcycle to illustrate his main points Pirsig explains:

> Two kinds of logic are used, inductive and deductive. Inductive inferences start with observations of the machine and arrive at general conclusions. For example, if the cycle goes over a bump and the engine misfires, and then goes over another bump and the engine misfires, and then goes over another bump and the engine misfires, and then goes over a long smooth stretch of road and there is no misfiring, and then goes over a fourth bump and the engine misfires again, one can logically conclude that the misfiring is caused by the bumps. That is induction: reasoning from particular experiences to general truths.
>
> Deductive inferences do the reverse. They start with general knowledge and predict a specific observation. For example, if, from reading the hierarchy of facts about the machine, the mechanic knows the horn of the cycle is powered exclusively by electricity from the battery, then he can logically infer that if the battery is dead the horn will not work. That is deduction.
>
> Robert Pirsig

One of the reasons why readers find Pirsig's explanation so easy to understand is because the author uses an effective pattern of organization and makes it clear to his readers. He divides logic into two categories, classifies them as inductive and deductive, and then illustrates each type with an example to show the reader how one type differs from the other. By recognizing the pattern of organization suggested by the introductory sentences in each paragraph and noting the transitional phrase, "for example," within each paragraph, readers can follow Pirsig's thought patterns *as they are reading*. They don't have to read the material a second or third time to figure out what Pirsig is saying. If, however, readers were provided with no organizational signals, they would probably have been confused. Suppose, for example, that Pirsig had written:

    . . . Now I want to talk about methods of finding one's way through these hierarchies [of thought]—logic.
    Inductive inferences start with observations of the machine and arrive at general conclusions. "If the cycle goes over a bump . . .

The reader would have to reread the paragraph to figure out that the term *inductive inferences* refers to a *specific type* of logical reasoning and that the sentence "If the cycle goes over a bump . . . " is actually the beginning of a *specific example* of inductive reasoning.

In conclusion, the ability of readers to recognize the writer's organization clearly affects their reading comprehension. It is up to you as a writer to make sure that through topic sentences, transitional markers, and so on, you make your purpose and organizational structure clear to your readers.

IMPROVING YOUR VOCABULARY: ETYMOLOGY

Notice that in the following discussion of the etymologies of words, the information is organized by division and classification. Among the bases of this organization are words divided into roots, prefixes, and suffixes; another basis is the language of origin, either Greek, Latin, or Old English. There could be still other ways to divide and classify words, such as levels of usage and time of most frequent usage. In the following brief paragraphs, words themselves are analyzed by division and classification.

Many words discussed in a dictionary include the history of those words; the dictionary gives in brief, coded form the *derivation* of the word and which language or languages it comes from. This derivation is known as its *etymology*. The word *etymology* derives from the Greek word *etymon* which means "true sense." When you add to "true sense" the suffix *-ology*, which means "study of," you have a reasonably accurate and memorable sense of the word.

Words come into English in two ways. Some come from the native stock; that is, as far back as their history goes, they are some form of English—either Old English (from the fourth century to the end of the eleventh) or Middle English (from the twelfth century through the fifteenth) or Modern English (from the sixteenth century to the present). For example, the history of the native word *woman* looks something like this.

Middle English: *wumman*
Old English: *wifmann,* from *wif,* a female, plus *mann,* a human being.

Other words came into English when, for reasons based on historical events, they were "borrowed" from other languages to become part of the English vocabulary. Such borrowed words tend to be longer and look more difficult than native words, but they are not more difficult because they are compounded from relatively few word parts, which give you at least a strong clue to the meanings of many words. Borrowed words are divided into roots, prefixes, and suffixes. Learning these relatively few components can help you with the meanings of thousands of words.

Roots

Roots are the basic, central portion of words, usually a Latin noun or verb. The five Latin roots most frequently used to develop English words are the following:

LATIN FORMS	MEANING	ROOT
1. facio, facere, factus, ficere, fictus	to do, to make	*fac, fect, fic*

More than 250 English words are built on this root, among them:
af*fec*t, af*fec*tion, dif*fic*ult, manu*fac*ture, per*fec*t

2. capio, capere, captus	to take, to seize, to grasp	*cap, capt, cept*

More than one hundred English words are based on this root, among them:
ac*cept*, *cap*able, contra*cept*ive, inter*cept*, re*cept*ion

3. mitto, mittere, missus	to let go, to send	*mit(t), mis(s)*

More than one hundred English words are based on this root, among them:
ad*mit*, com*mit*, dis*miss*, sub*mit*, trans*mit*

4. specio, specere, spectus	to look at, to look around	*spec, spect*

Almost two hundred words are formed from this root, among them:
ex*pect*, in*spect*, circum*spect*, *spec*ify, su*spic*ion

5. duco, ducere, ductus	to take, to lead, to draw	*duc, duct*

Almost one hundred English words are based on this root, among them:
con*duct*, e*duc*ation, pro*duct*, repro*duc*e, intro*duc*e

Prefixes

As you can see from the examples of the words built on Latin roots, there must be more to the word than just the root. Added to the roots are *affixes,* which are made up of *prefixes* (word parts put at the beginning of the word) and *suffixes* (word parts put at the end of the word).

Among the most common Latin prefixes are the following:

PREFIX	MEANING	EXAMPLE
ab-, abs-	away, from	*abs*cond *ab*original
ad-, ac-	to, toward	*ac*cept *ad*verse
ante-	before	*ante*cedent
circum-	around	*circum*stance
com-, con-	with, together	*com*pare *con*trast
contra-	against	*contra*dict
de-	down, away, reversal	*de*prive *de*scent
in-	not	*in*justice
in-	in, into	*in*trude *in*flate
inter-	among, between	*inter*mural *inter*fere
mal-	bad, wrong, ill	*mal*adjustment *male*factor
non-	not	*non*entity *non*conformist
post-	after	*post*pone *post*mortem
re-	back, backward, again	*re*call *re*collect *re*member
trans-	across	*trans*mit *trans*ition

The following Greek prefixes are also common and important. Their most frequent use is in technical and scientific writing.

PREFIX	MEANING	EXAMPLE
a-, an-	without, not	*a*theist, *ag*nostic
anti-	opposite, against	*anti*climax *anta*gonist

PREFIX	MEANING	EXAMPLE
dia-	across, through, between	*dia*gonal *dia*gnosis
eu-	well, good	*eu*logize *eu*phemism
hyper-	over, alone, beyond	*hyper*active
hypo-	below, under, less	*hypo*crite
para-, par-	beside, alongside of	*para*medic
peri-	around, encircling	*peri*meter
pro-	before (in time and place)	*pro*logue
syn-, sym-	with, together, like	*syn*onym *sym*pathy

Suffixes

These Latin and Greek suffixes are attached at the end of the roots.

SUFFIX	MEANING	EXAMPLE
-able, -ible	having the quality, capacity, or fitness	educ*able* incorrig*ible*
-al	having character of, pertaining to	poetic*al* form*al*
-ance, -ence,	action, process, quality, or state of	mainten*ance* compet*ence*
-ary	belonging or pertaining to, a place for	volunt*ary* avi*ary*
-ation	act, doing, being	consider*ation* civiliz*ation*
-er, -or	process of, one who does something	supp*er* do*er* act*or*
-ful	full of, characterized by	spoon*ful* beauti*ful*
-fy	to make	intensi*fy* modi*fy*
-ion	act or state of	tradit*ion* persuas*ion*
-ism	act, state, doctrine, or characteristic of	commun*ism* capital*ism*
-ist	one who acts, believes, works, or is skilled in	typ*ist* de*ist* dent*ist*

SUFFIX	MEANING	EXAMPLE
-ity	quality, state, degree, condition	inferior*ity* personal*ity* qual*ity*
-ive	having the quality of	addict*ive* compuls*ive* affirmat*ive*
-ize	to subject to, to make, to practice	critic*ize* penal*ize*
-less	without	form*less* bottom*less*
-ment	a state of action or being	amuse*ment*

ASSIGNMENTS

A. The more complex our technological world becomes, the more we see people being shoved into categories. Vine Deloria, Jr., the gifted Indian writer, contends that American blacks and Indians have been seriously victimized by the meaningless categories, the "conceptual prisons" into which they have been thrown. He warns his readers, "One day you may find yourself catalogued—perhaps as a credit-card carrying, turnpike-commuting, condominium-dwelling, fraternity-joining, church-going, sports-watching, time-purchase-buying, television-watching, magazine-subscribing, politically inert, transmigrated urbanite."

In order to avoid meaningless classification in your own writing, you have to do more than simply divide a subject into different categories. Your categories won't mean anything unless your readers learn something from them. Write an essay of division and classification on one of the following topics and make sure that your classification has a useful purpose. Your purpose might be to inform, to persuade, or to amuse your reader.

DIFFERENT METHODS OF DOING SOMETHING

studying for a test	balancing a budget
losing weight	dealing with an irate customer
disciplining children	coaching athletes
finding a job	teaching a class
training an animal	making people laugh
saving money	treating an illness
designing a car	solving a problem
planning a vacation	reaching an audience
arriving at the truth	fighting poverty
getting a date	selling a product

DIFFERENT TYPES OF PEOPLE

doctors	teachers	leaders	nurses
salespeople	parents	followers	drivers
newscasters	humorists	coaches	smokers
athletes	bosses	writers	drinkers
politicians	policemen	speakers	Christmas shoppers
students	musicians	liars	kids

B. W.H. Auden pretends that the following satiric poem is written by a governmental functionary writing an obituary in praise of a state "hero." Notice how Auden divides and classifies his information about the citizen on the basis of his patriotism, his social conformity, his life as a consumer, and his personal philosophies. The admiration expressed in this poem is, of course, only a mock emotion. Write a division and classification essay of your own on what attributes Auden thought this "hero" really had or make up a satire of your own on some other typical character in today's society, such as a typical television viewer, a typical consumer, or a typical sports fan.

THE UNKNOWN CITIZEN

(To JS/07/M/378 This Marble Monument Is Erected by the State)

He was found by the Bureau of Statistics to be
One against whom there was no official complaint,
And all the reports on his conduct agree
That, in the modern sense of an old-fashioned word, he was a saint,
For in everything he did he served the Greater Community.
Except for the War till the day he retired
He worked in a factory and never got fired,
But satisfied his employers, Fudge Motors Inc.
Yet he wasn't a scab or odd in his views,
For his Union reports that he paid his dues,
(Our report on his Union shows it was sound)
And our Social Psychology workers found
That he was popular with his mates and liked a drink.
The Press are convinced that he bought a paper every day
And that his reactions to advertisements were normal in every way.
Policies taken out in his name prove that he was fully insured,
And his Health-card shows he was once in hospital but left it cured.
Both Producers Research and High-Grade Living declare
He was fully sensible to the advantages of the Installment Plan
And had everything necessary to the Modern Man,
A phonograph, a radio, a car and a frigidaire.

W.H. Auden

8

Establishing Cause and Effect

RHETORIC

Rudyard Kipling explained his success as a newspaper reporter with the following little jingle:

> I kept six honest serving men
> They taught me all I knew
> Their names are What and Where and When
> And How and Why and Who.

Rudyard Kipling

In the cause-and-effect essays that are discussed in this chapter, the principle servingman is *why*. Some methods of essay development use several of Kipling's servingmen, and narrative really uses all of them. Explaining a process, which was discussed in chapter 5, is concerned largely with *how*. But explaining cause-and-effect relationships requires answering the question *why*.

Have you ever noticed how often young children ask "Why"? They're trying to get a grasp on their world. Kipling said his little daughter asked him "Two million wheres and seven million whys." Understanding the causal relationship is of immense intellectual importance. Without understanding *why*, you'll not only fail to perceive the present, but you'll also lose control over the future.

Causal Analysis Works in Two Directions

Cause-and-effect analysis permits the author to go in two directions—from cause to effect or from effect to cause. For example, suppose Alice's car clanks to a halt along the road and will not start again. What, she wants to know, is the cause of this situation. A little analysis by a mechanic reveals that the car is totally out of oil and has been for some time. This, Alice realizes, is the cause of her engine burning up. Having found the cause of this effect, she can reason that she must not forget oil in the future. Even in the simplest examples such as this, you can easily see that there could be two directions: stating the effect and then seeking the cause or identifying the cause and projecting the effects.

As you analyze any but the simplest situations, you will probably find that one cause-and-effect relationship leads to another. For example, Lincoln Steffans once described the Adam and Eve story as a causal chain. God accused Adam of causing the expulsion from Eden; Adam said Eve was the cause; Eve denied it, putting the blame on the serpent; Steffans said the ultimate cause was probably the apple.

To be convincing in presenting your casual chain, you must be informed. How well informed you need to be will depend on the scope of your paper, but whether it is short or long, you will want to write from a background of unbiased and current information. Information that is prejudiced or out-of-date will not be convincing.

Necessary and Sufficient Cause

As you try to isolate the cause for a given effect, you will notice that there is seldom one cause but usually several or many. How then do you determine *the* cause? Logicians have given the answer: You must make sure that it is both a *necessary* and a *sufficient* cause. If A is a necessary cause of B, then B must always occur when A does. If

A does not exist, *B* will not occur. If *A* is a sufficient cause of *B*, *A* must be important enough to call *B* into existence. To be a sufficient cause, *A* must be significant enough to create *B*.

The basic definition of *the cause* is that it is the necessary and sufficient condition that produces an effect. But cause must be considered in two other ways. First, you must distinguish between sufficient cause and contributing cause. *Sufficient cause* can create the result all by itself; *contributing cause* is simply one of a number of causes, not important enough alone to create the result.

Second, you must distinguish between proximate cause and ultimate cause. *Proximate cause* is the most obvious cause—the attention-getter. For example, a picture falls from a wall because the picture hanger has pulled out of its enlarged hole. But the ultimate cause—the real reason, the cause of the obvious cause of the falling of the picture was the continual shaking of the walls by passing trucks, which cracked the plaster around the picture hanger. Although it is logically important to go beyond the proximate cause, there is a failure of logic in searching too far afield for the ultimate cause. You must be wary of tenuous, remote causes. For example, to say "The child wouldn't have gotten run over if he hadn't gone to his grandfather's for the summer" is to link a cause and effect that are light-years apart.

The Chain of Cause and Effect

To find a cause, you must follow a *chain* of causes and effects in which each link gives some understanding of *the* cause. If you were trying to determine the cause of a national economic depression, you could not logically blame it on one or even several causes, even if they did contribute to the bad times. You would probably find that one cause and effect led to another associated or linked cause, thus establishing a chain. Consider the following example of a causal chain borrowed from a famous historical event.

During the Crimean War, an absurd but heroic event occurred that shook all of England, and it is still remembered today through a poem by Lord Tennyson.

THE CHARGE OF THE LIGHT BRIGADE

Half a league, half a league,
Half a league onward,
All in the valley of Death

Rode the six hundred.
"Forward the Light Brigade!
Charge for the guns!" he said.
Into the valley of Death
   Rode the six hundred.
"Forward, the Light Brigade!"
Was there a man dismayed?
Not though the soldier knew
   Someone had blundered.
Theirs not to make reply,
Theirs not to reason why,
Theirs but to do and die.
Into the valley of Death
   Rode the six hundred.

                                      Alfred, Lord Tennyson

The chain of cause and effect reflected here is very complicated. A brigade of cavalrymen was ordered to "charge the guns,"
that is, to attack an artillery emplacement. They attacked the wrong
one, and after a half-hour's fighting, only 190 men were left alive of
600. Why did they attack the overwhelmingly powerful guns and
ignore the closer ones, which were vulnerable? All of Europe asked
why.

The proximate cause is easy enough. They thought they were
following orders, and soldiers follow orders. But the ultimate cause
is far more obscure. Decades went by before a historian, Cecil
Woodham-Smith, wrote the book *The Reason Why* in an attempt to
trace the causes that resulted in the heroic, idealistic absurdity of
that blundering charge. She found that one of the primary causes
was the jealous hatred between the two brothers-in-law who were
the brigade's commanding officers. This hatred also had many
causes. In addition, the whole system of recruiting officers for the
army was wrong; officers bought their commissions rather than
earning them. As a result, none of the upper-echelon officers had
any active experience, including the commander-in-chief. What's
more, the officers actually leading the charge were unable to see the
terrain because of hills and woods, so they could not understand the
commands coming down from the general on the hill above them,
who could see. Thus, a chain of cause and effect led to disaster.

ORGANIZATION

As in all other standard essays, the basic organization is introduction, body, and conclusion. The content may vary, not just in subject matter, but in technique; that is, you may use differing modes to present your cause and effect. Content may be either factual or a matter of opinion. And, of course, tone (your attitude) may differ. Overall, however, the basic organization remains essentially constant.

Your introduction may follow any of the forms suggested in chapter 1 or any idea of your own so long as it fulfills its twofold purpose of catching the reader's interest and leading to the thesis statement. The thesis statement, in addition to reflecting your subject and attitude, should indicate in which causal direction your ideas are going—from cause to effect or from effect to cause.

The body may follow almost any method of development. The only restrictions are that the body must provide clear, relevant support for your thesis statement and be consistently clear about whether you are finding causes or projecting effects.

The conclusion, as always, should reinforce the controlling idea of the thesis statement. The conclusion might well include a remedy or a warning, especially if the essay's intent is to project effects.

Sometimes Peanuts Are Unwelcome

RUSSELL BAKER

Russell Baker, an extremely popular satirist who writes a column called "Observer" for the New York Times, *usually bases his ideas on current happenings. As in the following example, a relatively unimportant news item sets him off on a flight of comic fancy that is more than fancy before he is finished:*

Introduction

Roy Gallant, writing in the magazine *Nature and Science*, urges people to quit smiling at chimpanzees. This is sensible advice. People who begin by smiling at chimpanzees sometimes wind up talking to bears.

Mr. Gallant's advice is based on studies conducted by Dr. Desmond Morris, curator of mammals at the London Zoo. When a chimpanzee sees two rows of human teeth, he is not amused, according to Dr. Morris, but angered and frightened, and bares his own teeth in return.

The person smiling at the chimp misinterprets the ape's response, assumes that the chimp is smiling back at him, and smiles harder, thus infuriating the chimp and starting him down the road to neurosis.

It is not surprising that the chimpanzee resents being smiled at all the time. One need only put oneself in the chimp's shoes to appreciate his resentment. It is no picnic sitting behind bars having peanuts thrown at you by smilers.

Thesis Statement

This raises some unpleasant questions about the whole smile tradition in this country from zoo to White House. The theory behind it has always been that if you smile, the world will smile with you. Politicians, who are the most indefatigable smilers, hold that a handsome set of incisors is more valuable than a brain for winning elections, and even the solemn professions like undertaking and nuclear science assume that the smile is sound business practice.

Specific effects of various types of smiles: win elections, sell products, disguise misery, encourage misunderstandings

The papers are full of smilers. A general tells Congress that the world's nuclear storehouse is now big enough to provide the equivalent of a 35-ton dynamite explosion for each individual on earth, and the illustrating picture shows him smiling.

Barry Goldwater declares that the country is going to ruin, and smiles and smiles. At less cosmic levels, everybody can recite ugly experiences associated with smiles. There is the smile of the dentist when he says, "This may hurt a little—" The smile of the banker declaring you a hopeless credit risk. And the smile of the TV repairman explaining that he will have to take the set back to the shop.

If incoming smiles too often mean misery, outgoing smiles are likely to mean trouble. Smile while walking through any public square in America, and the panhandlers attack in platoons. What man has not let his smile at some time or other come to rest on a lovely stranger across a crowded room, only to note her escort glaring back with undisguised malevolence?

Comparisons to show effect of rationing smiles

The British ration their smiles. When they use one, it is effective. No one has ever seen a picture of a British politician smiling, although they are always announcing that Britian is going to ruin. Of course, the British do have that odd habit of smiling at dogs, but this is probably sounder than the American habit of smiling back at politicians.

The French think that the smile is overdone in America and favor less ambiguous gestures. A Frenchman, for example, will not smile at your wife across a crowded room; he will walk across, dismiss you and ask her what she is doing tomorrow afternoon. French politicans also know better than to smile at the voters. One could no more picture President de Gaulle smiling than imagine a toastmaster calling him "Chuck."

Precisely when or why Americans adopted the smile as the

national facial expression is unclear. There are no portraits of George Washington, Jefferson or Jackson smiling, and the one photograph of a Lincoln smile is a tragedy. Yet nowadays the whole country, in Scott Fitzgerald's phrase, lives by the contorted pan.

> *Conclusion—Collective effect of smiling too much: debases the value of a smile*

The trouble is not so much that it is ridiculous to get elected on strong teeth, or look cheerful about "overkill," or act happy about charging some wretch $67.50 for TV repairs. The trouble is that the smile becomes debased in the process.

People who are constantly smiled at by generals who have 35 tons of dynamite earmarked for them or by TV repairmen planning to deplete their bank balance are apt to reconsider the value of the smile and agree with Shakespeare that "one may smile, and smile, and be a villain."

In extreme cases, these people may develop hallucinations about being behind bars with peanuts raining in on them. Sometimes they go mad with the urge to bite back when they see two exposed rows of human teeth.

The Great American Cooling Machine

FRANK TRIPPETT

Frank Trippett is a longtime journalist who has worked as a reporter, photographer, and editor in newspapers in the South and on such national magazines as Look, Newsweek, *and* Time. *This essay presents the importance of air conditioning in our lives and projects its effects on us as individuals and as a group.*

"The greatest contribution to civilization in this century may well be air conditioning—and America leads the way." So wrote British Scholar-Politician S.F. Markham 32 years ago when a modern cooling system was still an exotic luxury. In a century that has yielded such treasures as the electric knife, spray-on deodorant and disposable diapers, anybody might question whether air conditioning is the supreme gift. There is not a whiff of doubt, however, that America is far out front in its use. As a matter of lopsided fact, the U.S. today, with a mere 5% of the population, consumes as much man-made coolness as the whole rest of the world put together.

Just as amazing is the speed with which this situation came to be. Air conditioning began to spread in industries as a production aid during World War II. Yet only a generation ago a chilled sanctuary during summer's stewing heat was a happy frill that ordinary people sampled only in movie houses. Today most Americans tend to take air conditioning for granted in homes, offices, factories, stores, theaters, shops, studios, schools, hotels and restaurants. They travel in chilled buses, trains, planes and private cars. Sporting events once associated with open sky and fresh air are increasingly boxed in and air cooled. Skiing still takes place outdoors, but such attractions as tennis, rodeos, football and, alas, even baseball are now often staged in synthetic climates like those of Houston's Astrodome and New Orleans' Superdome. A great many of the country's farming tractors are now, yup, air-conditioned.

It is thus no exaggeration to say that Americans have taken to mechanical cooling avidly and greedily. Many have become all but addicted, refusing to go places that are not air-conditioned. In Atlanta, shoppers in Lenox Square so resented having to endure natural heat while walking outdoors from chilled store to chilled store that the mall management enclosed and air-conditioned the whole sprawling shebang. The widespread whining about Washington's raising of thermostats to a mandatory 78°F suggests that people no longer think of interior coolness as an amenity but consider it a necessity, almost a birthright, like suffrage. The existence of such a view was proved last month when a number of federal judges, sitting too high and mighty to suffer 78°, defied and denounced the Government's energy-saving order to cut back on cooling. Significantly, there was no popular outrage at this judicial insolence; many citizens probably wished that they could be so highhanded.

Everybody by now is aware that the cost of the American way is enormous, that air conditioning is an energy glutton. It uses some 9% of all electricity produced. Such an extravagance merely to provide comfort is peculiarly American and strikingly at odds with all the recent rhetoric about national sacrifice in a period of menacing energy shortages. Other modern industrial nations such as Japan, Germany and France have managed all along to thrive with mere fractions of the man-made coolness used in the U.S., and precious little of that in private dwellings. Here, so profligate has its use become that the air conditioner is almost as glaring a symptom as the automobile of the national tendency to overindulge in every technical possibility, to use every convenience to such excess that the country looks downright coddled.

But not everybody is aware that high cost and easy comfort are merely two of the effects of the vast cooling of America. In fact, air conditioning has substantially altered the country's character and folkways. With the dog days at hand and the thermostats ostensibly up, it is a good time to begin taking stock of what air conditioning has done besides lower the indoor temperature.

Many of its byproducts are so conspicious that they are scarcely noticed. To begin with, air conditioning transformed the face of urban America by making possible those glassy, boxy, sealed-in skyscrapers on which the once humane geometries of places like San Francisco, Boston, and Manhattan have been impaled. It has been indispensable, no less, to the functioning of sensitive advanced computers, whose high operating temperatures require that they be constantly cooled. Thus, in a very real way, air conditioning has made possible the ascendency of computerized civilization. Its cooling protection has given rise not only to moon landings, space shuttles and Skylabs but to the depersonalized punch-cardification of society that regularly gets people hot under the collar even in swelter-proof environments. It has also reshaped the national economy and redistributed political power simply by encouraging the burgeoning of the sultry southerly swatch of the country, profoundly influencing major migration trends of people and industry. Sunbelt cities like Phoenix, Atlanta, Dallas and Houston (where shivering indoor frigidity became a mark of status) could never have mushroomed so prosperously without air conditioning; some communities—Las Vegas in the Nevada desert and Lake Havasu City on the Arizona-California border—would shrivel and die overnight if it were turned off.

It has, as well, seduced families into retreating into houses with closed doors and shut windows, reducing the commonalty of neighborhood life and all but obsoleting the front-porch society whose open casual folkways were an appealing hallmark of a sweatier America. Is it really surprising that the public's often noted withdrawal into self-pursuit and privatism has coincided with the epic spread of air conditioning? Though science has little studied how habitual air conditioning affects mind or body, some medical experts suggest that, like other technical avoidance of natural swings in climate, air conditioning may take a toll on the human capacity to adapt to stress. If so, air conditioning is only like many other greatly useful technical developments that liberate man from nature by increasing his productivity and power in some ways—while subtly weakening him in others.

Neither scholars nor pop sociologists have really got around to charting and diagnosing all the changes brought about by air conditioning. Professional observers have for years been preoccupied with the social implications of the automobile and television. Mere glancing analysis suggests that the car and TV, in their most decisive influences on American habits, have been powerfuly aided and abetted by air conditioning. The car may have created all those shopping centers in the boondocks, but only air conditioning has made them attractive to mass clienteles. Similarly, the artificial cooling of the living room undoubtedly helped turn the typical American into a year-round TV addict. Without air conditioning, how many viewers would endure reruns (or even Johnny Carson) on one of those pestilential summer nights that used to send people out to collapse on the lawn or to sleep on the roof?

Many of the side effects of air conditioning are far from being fully pinned down. It is a reasonable suspicion, though, that controlled climate, by inducing Congress to stay in Washington longer than it used to during the swelter season, thus presumably passing more laws, has contributed to bloated Government. One can only speculate that the advent of the supercooled bedroom may be linked to the carnal adventurism associated with the mid-century sexual revolution. Surely it is a fact—if restaurant complaints about raised thermostats are to be believed—that air conditioning induces at least expense-account diners to eat and drink more; if so, it must be credited with adding to the national fat problem.

Perhaps only a sophist might be tempted to tie the spread of air conditioning to the coincidentally rising divorce rate, but every attentive realist must have noticed that even a little window unit can instigate domestic tension and chronic bickering between couples composed of one who likes it on all the time and another who does not. In fact, perhaps surprisingly, not everybody likes air conditioning. The necessarily sealed rooms or buildings make some feel claustrophobic, cut off from the real world. The rush, whir and clatter of cooling units annoys others. There are even a few eccentrics who object to man-made cool simply because they like hot weather. Still, the overwhelming majority of Americans have taken to air conditioning like hogs to a wet wallow.

It might be tempting, and even fair, to chastise that vast majority for being spoiled rotten in their cool ascendancy. It would be more just, however, to observe that their great cooling machine carries with it a perpetual price tag that is going to provide continued and increasing chastisement during the energy crisis. Ultimately, the air conditioner, and the hermetic buildings it requires, may turn out to be a more pertinent technical symbol of the American personality than the car. While the car has been a fine sign of the American impulse to dart hither and yon about the world, the mechanical cooler more neatly suggests the maturing national compulsion to flee the natural world in favor of a technological cocoon.

Already architectural designers are toiling to find ways out of the technical trap represented by sealed buildings with immovable glass, ways that might let in some of the naturally cool air outside. Some have lately come up with a remarkable discovery: the openable window. Presumably, that represents progress.

How Does the Author Make His Point?

1. Why does the author open with a quotation that he obviously disagrees with? What about the title?
2. Starting with paragraph 5, trace the chain of effects from the proximate effects (high cost and easy comfort) to a series of subordinate effects, some of which have their *own* effects.
3. What is the author's tone? (You can probably get this immediately by reading the introduction and the conclusion, but find some examples from the body of the essay, too.)
4. What effect is the author trying for when he uses such nonwords as "yup" (in paragraph 2) and punch-cardification (in paragraph 6)?
5. What is the author's main point?

What Do You Think?

1. Do you think Trippett exaggerates the effects of air conditioning? If so, cite some examples where you see exaggeration. Does it really make us fat? (Is this a proximate or a subordinate effect?)
2. Do you agree that man's greatest inventions help him in some ways and weaken him in others? (See the last line in paragraph 7.) Cite some examples.
3. Do you think the air conditioner is a "more pertinent technical symbol of the American personality than the car"? Why or why not?

The Deadly Degrading Sport

Maurice W. Van Allen, M.D.

In the following editorial from the Journal of the American Medical Association, *Dr. Maurice W. Van Allen constructs a powerful argument against boxing through the skillfull use of cause-and-effect reasoning:*

How strange that, in this climate of preoccupation with health and physical fitness and with near-hysterical concern for every conceivable deleterious factor in the environment, so few raise their voices against boxing. How strange, when strident voices urge equality for all and promote and make capital of support for equal rights, that poor and minority youth are recruited and rewarded for sacrificing themselves to a spectacle for the more favored or whatever ethnic or fiscal group.

What factors contribute to this continued public spectacle of brutality and the literal sacrifice of minority youth for the profit and delectation of self-styled sportsmen?

In fairness to the boxing game and its proponents, let us review the widely shared ignorance about the effects of trauma on the brain and the implications of being knocked unconscious.

Head injury from falls and blows is a common incident in the animated cartoons of children's shows. The hero or villain, whether animal or human, is often momentarily stopped in his action by a blow to the head—the circumstances are entertaining, and the victim quickly recovers and is as fast and effective as before. This may happen repeatedly to the same character with no harmful effect. Children can grow up with the belief that head injury is amusing, recoverable, and of little consequence. Novels and television shows bludgeon their private eyes, heroes, and villains with never a suggestion of post-traumatic symptoms lasting more than a few minutes.

The football player who is stunned or senseless has had his "bell rung" or is "shaken up on the play." That he can walk off the field with help or even reenter the game is ample evidence of the triviality of the incident and its apparent short-lived consequences. No matter that memory of the incident may be lost and confusion be present for several days afterward. The sports commentators, whose own fortunes are invested heavily in the game, never allude to and are probably only vaguely aware of the implications of these brain injuries—hence, their prattle of euphemisms to cover only vague discomfort.

With this kind of folklore about brain injury, small wonder that those who enjoy and profit from regulated brawling and violence easily convince themselves that little harm is done in boxing. The "punch-drunk" fighter is an amusing oddity, seldom the object of pity and not, it seems, a catalyst of guilt.

The fight game provides an opportunity for ambitious youths to climb from scandalous social circumstances through a disgraceful "sports" opportunity to some kind of fame or hero status. We are told this in different terms by those who justify boxing and who find the bashing of others to be financially and emotionally rewarding.

In boxing, we are reassured by the concern of the announcers for facial cuts and by the referee, who will stop a fight when superficial hemorrhage may obscure the fighter's vision, or perhaps offend some in the audience and remind them of their involvement in the guilt of promoting a vicious and deadly game. At the end, some functionary will appear in formal evening attire to announce the winners. His ruffled shirt and black tie attest to the dignity of the proceedings and to the gentlemanly way in which they are conducted.

Perhaps you will say that, with human nature as it is, some important societal needs are served by this vicarious outlet of violence for the viciousness hidden in all of us and that a good fight by others relieves tensions and lubricates communal living. Others, in defending the recruitment of children to the fight game, will point to the advantages of the discipline that comes from preparation for fighting and to the moral benefits of fighting within a set of rules. They will emphasize the opportunity for the otherwise hopeless to achieve fame, no matter what the price to the brains of the unsuccessful and successful alike. No matter the basic degradation of those who fight for the entertainment of others even when victorious. The owners and managers of a "stable" of fighters recall those who solved the energy crisis created by the cotton gin.

We are assured by the television networks responsible for bringing us a boxing spectacle that an ambulance will be available throughout the bout, and of course that physcians are present at ringside—a flattering faith in the ability of modern medicine to repair irreversible damage to the nervous system. We are not so reassurred when clearly mismatched fighters are paired in the ring, and one game but less-talented gladiator is finally unmercifully beaten while the referee, for reasons of his own, allows a bout to proceed when the outcome is clear to all. The physical and mental consequences are smothered in euphemisms and suppressed by announcers, promoters, and audience.

We are reassured again, when we reflect on the respectability given to the sport by the Olympic Committee, since these self-appointed guardians of sportsman's virtues endorse fighting (under careful jurisdiction), suggesting that well-regulated sin is perhaps not very sinful after all.

Heroes usually arise from sacrifice, often in hazardous circumstances and at high cost. The high cost that is paid by the fighters in boxing is buried in emotional bookkeeping.

When a human or animal is struck on the head so that consciousness is lost, pathological changes—minute or larger hemorrhages; contusions often at the base, and tearing of nerve fibers that may not be easily identified—are all consequences of a blunt blow of sufficient force to render the subject unconscious. Detectable symptoms of a beating may not be apparent to a victim preoccupied by the pursuit that caused the injury but have been admitted by the more introspective who go on to other occupations.

The accumulative destructive effects of repeated blows, even when consciousness and posture are not lost, are well known and accepted.

Is now not the time to suppress exposure of this fragment of our savagery by the mass media and leave boxing to those who enjoy privately staged dogfights?

How Does the Author Make His Point?

1. How does the author attract your attention in the introduction?
2. What is the effect of seeing specific examples of "folklore about brain injury" at the beginning of the essay (paragraph 4 and 5)?

3. What is the effect of not seeing the medical facts about blows to the head until the *end* of the essay (paragraphs 13 and 14?)
4. Why is the author's concluding sentence effective?

What Do You Think?

1. Do you agree that most people are unaware of the real dangers of brain injuries, or do you think that many people are aware of the dangers but choose to ignore them?
2. Do you feel that the harmful moral and emotional effects of boxing that the author refers to are just as dangerous as the harmful physical effects?
3. How has this essay affected your perception of the function of the boxing referee in his "ruffled shirt and black tie"?
4. How might your response to this essay have differed if it had been written by someone other than an experienced physician?
5. What, in your opinion, is the most important point that the author is making in this essay?

From On Boxing

Joyce Carol Oates

Joyce Carol Oates, a highly regarded contemporary critic and writer of fiction, presents a little essay taken from her book about boxing, which she describes as "a mosaic of essays."

Why are you a boxer, Irish featherweight champion Barry McGuigan was asked. He said: "I can't be a poet. I can't tell stories. . . ."

Each boxing match is a story—a unique and highly condensed drama without words. Even when nothing sensational happens: then the drama is "merely" psychological. Boxers are there to establish an absolute experience, a public accounting of the outermost limits of their beings; they will know, as few of us can know of ourselves, what physical and psychic power they possess—of how much, or how little, they are capable. To enter the ring near-naked and to risk one's life is to make of one's audience voyeurs of a kind: boxing is so intimate. It is to ease out of sanity's consciousness and into another, difficult to name. It is to risk, and sometimes to realize, the agony of which *agon* (Greek, "contest") is the root.

In the boxing ring there are two principal players, overseen by a shadowy third. The ceremonial ringing of the bell is a summoning to full wakefulness for both boxers and spectators. It sets into motion, too, the authority of Time.

The boxers will bring to the fight everything that is themselves, and everything will be exposed—including secrets about themselves they cannot fully realize. The physical self, the maleness, one might say, underlying the "self." There are boxers possessed of such remarkable intuition, such uncanny prescience, one would think they were somehow recalling their fights, not fighting them as we watch. There are boxers who perform skillfully, but mechanically, who cannot improvise in response to another's alteration of strategy; . . . there are boxers performing at the peak of their talent who come to realize, mid-fight, that it will not be enough; there are boxers—including great champions—whose careers end abruptly, and irrevocably, as we watch. There has been at least one boxer possessed of an extraordinary and disquieting awareness not only of his opponent's every move and anticipated move but of the audience's keenest shifts in mood as well, for which he seems to have felt personally responsible—Cassius Clay/Muhammad Ali, of course. "The Sweet Science of Bruising" celebrates the physicality of men even as it dramatizes the limitations, sometimes tragic, more often poignant, of the physical. Though male spectators identify with boxers no boxer behaves like a "normal" man when he is in the ring and no combination of blows is "natural." All is style.

Every talent must unfold itself in fighting. So Nietzsche speaks of the Hellenic past, the history of the "contest"—athletic, and otherwise—by which Greek youths were educated into Greek citizenry. Without the ferocity of competition, without, even, "envy, jealousy, and ambition" in the contest, the Hellenic city, like the Hellenic man, degenerated. If death is a risk, death is also the prize—for the winning athlete.

In the boxing ring, even in our greatly humanized times, death is always a possibility—which is why some of us prefer to watch films or tapes of fights already past, already defined as history. Or, in some instances, art. (Though to prepare for writing this mosaic-like essay I saw tapes of two infamous "death" fights of recent times: the Lupe Pintor–Johnny Owen bantamweight match of 1982, and the Ray Mancini–Duk Koo-Kim lightweight match of the same year. In both instances the boxers died as a consequence of their astonishing resilience and apparent indefatigability—their "heart," as it's known in boxing circles.) Most of the time, however, death in the ring is extremely unlikely; a statistically rare possibility like your possible death tomorrow morning in an automobile accident or in next month's headlined airline disaster or in a freak accident involving a fall on the stairs or in the bathtub, a skull fracture, subarachnoid hemorrhage. Spectators at "death" fights often claim afterward that what happened simply seemed to happen—unpredictably, in a sense accidentally. Only in retrospect does death appear to have been inevitable.

If a boxing match is a story it is an always wayward story,

one in which anything can happen. And in a matter of seconds. Split seconds! (Muhammad Ali boasted that he could throw a punch faster than the eye could follow, and he may have been right.) In no other sport can so much take place in so brief a period of time, and so irrevocably.

Because a boxing match is a story without words, this doesn't mean that it has no text or no language, that it is somehow "brute," "primitive," "inarticulate," only that the text is improvised in action; the language a dialogue between the boxers of the most refined sort (one might say, as much neurological as psychological: a dialogue of split-second reflexes) in a joint response to the mysterious will of the audience which is always that the fight be a worthy one so that the crude paraphernalia of the setting—ring, lights, ropes, stained canvas, the staring onlookers themselves—be erased, forgotten. (As in the theater or the church, settings are erased by way, ideally, of transcendent action.) Ringside announcers give to the wordless spectacle a narrative unity, yet boxing as performance is more clearly akin to dance or music than narrative.

To turn from an ordinary preliminary match to a "Fight of the Century" like those between Joe Louis and Billy Conn, Joe Frazier and Muhammad Ali, Marvin Hagler and Thomas Hearns is to turn from listening or half-listening to a guitar being idly plucked to hearing Bach's *Well-Tempered Clavier* perfectly executed, and that too is part of the story's mystery: so much happens so swiftly and with such heart-stopping subtlety you cannot absorb it except to know that something profound is happening and it is happening in a place beyond words.

How Does the Author Make Her Point?

1. How appropriate is the little anecdote (the Barry McGuigan conversation) which Oates uses to introduce this essay?
2. Why do you think the author uses such sexually loaded words as "near-naked," "voyeurs," and "intimate" in the first paragraph? Can you find other examples of such suggestive words in the essay?
3. In paragraph 3, the author talks about different types of boxers. Is it a good division and classification? (Check chaper 7.) Why or why not?
4. To what other arts does the author compare boxing? Why do you think she does this? In which comparison is she most effective? Explain your answer.

What Do You Think?

1. Why do you think people box or go to boxing matches?
2. What fascination does boxing have even for essentially gentle people, those who wouldn't hurt anyone if they could help it? Why do women seem to be more bloodthirsty than men?
3. In another part of her book, Oates says, "If boxing is a sport, it is the most tragic of all sports?" What do you think she means by this? Do you agree? Why or why not?
4. How do you feel about boxing? Is it a "deadly degrading sport" or is it "something profound" as Oates describes it in her conclusion?
5. Why do you think the author includes a long paragraph on death in the ring (paragraph 5)?

Toward an Understanding of Accidental Knots

WILLIAM ALLEN

William Allen was born in Texas, went to undergraduate school in California, attended graduate school in Iowa, and teaches in Ohio; yet he considers himself a regional writer! He teaches creative writing and writes essays, short stories, and novels. In the following essay, he shows his talent in humor as he describes something that must have baffled all of us at one time or another—perhaps at Christmas when we tried to untangle the strings of lights we had packed so carefully the previous January:

One night a few weeks ago my birdbath caught on fire, and when I ran with what I thought was a neatly coiled hose to put out the blaze, I was yanked up hopelessly short. I looked back and the hose had six knots in it. All those knots appearing just like that seemed impossible, to say nothing of unjust, and it set off something in me that had been brewing for a long time. It made me decide that I was going to unravel forever the mystery surrounding what amounts to half a lifetime of accidental knots.

As a child I thought that any knots in my life must somehow be my fault. Back then I also noticed that knots I wanted tied often wouldn't stay tied—or they turned into knots totally unsuited to my purpose. Later, though I stopped taking the blame for knots, I still hadn't learned how they worked, the way I was sure other people had. Every time I found a knot where I didn't think there should be one, it troubled me. My phone cord has always been in a snarl—I'm used to that—but when it knotted around the stem of my empty wineglass during the night, I needed to know why. Before I died, I wanted to know why the once straight cord to the toaster on my kitchen counter became so knotted that it pulled the appliance up under the cupboard where it was useless, and finally one day caused the toaster to blow up.

I had always assumed a knot required that the end of something be free to go through a loop and then get pulled tight. This assumption was based on the way I had tied knots; but if I was correct, my problem with knots shouldn't exist. If you hold kite string at one end and tie it to a kite at the other, those enormous, hopeless clumps should never develop—especially if the carefully tied knots in the tail are always going to fall loose.

If this seems like a minor issue, let me say that almost everyone I have asked about knots agrees that they are mysterious and need to be better understood. These people also say that my initial conception of a knot ought to be right.

Now, I'm sure that somewhere, in some obscure treatise on some remote library shelf, the answer lies waiting. Sailors and mountain climbers and window washers—or anyone else who depends on the control of knots—certainly must know more than the average person. The cowboys who continually fool with their ropes in movies and rodeos must do so with understanding and purpose. Rope designers and ropemakers must know almost everything about knots. But the information has never reached me—and apparently never reached a good many other people as well. What I am about to tell you, then, I have learned on my own.

First, I bought ten feet of common manila rope, tossed it on the middle of the floor, and just watched it for a while. It didn't move, which didn't surprise me, so I left it there overnight.

Next morning I realized that, even though the rope hadn't moved, it looked tangled. I picked up the tangle and, sure enough, it didn't snake out into my ten-foot length of straight manila rope, the way it should have. It came up in a clump. I tried to shake loose the clump, then pulled on the ends to free it, but this only made it worse. What I had was a tightly tangled mess that required considerable effort to undo.

The rope hadn't been tangled when I bought it, or before I tossed it to the floor, but somehow the *act of tossing* had caused it to converge on itself. It had happened right in front of me, but I hadn't observed it until the next day—which made me aware that, so far, I was bringing an untrained eye to my task.

It became clear that the act of moving the rope in the slightest way tended to cause it to knot. But why? I inspected it more closely. It consisted of three smaller pieces of rope tightly twisted around each other, all with little clinging hemp burrs sticking out of them. Each of the three pieces was made of long, single strands of hemp twisted around each other. When I took it apart, it wanted to kink back up—as if the rope depended on knottiness to exist.

I noticed that if I tossed the rope in the air, freeing it from the force of gravity for a moment, the rope's inherent forces came into play. All the twisting that had gone into the making of the rope had created internal dynamics which made it seek to converge on itself, to continue to twine around itself—most obviously in the form of loops. And a few loops could form a support for yet more rope to gather and wrap around itself. Any collective movement of the rope—any pulling, for instance—made the loops smaller and tangles tighter. Eventually all this movement was likely to result in a real knot. The bend of a loop, if tight enough, could constitute that free end I originally felt necessary to the creation of a knot.

So now I postulated: *Given the opportunity, a length of something with an end or a substitute end will, in general, tangle rather than stay straight.*

But this only formulated the mystery, it didn't solve it. I recently ordered a martini with a twist and noticed that the lemon peel was unusually long, looking like a little yellow snake in my gin. Before the drink was gone, that twist had turned itself into a knot. At this moment, the cord to my desk lamp has a knot in it. (Some people would have plugged it in like that, of course, but I never would.) A couple of years ago I went to great lengths to make sure that the cords running to my new stereo speakers were straight. Now they're snarled and knotted to the point where the little wires inside are broken, causing static when I walk across the living room floor, and then I've got that problem with the vacuum cleaner cord.

When I vacuum the rug, it would be difficult for me consciously to make a knot in the cord, assuming that it was connected to both the wall and the cleaner. I think I would have to pick up my large Eureka upright and put it through an even larger, preformed loop in the cord. But lately I have watched the cord as I vacuum. It goes back and forth, twists this way and that, is constantly being turned—creating tension and a tendency to twine around itself. Then—and this was somehow a surprise to me in its obviousness—I *unplug the cord* in order to move from room to room. For long moments, there is a loose end—sometimes jerked and flying through the air if I'm tired or in a hurry—and with the tension on the cord being what it is, a knot sooner or later will occur.

It all makes sense, more or less.

The accidental knotting of my garden hose, however, remains unexplained. I have watched it for some time and can only theorize how a hundred feet of stiff rubber tubing can so easily develop knots. When I discovered those six knots, I thought back and realized that the hose hadn't been moved for over a year, during which time it had, I assumed, been lying in a state of unsnarled rest. The tension from the act of looping those coils the year before, and the tautness resulting from my race to the birdbath, could certainly explain some snarling, but six knots? The unlikelihood of it has caused me to look in other directions.

I live in the country, and quite a few animals come around that hose at night, drinking from a crock I leave there which is filled by a very slow leak at the point where the hose connects to the faucet. Dogs and cats and raccoons and opossums and who knows what else probably touch the hose from time to time, and just a nudge could activate the tension already in the rubber. Also, the weather could have any variety of effects. High winds and driving rains and accumulations of snow could move the hose from its natural inert state. The change in temperature could cause expansion and contraction—in other words, movement—to occur.

The grass and weeds growing under the hose, the erosion of dirt caused by the leaky faucet, the aging process of the rubber . . . all of these things could combine to make a knot or two while I lie in bed asleep.

But six? It's hard to believe. Possibly other forces, difficult to understand but in keeping with the laws of the universe, have contributed—such as the changing gravitational pull of the moon, or maybe a preceding configuration of the larger planets. But the laws themselves are snarled. We are told both that the universe is expanding and that the natural tendency of all matter is to converge, to pull in upon itself. I have read—and this is disputed—that our solar system originally formed from condensing hydrogen plasma which pulled in on itself and hardened into chunks that became planets and moons that are now locked into orbits about our sun, which is constantly trying to tug them into its fiery gases.

I've always assumed, as Newton did, that these matters had to do with gravity, but cosmologists say they have to do with something called "degree of curvature," and that the quintessence of curvature—don't ask me how—results in the mysterious black holes. Some say that the universe is in the shape of a saddle, except that it has a fourth dimension which perhaps keeps us from being able to see its tendency toward clumping. Other theorists see the universe as having the shape of a figure eight—

which we all know is just a yank away from a tangle or a snarl. Whether the universe is going to tie itself into a knot is still in dispute. The argument has to do with the need for a free end, which the universe supposedly doesn't have, but I personally think it might have a tightly bent loop somewhere, which could amount to the same thing.

Some or perhaps all of the forces in the universe may have contributed to the six knots that defeated me the night I ran to put out the fire in the birdbath. I just don't know. The problem is baffling. Despite all my research—or perhaps because of it—the number of knots in that length of rubber hose makes me want to consider the possibility that they occurred not by accident at all but by design.

How Does the Author Make His Point?

1. Why is the first paragraph effective? Does it follow the "rules" for an introduction given in chapter 1?
2. What was the author's original assumption about knots? What discoveries did he make that disprove this assumption?
3. Where does the introduction end and the body of the essay begin?
4. What does Allen's first experiment teach him?
5. What method does Allen use to develop his essay? Is this effective? Why or why not?
6. What is the purpose of the author's bringing in cosmic research in paragraphs 18 and 19? How does this link with his garden hose?

What Do You Think?

1. What is your explanation of the six knots in the narrator's hose?
2. Cite examples of other everyday occurrences that seem to defy explanation.
3. Is the purpose of this essay entirely to entertain? Does it raise any serious issues?

Cipher in the Snow

JEAN E. MIZER

Jean E. Mizer was a schoolteacher, and this essay reflects a personal experience that she had. Perhaps this is what makes it so terrifying.

It started with tragedy on a biting cold February morning. I was driving behind the Milford Corners bus as I did most snowy mornings on my way to school. It veered and stopped short at the hotel, which it had no business doing, and I was annoyed as I had to come to an unexpected stop. A boy lurched out of the bus, reeled, stumbled, and collapsed on the snowbank at the curb. The bus driver and I reached him at the same moment. His thin, hollow face was white even against the snow.

"He's dead," the driver whispered.

It didn't register for a minute. I glanced quickly at the scared young faces staring down at us from the school bus. "A doctor! Quick! I'll phone from the hotel. . . ."

"No use. I tell you he's dead." The driver looked down at the boy's still form. "He never even said he felt bad," he muttered, "just tapped me on the shoulder and said, real quiet, 'I'm sorry. I have to get off at the hotel.' That's all. Polite and apologizing like."

At school, the giggling, shuffling morning noise quieted as the news went down the halls. I passed a huddle of girls. "Who was it? Who dropped dead on the way to school?" I heard one of them half-whisper.

"Don't know his name; some kid from Milford Corners," was the reply.

It was like that in the faculty room and the principal's office. "I'd appreciate your going out to tell the parents," the principal told me. "They haven't a phone and, anyway, somebody from school should go there in person. I'll cover your classes."

"Why me?" I asked. "Wouldn't it be better if you did it?"

"I didn't know the boy," the principal admitted levelly. "And in last year's sophomore personalities column I note that you were listed as his favorite teacher."

I drove through the snow and cold down the bad canyon road to the Evans place and thought about the boy, Cliff Evans. His favorite teacher! I thought. He hasn't spoken two words to me in two years! I could see him in my mind's eye all right, sitting back there in the last seat in my afternoon literature class. He came in the room by himself and left by himself. "Cliff Evans," I muttered to myself, "a boy who never talked." I thought a minute. "A boy who never smiled. I never saw him smile once."

The big ranch kitchen was clean and warm. I blurted out my news somehow. Mrs. Evans reached blindly toward a chair. "He never said anything about bein' ailing."

His step-father snorted. "He ain't said nothin' about anything since I moved in here."

Mrs. Evans pushed a pan to the back of the stove and began to untie her apron. "Now hold on," her husband snapped. "I got to have breakfast before I go to town. Nothin' we can do now anyway. If Cliff hadn't been so dumb, he'd have told us he didn't feel good."

After school I sat in the office and stared bleakly at the records spread out before me. I was to close the file and write the obituary for the school paper. The almost bare sheets mocked the effort. Cliff Evans, white, never legally adopted by step-father, five young half-brothers and sisters. These meager strands of information and the list of D grades were all the records had to offer.

Cliff Evans had silently come in the school door in the mornings and gone out the school door in the evenings, and that was all. He had never belonged to a club. He had never played on a team. He had never held an office. As far as I could tell, he had never done one happy, noisy kid thing. He had never been anybody at all.

How do you go about making a boy into a zero? The grade school records showed me. The first and second grade teachers' annotations read "sweet, shy child"; "timid but eager." Then the third grade note had opened the attack. Some teacher had written in a good, firm hand, "Cliff won't talk. Uncooperative. Slow learner." The other academic sheep had followed with "dull"; "slow-witted"; "low I.Q." They became correct. The boy's I.Q. score in the ninth grade was listed at 83. But his I.Q. in the third grade had been 106. The score didn't go under 100 until the seventh grade. Even shy, timid, sweet children have resilience. It takes time to break them.

I stomped to the typewriter and wrote a savage report

pointing out what education had done to Cliff Evans. I slapped a copy on the principal's desk and another in the sad, dog-eared file. I banged the typewriter and slammed the file and crashed the door shut, but I didn't feel much better. A little boy kept walking after me, a little boy with a peaked, pale face; a skinny body in faded jeans; and big eyes that had looked and searched for a long time and then had become veiled.

I could guess how many times he'd been chosen last to play sides in a game, how many whispered child conversations had excluded him, how many times he hadn't been asked. I could see and hear the faces and voices that said over and over, "You're dumb. You're dumb. You're nothing, Cliff Evans."

A child is a believing creature. Cliff undoubtedly believed them. Suddenly it seemed clear to me: When finally there was nothing left at all for Cliff Evans, he collapsed on a snowbank and went away. The doctor might list "heart failure" as the cause of death, but that wouldn't change my mind.

We couldn't find ten students in the school who had known Cliff well enough to attend the funeral as his friends. So the student body officers and a committee from the junior class went as a group to the church, being politely sad. I attended the services with them, and sat through it with a lump of cold lead in my chest and a big resolve growing through me.

I've never forgotten Cliff Evans nor that resolve. He has been my challenge year after year, class after class. I look up and down the rows carefully each September at the unfamiliar faces. I look for veiled eyes or bodies scrounged into a seat in an alien world. "Look, kids," I say silently, "I may not do anything else for you this year, but not one of you is going to come out of here a nobody. I'll work or fight to the bitter end doing battle with society and the school board, but I won't have one of you coming out of here thinking himself into a zero."

Most of the time—not always, but most of the time—I've succeeded.

How Does the Author Make Her Point?

1. Why does Mizer open with Cliff Evans's death rather than telling the story in chronological order?

2. What do you learn about Cliff in the first paragraph?
3. What do you learn about Cliff's parents in the author's brief account of what happened in their home?
4. Whom does the author blame for what happened to Cliff Evans? What did happen to him? What, according to the author, caused his death?
5. How effective is the title? Could you write a better one?

What Do You Think?

1 Do things like this really happen in schools today? Can you think of any examples?
2. Can I.Q.'s really change as a result of other people's actions?
3. Can anything be done to ensure that nothing like what happened to Cliff Evans ever happens again?

Why I Lost Ho-Hum

LOLA KARNES (student)

This student skillfully uses specifically detailed causes to account for her changed attitude, the effect, of Comp. I, the cause.

My "ho-hum" attitude toward English Comp was quickly changed as the weeks of class unfolded. I had been writing paragraphs in business letters, civic and church organization reports, and letters to friends and family for more than twenty years. What could a class on writing paragraphs have to say to me? It became apparent with the first assignment that there was much to be learned and much to be enjoyed. Each week I was challenged to search my mind and emotions and relate personal experiences. New words were found and old words "came alive" and had new meaning. I no longer walked—I strutted, danced, staggered, pranced, ambled, and bounced. My dictionary became my much used friend. I learned new techniques of putting thoughts into words and was reminded of techniques I had been taught many years before. Conveying my thoughts in such a manner so as to be precisely understood became important to me. I could identify mistakes I had been making in my writing and was taught how to avoid them. Writing was fun, but in no way an effortless, boring experience. Organization, transition, sentence structure, wordiness, clichés, clarity, and simplicity were only a few of the characteristics I had to consider to achieve coherence and meaning in my paragraphs. Thought and effort had to be given to each assignment. Beyond the skills of writing, the grammar, and the fun with words, my mind was provoked to "think" about what I was writing and my instinctive thirst for knowledge was being satisfied. Whatever I had expected from English Comp, I certainly received much more. I now have a new awareness of writing and, when challenged to express myself on paper, will never say "ho-hum."

How Does the Author Make Her Point?

1. Written for a class in paragraph writing, this essay is in single-paragraph form rather than the multiparagraph form discussed in this

book. Analyze the structure of this single paragraph as compared with a multiparagraph essay.

2. In the topic sentence, why does the author use the term *ho-hum* instead of the more usual term *bored*?

3. What method of development does she use? Is it effective?

What Do You Think?

1. Does the writer cover most of the points studied in a first class in composition?

2. Are students usually aware of the value of what they learn?Do they sometimes evaluate classes better after five years—or ten?

INTEGRATING READING WITH WRITING SKILLS: RECOGNIZING CAUSE-AND-EFFECT RELATIONSHIPS

Recognizing cause-and-effect relationships is probably one of the first intellectual skills you learned as a child. Even as an infant, you probably quickly learned the cause-and-effect relationship between crying and getting attention. You discovered that crying produced positive results, largely because of the other cause-and-effect assumption made by your parents—the baby is crying because he needs something; therefore, if I seek out the cause of his tears and satisfy his needs, he will stop crying. By simply observing human behavior, you learn to recognize hundreds of cause-and-effect relationships. When you learned to read, your ability to recognize causes and effects became a fundamental part of reading comprehension.

There are three levels of reading comprehension: literal comprehension, critical comprehension, and affective comprehension. *Literal comprehension* includes the basic skills required for everyday reading. These include identifying main ideas and subordinate ideas, understanding logical sequence, and recognizing cause-and-effect relationships. Certain words are clues that a cause-and-effect relationship will follow (*why, reason, cause, result, consequence, effect*). Likewise, some transitional markers also indicate cause and effect (*so, because, since, thus, therefore, consequently, as a consequence, as a result*). *Critical comprehension* involves more subtle skills such as distinguishing between fact and opinion, recognizing bias and objectivity, and discovering slanted or loaded words. *Affective comprehension* demands even more subtle recognition to identify the writer's tone as evidenced in his use of straightforward statement, irony, satire, or ridicule.

Although cause-and-effect relationships are relatively simple in theory, in the hands of a good writer they can be both sophisticated and complex. Thomas Sowell's essay, "Crime and Punishment," begins with an effect, that is, that our legal system, relating to crime, does not work. Sowell attributes this to one generalized cause which, in turn, is supported by a series of specific cause-and-effect relationships. Read the essay analytically so that you can identify the overall cause and effect and find at least five supporting causal relationships.

EXERCISE
CRIME AND PUNISHMENT

Controversy has been raging for a long time between those who favor a "soft" approach and those who favor a "hard" approach to punishing criminals. But much of what actually happens in the legal system combines the worst features of both approaches.

The basic problem is that the law hands out penalties in installments. The first installment is likely to be turning the criminal loose after some sociological mumbo jumbo about "rehabilitation" or (the other magic word) "community" release. The young offender, especially, is likely to get the idea that the law is a paper tiger that can be defied and mocked. As he continues down the same road, the law slowly begins to act, sometimes only after many arrests and convictions.

But just as the law is slow to start punishing, it is slow to stop. Installments keep coming long after the criminal has stopped raising hell and may be trying to settle down to raise a family. A prison record dogs him wherever he goes, cutting off his opportunities, making him a social pariah and generally painting him into a corner. Would it not have been more humane, as well as more effective, to have given the young offender a quick rap across the knuckles, to let him know the law means business?

The ever more elaborate "rights" and "due process" which encircle the criminal have been criticized as unfair to the victim or to society. They may also be unfair to the criminal, especially the young offender who is repeatedly misled into believing that the law has no real teeth. By the time those teeth are finally sunk into him, it may be too late for his victims.

The soft-liners and the hard-liners both contribute to this tragic situation. The soft-liners dress up their indecision and cop-outs as deeper insight into the social causes of crime. Being poor, under-privileged, and discriminated against are supposed to cause crime. But in the midst of the worst depression in history, people in the tenements of Harlem could go sleep out in the park on hot summer nights. Today nobody would dare do that, even in affluent and over-privileged neighborhoods. Armed guards in public schools are another phenomenon of our affluent—and vacillating—times.

The hard-liners contribute to the problem by refusing to do anything about impossible prison conditions. Even a judge who has both feet on the ground and has the guts to enforce the law is going to hesitate to send a young man with a minor offense to an overcrowded prison snakepit, where he is likely to be terrorized and gang-raped.

It will cost hard cash to maintain enough prison capacity to eliminate overcrowding and the breakdown of internal prison disci-pline that goes with it. It will cost tax dollars to hire the quantity and quality of guards needed to put the prison population under control of the authorities instead of under the prison terrorists.

This isn't coddling criminals. This is protecting society. At the very least, it means giving the judge a place where he can send a young offender for a minor punishment rather than a dehumanizing trauma. Right now, there is nothing much in between letting him go scot-free and letting him be devastated as a human being.

Politicians like to spend money on constituents who will vote for them, or on groups toward whom the general public feels sympa-thetic. No politician wants to champion the cause of more money for jailbirds. The public itself has to demand enough prison facilities and prison personnel to allow a conscientious judge to let criminals know from the outset that the law means business.

Money is absolutely necessary, but money alone will not do it. The whole criminal justice area needs to be cleansed of the excuse-mongers, faddists, sentimentalists, and assorted zanies and hustlers who infest the system. Enormous power has been put into the hands of anonymous little cliques who can parole murderers or leave con-victed drug-pushers at large in "rehabilitation" programs or put hoodlums back on the street in "community" organizations.

The people to whom such powers have been delegated are usu-ally elected by nobody, accountable to nobody, and meet no qualifica-tions standard other than talking the rest of us into putting them on parole boards or funding their high-sounding programs. If "prison reform" means continuing to subsidize this crowd, it has no chance. It ought to mean adequate facilities to house prisoners and protect the public.

Thomas Sowell

IMPROVING YOUR VOCABULARY: SOURCES OF NEW WORDS

The English language is in a constant state of growth. In 1982, for example, William Morrow & Company published a book, *New Words,* consisting of 8,500 terms that had not yet been included in standard dictionaries. Unprecedented advances in science and technology, together with a revolution in modern communications, have created a rapidly changing world in which the human mind is constantly bombarded with information. Each new discovery, each new cultural change brings with it a new set of words and ideas. Consider, for example, computer technology—a virtual language in itself, complete with "extended dialects." Someday the terms *byte, BASIC,* and *bubble sort* may be as familiar to you as *boy, baseball,* and *bubble gum.*

If you have any doubts about the vitality of the English language, just walk into the nearest library. You will find that the standard dictionary no longer satisfies the reader's vocabulary needs. In addition to basic dictionaries dealing with legal language or computer terminology or slang expressions, you will also find dictionaries as specialized as *The Dictionary of Weeds of Western Europe,* or *The Dictionary of Africanisms: Contributions of Sub-Saharan Africa to the English Language,* as well as dictionaries on topics as diverse as the underworld, the New Testament, and chemical additives. In fact, there are over one thousand different dictionaries in print today, and each of them reflects the various ways in which words are born. In the section that follows, you will find ten different ways in which the English language has grown. These words are grouped under headings that indicate what discipline or area of society they evolved from. Try to find five more for each category.

1. CHANGING LIFE STYLES

alimony	agribusiness	hijacker
credit card	skyscraper	brunch
jeans	laundromat	waterbed
condominium	casino	pizza

2. SCIENCE AND TECHNOLOGY

cassette	quarks	cryonics
microchip	seismograph	supersonic
robotics	turbojet	photocopy
odometer	diode	atomic

3. MEDICINE

prosthesis	hypodermic	interferon
oncology	vaccination	chemotherapy
steroid	radiology	cybernetics
pacemaker	biopsy	biofeedback

4. LITERATURE AND MYTHOLOGY

scrooge	malapropism	Frankenstein
cynic	argonaut	titan
Uncle Tom	Pandora's box	Achilles's heel

5. PROPER NAMES

jacuzzi (Roy Jacuzzi)
maverick (Samuel Maverick)
ghetto (Island of Gheto, Venice)
bloomers (Amelia Jenks Bloomers)
boycott (Capt. Charles Boycott)
lynch (William Lynch)
chauvinist (Nicolas Chauvin)
gerrymander (Gov. Elbridge Gerry)
guillotine (Joseph Guillotin)
stetson (John Stetson)
limerick (county of Limerick, Ireland)

6. MILITARY HISTORY

blitz	Nazi	boondocks
submarine	cannon	grenade
sergeant	cadet	air raid

7. POPULAR ENTERTAINMENT

rock	soul	reprise
acid rock	blues	whodunit
new wave	funnies	western
punk rock	sitcom	gothic

8. RELIGION

mecca	ecumenical	rabbi
heaven	hell	pulpit
priest	monastery	rosary
Bible	psalm	baptism

9. SPORTS

bogey	welterweight	switch-hitter
caddy	aquatics	coxswain
grand slam	umpire	bodysurfer
speedway	quarterback	sportscast

10. PSYCHOLOGY

neurosis	inhibition	complex
psychosis	cognitive	psychosomatic
fixation	affective	phobia
conditioning	maturation	reinforcement

To acquire more knowledge, you need to enlarge your vocabulary, because *thinking depends on the language you have to think with*. For example, much of the first semester of study of any intellectual discipline is spent learning its specialized vocabulary. Often, the "new" words are really just new meanings of already established words. For example, under Popular Entertainment above, acid rock and punk rock are merely variations of *rock*. Similarly, under Religion, all of the words belong to a cluster of religious associations. For example, heaven and mecca are different terms for the same concept, as are priest and rabbi. Heaven and hell, likewise, are associated by being opposites.

After reading the next paragraph, inspect the words listed in the preceding ten categories to see if you can identify which way they entered the language: extension of meaning, compounding, borrowing, or some other method among those discussed in the vocabulary sections.

New words are also created when existing words change their function. For example, many words first entered the language as nouns—the names of things—but through extension of meaning, these same nouns came to function as verbs. As verbs, they are usually strong and emphatic.

Here is one student's attempt at discovering nouns that can be used effectively as verbs.

comb	bite	play
brush	pop	saw
dance	cook	fish
drill	love	hit
dress	turn	cut

Jeff Watson (student)

Look at the following list of such words, all taken from parts of the body. Use these in sentences so that it is obvious how strong these verbs can be. Then make up a list of twenty-five other nouns which can also be converted into verbs.

nose	knuckle	arm	jaw
eye	muscle	neck	bone
foot	mouth	beard	skin
finger	nail	elbow	head
hand	toe	thumb	leg
stomach	knee	lash	gut
mind	back	curl	blood

ASSIGNMENT

One of the most common errors made in cause-and-effect reasoning is seeing only one cause where actually many exist. Consider the following explanations of the unemployment problem:

> *"It's the greedy unions who are putting Americans out of work."*
> *"It's all those corporate vultures moving their companies to foreign countries for cheap labor that's robbing us of our jobs."*
> *"It's all due to mismanagement."*
> *"Computer technology is what is putting us all out of work."*
> *"It's the government's fault."*

None of these reasons alone provide a sufficient explanation of the causes of unemployment, but together they begin to shed some light on the problem.

Each of the topics below suggests a problem with multiple causes. Choose one of the problems and consider its possible contributing causes before you write your cause-and-effect essay.

Juvenile delinquency
Racial prejudice
Cheating in college
Declining reading levels
Teenage pregnancy
Anorexia nervosa
Poverty
Low-quality merchandise
White-collar crime
Depression
The common cold
Alcoholism

Drug use among athletes
Low voter turnout
Wife beating
Vanishing wildlife
Changing attitudes toward work
Misuse of the English language
Unemployment
Classroom discipline problems
Changing weather patterns
Declining church membership
Increasing illiteracy rate
Suicide

Rising medical costs
Increased divorce rate
Child abuse
Sex discrimination
Violence in the classroom

Student apathy
Censorship in the classroom
Low-quality TV programming
Religious cult violence
Aversion to English class

9

Defining

RHETORIC

Combining Methods of Development

In many of the essays you write, you will be using a combination of the methods explained in this book. In a narrative, for example, you might want to *describe* the setting or the characters, to compare the emotions you felt, to divide and *classify* the actions you took, and to give *examples* to vivify your narrative. If defining a word, you might use a short *narrative* or anecdote to demonstrate how the word is used, a *comparison or contrast* to discriminate between the term you're defining and other similar words, *examples* to clarify the meaning, and *division and classification* to show how the various meanings of the word may be divided or how the word fits into a larger category.

Combining methods gives you increased flexibility and range. Choose the method or methods that best serve your purpose, that best convey your thoughts to your reader. You may develop each paragraph by a different method or even combine the methods within a paragraph.

The following essay shows how methods of development can be combined:

NOTES ON THE SATURNALIA OF HALLWAY LIFE: LIBIDINOUS SCRIMMAGING AND OTHER WEAPONS IN THE ARSENAL OF DISTRACTION

Edmund Janko teaches English at Bayside High School in Bayside, New York, and is a freelance writer. Note how, in the following essay, he uses narration, contrast, fact, negation, analogy, cause and effect, and examples to explain why students don't learn very much in the classroom today.

[Narrative: a short anecdote to set the scene.]

She toyed with her boyfriend's hair, pecked at his lips, and snuggled deeper into his arms, but since she's really a good girl and no rampaging wanton, she lovingly pushed him away when the bell rang and went into the classroom to take her seat. My heart sank.

[Author contrasts the power of the academic with the power of love and begins an extended contrast between the rise in SAT scores and the real situation.]

I had been reviewing my lesson on *Othello*, but what chance did my super-subtle insights into Shakespeare have against the lingering warmth of a young man's embrace? And I could imagine how distracted the poor guy was somewhere down the hall where one of my colleagues was probably raving on about Metternich's foreign policy.

[Thesis statement: author gives the major cause of poor academic achievement.]

That same morning, a story about the latest S.A.T. results made front-page news, but I knew that no reporter would be around to cover my student's burgeoning libido. However, from what I see, usually standing in my classroom doorway with a good view of the saturnalia of hallway life, that's the real story in education today.

[Analogy: author likens educators to generals and likens the battle for students' attention to war. This analogy recurs throughout the essay.]

I know that old notions die hard, and that's probably why a minute rise in S.A.T. scores made a splash. Obviously, a lot of people think that sort of thing makes a difference. Reading and mathematics test results have become something of an academic body count for the field marshals and generals of education. And, fortified by the latest communiques, they comfortably claim that "we're winning," or, as my union newspaper tells it, "We're on the right track." One could easily have visions of hordes of us good guys advancing on all fronts, across the steppes of Central Asia. Moscow has fallen! On to Gopher Prairie!

But to sustain such a rosy vision, you have to stay away from classrooms and students. We teachers know all too well what's really happening on the front line.

[Cause and Effect.]

Which brings me back to my amorous students and the reasons why no practicing teacher that I know got excited over the latest test results. Those who are cheered by these statistics tend to assume that improved skills will be converted into better performance. But over the last few years, I, for one, never doubted my students' abilities. What I saw decline was not brainpower, but willpower. Our main problem now in the classroom is that our young people are hopelessly distracted.

[First cause: specific examples to support first cause.]

For one thing, the sexual revolution, which some misguided free spirits would call a salutary release of crushing inhibitions, has radicalized our teenyboppers, and student-watching has become a kind of voyeurism or soft porn on the hoof.

Yesterday, for example, before my sophomore class began, a local gridiron Adonis came into my room to nibble at the neck of his girlfriend before an admiring audience. And last term, the curly haired girl in the back row would periodically, with studied casualness, drop her hand onto the thigh of the boy across the aisle. When, with consummate avuncular tact, I spoke to her about it, she just smiled and said the boy was "just a friend." I blush to think of her tactile relations with a guy she liked a lot.

All this, along with the embracing, fondling, and kissing in our hallways and classrooms, is clearly just the tip of the erotic iceberg. Teenage pregnancy and venereal disease are rising, certainly with a substantial investment of time, effort, and preoccupation.

Effect: author gives one effect of the "scrimmaging in the hall."

This libidinous scrimmaging leads to further distraction. A significant part of classroom time is filled with combing, primping, and all-around mirror gazing. Five or ten minutes before the end of the period, covertly or blatantly, out come the combs, tweezers, skin lotion, and mirrors, frantic preparation for the five-minute "nibble and nuzzle session" between classes. Nor is this foppishness confined to girls. A young Dorian Gray in the first row carries a notebook-sized mirror which he pops open at intervals to reassure himself that age hasn't withered his fragile beauty. Crow's feet at 15 can be crushing.

Second cause

Not all students, of course, are votaries of Eros. Those who swear allegiance to Morpheus are probably more numerous. Large numbers of students pass their day in semi-stupor or in a daze of greater or lesser befuddlement. I've been told that on some school buses, marijuana smoking is so blatant and widespread that the driver sometimes stops and refuses to move unless the kids "cool" it.

But most often, the driver is anxious to make his or her run as quickly and painlessly as possible. So a lot of my students literally tumble from the bus into my classroom. Some put their foreheads on the desk, while others sit passively while questions, assignments, and miscellaneous profundities whiz harmlessly over their heads. There is some alcohol around, too, but most of the damage is done by the forbidden weed.

Third cause

If sex, pot, and booze have sent us reeling to the ropes, miniaturization is bound to finish us off. The kids' culture is frantic, frenetic, and hypnotic, and now they can take it wherever they go, even into the classroom.

War analogy

Up until now, we've generally been successful in our war against radios, but the "Walkman" types are formidable new weapons in the distraction arsenal, cruise missiles of diversion that are being deployed at an accelerated rate.

It's becoming harder to detect the thin strands of wire curling from pockets or book bags or purses up into the tiniest of headsets. And I've already seen "computer" games that can fit in the palm of a hand or, more likely, inside a copy of Hamlet. So, when the not-too-distant day arrives when wrist-watch television sets are sold for under $50, it'll be time for us to hoist the white flag. No student will ever

look at a teacher again. (Who knows, I might even welcome the anonymity when I crawl off to ignominious retirement.)

Return to SAT score contrast

So, though the romantic tales of improved scores may well keep
old men by the fire or administrators by their graphs, we teachers
know that, as surely as the sun will rise, tapes will turn, grass will grow,
and love will bloom in the land.

Edmund Janko

There are several kinds of definitions and many ways that
words can be defined. The following pages give you some of the
more common ones.

Limited Definition

A limited definition may be enlightening, even if it is developed
by only one method. The most frequent type of brief definition, for
example, is by *synonym*.

Q: What do you mean, otiose?

A: I mean lazy, ineffective, futile.

This brief definition serves its purpose, but other types of brief
definition are rarely helpful to anyone who doesn't already know
something about the subject. To say, for instance, that examples of a
palindrome are "Able was I ere I saw Elba" and "Madame, I'm
Adam" isn't much help without some other methods of definition.
Indeed, some English instructors request students to combine at
least three methods of defining in an extended definition. For readers who have no previous knowledge of a subject, one or two methods seldom supply enough information.

Extended Definition

Abstract words, such as *honor, glory, integrity, morality, grace, courage, progress,* are the ones that most often call for an extended definition. Since these words do not refer to objects or natural facts but to
abstractions—concepts in somebody's mind—their meanings are
always hard to pin down. Scores of essays have been written to
define such terms and the other abstractions represented by the
phrases and slogans of our time: *civil rights, women's liberation, nuclear
deterrence, welfare state, peace with honor, fiscal responsibility,* and so on.

Common Methods and Techniques for Developing a Definition

Formal Definition

Most dictionary definitions follow the general pattern of formal definition. First, the term to be defined is placed in the class to which it logically belongs; then differentiating details are used to show how the term being defined differs from other members of the class.

TERM	CLASS	DIFFERENTIATING DETAIL
muscadine	American grape	grows in Southeast US.,has small leaves, small clusters of large, thick-skinned, musky fruit of dull purple

NOTE: The amount of differentiating detail may be expanded almost indefinitely, depending upon your purpose.

Defining by Example

One of the most natural methods of explaining what a term means is to cite examples. An essay explaining classical Greek drama would probably cite examples from the works of Aeschylus, Sophocles, and Euripides. An essay defining modern drama might well cite examples from the works of Eugene O'Neill, Arthur Miller, and Tennessee Williams. A current essay on comedians would almost certainly use examples such as Johnny Carson, Bob Hope, Steve Martin, Richard Pryor, and Eddie Murphy.

Defining by Synonym or Metaphor

In trying to explain what something is or what it means, you often look around for something similar that will help you to show the meaning. In attempting to explain what *onerous* means, you might use a number of words of similar meaning, such as *troublesome, burdensome, oppressive, galling.*

In defining by metaphor, the principle is the same, but what is used to illustrate the meaning is a nonliteral comparison. To show what a tropical storm is like, D.H. Lawrence describes its sudden onset through a figure of speech: "as if a membrane in the air had been ripped."

Defining by Narration

Often a little story, fable, or anecdote may illuminate the meaning of a particular term. The story of one family's suffering in a bigoted community might shed light on what racial prejudice means to its victims.

Defining by Process

Some mechanical things can best be defined in terms of the operation or process they perform. Some diseases, such as *myasthenia gravis,* might be defined by describing the process of change that takes place within the nerves and muscles. A volcanic eruption could scarcely be defined without describing the process, and some scientists attempt to explain the origin of the universe through the "big bang" theory—a process that appears to be continuing after billions of years.

Defining by Comparison and Contrast

Comparing or contrasting a term with similar terms may serve to illuminate its meaning. An essay on socialism, for example, might eliminate confusion by clearly distinguishing between communism and socialism.

Defining by Division and Classification

Almost any complex term (or complex idea that the term represents) can be made clearer by dividing and classifying the various aspects of its meaning. You might, for example, examine the meaning of the term *addictive personality* by classifying the various traits associated with addictive behavior.

Defining by Negation

Although you can never completely define something by saying what it is not, negation can often help you to limit and classify your meaning by clearing away mistaken assumptions. To answer a child's question about what whales are, you might have to begin by showing that whales are *not* fish.

Defining by Word Origin

The origin and historical development of a word may shed a good deal of light on its meaning. The word *excoriate,* for instance, originally meant "to strip off the skin." That original meaning carries over to the modern sense of the word: to severely upbraid someone, to administer a tongue-lashing. You might even hear someone say such things as, "The boss will take George's hide off when he finds out what George did."

ORGANIZATION

The basic organization remains the same three-part structure of introduction, body, and conclusion. And any of the previously discussed methods may be used in your introduction, so long as it brings sharply into focus the term to be defined and your attitude or approach. Then any combination of methods may be used in developing the extended definition in the body of your essay, provided these methods serve to clarify your meaning. To define *contract,* for example, you might classify contracts according to various types; you might use a narrative, a brief case history, to show why certain contracts are unenforceable; you might use examples to illustrate why contracts should be in writing; and you almost certainly would need to provide brief definitions for various other terms, such as, *assent, mutuality, consideration,* and *legal capacity.* Usually, an effective conclusion of an extended definition pulls together the various aspects of meaning you have discussed and concludes with a clear statement of the term's essential meaning—a restatement of the thesis sentence.

Fifteen

BOB GREENE

Bob Greene, a columnist for the Chicago Tribune, *established himself as a first-class journalist when he was in his early twenties and has, since then, written a column for* Esquire *magazine and a half dozen books. As a writer, he says, "I basically consider myself to be a storyteller . . . of the little stories I find while traveling around the country."*

In "Fifteen," Greene defines what it is to be a fifteen-year-old boy in today's suburban society.

"This would be excellent, to go in the ocean with this thing," says Dave Gembutis, fifteen.

He is looking at a $170 Sea Cruiser raft.

"Great," says his companion, Dan Holmes, also fifteen.

This is at Herman's World of Sporting Goods, in the middle of the Woodfield Mall in Schaumberg, Illinois.

The two of them keep staring at the raft. It is unlikely that they will purchase it. For one thing, Dan has only twenty dollars in his pocket, Dave five dollars. For another thing—ocean voyages aside—neither of them is even old enough to drive. Dave's older sister, Kim, has dropped them off at the mall. They will be taking the bus home.

Fifteen. What a weird age to be male. Most of us have forgotten about it, or have idealized it. But when you are fifteen . . . well, things tend to be less than perfect.

You can't drive. You are only a freshman in high school. The girls your age look older than you and go out with upperclassmen who have cars. You probably don't shave. You have nothing to do on the weekends.

So how do you spend your time? In 1982, most likely at a mall. Woodfield is an enclosed shopping center sprawling over 2.25 million square feet in northern Illinois. There are 230 stores at Woodfield, and on a given Saturday those stores are cruised in and out of by thousands of teenagers killing time. Today two of those teenagers are Dave Gembutis and Dan Holmes.

Dave is wearing a purple Rolling Meadows High School Mustangs windbreaker over a gray M*A*S*H T-shirt, jeans, and Nike running shoes. He has a red plastic spoon in his mouth, and will keep it there for most of the afternoon. Dan is wearing a white Ohio State Buckeyes T-shirt, jeans, and Nike running shoes.

We are in the Video Forum store. Paul Simon and Art Garfunkel are singing "Wake Up Little Susie" from their Central Park concert on four television screens. Dave and Dan have already been wandering around Woodfield for an hour.

"There's not too much to do at my house," Dan says to me.

"Here we can at least look around," Dave says. "At home I don't know what we'd do."

"Play catch or something," Dan says. "Here there's lots of things to see."

"See some girls or something, start talking," Dave says.

I ask them how they could start a conversation with girls they had never met.

"Ask them what school they're from," Dan says. "Then if they say Arlington Heights High School or something, you can say, 'Oh, I know somebody from there.'"

I ask them how important meeting girls is to their lives.

"About forty-five percent," Dan says.

"About half your life," Dave says.

"Half is girls," Dan says. "Half is going out for sports."

An hour later, Dave and Dan have yet to meet any girls. They have seen a girl from their own class at Rolling Meadows High, but she is walking with an older boy, holding his hand. Now we are in the Woodfield McDonald's. Dave is eating a McRib sandwich, a small fries, and a small Coke. Dan is eating a cheeseburger, a small fries, and a medium root beer.

In here, the dilemma is obvious. The McDonald's is filled with girls who are precisely as old as Dave and Dan. The girls are wearing eye shadow, are fully developed, and generally look as if they could be dating the Green Bay Packers. Dave and Dan, on the other hand . . . well, when you're a fifteen-year-old boy, you look like a fifteen-year-old boy.

"They go with the older guys who have the cars," Dan says.

"It makes them more popular," Dave says.

"My ex-girlfriend is seeing a junior," Dan says.

I ask him what happened.

"Well, I was in Florida over spring vacation," he says. "And when I got back I heard that she was a Cinderella Rockefella one night, and she was dancing with this guy, and she liked him and he drove her home and stuff."

"She two-timed him," Dave says.

"The guy's on the basketball team," Dan says.

I ask Dan what he did about it.

"I broke up with her," he says, as if I had asked the stupidest question in the world.

I ask him how he did it.

"Well, she was at her locker," he says. "She was working the combination. And I said, 'Hey, Linda, I want to break up.' And she was opening her locker door and she just nodded her head yes. And I said, 'I hear you had a good time while I was gone, but I had a better time in Florida.'"

I ask him if he feels bad about it.

"Well, I feel bad," he says. "But a lot of guys told me, 'I heard you broke up with her. Way to be.'"

"It's too bad the Puppy Palace isn't open," Dan says.

"They're remodeling," Dave says.

We are walking around the upper level of Woodfield. I ask them why they would want to go to the Puppy Palace.

"The dogs are real cute and you feel sorry for them," Dan says.

We are in a fast-food restaurant called the Orange Bowl. Dave is eating a frozen concoction called an O-Joy. They still have not met any girls.

"I feel like I'd be wasting my time if I sat at home," Dan says. "If it's Friday or Saturday and you sit home, it's considered . . . low."

"Coming to the mall is about all there is," Dave says. "Until we can drive."

"Then I'll cruise," Dan says. "Look for action a little farther away from my house, instead of just riding my bike around."

"When you're sixteen, you can do anything," Dave says. "You can go all the way across town."

"When you have to ride your bike . . ." Dan says. "When it rains, it ruins everything."

In the J.C. Penny store, the Penny Fashion Carnival is under way. Wally the clown is handing out favors to children, but Dave and Dan are watching the young female models parade onto a stage in bathing suits.

"Just looking is enough for me," Dan says.

Dave suggests that they head out back into the mall and pick out some girls to wave to. I ask why.

"Well, see, even if they don't wave back, you might see them later in the day," Dan says. "And then they might remember that you waved at them, and you can meet them."

We are at the Cookie Factory. These guys eat approximately every twenty minutes.

It is clear that Dan is attracted to the girl behind the counter. He walks up, and his voice is slower and about half an octave lower than before.

The tone of voice is going to have to carry the day, because the words are not all that romantic:

"Can I have a chocolate-chip cookie?"

The girl does not even look up as she wraps the cookie in tissue paper.

Dan persists. The voice might be Clark Gable's:

"What do they cost?"

The girl is still looking down.

"Forty-seven," she says and takes his money, still looking away, and we move on.

Dave and Dan tell me that there are lots of girls at Woodfield's indoor ice-skating rink. It costs money to get inside, but they lead me to an exit door, and when a woman walks out we slip into the rink. It is chilly in here, but only three people are on the ice.

"It's not time for open skating yet," Dan says. "This is all private lessons."

"Not much in here," Dave says.

We sit on benches. I ask them if they wish they were older.

"Well," Dan says, "when you get there, you look back and you remember. Like I'm glad that I'm not in the fourth or fifth grade now. But I'm glad I'm not twenty-five, either."

"Once in a while I'm sorry I'm not twenty-one," Dave says.

"There's not much you can do when you're fifteen. This summer I'm going to caddy and try to save some money."

"Yeah," Dan says. "I want to save up for a dirt bike."

"Right now, being fifteen is starting to bother me a little bit," Dave says. "Like when you have to get your parents to drive you to Homecoming with a girl."

I ask him how that works.

"Well, your mom is in the front seat driving," he says. "And you're in the back seat with your date."

I ask him how he feels about that.

"It's embarassing," he says. "Your date understands that there's nothing you can do about it, but it's still embarassing."

Dave says he wants to go to Pet World.

"I think they closed it down," Dan says, but we head in that direction anyway. I ask them what the difference is between Pet World and the Puppy Palace.

"They've got snakes and fish and another assortment of dogs," Dan says. "But not as much as the Puppy Palace."

When we arrive, Pet World is, indeed, boarded up.

We are on the upper level of the mall. Dave and Dan have spotted two girls sitting on a bench directly below them, on the mall's main level.

"Whistle," Dan says. Dave whistles, but the girls keep talking.

"Dave, wave to them and see if they look," Dan says.

"They aren't looking," Dave says.

"There's another one over there," Dan says.

"Where?" Dave says.

"Oh, that's a mother," Dan says. "She's got her kid with her."

They return their attention to the two downstairs.

Dan calls to them: "Would you girls get the dollar I just dropped?"

The girls look up.

"Just kidding," Dan says.

The girls resume their conversation.

"I think they're laughing." Dan says.

"What are you going to do when the dumb girls won't respond," Dave says.

"At least we tried," Dan says.

I ask him what response would have satisfied him.

"The way we would have known that we succeeded," he says, "they'd have looked up here and started laughing."

The boys keep staring at the two girls.

"Ask her to look up," Dan says. "Ask her what school they go to."

"I did," Dave says. "I did."

The two boys lean over the railing.

"Bye, girls," Dave yells.

"See you later," Dan yells.

The girls do not look up.

"Too hard," Dan says. "Some girls are stuck on themselves, if you know what I mean by that."

We go to a store called the Foot Locker, where all the salespeople are dressed in striped referee's shirts.

"Dave!" Dan says. "Look at this! Seventy bucks!" He holds up a pair of New Balance running shoes. Both boys shake their heads.

We move on to a store called Passage to China. A huge stuffed tiger is placed by the doorway. There is a PLEASE DO NOT TOUCH sign attached to it. Dan rubs his hand over the tiger's back. "This would look so great in my room," he says.

We head over to Alan's TV and Stereo. Two salesmen ask the boys if they are interested in buying anything, so they go back outside and look at the store's window. A color television set is tuned to a baseball game between the Chicago Cubs and the Pittsburgh Pirates.

They watch for five minutes. The sound is muted, so they cannot hear the announcers.

"I wish they'd show the score," Dave says.

They watch for five minutes more.

"Hey, Dave," Dan says. "You want to go home?"

"I guess so," Dave says.

They do. We wave goodbye. I watch them walk out of the mall toward the bus stop. I wish them girls, dirt bikes, puppies, and happiness.

HOW DOES THE AUTHOR MAKE HIS POINT?

1. What varying techniques of defining does Greene use?
2. Greene quotes the boys as saying they have two equally strong interests in life. How do the boys display these interests as they wander through the mall?
3. Does Greene show a consistent attitude toward the boys? Support your answer by direct quotation.

What Do You Think?

1. What do you think is the primary characteristic of these boys?
2. Why do the girls not seem to be interested in the boys?
3. What do you think is the thesis statement for this essay of definition?

Concerning Tolerance

DOROTHY THOMPSON

Dorothy Thompson, an extremely influential columnist of a generation ago, focused her attention on international politics. She was an early proponent of the theory that America could not stand apart from the rest of the world but had to act and react in the larger world community. In this essay, she warns us that the American devotion to freedom and tolerance may blind us to dangers threatening us from those who would exploit these beliefs.

The open mind has been greatly praised, but somebody once said that an open mind was often a mind with nothing in it. It has also been said that "to understand all is to forgive all," but it is perhaps truer to say that to understand nothing is to forgive everything.

Every saw and every truism needs inspection. Words need periodic inspection. And one word that needs some reconsideration is the great word "tolerance." For it has been abused past recognition. From being a positive expression of respect for other people's rights, it has become a weasel word for the avoidance of responsibility.

The Latin root of the word "tolerance" refers to things that can be borne, endured, are supportable. The intrinsic meaning of "tolerance" is the capacity to sustain and endure, as of hardship. From this comes the inferential meaning of patience with the opinions and practices of those who differ. It is interesting that the word is used in connection with the coining of money and with machinery, to indicate the margin within which coins may deviate from the fixed standard, or the dimensions or parts of a machine from the norm.

But the word "tolerance" does not suggest that everything is supportable and that any amount of deviation is allowable. It suggests that one's principles and standards should be tempered with patience, and with readiness to subject them to modification, through practical or intellectual tests. But it does not suggest that one should have no principles or standards. In the contemporary world, I find that for many people this is, however, exactly what they mean by tolerance: a vapid openness to the condoning of anything. Tolerance carried to this conclusion is anarchy. It is not an instrument of civilization, but an instrument of barbarism.

We are not tolerant of diphtheria bacilli, tuberculosis germs, or cancer cells. We do not assert their right also to live and work. We know that they cannot continue to exist if the organism which they have entered, or in which they have grown, is also to continue to exist. Therefore we eradicate them with the greatest intolerance. We know that there is no way for noncancerous tissue to come to an agreement with cancerous tissue. There is no possible *modus vivendi* between them. Therefore, a cancer is eradicated.

But in our social and political life we seem to think that democracy is only a casual host for the entertainment of all conceivable viewpoints and organizations, including those whose clear intention is to destroy the host. Instead of allowing that margin, even a very wide margin, for variation which is the essence of tolerance, we entertain those in whom there is no speck of tolerance whatsoever for democracy itself, or for tolerance itself, and who seek to substitute for ordered popular government under law a regime of dictatorship and violence.

The margin of tolerance in a democracy, or in any other organized and civilized state ruled by law, stops when standards essential to the continuance of an orderly and civilized community are seriously menaced. It is impossible, for instance, to continue any sort of orderly, civilized, and legal community at all if the police powers are captured, by whatever legal methods, by gangsters, and then used to destroy the law, the courts, private property, all civilian immunities, and to kill people arbitrarily, without indictment or trial.

It is of not the slightest consequence, for instance, that the American Communist Party is a legal organization, that it pays lip service to democracy—and, indeed, calls itself democracy's agent—and that it does not seek to make its way by throwing bombs or by any other acts of violence, but uses instead the legal methods of persuasion and organization, assisted by more dubious instruments of slander and intimidation. Its object is what is important, and its object is to destroy the law, and to substitute for law the absolute dictatorship of a party itself dictatorially ruled, and acting as the self-appointed agents of what they choose to delineate as the proletariat, or "working masses." This is demonstrably the object of the Communist Party. This is the actual form of organization that exists in Soviet Russia, and it is a form of organization that has been consistently praised and never denounced by any Communist Party leader—or by any one of them who has continued thereafter to hold his position. The American Communist Party is in alliance with the Communist Party of Russia. And, therefore, the American Communist Party is outside the bounds of possible tolerance by anyone who is not a Communist, for the achievement of its objective is incompatible with the continuance of our existence as a civilized community ruled by law.

Exactly the same thing holds true for the German-American Bund and its kindred and supporting organizations. The legality of their methods does not obscure the fact that their object is to destroy the essential integrity of this country both as an independent power and as an organized commonwealth. If anyone doubts that, after what has happened in Central Europe, he is verging on feeble-mindedness. Their program is to deprive millions of our citizens of their citizenship rights and make them "subjects" of the rest of us. The pattern of society which is their model is the dictatorship of a gang, knowing no limitations of ethics or law, and ruling with total arbitrariness. As I write these lines, this regime, if you can call it a regime, is engaged on an international plunder expedition.

It is impossible to tolerate the absolutely incompatible. Tolerating then leads either to the destruction of order and civilization by capitulation, or to civil war. It cannot possibly lead anywhere else. You cannot make a "pact" with Communism or Nazism. They demand all or nothing; that is their nature. Therefore there is, in respect of them, no supportable plea for the rights of liberty. Al Capone could not appeal to civil liberties for the right openly to organize his gang, with the protection of the police. No state can tolerate that which is hostile to the very concept of the state as such.

In this country we can tolerate every political group, from the right to the left, Socialists and Bourbons, provided they are not acting as agents of foreign powers and do not have as their object the substitution of the legally ordered society by the rule of violence. To extend tolerance to such is to abdicate intelligence and prepare for the extermination of tolerance itself.

How Does the Author Make Her Point?

1. What type of introduction does the author use? Is it effective? Why or why not?
2. What is the meaning of *saw* and *truism* in the second paragraph
3. Give the thesis in one sentence.
4. What is the purpose (in paragraph 3) of referring to the entymology of the word and its meaning in reference to machinery? How do these definitions differ from what most people think *tolerance* means (paragraph 4)?
5. What technique does the author use in paragraph 5? Is it effective?
6. On what basis does Thompson condemn the American Communist party and the German American Bund? What does this argument have to do with her subject?

What Do You Think?

1. Do you agree with the author's stand against the Communist and Neo-Nazi party? Why or why not?
2. What is your definition of *tolerance*? Do you set any limits on tolerance? In what cases would you be intolerant?
3. Do you think Thompson's argument is fair? Can you find any holes in it?

The Tragic Fallacy

Joseph Wood Krutch

Joseph Wood Krutch, a scholar and writer on a wide range of learned topics including botany, biology, and conservation, was primarily interested in drama. He was for many years the drama critic of the magazine Nation *and a contributor to* The American Scholar, *the publication of the Phi Beta Kappa society. In this excerpt from a famous essay called "The Tragic Fallacy," Krutch defines* tragedy.

Comedy laughs the minor mishaps of its characters away; drama solves all the difficulties which it allows to arise; and melodrama, separating good from evil by simple lines, distributes its rewards and punishments in accordance with the principles of naive justice which satisfies the simple souls of its audience, which are neither philosophical enough to question its primitive ethics nor critical enough to object to the way in which its neat events violate the laws of probability. Tragedy, the greatest and most difficult of the arts, can adopt none of these methods; and yet it must reach its own happy end in its own way. Though its conclusion must be, by its premise, outwardly calamitous, though it must speak to those who know that the good man is cut off and that the fairest things are the first to perish, yet it must leave them, as *Othello* does, content that this is so. We must be and we are glad that Juliet dies and glad that Lear is turned out into the storm.

We accept gladly the outward defeats which it describes for the sake of the inward victories which it reveals. Juliet died, but not before she had shown how great and resplendent a thing love could be; Othello plunged the dagger into his own breast, but not before he had revealed the greatness of soul which makes his death seem unimportant. Had he died in the instant when he struck the blow, had he perished still believing that the world was as completely black as he saw it before the innocence of Desdemona was revealed to him, then, for him at least, the world would have been merely damnable, but Shakespeare kept him alive long enough to allow him to learn his error and hence to die, not in despair, but in the full acceptance of the tragic reconcilation to life. Perhaps it would be pleasanter if men could believe what the child is taught—that the good are happy and that things turn out as they should—but it is far more important to be able to believe, as Shakespeare did, that however much things in the outward world would may go awry, man has, nevertheless, splendors of his own and that, in a word, Love and Honor and Glory are not words but realities.

Thus for the great ages tragedy is not an expression of despair but the means by which they saved themselves from it. It is a profession of faith, and a sort of religion; a way of looking at life by virtue of which it is robbed of its pain. The sturdy soul of the tragic author seizes upon suffering and uses it only as a means by which joy may be wrung out of existence, but it is not to be forgotten that he is enabled to do so only because of his belief in the greatness of human nature and because, though he has lost the child's faith in life, he has not lost his far more important faith in human nature. A tragic writer does not have to believe in God, but he must believe in man.

How Does the Author Make His Point

1. How much of the first paragraph is introduction and what form does this introduction take?
2. Where is the thesis statement? Why does it seem at first glance to be a contradiction?
3. How does the final sentence support the thesis statement?

What Do You Think?

1. What are the methods of definition which Krutch uses?
2. Would life be "pleasanter if man could believe what the child is taught"?
3. Do you believe in the happy ending—either in the popular sense or in the more subtle sense—in which Krutch believes?

The Mischief of Language

LEO ROSTEN

*Perhaps best known as the creator of H*Y*M*A*N K*A*P*L*A*N,
Leo Rosten is a wise and witty observer of American life. In the following
passage from* Rome Wasn't Burned in a Day, *he provides his own
humorous definitions and observations on verbal fumbles.*

A malaprop, according to the Fowlers' *The King's English*
(". . . and so is the Queen!" cried Dizzy Dean), is a word used "in
the belief that it has the meaning really belonging to another
word that resembles it." Most malaprops are as dreary as that
definition. The ones that most delight us are those that convert a
platitude into a laugh ("A rolling stone gathers no moths"), or
that titillate the mind with a revelation that has been lying around
for centuries, waiting to be uttered ("Rome is full of fallen
arches"), or that transform a cliche into an epigram—an
inadvertent, unintended epigram, to be sure, but an aphorism
nonetheless, pointed, memorable, a crisp distillation of a larger
truth. "An oral contract isn't worth the paper it's written on."

Hobbes brilliantly described "the passion of laughter" as
"sudden glory arising from sudden conception of some eminence
in ourselves by comparison with the inferiority of others." This
lovely insight explains why we feel superior, no less than amused,
when we read such marvelous blunders as "Radium was
discovered by Madman Curry," or "Underneath those shabby
trousers beats a heart of gold." Each is a sudden, risible occasion
for vainglory.

The cave men (whose descendents the theologians treat as
fallen angels and the Darwinians as ascended apes) probably
laughed their heads off when a baboon slipped on a banana peel.
It took centuries, I presume, before some Homo sapiens reached
the cerebral sophistication required to place a coconut where
some sap would be sure to be conked by it.

The practical joker must have been the earliest wit in human
history—and remains the most enduring. He is found in every
primitive society, anthropologists tell men, as well as in

Switzerland. I say Switzerland not because I am anti-Swiss but because I have come to the conclusion that anything that can get a laugh in the yodel belt will tickle the ribs of men anywhere else.

It is my guess that our ancestors first laughed at a prat fall; later, laughter accompanied a practical joke ("monkey business"); later still snickers followed some mistaken grunt of "Blgh" instead of "Ugh." Men fell on their butts long before they burbled a boo-boo, because you must *have* a word, and know it, and have it understood by your peers before its misuse will trigger a giggle.

The treasury of verbal bobbles is enriched each hour each day in every land on earth. Was there ever a child who did *not* come a cropper with a word? When my daughter was eight, she described something she had seen "as I was towardsing home"; when she was ten, she told a story that ended flatly, "This is my virgin of what happened"; when she was eleven, she sighed morosely, "I am a middle-aged child."

In a Winnetka kindergarten some years ago, one lad drew a man with tiny creatures creeping all over him. When the foolish teacher asked what the drawing meant, young Raphael explained: "That's John, with all the mice on him." What John? What Mice? "From the poem: 'Diddle, diddle dumpling, mice on John' " I can find no way of faulting such peerless imagery. Or that of the tot who sang, "London britches falling down. . . ." These delightful inventions are not, of course, in the same immortal league as the line, uttered by a child, which has surely been savored ten thousand times: "The equator is a menagerie lion that runs around the middle of the earth."

Given the ancient lineage and unceasing prediction of verbal goofs, it strikes me as astonishing that we had no name for the malaprop until the seventeenth century. I say the seventeenth century even though the word "malapropism" is usually associated with Mrs. Malaprop, a character in Sheridan's *The Rivals*, first performed in 1775. It turns out that Dryden preceded Sheridan by a century, when he enlisted a French phrase, *mal à propos*, to describe some false use of a word. But *mal à propos* happens to be quite inexact. It means improper, unseasonable, not pertinent—none of which is precisely what a malapropism is.

The length of time it took English writers and linguists to devise some name for amusing verbal fluffs is all the more striking if we consider how large is the supply of Greek or Latin roots available for English neologisms—itself a good example of word-building. Consider the array of technical terms we do use when we want to name, not describe, other forms of language play or ploy: oxymoron, metathesis, litotes, synecdoche, polyonymy, mimesis, paronomasia, metonymy. They look outlandish, but they are exact and authorative.

Malapropists galore surely flourished in England and America long before Mrs. Malaprop, the matron saint of word-manglers, appeared on the scene. The pun was always a thigh-slapper ("pun, by the way, is a Drydenian latecomer to English, too). The Elizabethans yakked their heads off over verbal incongruities. Shakespeare created word-bumblers like Dogberry, Mistress Quickly, Bottom, and the Gravedigger in *Hamlet*. Fielding named one of his characters Mrs. Slipslop, to emphasize her bungling of our pliant tongue.

Ireland's writers, all survivors of the Irish bull ("Ireland is overrun by absentee landlords"), have long employed jocular word jugglery, from Wilde to Joyce to O'Casey ("The World is in a state of chassis"). Englishmen, incidentally, have been patsies for a pun since the day a Londoner threw a sandwich at a pub mirror with the blasé quip, "Is that not food for reflection?" But American humorists have long seemed to prefer antic spelling as a lever of laughter. Linguistic crotchets are as old as American journalism: Josh Billings, Artemus Ward, Mark Twain, and Kin Hubbard took impudent liberties with England's prose. And spiritual sisters to Mrs. Malaprop enlivened American letters in the form of Mrs. Partington, the brain child of one B. P. Shillaber, and Mrs Spriggins, a *faux pas* female sired by John Bangs in the old comic magazine *Life*. *1066 and All That* by W. C. Sellar and R. J. Yeatman was a 1930's carnival of historical and verbal doozies. The tradition has been carried on nobly by Richard Armour.

Ring Lardner was a genius at depicting idiots through their idiom (*You Know Me, Al*); he raked fools, scoundrels, and sharpies with murderous parody ("Although he was not a good fielder, he was not a good hitter, either") or exquisite genteelisms ("Shut up," he explained). William Faulkner used dialect with contrapuntal power; James Thurber, Anita Loos, and Dorothy Parker deployed solecisms to deadly effect. S.J. Perelman is both an incomparable punster and a wizard of verbal miscegenation. Arthur Kober pinpointed the argot of the bygone Bronx for history (*Dear Bella*). And I daresay that H*Y*M*A*N K*A*P*L*A*N committed enough malapropian misdemeanors to keep the *mavens* at Oxford busy for a generation.

I often wonder why we do not hear, or hear of, far more bloomers and bloopers, considering the endless opportunities that present themselves in a language so rich in words, metaphors, similes, and slang—all begging to be butchered. Verbal mischief is ever latent and omnitempting in the English tongue.

> If crockery is a collection of crocks, then flattery is a collection of flats, scullery is a collection of skulls, sorcery a collection of sources, and monastery a collection of monsters. . . [and] if jewelry is a collection of jewels, then husbandry is a collection of husbands, infantry is a collection of infants, vestry a collection of vests, and pantry a collection of pants . . . (from *Humorous English* by Evan Esar).

Or consider the realm of print, a veritable paradise for the all-thumbed. Recently, in checking the printers' galleys of an article I had written, I read, with utter astonishment: "The rapists tell us. . . ." I placed an icepack on my head after I realized that "the rapists" was some typesetter's Freudian spatial improvement upon "therapists."

This kind of malaprintism, to coin a word, is the unending nightmare of editors and the recurring delight of readers. American folklore has sanctified the newspaper that referred to "Patrick Clancy, a defective on the police force," and hastily changed it in the next edition to "Patrick Clancy, a detective on the police farce."

Sports-page editors learned from ghastly experience never, never to let the phrase "Babe Ruth's hits" get past them. The cherubic perversity of printers has produced more than one obituary announcing that someone "did eat his home last night," or that some king, president, or mayor was overtired because of "his official cuties." These katzenjammers are another order from such transmutations of logic as have plagued the Chicago *Tribune* ("He got up, dressed, and took a shower") or *The New York Times* ("He clung to the sill by his fingerprints").

"Typos," as typographical hanky-panky is called, seem to prove the validity of what some unknown sage has defined as Murphy's Law: "If something can go wrong, it will." In the reign of unhappy Charles I, the so-called Wicked Bible appeared, an unforgettable edition of Holy Scripture in which an errant (or diabolic) printer rendered the Seventh Commandment as: "Thou shall commit adultery." As the Van Buren, Arkansas, *Press Argus* ruefully observed centuries later, "It's nearly as hard to correct a typographical error as it is to get a woman unpregnant." Incidentally, for all of these journalistic gems, I am grateful to Earle Tempel's *Press Boners* (Pocket Books, New York: 1967).

But deeper, darker things are involved here. We have learned from Sigmund Freud that "typos" and slips of the tongue, malaprops and misnomers are not entirely innocent or accidental. Man's mistakes, no less than his dreams, are packed with meaning. *The Interpretation of Dreams* and *Wit and the Unconsciousness* are treasuries of dazzling revelations about comic errors that are, in fact, not errors but stratagems that evade the censors of the self.

Comedy is a complex masquerade for anxiety, hostility, or ambivalence, or the unconscious need to diminish guilt by making light of what is taboo. Murder oft peeps through the masks of our wit. The corniest joke may convey feelings we are afraid to confront and reluctant to acknowledge, but can and do express from behind the protective visors of jest. And just as "free association" is never free, but is governed and guided by emotions ordinarily repressed, so humor is the unwitting messenger of truths that churn behind the camouflage of levity. There is method in our boners as well as our madness.

I have been collecting linguistic gewgaws ever since I wore knickers. In Hollywood, where I was indentured for a decade, no week passed unbrightened by some sparkling muff from one or another producer, director, or actor. The moviemakers from Mittel-europa were especially fecund joy-givers to screenwriters. One Budapestian impresario solemnly invited me to cook up a story that would contain "a generous dearth of hearthrobs about a great feedle-player—someone like Sascha Heifetz."

Every so often, I run across a line that strikes me as very funny, even though it is not, strictly speaking, a malaprop; why speak strictly at a time like this? Back in 1887, a testimonial advertisement featured an unshaved hobo saying, "I used your soap two years ago and have not used another since then." I do not think we should allow that to be lost in the humorless abysses of the past. I also dream of the day when some farsighted foundation will establish a museum for menus, store signs, theater marquees, and church plaques that clearly deserve immortality:

Today's Special
Barely Soup
* * *

GOOD CLEAN DANCING
EVERY NIGHT
EXCEPT SUNDAY
* * *

NOW PLAYING
Adam and Eve
—with a cast of thousands!
* *

TODAY'S SERMON:
"HOW MUCH CAN A MAN DRINK?"
WITH HYMNS FROM
A FULL CHOIR

Other such near-miss malaprops too delicious to exclude include such nifties as "Keeping a secret from him is like trying to sneak the dawn past a rooster" (Fred Allen), "No man ever forgets where he buried a hatchet" (Kin Hubbard), "She's beautiful, an angel—with spurs" (Joe Pasternak), "He looks like a dishonest Abe Lincoln" (of Harold Ross), or "You certainly have a ready wit: Let me know when it's ready" (Henny Youngman).

The actual origin of a funny anecdote, a pun, a snapper, or a retort is often hopelessly entangled in the chain of conversational communications. It is just inevitable that the whoppers of one man will be attributed to another. This is especially true in the case of such a virtuoso as Samuel Goldwyn, whose gallery of malaprops has constantly been enlarged by cacologies that originated elsewhere. I have more than once heard an ad lib at, say, the Brown Derby or Sardi's and read it in a gossip column the next day as having been coined by Mr. Goldwyn. I even have heretical doubts that the esteemed neologist actually coined the deathless "in two words: Umpossible!" I say this because Jock Lawrence, then Goldwyn's press agent, used to beg many of us for gaffes he would then pass on to the Hollywood press—as 24-karat Goldwynisms.

I learned long ago not to be surprised by popular but incorrect attributions. After all, such historical utterances as "Go west, young man," "We have nothing to fear but fear itself," " . . . the Iron Curtain," "Ask not what your country can do for you; ask what you can do for your country" were *not* originated by, respectively, Horace Greeley, Franklin D. Roosevelt, Winston Churchill, John F. Kennedy. (The encouragement to go westward was first made by John L. Soule in an 1851 edition of the *Terre Haute Express.* In words only slightly different, Henry David Thoreau first wrote there was nothing to fear in his *Journal,* also in 1851. "The Iron Curtain" was first coined by Joseph Goebbels in 1945, and the admonishment, "Ask not . . ." was made, not quite verbatim, by Cicero, addressing the Senate of Rome in 63

B.C. The familiar "Any man who hates dogs and babies can't be all bad" is usually credited to W. C. Fields, but the line was uttered not by him but *about* him, by a young speaker at a Masquers' Club dinner in the great man's honor. I ought to know; I was there.

Or again: I always thought it was in a debate in the House of Commons that Gladstone, stung beyond endurance by Disraeli's barbs, cried, "You, sir, will die either on the gallows or of some loathsome disease!"—only to hear Disraeli retort, "That, sir, depends upon whether I embrace your principles or your mistress." Only yesterday (and I *do* mean yesterday) did I learn that the incomparable exchange took place in the eighteenth century, between the Earl of Sandwich and John Wilkes, a libertine of exceptional agility.

One final caveat: Never underestimate the ancestry of a squib. "Athens is a great place to visit, but I wouldn't want to live there" sounds as contemporary as bubble gum, but that putdown was tossed off by Isocrates, a ghost writer of the fourth century B.C. You would be startled by the number of current japeries that can be traced back to Epictetus, Marcus Aurelius, Gracián, Erasmus, Montaigne, Francis Bacon, Voltaire, Samuel Johnson, La Rochefoucauld, Whistler, G. K. Chesterton, Wilde, Mark Twain, Bernard Shaw, Stephen Leacock, Wilson Mizner, George S. Kaufman, *et*, as they say, *cetera*.

As a seasoned tautologist would put it: Some things are so unexpected that no one is prepared for them.

How Does the Author Make His Point?

1. How does Rosten make use of the devices of formal definition by giving them a new twist?
2. What method of definition does Rosten employ most frequently?
3. How would you characterize the author's tone?
4. What makes the author's conclusion effective?

What Do You Think?

1. In your opinion, does humor serve any function other than making people laugh? Can you think of any personal experiences where humor acted as an "unwitting messenger of truth"?

2. Many professional comedians are often rather shy offstage. Can you find anything in Rosten's essay that might explain this phenomenon?
3. Have you ever been guilty of a malapropism? Have you either read or heard any "verbal doozies" that would have served as good examples for this essay?

Barrier Signals

DESMOND MORRIS

Desmond Morris is a zoologist, a writer, a painter, a researcher, and a people watcher. As a writer, he is best known for his books The Naked Ape *and* The Human Zoo. *In both of these works, he uses his knowledge of animal behavior to explain human behavior, as he does in this excerpt from* Manwatching. *As an artist, Morris once exhibited his own paintings in a one-man show; at another time, he held a sale of abstract paintings done by chimpanzees!*

People feel safer behind some kind of physical barrier. If a social situation is in any way threatening, then there is an immediate urge to set up such a barricade. For a tiny child faced with a stranger, the problem is usually solved by hiding behind its mother's body and peeping out at the intruder to see what he or she will do next. If the mother's body is not available, then a chair or some other piece of solid furniture will do. If the stranger insists on coming closer, then the peeping face must be hidden too. If the insensitive intruder continues to approach despite these obvious signals of fear, then there is nothing for it but to scream or flee.

This pattern is gradually reduced as the child matures. In teenage girls it may still be detected in the giggling cover-up of the face, with hands or papers, when acutely or jokingly embarrassed. But by the time we are adult, the childhood hiding, which dwindled to adolescent shyness, is expected to disappear altogether, as we bravely stride out to meet our guests, hosts, companions, relatives, colleagues, customers, clients, or friends. Each social occasion involves us, once again, in encounters similar to the ones which made us hide as scared infants and, as then, each encounter is slightly threatening. In other words, the fears are still there, but their expression is blocked. Our adult roles demand control and suppression of any primitive urge to withdraw and hide ourselves away. The more formal the occasion and the more dominant or unfamiliar our social companions, the more worrying the moment of encounter becomes. Watching people under these conditions, it is possible to observe the many small ways in which they continue 'to hide behind their mother's skirts.' The actions are still there, but they are transformed into less obvious movements and postures. It is these that are the Barrier Signals of adult life.

The most popular form of Barrier Signal is the Body-cross. In this, the hands or arms are brought into contact with one another in front of the body, forming a temporary 'bar' across the trunk, rather like a bumper or fender on the front of a motor-car. This is not done as a physical act of fending off the other person, as when raising a forearm horizontally across the front of the body to push through a struggling crowd. It is done, usually at quite a distance, as a nervous guest approaches a dominant host. The action is performed unconsciously and, if tackled on the subject immediately afterwards, the guest will not be able to remember having made the gesture. It is always camouflaged in some way, because if it were performed as a primitive fending-off or covering-up action, it would obviously be too transparent. The disguise it wears varies from person to person. Here are some examples:

The special guest on a gala occasion is alighting from his official limousine. Before he can meet and shake hands with the reception committee, he has to walk alone across the open space in front of the main entrance to the building where the function is being held. A large crowd has come to watch his arrival and the press cameras are flashing. Even for the most experienced of celebrities this is a slightly nervous moment, and the mild fear that is felt expresses itself just as he is halfway across the 'greeting-space'. As he walks forward, his right hand reaches across his body and makes a last-minute adjustment to his left cuff-link. It pauses there momentarily as he takes a few more steps, and then, at last, he is close enough to reach out his hand for the first of the many handshakes.

On a similar occasion, the special guest is a female. At just the point where her male counterpart would have fiddled with his cuff, she reaches across her body with her right hand and slightly shifts the position of her handbag, which is hanging from her left forearm.

There are other variations on this theme. A male may finger a button or the strap of a wristwatch instead of his cuff. A female may smooth out an imaginary crease in a sleeve, or re-position a scarf or coat held over her left arm. But in all cases there is one essential feature: at the peak moment of nervousness there is a Body-cross, in which one arm makes contact with the other across the front of the body, constructing a fleeting barrier between the guest and the reception committee.

Sometimes the barrier is incomplete. One arm swings across but does not actually make contact with the other. Instead it deals with some trivial clothing-adjustment task on the opposite side of the body. With even heavier camouflage, the hand comes up and across, but goes no further than the far side of the head or face, with a mild stroking or touching action.

Less disguised forms of the Body-cross are seen with less experienced individuals. The man entering the restaurant, as he walks across an open space, rubs his hands together, as if washing them. Or he advances with them clasped firmly in front of him.

Such are the Barrier Signals of the greeting situation, where one person is advancing on another. Interestingly, field observations reveal that it is most unlikely that both the greeter *and* the greeted will perform such actions. Regardless of status, it is nearly always the new arrival who makes the body-cross movement, because it is he who is invading the home territory of the greeters. They are on their own ground or, even if they are not, they were there first and have at least temporary territorial 'rights' over the place. This gives them an indisputable dominance at the moment of the greeting. Only if they are extremely subordinate to the new arrival, and perhaps in serious trouble with him, will there be a likelihood of them taking the 'body-cross role'. And if they do, this will mean that the new arrival on the scene will omit it when he enters.

These observations tell us something about the secret language of Barrier Signals, and indicate that, although the sending and receiving of the signals are both unconsciously done, the message gets across, nonetheless. The message says: 'I am nervous but I will not retreat'; and this makes it into an act of subordination which automatically makes the other person feel slightly more dominant and more comfortable.

The situation is different after greetings are over and people are standing about talking to one another. Now, if one man edges too close to another, perhaps to hear better in all the noise of chattering voices, the boxed-in companion may feel the same sort of threatening sensation that the arriving celebrity felt as he walked towards the reception committee. What is needed now, however, is something more long-lasting than a mere cuff-fumble. It is simply not possible to go fiddling with a button for as long as this companion is going to thrust himself forward. So a more composed posture is needed. The Favorite Body-cross employed in this situation is the arm-fold, in which the left and right arms intertwine themselves across the front of the chest. This posture, a perfect, frontal Barrier Signal, can be held for a very long time without appearing strange. Unconsciously it transmits a 'come-no-farther' message and is used a great deal at crowded gatherings. It has also been used by poster artists as a deliberate 'They-shall-not-pass!' gesture, and is rather formally employed by bodyguards when standing outside a protected doorway.

The same device of arm-folding can be used in a sitting relationship where the companion is approaching too close, and it can be amplified by a crossing of the legs *away* from the companion. Another variant is to press the tightly clasped hands down on the crotch and squeeze them there between the legs, as if protecting the genitals. The message of this particular form of barrier is clear enough, even though neither side becomes consciously aware of it. But perhaps the major Barrier Signal for the seated person is that ubiquitous device, the desk. Many a businessman would feel naked without one and hides behind it gratefully every day, wearing it like a vast, wooden chastity-belt. Sitting beyond it he feels fully protected from the visitor exposed on the far side. It is the supreme barrier, both physical and psychological, giving him an immediate and lasting comfort while he remains in its solid embrace.

How Does the Author Make His Point?

1. What is the thesis statement? Does the author place it effectively? Explain.
2. In what ways do barrier signals change from childhood to adulthood?
3. What are the types of body-cross? Which are the least sophisticated? What causes the differences between the actions of men and those of women? Since the essay refers to types of barrier signals, why is it not a classification essay?
4. Why is it the "greeted" and not the "greeter" who usually employs the body-cross?
5. Name the other forms of the body-cross mentioned in the essay.

What Do You Think?

1. Do you use any of these barrier signals? Would you know if you did?
2. Does it bother you to have to talk to someone across a desk? Do you think people use their desks as barriers? Are "outer" offices and secretaries barrier signals?
3. Why do you think people need these barriers? What do they mask?
4. Observe people around you, looking for barriers they use. If you are observant, you should have a list of them in one day.

What Is Poverty? Listen.

CURTIS ULMER

Taken from a book entitled Teaching the Culturally Disadvantaged Adult, *the following poignant essay creates a definition by piling up vivid details:*

You ask me what is poverty? Listen to me. Listen without pity. I cannot use your pity. Listen with understanding.

Poverty is living in a smell that never leaves. It is a smell of young children who cannot walk the long dark way in the night. It is the smell of milk which has gone sour because the refrigerator doesn't work, and it costs money to get it fixed. It is the smell of rotting garbage.

Poverty is being tired. I have always been tired. They told me at the hospital when the last baby came that I had chronic anemia and that I needed a corrective operation. I listened politely. The poor are always polite. The poor always listen. They don't say that there is no money for the iron pills or better food or worm medicine. Or that an operation is frightening and costs so much. Or that there is no one to take care of the children.

Poverty is dirt. You say, "Anyone can be clean." Let me explain about housekeeping with no money. Every night I wash every stitch my schoolage child has on and hope her clothes dry by morning. What dishes there are, I wash in cold water with no soap. Even the cheapest soap has to be saved for the baby's diapers. Why not hot water? Hot water is a luxury. I do not have luxuries.

Poverty is asking for help. I will tell you how it feels. You find out where the office is that you are supposed to visit. You circle the block for four or five times, then you go in. Everyone is busy. Finally someone comes out and you tell her you need help. That is never the person you need to see. You go to see another person and, after spilling the whole shame of your life all over the desk between you, you find that this isn't the right office after all.

Poverty is looking into a black future. Your children won't play with my boys. My boys will turn to other boys who steal to get what they want. And for my daughter? At best there is for her a life like mine.

"But," you say to me, "there are schools." Yes, there are schools. But my children have no books, no magazines, no pencils, no crayons or paper. And most important of all, they do not have health. They have worms. They have infections. They do not sleep well on the floor. They do not suffer from hunger, but they do suffer from malnutrition.

Poverty is cooking without food and cleaning without soap. Poverty is an acid that drips on pride until all pride is worn away. Some of you say that you would do something in my situation. And maybe you would—for the first week or month. But for year after year after year?

How Does the Author Make Her Point?

1. What is the thesis statement?
2. Discuss the effectiveness of the topic sentences.
3. What is the effect of the short, simple sentences?
4. What is the tone of the essay?
5. Where does the author use parallelism? Find at least five examples.

What Do You Think?

1. Do you agree with the implication in the last two sentences?
2. Are there any statements in this essay that you disagree with, that you think are not true?
3. Which of the conditions that the author mentions would bother you most? Explain why.
4. Did this essay change, in any way, your previous attitude toward the poor?
5. Do you think that there is no way out for the poor, that they are trapped in their poverty?

INTEGRATING READING SKILLS WITH WRITING SKILLS: DISCOVERING MEANING THROUGH CONTEXT

After over a hundred years of research into the origins of human intelligence, psychologists have concluded that vocabulary is still the single most valid indicator of a person's IQ. Unfortunately, however, few people take an active interest in expanding their vocabulary. Most high school graduates let their library cards expire, and the average college graduate reads fewer than three books per year! What these individuals do not realize is that learning new words is just as important to an adult as it is to the first or second grader who is trying to learn how to read. What you, as a student, must realize is that if you want to become a good thinker, a good reader, and a good writer, you simply can't ignore words that you don't understand. You have to try to find out what they mean.

The first thing you should do when you encounter a new word is to see how that word is used in the sentence. You would be surprised how often you can determine the general meaning of a word simply by examining the words that surround it—its *context*. Reading authority Brenda Smith points out several different types of contextual clues, such as examples, definition, comparison, and contrast* that can help you determine the meaning of a word. For example, if you were reading the Bible, you might come across a number of words that you wouldn't understand. Consider these words, for instance:

terebinth	licentiousness
shoal	girds
presumptuously	prudent
prostrate	

Some of these words are probably part of your *passive* vocabulary; that is, you have heard them or seen them before, but you don't really know what they mean. After you have looked at them carefully in their contexts, you can get a fairly good idea of what they mean—even for example *terebinth*, which you have probably never seen nor heard. A study of their contexts will permit you to use the words yourself; that is, you will have added them to your *active* vocabulary.

---

* See *Breaking Through:* Beginning College Reading (Glenview, Illinois: Scott, Foresman and Company, 1983), pp. 52–53.

Explanatory Details:

> . . . it will be burned again like a *terebinth* or an oak whose stump remains standing when it is felled. (Isaiah 6:13)

It's not hard to figure out that a terebinth is a tree. If you looked the word up in a dictionary, you would also learn that the terebinth was man's original source of turpentine.

> "Put out into the deep and let down your nets for a catch." And Simon answered, "Master, we toiled all night and took nothing! But at your word I will let down the nets." And when they had done this, they enclosed a great *shoal* of fish; and as their nets were breaking, they beckoned to their partners in the other boat to come and help them. (Luke 5:4–7)

You don't need a dictionary to figure out that "a great *shoal* of fish" must mean one heck of a lot of fish!

Example:

> The man who acts *presumptuously*, by not obeying the priest who stands to minister there before the Lord, . . . that man shall die. (Deuteronomy 17:12)

The phrase "by not obeying the priest" provides a specific example which illustrates the meaning of presumptuous—overstepping one's bounds.

Definition:

> There the evildoers lie *prostrate* They are thrust down, unable to rise. (Psalm 36:12)

> They have become callous and have given themselves up to *licentiousness*, Greedy to practice every kind of uncleanness. (Ephesians 4:19)

In both passages, the second line actually defines the word in question.

Comparison

> May it be like a garment which he wraps round him Like a belt with which he daily *girds* himself. (Psalm 109:19)

The reader can clearly see the connection between belt and garment and thus also between "girds" and "wraps round."

Contrast:

> A *prudent* man sees danger and hides himself; but the simple go on, and suffer for it. (Proverbs 27:12)

Seeing the prudent man as the opposite of the simple man who isn't smart enough to protect himself from danger, you can figure out that prudence must have something to do with wisdom or intelligence.

How Context Affects Meaning

Open an unabridged dictionary of the English language and you will find several hundred thousand words, nearly all of which are followed by more than one definition. Most words have several meanings. That's why you always have to see how a word is used in a sentence before you can determine what it means. For example, if you look up *word* in Webster's, you will find ten different definitions listed. Read the following sentences and notice how the term *word* or *words* takes on a different meaning, depending on the context in which it is used:

1. How could you reveal my secret? You gave me your *word*. (word = promise)
2. "A *word* to the wise," said the nurse, "get a second opinion." (word = advice)
3. Could I have a *word* with you? (word = private conversation)
4. Have you had any *word* from your lawyer (word = news, information)
5. Bob is upset because he and his wife had *words* about Larry's drinking. (word = argument)
6. "Heaven and earth shall pass away, but my *words* shall not pass away." (word = truth) (New Testament)
7. "Clearness is the most important matter in the use of *words*." (word = language) (Quintilian)
8. "A man of *words* and not of deeds is like a garden full of weeds." (word = thoughts as opposed to actions) (James Howell)

IMPROVING YOUR VOCABULARY

Context

For both readers and writers, the dictionary is the most useful of all reference tools. Nevertheless, using the dictionary is not the most common method of determining the meaning of a word; the most common way to understanding is through *context,* the words surrounding the word under consideration.

Suppose you heard a friend say,"Jack gives me a pain when he kowtows to the instructor hoping for a good grade. Why doesn't he do his work like the rest of us?" Perhaps, you're unfamiliar with the word *kowtow,* but you could still guess approximately what it means—to flatter or to overpraise someone. For many purposes, this meaning through context would be sufficient for you to recognize it whenever you see it or hear it, thus making it a part of your *passive* vocabulary.

Through continuing awareness of context, you move words from your passive to your active vocabulary, thus enlarging the number of words you can put to use. Such a progression from passive to active is the standard pattern of growth for an individual's vocabulary.

Refer to the essay in the first part of this chapter, "Notes on the Saturnalia of Hallway Life," and look carefully at the contexts of the following words:

wanton	Saturnalia	tactile
burgeoning	amorous	erotic
libido, libidinous	consummate	voyeurism

Can you guess their meanings?

Remembering that the author likens the classroom to a battle-field might help you guess the meaning of the following words:

communiques
salutary
arsenal
deployed

Context should give you a clue to the meaning of these words:

covertly	votaries
blatantly	profundities
foppishness	frenetic

These words you may have to look up: (But only two!)

avuncular

ignominious

For the groups of words listed above, write down the meanings you guessed in one list; then, beside those meanings, write down the dictionary definitions. Even if you didn't guess accurately many of the unknown words, paying attention to context will increase your skill in vocabulary building.

How Meanings Change

Words are symbols that point to specific objects or ideas. These objects or ideas are called *referents*—things referred to. The *meanings* of words come from general agreement among people sharing a language that a particular combination of letters will have a specific referent. As distinguished linguist W. Nelson Francis explains, "Words do not have meaning; people have meanings for words."

Since the meaning of a word is not fixed within the word itself but is lent to it by people using the language, it follows that meaning may change when events or living conditions give people needs for new meanings or when people no longer need an old meaning. Two of the main ways in which meanings change are by *extension* and by *limitation;* words are said to have acquired new meanings by extension or to have lost them by limitation.

Extension

Most common words have a number of meanings. The word *man,* as given in *The American Heritage Dictionary of the English Language,** for instance, has approximately twenty different meanings, all, or almost all, of which are well-known extensions.

---

* Copyright © 1973 Houghton Mifflin Company. Reprinted by permission from *The American Heritage Dictionary of the English Language.*

Man (măn) *n. pl.* **men** (měn). **1.** An adult male human being, as distinguished from a female. **2.** Any human being, regardless of sex or age; a member of the human race; a person. **3.** The human race; mankind. Used without an article: *the accomplishments of man.* **4.** *Zoology.* A member of the genus *Homo,* family Hominidae, order Primates, class Mammalia, characterized by erect posture and an opposable thumb; especially, a member of the only extant species, *Homo sapiens,* distinguished by the ability to communicate by means of organized speech and to record information in a variety of symbolic systems. **5.** A male human being endowed with such qualities as courage, strength, and fortitude, considered characteristic of manhood. **6.** *Theology.* In Christianity and Judaism, a being composed of a body and a soul or spirit. **7.** A husband, lover, or sweetheart. Now used chiefly informally, except in the phrase *man and wife.* **8.** An enlisted serviceman of the armed forces. Used chiefly in the plural: *officers and men.* **9.** Any workman, servant, or subordinate, as opposed to an employer or master. **10.** *Informal.* Fellow. Used as a term of address. **11.** One who swore allegiance to a lord in the Middle Ages; a liegeman; vassal. **12.** Any of the pieces used in chess, checkers, backgammon, and other board games. **13.** *Nautical.* A ship. Used in combination: *merchantman; man-of-war.*—**as one man.** Unanimously: *They answered him as one man.*—**be one's own man.** To be independent in judgment and action—**man and boy.** From childhood on: *Man and boy, I've lived here 40 years.*—**The man.** *Negro Slang.* A white man. Used disparagingly.—**to a man.** Including everyone; without exceptions.—*tr.v.* **manned, manning, mans. 1.** To supply or furnish with men for defense, support, or service: *manning a ship.* **2.** To be stationed at in order to defend, care for, or operate: *man the guns.*—*adj.* **Male.**—*interj.* Used as an expletive to indicate excitement or to draw attention: *Man! it's hot in here.* [Middle English *man* (plural *men*). Old English *mann* (plural *menn*).]

Despite the multiple meanings, users have no difficulty in deciding which meaning is meant because of context.

The entry under *mad,* as defined in the same dictionary, lists the following extended definitions:

> **mad** (mad) *adj.* **madder, maddest. 1.** Suffering from a disorder of the mind; insane: *"Honora was eccentric, but Maggie told everyone in the village that she was mad."* (John Cheever). **2.** As if insane; temporarily or apparently deranged by violent sensations, emotions, or ideas: *"I tell thee I am mad/In Cressid's love."* (Shakespeare). **3.** *Informal.* Feeling or showing strong liking or enthusiasm. Used with *about, for* or *over:* *"You probabaly know how mad he is about sports."* (Peter Taylor). **4.** *Informal.* Angry; resentful: *"He'd be so mad he missed it he wouldn't speak to me for days."* (Harper Lee). **5.** Lacking restraint or reason; wildly foolish;

senseless: *"Ah, will you stop telling me your mad dreams."* (Eugene O'Neill). **6.** Marked by extreme excitement, confusion, or agitation; frantic: *a mad scramble for the bus.* **7.** Boisterously gay; hilarious: *have a mad time.* **8.** *Slang.* Delightfully unusual; humorously pointless: *mad conversation in double talk.* **9.** Affected by rabies; rabid.—**have a mad on.** *Slang.* To sulk; be angry.—**like mad.** *Slang.* Wildly; impetuously: *He drove like mad.*—*v.* **madded, madding, mads.**—*tr rare.* To madden or make mad.—*intr. Rare.* To act, be, or become mad. [Middle English *madd.* Old English *gemædd*, past participle of *gemædan*, to madden, from *gemād.* mad.]

Even though new words are created all the time, people are likely to use an old word if they can extend its meaning to cover the new concept—as W. Nelson Francis points out.

Therefore, when some new aspect of the outside world requires a new segment of meaning, an existing word often has its range of meaning extended to cover the new area. The vocabulary of railroading, for example, had to be built up quite rapidly to meet the numerous new objects, events, and occupations which this new mode of transport created. It is true that some new words, like *locomotive*, were created. But, for the most part, words which had already been in the language for a long time were simply extended to cover those new segments of meaning which most closely resembled their existing ones. For the way along which the trains traveled, the old word *road* was used. The iron *rails* took their name from similarly shaped wooden parts of a fence. Collectively they made up the *track*, whose older meaning was "a path." A place where the track divided was called a *switch*, from an old word meaning originally a long slender twig or branch. A string of cars pulled by a locomotive naturally took on the name *train* (at first *train of carriages*), extended from the meaning "a body of persons, animals or vehicles travelling together in order, esp. in a long line or procession" (OED) which it had had since the fifteenth century. Various words previously used to describe vehicles drawn by horses had their meanings extended to cover the new vehicles: *carriage, coach, car* (in America), *van* (in Britain). Places where the trains stopped came to be called *stations,* by extension of the meaning of a word already used to describe places on a highway where stage-coaches stopped to change horses or passengers. A piece of paper entitling one *to ride* on the train was called a *ticket,* a word which had been used in this general sense in the theatre since the seventeenth century. Devices used to indicate the state of the track ahead were called *signals,* a word which already had the general meaning of "indicator," or *semaphores,* a word made up of Greek roots ("sign-carrier") during the Napoleonic wars to describe a device for sending messages.

W. Nelson Francis

Limitation

The opposite of extension is limitation, in which the meanings of a word dwindle, either because their referents no longer exist or because other words have replaced them. The word *doublet,* for instance, is limited now to a garment for a stage costume, since men no longer customarily wear doublets. And the word *starve,* which once meant simply *to die* now has only the limited sense of to die from hunger. The word *deer* was once a general term for any animal, but now it is limited to one specific family of animals. The ultimate limitation occurs, of course, when no meanings exist any longer for a word, and it drops out of the language.

ASSIGNMENT

Many well-known figures have been able to capture the essence of an idea in a brief but powerful definition. In the following examples, the authors have used various methods of definition (formal, negation, example, comparison) to convey their specific understanding of an abstract term. Read the definitions and use them as thought provokers to help you choose a topic. Then write an essay defining one of the terms covered in the definitions or another abstract term that came to mind after reading one of the definitions. Make sure that your thesis statement is clear and that you use several different methods of definition to develop the body of your essay.

Charity: A bone to the dog is not charity. Charity is the bone shared with the dog, when you are just as hungry as the dog.

Jack London

Fanatic: A fanatic is one who can't change his mind and won't change the subject.

Winston Churchill

Hypocrite: The man who murdered both his parents and pleaded for mercy on the grounds that he was an orphan.

Abraham Lincoln

Cynic: A cynic is a man who knows the price of everything and the value of nothing.

Oscar Wilde

Wealth: He is rich or poor according to what he *is*, not according to what he *has*.

Henry Ward Beecher

Democracy: It's the right to make the wrong choice.

John Patrick

Courage: Courage is grace under pressure.

Ernest Hemingway

Education: Education is a progressive discovery of our ignorance.

Will Durant

Conscience: Conscience is a mother-in-law whose visit never ends.

H.L. Mencken

Failure: Defeat is not the worst of failures. Not to have tried is the true failure.

George Edward Woodberry

Patience: Patience is a minor form of despair, disguised as a virtue.

Ambrose Bierce

Insanity: Insanity is often the logic of an accurate mind overtaxed.

Oliver Wendell Holmes

Pride: Pride is an admission of weakness; it secretly fears all competition and dreads all rivals.

Fulton J. Sheen

Miser: He doesn't possess his gold; his gold possesses him.

La Fontaine

Gossip: Gossip is the art of saying nothing in a way that leaves practically nothing unsaid.

Walter Winchell

Wife: A wife is a gift bestowed upon man to reconcile him to the loss of paradise.

Johann Wolfgang von Goethe

Work: Nothing is really work unless you would rather be doing something else.

James Matthew Barrie

Pain: Pain is no evil, unless it conquers us.

Charles Kingsley

Tact: The ability to describe others as they see themselves.

Abraham Lincoln

Politics: Politics is the conduct of public affairs for private advantage.

Ambrose Bierce

Marriage: Marriage, a market which has nothing free but the entrance.

Montaigne

Enemy: An enemy is anyone who tells the truth about you.

Elbert Hubbard

America: America is a large, friendly dog in a very small room. Every time it wags its tail, it knocks over a chair.

Arnold J. Toynbee

Book: A book is a mirror: if an ass peers into it, you can't expect an apostle to look out.

G.C. Lichtenberg

Drunkenness: Drunkenness is temporary suicide; the happiness that it brings is merely negative, a momentary cessation of unhappiness.

Bertrand Russell

10

Persuading

RHETORIC

For a number of people who theorize about writing, all writing is persuasion. Their idea is that anyone who goes to all the work of writing something well (and it is a lot of work) does it only to persuade someone else to think something, feel something, or do something that he or she might not have thought, felt, or done without the persuasive writing. Whether or not this theory is correct, much writing is persuasive. The persuasive writer creates new sympathies and perceptions in the reader through two kinds of appeals: the emotional and the logical. Usually, these two must work together.

Emotional Appeals

Although emotional appeals can be overdone, a legitimate appeal may be made to readers' self-interest, their need for survival, safety, love, and esteem. A legitimate appeal may be made to their feelings, pity, loyalty, generosity, and patriotism. Feelings are a powerful addition to logical appeals.

Logical Appeals

If you don't want to be exploited by unscrupulous writers who want your money, your voice or your vote, you must be able to distinguish between a good argument and a bad one. If you want to write honest but effective persuasion, your own reasoning must be free of fallacies, wrong thinking that leads to gross error.

Logicians have identified a number of fallacies so that they can be avoided. Some of the common ones are described in the following paragraphs:

Hasty Generalization

Jumping to conclusions is a widespread and dangerous fallacy. It means reaching a conclusion without enough evidence to support it. The hasty generalization frequently uses the words *all or none*. It can be demolished by giving any evidence against it.

> Hasty Generalization: Women are terrible drivers. (This implies *all* women.)
> Evidence Against: Mrs. Wargetz is a fine driver.
> Therefore: Hasty generalization is proved wrong.
> Hasty Generalization: No child goes to bed cheerfully.
> Evidence Against: After his hike, Johnny was very happy to hit the sack.
> Therefore: Hasty generalization is proved wrong.

Remember that you must have enough evidence to support a generalization. And most generalizations that have *all* or *none* in them should be qualified. For instance, some women are poor drivers because their husbands seldom let them drive.

Either-Or Fallacy

This fallacy comes from the oversimplified thinking that sees only two possible answers to a complex question. There are more answers than good or bad, black or white, love it or leave it. "Either you back me on this, or you are not my friend." It is quite possible that a logical disagreement on an issue has no influence on the emotional basis of a friendship.

Post Hoc Fallacy

The hasty generalization and the either-or fallacy come from reaching a conclusion on too little evidence. The *post hoc* fallacy is based on no real evidence but on a misunderstanding of assumed evidence. The *post hoc* fallacy is a confusion of a time sequence with a cause-and-effect sequence. (The whole name of the fallacy is *post hoc, ergo propter hoc,* which is translated as: "after this, therefore because of this.") For instance, an illogical thinker might say: "Old Mrs. Seidel got a telegram and less than an hour later she had a heart attack. She must have received terrible news." It's possible she did; it's equally possible she got a singing telegram wishing her happy Mother's Day.

Remember that even an apparent cause-and-effect relationship may be just a coincidence.

Circular Reasoning

This kind of nonthinking usually happens when enthusiastic people are making value judgments. They simply say the same thing twice, linking the two statements together with a "therefore" or a "because." For example: "The senator had a poverty-stricken childhood because his parents were poor." Or, "Circular reasoning is a fruitless discussion; therefore, nothing important is said."

Misuse of Authority

An authority is an authority only when he is speaking about something he knows. Henry Ford's well-known boner that "history is bunk" is a prime example of the fallacious use of authority. If Ford had wished to pose as an authority, he should have spoken on cars and their manufacture.

False Analogy

Analogy, a kind of comparison, reasons by parallel cases. If you notice that Case A is very much like Case B, you may assume that what is true for A is also true for B. This is helpful in explaining, but in reasoning it is weak because the similarities are only partial, not complete.

A well-know analogy compares the federal government to the "ship of state." People who think the president should have more power argue that a ship runs much better is there is only one captain. Therefore, their analogy goes, the president should be like the captain and have all the power of Congress and the courts. The analogy is false because the federal government has only the most superficial resemblance to a ship. But the fallacy is dangerous because careless thinkers are so busy agreeing about the captain that they forget the government.

The Majority-Is-Always-Right and Large Numbers

The majority and *large numbers* are closely related fallacies. Assuming everyone is equally well-informed and objective, the majority could well be right. If not, a well-informed minority might easily be correct.

As for *large numbers*, consider a statement like "Five million Americans choose Burpy Cola two times out of three." Now, this is fairly impressive at first glance. But out of 230 million Americans, how many are there who might drink soft drinks?

There are many other fallacies, but the important thing to remember is this: If you become aware of fallacies, you will probably be able to detect them in others' writing and to avoid them in your own.

ORGANIZATION

Prewriting

The persuasive essay is contructed in the same basic form as the other types of essays discussed in this book. It differs from them only in its aim—to persuade. That aim, however, influences every technique you decide upon, every word you choose.

In selecting your topic, it is important to choose something you care about because if *you* don't care, neither will your *reader*. Your indifference will show in spite of *you* and turn away your reader. You don't have to select a topic that's earthshaking (there really aren't many of those); but you do need to select a topic that arouses your love or amusement or anger or whatever. The feeling your topic arouses in you will determine your attitude toward it and toward the audience you want to persuade to agree with you.

Although your topic may range from the trivial to the profound and your attitude is your own free expression, they must be in some accord. For instance, you will not be very persuasive if you attempt to be funny about child abuse or impassioned and tragic about bumper stickers.

Thesis Statement

The thesis statement is vital in persuasion. You must make totally clear to your readers what you want them to think or perhaps to do. The thesis statement may come at the very beginning of your essay or after an introduction. It is usually brief, but wherever it comes, it must be clear and it must clearly be the thesis statement.

In a book on how to write, called *The Reader over Your Shoulder,* Robert Graves and Alan Hodge give a series of "Principles of Clear Statement." For Principle Nine, they make this thesis statement.

"No word or phrase should be ambiguous."

They go on to give several examples of trouble arising from ambiguous phrasing.

It is often very difficult to compose an English sentence that cannot possibly be misunderstood. From the Minutes of a Borough Council Meeting:

Councillor Trafford took exception to the proposed notice at the entrance of South Park: "No dogs must be brought to this Park except on a lead." He pointed out that this order would not prevent an owner from releasing his pets, or pet, from a lead when once safely inside the Park.

The Chairman (Colonel Vine): What alternative wording would you propose, Councillor?

Councillor Trafford: "Dogs are not allowed in this park without leads."

Councillor Hogg: Mr. Chairman, I object. The order should be addressed to the owners, not to the dogs.

Councillor Trafford: That is a nice point. Very well then: "Owners of dogs are not allowed in this Park unless they keep them on leads."

Councillor Hogg: Mr. Chairman, I object. Strictly speaking, this would prevent me as a dog-owner from leaving my dog in the back-garden at home and walking with Mrs. Hogg across the Park.

Councillor Trafford: Mr. Chairman, I suggest that our legalistic friend be asked to redraft the notice himself.

Councillor Hogg: Mr. Chairman, since Councillor Trafford finds it so difficult to improve on my original wording, I accept. "Nobody without his dog on a lead is allowed in this Park."

Councillor Trafford: Mr. Chairman, I object. Strictly speaking, this notice would prevent me, as a citizen who owns no dogs, from walking in the Park without first acquiring one.

Councillor Hogg: (with some warmth): Very simply, then: "Dogs must be led in this Park."

Councillor Trafford: Mr. Chairman, I object: this reads as if it were a general injunction to the Borough to lead their dogs into the Park.

Councillor Hogg interposed a remark for which he was called to order; upon his withdrawing it, it was directed to be expunged from the Minutes.

Robert Graves and Alan Hodge

In his introduction to *History of English Literature*, the great French critic Hippolyte Taine gives a short introduction and a thesis statement that gives direction, organization, and unity to a vast book of three volumes. His ideas, widely accepted now, were considered so daring that he was dismissed from his university. His book aimed to persuade scholars throughout Europe to accept his views on the relationship between history and literature.

> History has been transformed, within a hundred years in Germany, within sixty years in France, and that by the study of their literatures.
>
> It was perceived that a literary work is not a mere individual play of imagination, the isolated caprice of an excited brain, but a transcript of contemporary manners, a manifestation of a certain kind of mind. It was concluded that we might recover, from the monuments of literature, a knowledge of the manner in which men thought and felt centuries ago. The attempt was made, and it succeeded.
>
> Hippolyte Taine

Development

All methods of development can be successfully used in persuasion. Most often, a combination of methods works best. Graves and Hodge, however, use only examples to support their "Principles of Clear Statement." For all twenty-five principles, they announce the principle and show by several examples the obscurity that results from ignoring it. Taine, as might be expected in so large a book, uses many modes: definition, description, narration, and, above all, causal analysis.

You will find that the thesis statement, when clearly and forcefully stated, not only is persuasive in itself but directs you to the most effective methods of developing it.

Conclusion

As you have already heard several times at least, the conclusion is important because it is the last thing you leave in the reader's mind. The importance of the conclusion in a persuasive essay is obvious. It is your last chance to make your point. Therefore, you should restate the topic and reinforce the attitude with the most eloquent closing sentences you can muster.

The Future Is Now

ROSE LEE HAYDEN

Rose Lee Hayden is currently executive director of the National Council on Foreign Languages and International Studies. In the following essay, she uses a number of persuasive techniques to make her point that Americans are falling behind other countries in meeting international problems. One remedy is to learn the languages and cultures of the other peoples with whom we share the world.

Introduction—notice terms expressing attitude—"nonsense," "ridiculous," "baloney"

One often is exposed to nonsense when questioning why American citizens choose not to learn foreign languages. One ridiculous prevailing prejudice is that somehow people from other nations are born with a genetic code that enables them to unravel other languages with ease, while Americans simply lack the native ablility to learn about other peoples, cultures, and languages. Baloney! Other nations and peoples are more successful because they are motivated to learn other languages, they invest in instruction, and students spend a lot of time dedicating themselves to a degree of mastery.

Thesis statement

It is obvious that people in other lands have different *attitudes* toward language learning.

Body—reasons why Americans are reluctant to learn another language

People are motivated to learn English or other world-use languages, since language acquisition often is tied to social mobility. In the United States, speaking a second language, usually a language of immigration, was considered by many a mark of inferior social status.

Finally, few other educational systems are as comprehensive as that of the U.S. Most systems are highly elitist, with distinct tracks for leaders and followers. The U.S. system is one of the few in which so many people have access to education at all levels. The real challenge is to retain that broad access and assure excellent instruction.

Use of authoritative source of statistical data to support thesis statement

Congressman Paul Simon once surveyed 74 nations to learn what languages were required in schools around the world. Even countries like Botswana require more languages by the fourth grade than U.S. schools require altogether. To get into a university in Austria, a student must have eight years of a living foreign language plus four years of Latin. In the Arab Emirates, English is required from fifth through twelfth grades, while Egypt requires six years of English study, starting in the sixth grade. Honduras expects its students to fulfill a five-year foreign language requirement, and India has a complex system requiring all students to study two languages other than the mother tongue. Swedish students have taken English for nine full years by the time they graduate from high school, and have also studied either French or German from grade seven on. Almost all Soviet students take one foreign language in high school, one is required for university graduation; and a second or third foreign language is required in graduate school. But in the United States, one high school in five offers no instruction in any foreign language—modern or ancient.

Definition of problem on a national basis

The United States is entering a phase in which the most dynamic areas of federal policy are likely to be foreign affairs, defense, and economics—particularly as it relates to control of inflation, reindustrialization, energy self-sufficiency, and export promotion. In such circumstances, widespread knowledge of other languages and cultures is central to America's national security.

Causal analysis—five reasons for changing educational system

There are at least five excellent reasons for closing the gap between the U.S. educational system and the national interest. The first reason for Americans to globalize education is elemental—survival. The U.S. must be able to handle sustained communications in order to survive in a competitive, nuclear system. The second reason is humanitarian. The "haves" of this world must learn to care about and share with others, just to claim human decency. Without intercultural understanding, the world grows daily more unstable.

Another reason for attempting to relate to other peoples and cultures is inherently selfish—the need for shared brain power. Scientific breakthroughs respect no national borders. Knowledge must be shared to attack the seemingly intractable world problems of energy, crime, injustice, disease, hunger, and overpopulation.

One way to prevent a national nervous breakdown is to be tuned to the dazzling diversity and joy of human expression around the world. Full appreciation of human existence—in music, dance, drama, the arts, sports, food, literature, religion—is unattainable without an education that opens the mind and cultivates taste.

Finally, democratic leadership that is dedicated to a peaceful world order requires a citizenry sophisticated enough to be able to cope with international realities and meet global challenges.

Generalizing—summing up of points made

Of all the resources that make American diplomacy effective, few are as neglected as the educational, linguistic, and cultural components of foreign policy. All the weapons in an expensive arsenal are insufficient for a nation that underinvests in the political, economic, educational, and cultural alliances that can counteract the distorted world image of America. Through the sharing of basic human values, Americans can shape international events rather than merely coping with them.

Conclusion—a warning

The secure future of the U.S. will require at least a minimal cadre of experts about other peoples and cultures; professionals in business and government who can negotiate across national borders; scientists and technicians who can extend and share human knowledge on a global basis; and citizens knowledgeable enough to support tough leadership decisions in a dangerous and complicated world.

An English-Speaking World

ROBERT MCCRUM, WILLIAM CRAN, AND ROBERT MCNEIL

The following message opened the PBS television series, The Story of English. *This series was presented a number of times and was subsequently made into a book recording the widespread takeover of the world's languages by English.*

On 5 September 1977, the American spacecraft Voyager One blasted-off on its historic mission to Jupiter and beyond. On board, the scientists, who knew that Voyager would one day spin through distant star systems, had installed a recorded greeting from the people of the planet Earth. Preceding a brief message in fifty-five different languages for the people of outer space, the gold-plated disc plays a statement, from the Secretary-General of the United Nations, an Austrian named Kurt Waldheim, speaking on behalf of 147 member states—in English.

The rise of English is a remarkable success story. When Julius Caesar landed in Britain nearly two thousand years ago, English did not exist. Five hundred years later, *Englic,* incomprehensible to modern ears, was probably spoken by about as few people as currently speak Cherokee—and with about as little influence. Nearly a thousand years later, at the end of the sixteenth century, when William Shakespeare was in his prime, English was the native speech of between five and seven million Englishmen and it was, in the words of a contemporary, "of small reatch, it stretcheth no further than this iland of ours, naie not there over all".

Four hundred years later, the contrast is extraordinary. Between 1600 and the present, in armies, navies, companies and expeditions, the speakers of English—including Scots, Irish, Welsh, American and many more—travelled into every corner of the globe, carrying their language and culture with them. Today, English is used by at least 750 million people, and barely half of those speak it as a mother tongue. Some estimates have put that figure closer to one billion. Whatever the total, English at the end of the twentieth century is more widely scattered, more widely spoken and written, than any other language has ever been. It has become *the* language of the planet, the first truly global language.

The statistics of English are astonishing. Of all the world's languages (which now number some 2700), it is arguably the richest in vocabulary. The compendious *Oxford English Dictionary* lists about 500,000 words; and a further half million technical and scientific terms remain uncatalogued. According to traditional estimates, neighbouring German has a vocabulary of about 185,000 words and French fewer than 100,000, including such Franglais as *le snacque-barre* and *le hit-parade*. About 350 million people use English vocabulary as a mother tongue: about one-tenth of the world's population, scattered across every continent and surpassed, in numbers, though not in distribution, only by the speakers of the many varieties of Chinese. Three-quarters of the world's mail, and its telexes and cables, are in English. So are more than half the world's technical and scientific periodicals: it is the language of technology from Silicon Valley to Shanghai. English is the medium for 80 per cent of the information stored in the world's computers. Nearly half of all business deals in Europe are conducted in English. It is the language of sports and glamour; the official language of the Olympics and the Miss Universe competition. English is the official voice of the air, of the sea, and of Christianity: it is the ecumenical language of the World Council of Churches. Five of the largest broadcasting companies in the world (CBS, NBC, ABC, BBC, CBC) transmit in English to audiences that regularly exceed one hundred million.

English has a few rivals, but no equals. Neither Spanish nor Arabic, both international languages, have this global sway. Another rival, Russian, has the political and economic under-pinning of a world language, but far from spreading its influence outside the Soviet empire, it, too, is becoming mildly colonized by new words known as *Russlish* for example, *seksapil* (sex appeal) and *noh-khau* (know-how), Germany and Japan have, in matching the commercial and industrial vigour of the United States, achieved the commercial precondition of language-power, but their languages have also been invaded by English, in the shape of *Deutchlish* and *Japlish*.

The remarkable story of how English spread within predominantly English-speaking societies like the United States, Canada, Australia and New Zealand is not, with the benefit of hindsight, unique. It is a process in language that is as old as Greek, or Chinese. The truly significant development, which has occurred only in the last one hundred years or so, is the use of

English, taking the most conservative estimates, by three or four hundred million people for whom it is not a native language. English has become a *second* language in countries like India, Nigeria or Singapore where it is used for administration, broadcasting and education. In these countries, English is a vital alternative language, often unifying huge territorities and diverse populations. When Rajiv Gandhi appealed for an end to the violence that broke out after the assassination of his mother, Mrs. Indira Gandhi, he went on television and spoke to his people in English. In anglophone Africa, seizures of power are announced in English. Then there is English as *foreign* language, used in countries (like Holland or Yugoslavia) where it is backed up by a tradition of English teaching, or where it has been more recently adopted, Senegal for instance. Here it is used to have contact with people in other countries, usually to promote trade and scientific progress, but to the benefit of international communication generally. A Dutch poet is read by a few thousands. Translated into English, he can be read by hundreds of thousands.

How Do the Authors Make Their Point?

1. Is the introduction effective? Why?
2. What is the thesis statement?
3. What method of development do the authors use most to support the thesis statement? What method is used in the introduction and in the final paragraph?

What Do You Think?

1. How do you account for the rapid rise in the number of English speakers in the world?
2. Do you ever feel embarrassed at your inablility to use another language when you see children and people with far fewer advantages than you have who are fluent in your language?
3. Does the message of this article lessen the importance of learning another language, which Rose Lee Hayden emphasizes in her essay?

An Open Letter to Black Parents: Send Your Children to the Libraries

ARTHUR ASHE

Arthur Ashe was a world renowned tennis champion who has become a professional writer. In this brief essay, he attempts to persuade black parents that sports are not the primary answer to the problems of black culture.

Since my sophomore year at University of California, Los Angeles, I have become convinced that we blacks spend too much time on the playing fields and too little time in the libraries.

Please don't think of this attitude as being pretentious just because I am a black, single, professional athlete. I don't have children, but I can make observations. I strongly believe the black culture expends too much time, energy and effort raising, praising and teasing our black children as to the dubious glories of professional sport.

All children need models to emulate—parents, relatives or friends. But when the child starts school, the influence of the parent is shared by teachers and classmates, by the lure of books, movies, ministers and newspapers, but most of all by television. Which televised events have the greatest number of viewers?— Sports—the Olympics, Super Bowl, Masters, World Series, pro basketball play-offs, Forest Hills. ABC-TV even has sports on Monday night prime time from April to December. So your child gets a massive dose of O.J. Simpson, Kareem Abul-Jabbar, Muhammad Ali, Reggie Jackson, Dr. J. and Lee Elder and other pro athletes. And it is only natural that your child will dream of being a pro athlete himself.

But consider these facts. For the major professional sports of hockey, football, basketball, baseball, golf, tennis and boxing, there are roughly only 3,170 major league positions available (attributing 200 positions to golf, 200 to tennis and 100 to boxing). And the annual turnover is small. We blacks are a subculture of about 28 million. Of the 13½ million men, 5 to 6 million are under 20 years of age, so your son has less than one chance in 1,000 of becoming a pro. Less than one in a thousand.

Would you bet your son's future on something with odds of 999 to 1 against you? I wouldn't.

Unless a child is exceptionally gifted you should know by the time he enters high school whether he has a future as an athlete. But what is more important is what happens if he doesn't graduate or doesn't land a college scholarship and doesn't have a viable alternative job career. Our high school dropout rate is several times the national average, which contributes to our unemployment rate of roughly twice the national average.

And how do you fight the figures in the newspapers every day? Ali has earned more than $30 million boxing, O. J. just signed for $2-1/2 million, Dr. J. for almost $3 million, Reggie Jackson for $2.8 million, Nate Archibald for $400,000 a year. All that money, recognition, attention, free cars, girls, jobs in the offseason—no wonder there is Pop Warner football, Little League baseball, National Junior Tennis League tennis, hockey practice at 5 A.M. and pickup basketball games in any center city at any hour.

There must be some way to assure that the 999 who try but don't make it to pro sports don't wind up on the street corners or in the unemployment lines. Unfortunately, our most widely recognized role models are athletes and entertainers—"runnin'" and "jumpin'" and "singin'" and "dancin'." While we are 60 percent of the National Basketball Association, we are less than 4 percent of the doctors and lawyers. While we are about 35 percent of major league baseball, we are less than 2 percent of the engineers. While we are about 40 percent of the National Football League, we are less than 11 percent of construction workers such as carpenters and bricklayers.

Our greatest heroes of the century have been athletes—Jack Johnson, Joe Louis and Muhammad Ali. Racial and economic discrimination forced us to channel our energies into athletics and entertainment. These were the ways out of the ghetto, the ways to get that Cadillac, those alligator shoes, the cashmere sport coat.

Somehow, parents must instill a desire for learning alongside the desire to be Walt Frazier. Why not start by sending black professional athletes into high schools to explain the facts of life? I have often addressed high school audiences and my message is always the same. For every hour you spend on the athletic field, spend two in the library. Even if you make it as pro athlete, your career will be over by the time you are thirty-five. So you will need that diploma.

Have these pro athletes explain what happens if you break a leg, get a sore arm, have one bad year or don't make the cut for five or six tournaments. Explain to them the star system, wherein for every O.J. earning millions there are six or seven others making $15,000 or $20,000 or $30,000 a year.

But don't just have Walt Frazier or O.J. or Abdul-Jabbar address your class. Invite a benchwarmer or a guy who didn't make it. Ask him if he sleeps every night. Ask him whether he was graduated. Ask him what he would do if he became disabled tomorrow. Ask him where his high school athletic buddies are.

We have been on the same roads—sports and entertainment—too long. We need to pull over, fill up at the library and speed away to Congress and the Supreme Court, the unions and the business world. We need more Barbara Jordans, Andrew Youngs, union cardholders, Nikki Giovannis and Earl Graveses. Don't worry: we will still be able to sing and dance and run and jump better than anybody else.

I'll never forget how proud my grandmother was when I graduated from U.C.L.A. in 1966. Never mind the Davis Cup in 1968, 1969, and 1970. Never mind the Wimbledon title, Forest Hills, etc. To this day, she still doesn't know what those names mean. What matters to her was that of her more than thirty children and grandchildren, I was the first to be graduated from college, and a famous college at that. Somehow, that made up for all those floors she scrubbed all those years.

How Does the Author Make His Point?

1. What is the thesis sentence?
2. Why does he put his essay in the form of a letter?
3. Why does he mention entertainment but spend most of his essay on sports?
4. Can you give some examples of logical appeals and emotional appeals in this essay?
5. From his title on, Ashe limits his audience. What techniques does he use to identify with that audience?

What Do You Think?

1. On what grounds would you agree or disagree with Ashe that the black culture puts too much emphasis on sports?
2. What facts does he marshal to support his point?
3. Why wouldn't his argument apply equally to whites?
4. Why is the paragraph about his grandmother the conclusion?

Criminology

H. L. MENCKEN

H. L. Mencken, the editor of the Baltimore Sun newspapers, was a respected reporter, critic, columnist, and the writer of a highly important book called The American Language. *He was noted for the vigorous expression of his frequently controversial ideas. He has been called "the most powerful personal influence on a whole generation of educated people" throughout the twenties, well into the fifties. In this essay, he is presenting an individualistic and persuasive analysis of the problems with the criminology system in the United States.*

The more I read the hand-books of the new criminology, the more I am convinced that it stands on a level with dogmatic theology, chiropractic and the New Thought—in brief, that it is mainly buncombe. That it has materially civilized punishment I do not, of course, deny; what I question is its doctrine as to the primary causes of crime. The average man, as everyone knows, puts those causes in the domain of free will. The criminal, in his view, is simply a scoundrel who has deliberately chosen to break the law and injure his fellow-men. *Ergo,* he deserves to be punished swiftly and mercilessly. The new criminologists, in swinging away from that naive view, have obviously gone too far in the other direction. They find themselves, in the end, embracing a determinism that is as childlike as the free will of the man in the street. Crime, as they depict it, becomes a sort of disease, either inherited or acquired by contagion, and as devoid of moral content or significance as smallpox. The criminal is no longer a black-hearted villain, to be put down by force, but a poor brother who has succumbed to the laws of Mendel and the swinish stupidity of society. The aim of punishment is not to make him sweat, but to dissuade and rehabilitate him. In every pickpocket there is a potential Good Man. All this, gradually gaining credit, has greatly ameliorated punishments. They have not only lost their old barbaric quality; they have also diminished quantitatively. Men do not sit in prison as long as they used to; the parole boards turn them out almost as fast as the cops shove them in. The result is a public discontent that must be manifest. Whenever a criminal of any eminence comes to trial there are loud bellows against any show of mercy to him, and demands that he be punished to the limit. One never hears complaints any more that the courts are too savage; one hears only complaints that they are too soft and sentimental.

I am a congenital disbeliever in laws, and have only the most formal respect for the juridic process and its learned protagonist; nevertheless, it seems to me that there is a certain reasonableness in this unhappiness. For what it indicates, basically, is simply the inability of the average man to grasp the determinism of the new criminologists. He cannot imagine an apparently voluntary act that is determined, or even materially conditioned, from without. He can think of crime only in terms of free will, and so thinking of it, he believes that it ought to be punished in the ancient Christian manner, i.e., according to the damage flowing out of it, and not according to the temptations behind it. Certainly this is not an illogical ground to take. In all the other relations of life the average man sees free will accepted as axiomatic: he could not imagine a world in which it was denied. His religion is based squarely upon it: he knows, by the oath of his pastor, that his free acts can lift him to Heaven or cast him down to Hell. He works as a matter of free will, and is punished inevitably if he lags. His marriage, as he sees it, was a free will compact, and though he has some secret doubt, perhaps, that its issue came that way, he nevertheless orders his relations with his children on the same basis, and assumes it in judging them. In other words, he lives in a world in which free will is apparently omnipotent, and in which it is presumed even when there is no direct evidence for it. All his daily concerns are free will concerns. Well, what the criminologists ask him to do is to separate one special concern from the rest, and hand it over to determinism. They damn legislators for passing harsh laws, and judges and jailers for executing them— free will. They denounce society for "coercing" morons into crime—free will again. And then they argue that the criminals are no more than helpless victims of circumstance, like motes dancing along a sunbeam—determinism in its purest and sweetest form.

No wonder the plain man balks! Suppose an analogous suspension of the usual rules were attempted in some other field. Suppose it were argued seriously that free will had nothing to do with, say, the execution of contracts. Suppose an employer who failed to pay his workmen on Saturday were excused on the ground that he was the helpless victim of an evil heredity or of the stupidity of society, and thus not to be blamed for dissipating his money on Ford parts, women, foreign missions, or drink? Suppose the workman who had got out a mechanic's lien against him and sought to levy on his assets were denounced as a cruel and medieval fellow, and at odds with human progress? Certainly there would be a horrible hullabaloo, and equally certainly it would be justified. For whatever the theoretical arguments for determinism—and I am prepared to go even further in granting them than the criminologists go—it must be plain that the everyday affairs of the world are ordered on an assumption of free will, and that it is impossible, practically speaking, to get rid of it. Society itself, indeed, is grounded upon that assumption. Imagining it as determined is possible only to professional philosophers, whose other imaginings are surely not such as to give any authority to this one. The plain man simply gives up the effort as hopeless—and perhaps as also a bit anarchistic and un-Christian. So he is sniffish when the new criminologists begin to prattle their facile determinism, and when he observes it getting credit from the regular agents of the law, he lets a loud whoop of protest. I do not believe he is naturally cruel and vindictive; on the contrary, he is very apt to be maudlinly sentimental. But sentiment is one thing, and what seems to him to be a palpably false philosophy is quite another. He no more favors letting criminals go on the ground that they can't help themselves than he favors giving money to foreign missions, or the Red Cross, or the Y.M.C.A on the ground that it is his inescapable duty. In all of these cases he is willing to be persuaded, but in none of them is he willing to be dragooned.

Thus I fear that the criminologists of the new school only pile up trouble for themselves, and indirectly their pets, when they attempt to revise so radically the immemorial human view of crime. If they kept quiet in the department of responsibility, they would be heard with far more attention and respect in the department of punishment, where they really have something opposite and useful to say. Their influence here, in fact, is already immense, and it works much good. Our prisons are no longer quite as sordid and demoralizing as they used to be. They are still bad enough, in all conscience, but they are not as bad as they were. Here there is room for yet more improvement, and it cries aloud to be made. The men to work out its details are the criminologists. They have studied the effects of the prevailing punishments, and know where those punishments succeed or fail. They are happily devoid of that proud ignorance which is one of the boasts of the average judge, and they lack the unpleasant zeal of district attorneys, jail wardens and other such professional blood-letters. They need only offer the proofs that this or that punishment is ineffective to see it abandoned for something better, or, at all events, less obviously bad. But when they begin to talk of criminals in terms of pathology, even of social pathology, they speak a language that the plain man cannot understand and doesn't want to hear. He believes that crime, in the overwhelming majority of cases, is a voluntary matter, and that it ought to pay its own way and bury its own dead. He is not bothered about curing criminals, or otherwise redeeming them. He is intent only upon punishing them, and the more swiftly and certainly that business is achieved the better he is satisfied. Every time it is delayed by theorizing about the criminal's heredity and environment, and the duty that society owes to him, the plain man breaks into indignation. Only too often that indignation has been wreaked upon criminology and the criminologists. More American States, of late, have gone back to capital punishment than have abandoned it. What set the tide to running that way was surely not mere blood-lust. It was simply a natural reaction against the doctrine that murder is mainly an accidental and unfortunate matter, and devoid of moral content, like slipping on an icy sidewalk or becoming the father of twins.

How Does the Author Make His Point?

1. What is the difference between what the "average man" sees as the cause of crime and the view of the "new criminologist"? Who is winning? What is the result of this winning?
2. What does the "average man" believe? Why?
3. What device does Mencken imply in the third paragraph? Is it effective? Why or why not?
4. On whose side is Mencken? Where does he express these views?
5. Does Mencken come across as reasonable or as unreasonable? How does his word choice reveal his tone?

What Do You Think?

1. Whose side are you on in this controversy—the criminologists', or the average man's? Why?
2. Point out the contradictions in the criminologists' philosophy that Mencken expresses. Can you think of any other?
3. Does Mencken's word choice make him more or less persuasive?

The English Language Is My Enemy

OSSIE DAVIS

Ossie Davis, a very successful writer, playwright, and actor, gave a speech before the American Federation of Teachers, AFL-CIO in 1967. It was later printed in their magazine American Teacher. *Since that time it has been reprinted frequently and has been a source of much debate.*

In the introduction to his speech, Ossie Davis gave an interesting definition of education. Education, he said, is "preparing oneself . . . intellectually for a mature life."

I will define communication as the primary means by which the process of education is carried out.

I will say that language is the primary medium of communication in the educational process and, in this case, the English language. I will indict the English language as one of the prime carriers of racism from one person to another in our society and discuss how the teacher and the student, especially the Negro student, are affected by this fact.

The English language is my enemy.

Racism is a belief that human races have distinctive characteristics, usually involving the idea that one's own race is superior and has a right to rule others.

But that was not my original topic—I said that English was my goddamn enemy. Now why do I use "goddamn" to illustrate this aspect of the English language? Because I want to illustrate the sheer gut power of words. Words which control our action. Words like "nigger," "kike," "sheeny," "dago," "black power"— words like this. Words we don't use in ordinary decent conversation, one to the other. I choose these words deliberately, not to flaunt my freedom before you. If you are a normal human being these words will have assaulted your senses, may even have done you physical harm, and if you choose, you could have me arrested.

Those words are attacks upon your physical and emotional well being; your pulse rate is possibly higher, your breath quicker;

there is perhaps a tremor along the nerves of your arms and your legs; sweat begins in the palms of your hands, perhaps. With these few words I have assaulted you. I have damaged you, and there is nothing you can possibly do to control your reactions—to defend yourself against the brute force of these words.

These words have a power over us, a power that we cannot resist. For a moment you and I have had our deepest physical reaction controlled, not by our own wills, but by words in the English language.

A superficial examination of Roget's Thesaurus of the English Language reveals the following fact: The word "whiteness" has 134 synonyms, 44 of which are favorable and pleasing to contemplate. For example: "purity," "cleanness," "immaculateness," "bright," "shiny," "ivory," "unsullied," "innocent," "honorable," "upright," "just," "straightforward," "fair," "genuine," "trustworthy,"—and only 10 synonyms which I feel to have been negative and then only in the mildest sense, such as "gloss-over," "whitewash," "gray," "wan," "pale," "ashen," etc.

The word "blackness" has 120 synonyms, 60 of which are distinctly unfavorable, and none of them even mildly positive. Among the offending 60 were such words as "blot," "blotch," "smut," "smudge," "sullied," "begrime," "soot," "becloud," "obscure," "dingy," "murky," "low-toned," "threatening," "frowning," "foreboding," "forbidding," "sinister," "baneful," "dismal," "thundery," "wicked," "malignant," "deadly," "unclean," "dirty," "unwashed," "foul," etc. In addition, and this is what really hurts, 20 of those words—and I exclude the villainous 60 above—are related directly to race, such as "Negro," "Negress," "nigger," "darkey," "blackamoor," etc.

If you consider the fact that thinking itself is subvocal speech (in other words, one must use words in order to think at all), you will appreciate the enormous trap of prejudgment that works on any child who is born into the English language.

Any creature, good or bad, white or black, Jew or Gentile, who uses the English language for the purposes of communication is willing to force the Negro child into 60 ways to despise himself, and the white child, 60 ways to aid and abet him in the crime.

Language is a means of communication. This corruption, this evil of racism, doesn't affect only one group. It doesn't take white to make a person a racist. Blacks also become inverted racists in the process.

A part of our function, therefore, as teachers, will be to reconstruct the English language. A sizeable undertaking, but one which we must undertake if we are to cure the problems of racism in our society.

The English language must become democratic. It must become respectful of the possiblities of the human spirit. Racism is not only reflected in words relating to the color of Negroes. If you will examine some of the synonyms for the word Jew you will find that the adjectives and the verb of the word Jew are offensive. However, if you look at the word Hebrew you will see that there are no offensive connotations to the word.

When you understand and contemplate the small difference between the meaning of one word supposedly representing one fact, you will understand the power, good or evil, associated with the English language. You will understand also why there is a tremendous fight among the Negro people to stop using the word "Negro" altogether and substitute "Afro-American."

We come today to talk about education. Education is the only valid transmitter of American values from one generation to another. Churches have been used from time immemorial to teach certain values to certain people, but in America, as in no other country, it is the school that bears the burden of teaching young Americans to be Americans.

Schools define the meaning of such concepts as success. And education is a way out of the heritage of poverty for Negro people. It's the way we can get jobs.

I have had occasion (and with this I'll come to a close) to function as a teacher—I'm a bootleg teacher. I teach Sunday school, it's the closest I can get to the process—I teach boys from 9 to 12, and I have the same problem with getting them to appreciate the spoken and written word as you do, in your daily classrooms. Most of them can't read. I don't see how they're going to get, not only to Heaven—I don't see how they're going to get to the next grade unless they can command some of these problems that we have.

But, more importantly, I am also involved in the educational process. And those of us who are involved in culture and cultural activities do ourselves and our country and our cause a great injustice not to recognize that we, too, are communicators and have therefore a responsibility in the process of communication. I could be hired today to communicate to the great American public my great delight in smoking a cigarette, but I know that a cigarette could cause you cancer and I would be paid for that. I could be used to do many other things in the process of communications from the top to the bottom.

I have a responsibility to show that what I do, what is translated through me, is measured by the best interest of my country and my people and my profession. And in that I think we are all together.

How Does the Author Make His Point?

1. What is the thesis statement?
2. What are the primary modes of development the author uses?
3. Who is the audience for Davis's article? He had a specific audience when he gave it as a speech. How does the audience for the magazine article differ from the original audience?
4. What is his tone?

What Do You Think?

1. How, specifically, does the author expect us to "reconstruct the English language"?
2. What does he mean by the "brute power" of words?
3. Does Davis persuade you that the English language is his enemy?

Is the English Language Anybody's Enemy?

MURIEL R. SCHULZ

In a publication devoted to semantics, Muriel R. Schulz offered a counterargument to Ossie Davis's position in the preceding article. Her thesis is expressed in her title.

Ossie Davis started it. In an article, "The English Language Is My Enemy," he complained that in English we equate the word white with good things and black with evil. White is associated with pleasant, favorable attributes (pure, innocent, clean), while black is associated with feared, unfavorable ones (foul, sinister, dismal). Mixed in among the synonyms for black are words denoting race (black, nigger, darky), and this association with evil is just one more burden the Blacks are forced to carry in our society. He suggested that if we were to compare the connotations of the word Jew (unfavorable) with those of the word Hebrew (neutral), we would understand why he was fighting to stop using the word Negro (unfavorable) and to substitute Afro-American (neutral).

We were not very far into the Women's Movement of the Sixties before women, too, discovered the English language to be their enemy. It is contemptuous of them, having a great wealth of derogatory labels like whore, slut, slattern, hag, bag, and witch. It derides female characteristics by the easy insult, using feminine terms, such as sissy, old maidish, and effeminate, as scornful slurs. It implies that some qualities (weakness, frivolity, timidity, and passivity, for example) are appropriate only to women, while others (like courage, power, forcefulness, and bravery) are available only to men. It renders women invisible, by considering masculine to be the norm for such terms as doctor, professor, lawyer, and worker, by subsuming women under the cover terms man and mankind, and by using the masculine pronoun whenever sex is unknown or unspecified (as in "Everyone must have his ticket punched"). Women wonder, with some justice, just what the effect is upon the female child, who is forming a sense of her own identity, when she finds herself alternately abused and ignored by her own language.

But is our language so one-sided? Are Blacks and women dealt with more harshly than men? Have race and sex provided categories subject to a kind of linguistic abuse that doesn't operate against White Anglo-Saxon males?

Not at all! English is rich in scathing terms for men. Consider, for example, the synonyms for scoundrel, "a bold, selfish man who has very low ethical standards." We have cur, dog, hound, mongrel, reptile, viper, serpent, snake, swine, skunk, polecat, insect, worm, louse, and rat in animal metaphors as well as bounder, knave, rotter, rascal, rogue, villain, blackguard, shyster, heel, stinker, son of a bitch, bastard, and many more. Our language enables us to make fine distinctions in describing villainy, and English attributes this quality to the male. When the grizzled old prospector curls his lip and snarls, "You dirty, low-down varmint," we automatically assume that his adversary is a man.

Our terms for people who drink too much are also primarily masculine in reference. Statistics argue that a large percentage of our alcoholics are women, but English doesn't carry such a message. The synonyms for inebriate, whether happy or obnoxious, habitual or temporary, seem to be coded primarily "male"; for example, boozer, drunkard, tippler, toper, swiller, tosspot, guzzler, barfly, drunk, lush, boozehound, souse, tank, stew, rummy, and bum.

In a similar way, our words for law-breakers seem to have masculine reference: crook, felon, criminal, conspirator, racketeer, gangster, outlaw, convict, jailbird, desperado, and bookie all designate males. And when used figuratively, the reference remains masculine. Any man who bests another in a money transaction may earn the epithet of "dirty crook," and when we hear the phrase, we have no doubt of the sex of the person so named.

We are most venomous in characterizing men sexually. Women complain of the richness of vocabulary denoting them as sex objects, but at least many of these are positive, admiring terms. Not so the words which designate a man as a sexual being. Of rapist, debaucher, despoiler, seducer, rip, betrayer, deceiver, ravisher, ravager, violator, defiler, rake, and dirty old man, perhaps only the last two can be said to have positive connotations. In an article, "Our Sexist Language," Ethel Strainchamps has pointed out an ironic double standard which operates against men in our society: "If a man watches a woman undressing before a window, he can be arrested as a Peeping Tom. If a woman watches a man undressing before a window, the man can be arrested for indecent exposure." Voyeur and exhibitionist are both masculine terms.

Thus, men come in for a share of abuse in English, too. What we see operating is a natural function of language, one which Stuart Flexner noticed when he was gathering materials for his *Dictionary of American Slang*. There is no rich vocabulary of slang for attractive, chaste women, nor for good, amiable wives and mothers, for sober, hardworking men, nor for intelligent, attractive older people. Commenting on these improverished areas, he remarked, "Slang—and it is frequently true for all language levels—always tends toward degradation rather than elevation." It may not be an admirable quality, but it does appear to be human nature. The chant, "Sticks and stones may break my bones, but names can never hurt me," is acknowledgment that we can use names in an attempt to get at others, to categorize them as Other, to label what we dislike in them (and in ourselves). Language is potentially everyone's enemy, whether he or she is old (geezer, old fool, codger, fogey, crone) or young (squirt, young punk, hippie), whether a farmer (yokel, hick, rube, bumpkin, clod) or a laborer (menial, flunky, hack, drudge), whether a physician (quack, croaker, pill pusher, butcher) or an attorney (shyster, ambulance chaser).

Can we eliminate this use of language? The slogan, "Black is Beautiful," seems to have succeeded in de-mythicizing the word Black, removing from it our associations with evil, as well as removing from it the suggestions it carried when used as a label by a White Southerner in the Fifties. Having neither the euphemistic qualities of Colored person nor the stigma of Nigger, it has given us a fairly neutral label, relatively free of the associations and stereotypes of the past. Women introduced Ms. and chairperson and have suggested new neutral pronouns as a means of escaping from under the cloak of masculine reference. And they have urged us all to become aware of the unfavorable connotations of many of the words we use denoting women and to avoid abusive terms. But if Whites continue to think of Blacks as Other, and if men continue to think of women as Other, we will find the old associations drifting to the new terminology. As Simone de Beauvoir says in *The Second Sex*, "The category of the Other is as primordial as consciousness itself. In the most primitive societies, in the most ancient mythologies, one finds the expression of a quality—that of Self and the Other." We should not be surprised to find this opposition expressed in language. Language is nobody's enemy. It is simply used to express the hostility and fear toward others. Whether the difference is one of race, or sex, or religion, or behavior does not matter. The human responds to differences with suspicion and distrust, and those responses are going to be expressed in language.

How Does the Author Make Her Point?

1. What type of introduction does the author use (paragraphs 1 and 2)? Why is it effective here?
2. What is the basic method of development used here?
3. Into what categories does the author divide words? Is this a logical classification?
4. What other methods are used?

What Do You Think?

1. Can you think of any other group that has been maligned by our language? Support your answer by listing some derogatory words that seem to be meant for that group alone.
2. Were you convinced that "language is nobody's enemy"?
3. What is your opinion of the new nonsexist terms such as *chairperson* and *Ms*?

Student Essay:
Escape

ROBERT A. WOLFE

In this essay, a student attempts to persuade us to accept his interpretation of the relationships between the artist and his art and the artist and his audience.

Franz Kafka's "First Sorrow" presents to the readers the tenuous and tentative relationship of the artist and the society that feeds him and feeds off him. The trapeze artist dedicates his life to perfecting his skill, yet in the process, he eventually suffers from the loss of all that he has sacrificed in his quest. As "All his needs . . . were supplied by relays of attendants . . ." he remains aloft, above and separate from society continuously. But this is tolerated and accepted as the artist's due, as it leads to the perfection of his art.

Undisturbed by the mundane cares of those below, the (trapeze) artist strives and thrives. He does not share the problems of the society that provides and supports his egocentric and pretensive perch above our common and humdrum lives. "Nothing disturbed his seclusion . . ." as he practiced his art. He could remain there forever, unencumbered by life and society's problems, but for the interruptions in moving from one town to the next, interruptions that society's agent, the manager, kept at a minimum so as to reduce the artist's anxieties and "save" him from life's requirements.

Yet the artist would suffer during these times, as short as they were, because on the ground he is forced to confront the demands of society. The artist feels awkward and embarrassed while on the ground. He no longer is in a position to be "looked up to" and revered for his "most difficult" art. When asked to compete, like the average person within the normal activities of life, he knows that he is inadequate. It is only on his perch, high above the crowd and removed from the sundry demands of life, that he is able to thrive and flourish.

Yet the artist is unable to remain content in the pursuit of his art. As he suffers through an unavoidable passage through society and the real world, he bites his lip and states, not requests nor demands, that "he must in the future have *two* trapezes for his performances instead of only one . . . ." Although society, in the form of the manager, unhesitatingly agrees and supports this, as a logical refinement of art, the artist bursts into tears. In spite of the support and nurturing caresses of society's agent, the artist suffers the agony of confronting his being alone. His vaunted position is creating a schism between his artistic fulfillment and his personal isolation. The artist has reached a point where the pursuit of his art, once all-consuming and satisfying, can no longer totally sustain him. It no longer gives the innocent fulfillment that once carried him along in his search for excellence. He can no longer live with and only for his art. He discovers and is discovered by needs that his art, as near perfection as he has been able to make it, cannot fulfill.

The symbolism of the two trapezes, I believe, represents not only, as some have said, the need for "someone to share his life," but also an artist's need to transcend the limitations or envelope of his art. I believe the second trapeze represents the need for evolution in each art form. Not only does the artist eventually suffer with the need for personal love and fulfillment created from his obsession and its resulting isolation, but he must remain always and continuously a slave to the unceasing demands of art. Once artists have signed on for the pursuit of excellence, they forever increase their output. They must, without fail, find new, more, and better ways to satisfy their mistress's (art) voracious and unending appetite.

Kafka illustrates this relationship between artist and society well, if somewhat obliquely. It has always facinated me that society's ostracizing, directly or indirectly, of the creative personality often leads to many of the greatest innovations and advancements in the sciences as well as the arts. Kafka's "First Sorrow" shows us the realities of a relationship that nurtures through isolation.

How Does the Author Make His Point?

1. What is the thesis statement?
2. What is the author's primary method of support for this thesis?
3. What is the artist's predicament, according to the author? Does he see a solution?

What Do You Think?

1. Do you agree that artists in general have this relationship to their art?
2. Do audiences demand too much? Why do even the most popular television programs stay on the air only a few years?
3. Do you think it is possible to give too much of yourself for excellence?

INTEGRATING READING SKILLS WITH WRITING SKILLS: DISTINGUISHING BETWEEN FACT AND OPINION

gullible—easily cheated, deceived, duped, hoodwinked, fooled, tricked, or bamboozled

No one likes to be called gullible, yet millions of dollars are made every day by those who depend on the gullibility of the reading public. Full-color promotional brochures advertising worthless parcels of land as "pieces of paradise"; official-looking get-rich-quick newsletters designed to swindle unsuspecting victims out of their life savings, cheap 50-cent tabloids (conveniently placed near supermarket checkout counters) purporting to reveal the "true facts" about Hollywood's hottest stars . . . they all have one thing in common: they thrive on the reader's failure to separate fact from opinion.

The reader's failure to read critically does not necessarily stem from a lack of intelligence. More often than not, it stems from a lazy, untrained mind. The distinction between facts and opinions is not always clear-cut. Separating facts from opinions, therefore, is often more difficult than identifying main ideas and supporting details or recognizing the author's pattern of organization. It takes more concentration, and many readers simply do not want to take the time or the effort to read critically. To make matters worse, the reader is often at the mercy of writers who carelessly confuse facts and opinions by misusing the word *fact*. Expressions such as "the fact is" or "due to the fact that" or "in spite of the fact that" are often followed by an opinion—not a fact. Consider the following statement, for example:

In spite of the fact that most professional athletes are very well paid, some of them are still demanding exorbitant salary increases.

The statement following "the fact that" is *not* a fact. "Most professional athletes are very well paid" is a *judgment,* and whether or not it is a valid judgment is open to question. You would have to examine the facts regarding the salaries of professional athletes in order to determine the validity of the statement. If you are already inclined to agree with the *opinion,* however, you might readily accept the statement as fact without even questioning it. You would then be in danger of drawing false conclusions. If you want to be able to read critically, you must first make sure that you understand what a fact is.

The word *fact* comes from the Latin verb *facere,* meaning *to do, to act.* A fact, then, is something that actually *happened* or something that *existed* in the past or *exists* in the present. A prediction cannot be a fact because it involves speculation about something that has not yet happened or something that does not yet exist. A factual statement is thus a statement that can be proven true or false. Its beauty lies in its neutrality. A fact carries no interpretation, no positive or negative attitude. It either happened or it didn't; it either exists or it doesn't.

It is only when you begin to interpret facts that you arrive at an opinion. For example, the statement "Hitler became chancellor of Germany on January 30, 1933" is a fact; however, the statement "Hitler ruthlessly seized power in Germany on January 30, 1933" is part fact, part judgment. The phrase "ruthlessly seized power" suggests a particular interpretation of the facts. Whether or not Hitler ruthlessly seized power is a matter of opinion. Noted historian A.J.P. Taylor, for example, argues very convincingly that there was nothing sudden at all about Hitler's rise to power. The statement "Hitler was a ruthless, deranged dictator" is a judgment, an opinion. It may be a valid opinion, immediately recognized as such by intelligent readers who are familiar with the facts, but, nevertheless, it is an opinion—based on an *interpretation* of the facts.

EXERCISE

RESCUE FOUNDERING EDUCATION

In the following essay, the author uses both facts and judgments to support his thesis: American society remains poorly educated. Read the essay carefully and separate the factual evidence from the judgmental supports. Then underline only the factual statements.

WASHINGTON—American society remains poorly educated. Student performance is lower than in 1957 at the time of Sputnik, when many so-called reforms were initiated. Some curricula involve expensive gimmicks, trivial courses, and quick fixes of dubious value. Teachers are often poorly trained and misused on nonacademic tasks. Many students have settled for easy, so-called relevant and entertaining courses. They and their parents are deceived by grade inflation. And the lack of national standards of performance blinds everyone to how poor our education system is.

There should be a return to the ideal of a truly liberal education based on the three R's, which result in the ability to read intelligently, to think precisely, to speak fluently and to write clearly. Mandatory academic courses must be given priority over electives.

A nationwide system of standardized performance exams throughout the student's school years should be established. The Scholastic Aptitude Test exams, toward the end of high school, come too late to do much good.

Teachers should be paid more but only in return for demonstrating high standards.

Our secondary schools are trying to do too many things for too many constituencies. The result of such educationally irrelevant activities has been a definite decline in time and resources devoted to teaching and learning. By choosing easy, "relevant" and entertaining courses, students exhibit a long-term decline in academic performance. This is evidenced by S.A.T. scores. Over 20 years, S.A.T. verbal scores declined 42 points; mathematical scores declined 26 points. Recent minor reversals in this trend are statistically insignificant. In any event, it is too early to be sure of any long-term upward movement.

Just how bad things have become is illustrated by the fact that all four major users of high school graduates—business, industry, colleges, the military—must conduct remedial courses in math and English. The military spends some $60 million a year in developing basic reading skills. Between 25 and 40 percent of enrolled college freshman require remedial work. Our inadequacies are increasingly obvious, especially in technical and scientific areas. We simply do not educate our youths so they can perform effectively in modern, technologically demanding jobs.

Hyman G. Rickover

Understanding How Language Affects Tone

To reach the level of comprehension needed to understand persuasive writing, you must be able to do more than separate fact from opinion. You must also be able to recognize the author's tone—the author's attitude toward the topic. Understanding how the author feels about a topic is sometimes a twofold task. First, you've got to understand how language affects tone (how the author's choice of words reveals an attitude); and second, you've got to be able to read between the lines (recognize the importance of what the author is *implying* as well as what the author is stating directly).

Each of the following passages contains words that reveal the author's attitude toward the subject. The first selection about Franklin D. Roosevelt contains very positive emotive language. It appeared as part of a lengthy article about FDR published in the *Philadelphia Record* on April 13, 1945—the day after Roosevelt died. Notice how both the heading and the italicized words reveal the author's sympathetic attitude toward the late president.

COURAGE AND CONFIDENCE

Perhaps his *resiliency* can be traced to the dread poliomyelitis—infantile paralysis—which struck him down in middle life. Such overwhelming misfortune would have crushed a lesser man, but Franklin Roosevelt, at 39, refused to become a hopeless cripple.

His fight is an *epic of courage* and sheer force of *will*; after that *victory*, nothing could daunt him . . . .

Franklin Roosevelt not only had an *indomitable spirit* himself; he could transfuse his *never-failing confidence* into other people.

The Philadelphia Record

The next passage deals with the Nixon presidency. It was taken from the memoirs of Justice William O. Douglas, a thirty-six-year veteran justice of the Supreme Court and one of its most distinguished liberal activists. He was never allied with Richard Nixon, either personally or politically, and his choice of words in this particular paragraph clearly reveals a negative tone.

The Nixon-Agnew *regime* reflected both *crude* and subtle *corruption*. The Agnew activities were those of a *common crook*—receiving kickbacks from contractors and not reporting the revenues as income. The Nixon activities, among others, ran to cutting income tax corners to profit a president. Beyond that was the use of the office of the president not "to execute the laws faithfully," as required by the Constitution, but to *badger, beat,* and *destroy* anyone who asserted a first amendment right to disagree with the administration or register a protest against its policies or acts. This was the first time in history that both president and vice president *polluted* and *desecrated* their high positions of trust and public confidence.

William O. Douglas

Reading between the Lines

If you want to deal with persuasive writing effectively, either as a reader or as a writer, you've got to appreciate the importance of tone. Looking at persuasive writing from a reader's point of view and seeing how word choice can influence the reader's interpretation of the author's tone should persuade you, the writer, to choose your words carefully. Sometimes even what you *don't* say can influence the reader. For example, if you said the members of your family were very supportive and mentioned only your father, your siblings, and your grandparents, the absense of your mother's name would certainly tell the reader something. At times, in fact, the author says just as much—if not more—through the power of suggestion as he or she does through the written word. In these cases, the reader who cannot read between the lines and recognize the author's assumptions, implications, and inferences can easily misinterpret the author's attitude toward the subject.

In the following example, the reader can deduce a great deal about the author's attitude by reading between the lines. The subject is faith healers, and the passage was taken from James Morris's book, *The Preachers*. What follows is the opening of chapter 1, a biographical sketch of the late Asa Alonzo Allen, "the best known and most successful practicing faith healer in the country as the 1970s began."

> Son, let me tell you something. Do you know when you can tell a revival meeting is over? Do you know when God's saying to move on to the next town? When you can turn people on their head and shake them and no money falls out, then you know God's saying "Move on, son."

from A. A. Allen's message to brother Marjoe

Except for the threat of high winds or an occasional tornado, late spring and early summer are the best times for miracles all across the deep South and in most parts of the Southwest. For the 1970 season, this proved to be true in a most unusual way. People were being miraculously healed during the service under the Reverend A.A. Allen's big revival tent before he or his associate healers had a chance to lay a hand on them. Even while the congregation was singing, the crippled, the blind, and the deaf were rushing to the pulpit ramp declaring they had been healed. God was even filling and cleaning people's teeth during the opening prayer. It was an unprecedented season of many miracles, and no one was happier to report them than radio evangelist Asa Alonzo Allen, who announced he felt like dancing in the spirit. His broadcasts boasted he was "God's man of faith and power," and he credited the Lord for any growth in his ministry, an increase that often came not only from his tent revivals, but also through his radio broadcasts, television programs, his magazine and books, or the sale of his records.

He wrote that he was especially impressed with the great miracles being wrought in his ministry that spring, an observation that confounded some of his critics, who suggested his ministry already boasted of miracles beyond the belief of a medieval sorcerer: has not an arm instantly grown six inches? What of the baby whose skull has been partly re-created in a moment? A prayer had caused a safety pin to come sailing out of a woman's stomach, and a breast removed by surgery was miraculously restored to one of his female followers. If St. Peter's shadow and St. Paul's handkerchiefs healed the sick and cast out devils, his own ministry could boast quite as much, if not more. Even the dead had been brought back to life.

James Morris

There are several things that you can learn about the tone of this passage by being observant and reading between the lines. For example, the quotation that the author selected to open the chapter not only grabs the reader's attention but also suggests that the author's attitude toward Allen is not one of deep reverence and respect—amusement or skepticism perhaps, but not admiration. This tone is reinforced in the first paragraph, where the observant reader detects a light, somewhat cynical attitude toward "miracles" in general and Reverend Allen's in particular, even without the author explicitly stating: "I am skeptical about the so-called 'miracles' performed by faith healers in general, including those of Reverend Allen." Similarly, in the second paragraph, the author doesn't have to come right out and say that "some of Reverend Allen's 'miracles' are simply too far-fetched to believe" or that "Allen's critics are probably right." The well-chosen examples say it for him.

As Morris's excerpt illustrates, you can't look at an author's words in isolation. You always have to consider the words in conjunction with attitudes. For example, by the time you read the last sentence, you should understand the general tone of the passage well enough to understand that when the author states that Reverend Allen resurrected the dead, he is suggesting that some of Allen's "miracles" were preposterous.

IMPROVING YOUR VOCABULARY

Synonyms And Antonyms

Many words have *synonyms*, words close in meaning to them, as *hope* is close to *expect*. When words have synonyms, good dictionaries usually list them (and sometimes the antonyms, words meaning the opposite) toward the end of the entry. Since there are no exactly equal synonyms, the dictionary will distinguish among them so that you can use them precisely. For example, *The American Heritage Dictionary of the English Language,** after giving eleven different meanings for *love* as a noun and seven for *love* as a verb, lists four synonyms and shows the differences among their meanings.

> **Synonyms**: *love, affection, devotion, fondness, infatuation.* These nouns refer to feelings of attraction and attachment experienced by persons. *Love* suggests a feeling more intense and less susceptible to control than that associated with the other words of this group. *Affection* is a more unvarying feeling of warm regard for another person. *Devotion* is dedication and attachment to a person or thing; contrasted with *love,* it implies a more selfless and often a more settled feeling. *Fondness,* in its most common modern sense, is rather strong liking for a person or thing. *Infatuation* is extravagant attraction or attaction to a person or thing, usually short in duration and indicative of folly or faulty judgment.

Synonyms are important to you as both reader and writer because choosing among synonyms permits you to be *precise* in understanding what you read and in conveying your meaning. One of the values of precision is that, when you are precise, you can also be *concise.* When you are precise, you don't have to qualify a word to make a point clear. For example, if you forget the word *affection* but wish to express it, you'd have to say something like this: "He loved her in a warm but rather mild, controlled way which was unvarying," rather than saying, "He felt affection for her." As long as you know what you mean, you can find *some* way to say it. However, some ways are more effective than others. Careful choice among synonyms increases your effectiveness.

Synonyms are not the only way to develop your vocabulary. *Antonyms,* words which are opposite in meaning, also add to the precision and conciseness of your vocabulary. (They are particularly helpful in contrast and in definition.) And often, the first thought that you associate with a word is its antonym. For example,

> up—down
> black—white
> rich—poor

One way to improve your vocabulary is to learn new sets of opposites for common words. The following words, for example, might suggest specific antonyms:

> *thin* might suggest *fat*
> *underweight* might suggest *overweight*

But with the aid of a dictionary or a thesaurus, you can discover synonym-antonym combinations that you hadn't thought of. For example, instead of *thin/fat,* you might come up with *svelte/pursy* or *reedy/corpulent.* Other examples include

> *humble/proud unpretentious/grandiloquent*
> *happy/sad blithe/rueful*
> *sloppy/neat frowzy/meticulous*
> *calm/nervous phlegmatic/tremulous*
> *cowardly/courageous pusillanimous/intrepid*

Try this exercise with some common sets of antonyms and see how many new words you can add to your vocabulary.

Slanting

Slanting consists of the selection of words, the positioning of words, and the emphasis that we use to communicate our attitudes toward a subject. Even before we express in words what we wish to say, our knowledge about our subject is chosen by a process of selection. We know what we have observed; what we have observed is determined by a number of qualities within us. For example, suppose three people are looking in a jeweler's window at a display of engagement rings: one person is the owner of the store; a second person is a young woman who is about to become engaged; the third person is a jewel thief. What these three people unconsciously select to see in the window display will vary widely. The jeweler will be interested in how his merchandise looks and will wonder if it appeals to potential customers; the young woman will admire the diamonds and decide which among them is her favorite and will wonder if it is affordable; the jewel thief, obviously, will question things differently from the first two viewers. The details observed will, in turn, determine what will be remembered about this particular window. Thus, even before any communication is attempted, a selection has been made.

If these three people describe the window, they will be reporting different facts with different words. The words that are chosen—sometimes almost unconsciously—reflect the favorable or unfavorable attitude of the viewer. The viewer changes his wording to convey his attitude in one of three possible ways: he may slant his words to show approval, to show disapproval, or to show a balance between the two.

The choice, the selection of words, is the strongest way of slanting your attitude. Two other ways, however, can be selected to show a favorable or unfavorable attitude. One of these is the use of connectives. There is a difference, slight but strong, between the use of *and* and *but* and many other connectives. Word order also slants by emphasis. That is, if you say "He was a wise, old man," you are giving slight emphasis to *old* because the last position in sentence is the strongest. Conversely, if you say "He is an old, wise man," you would be emphasizing *wise*.

Some words are strongly slanted through the use of *charged* words. The following two passages are made up of highly charged expressions. Read them carefully and underline those words that seem to you to be charged.

> Corlyn paused at the entrance to the room and glanced about. A well-cut black dress draped subtly about her slender form. Her long blonde hair gave her chiseled features the simple frame they required. She smiled an engaging smile as she accepted a cigarette from her escort. As he lit it for her she looked over the flame and into his eyes. Corlyn had that rare talent of making every male feel that he was the one man in the world.
>
> She took his arm and they descended the steps into the room. She walked with an effortless grace and spoke with equal ease. They each took a cup of coffee and joined a group of friends near the fire. The flickering light danced across her face and lent an ethereal

quality to her beauty. The good conversation, the crackling logs, and the stimulating coffee gave her a feeling of internal warmth. Her eyes danced with each leap of the flames.

Corlyn halted at the entrance to the room and looked around. A plain black dress hung on her thin frame. Her stringy bleached hair accentuated her harsh features. She smiled an inane smile as she took a cigarette from her escort. As he lit it for her she stared over the lighter and into his eyes. Corlyn had a habit of making every male feel that he was the last man on earth.

She grasped his arm and they walked down the steps and into the room. Her pace was fast and ungainly, as was her speech. They each reached for some coffee and broke into a group of acquaintances near the fire. The flickering light played across her face and revealed every flaw. The loud talk, the fire, and the coffee she had gulped down made her feel hot. Her eyes grew more red with each leap of the flames.

ASSIGNMENT

The real test of your ability to persuade occurs when you have to face an audience that doesn't share your opinion. It wouldn't take much effort to persuade a member of the National Rifle Association to oppose gun control, but trying to convince the widow of a man who was brutally murdered with an illegally purchased handgun might not be such an easy task. Good persuasive writing, then, must be directed toward the neutral, the unsympathetic, or the openly hostile audience. In each of the suggestions listed below, you must take an unpopular stand (unpopular in terms of your audience) on a specific issue. Look at each topic carefully. Then choose one that you feel strongly about and write a good persuasive essay directed at the prescribed audience.

1. Try to convince an unemployed American steelworker that pollution control legislation is important—even if it sometimes leads to the loss of jobs.
2. Try to convince a healthy, capable, sixty-four-old widower who loves his job that mandatory retirement is a good idea.
3. Try to convince a group of executives from the American Tobacco Company that smoking in public places should be prohibited.
4. Try to convince a conservative Roman Catholic cardinal that the priesthood should be open to women.

5. Try to convince an auditorium full of college-bound high school students that American colleges and universities should expel students for cheating.

6. Try to convince a group of angry parents that teachers have as much right to strike as the members of any other occupation.

7. Try to convince a high school dropout who is making $50,000 a year selling cosmetics that education is important.

8. Try to convince a convention of fundamentalist preachers that there is something inherently wrong with the idea of censorship in a democracy.

9. Try to convince a nurse who works in a clinic for victims of child abuse that elementary school teachers should be able to paddle students without fear of having lawsuits filed against them.

10. Try to convince a man who has been married and divorced three times that alimony laws are necessary.

11. Try to convince a fifty-seven-year-old Appalachian coal miner that mental labor can be just as exhausting as physical labor.

12. Try to convince a vocal antiunion coworker who has just been promoted to middle management that unions are a necessary evil.

13. Try to convince your local bartender that, by law, bartenders should be subject to legal action for serving drinks to someone who is clearly intoxicated.

14. Try to convince your twelve-year-old son who hates school that he should spend more time reading and less time watching TV.

15. Try to convince a group of young doctors to support a bill which would significantly reduce the cost of health care in the U.S.

16. Try to convince the owner of a 500-acre farm that the use of pesticides must be more strictly regulated.

17. Try to convince the president of the Society for the Prevention of Cruelty to Animals that the progress of medical research would be seriously impaired without the use of animals in laboratory testing.

18. Try to convince the residents of Heavenly Heights, the most affluent section of your neighborhood, that they should let your local Human Welfare Agency build a shelter in Heavenly Heights for the temporary housing of battered wives and unwed mothers.

19. Try to convince a university archaeology professor who is walking on a publish-or-perish tightrope that he should abandon his excavation project at the Navajo burial site out of respect for the tribal descendants who are still living near the burial site.

20. Try to convince your immature sixteen-year-old daughter who thinks she has fallen madly in love with the boy next door that she is too young to get married.

11

Writing About Literature

In writing about literature, writing is your second intellectual activity. Your first is to *read* the literature, find your response to it, and then express it in your writing. The writing itself is perhaps the easiest of all the types of writing you are being asked to do because you don't have to search for something to write about. Your mind, responding to the mind of the writer of the literature, supplies your subject and attitude almost spontaneously.

Thinkers for centuries have tried to determine why readers respond in this vigorous way. Many answers have been suggested, but none have been completely satisfactory. Perhaps the simplest answer concerns the human desire for more extensive experience and the need for interpretation of experience. Even the most fortunate life is limited in comparison with the whole range of possible experience, but literature annihilates time and space to supply vicarious living that transcends any one life. Not only does literature supply a wider range of experience, but also, by presenting an experience comparable to the reader's own, it supplies interpretation and understanding.

But whether you are reading for experience or for interpretation, no matter what assignment you may be given or what approach you may choose, there is no substitute for thorough study of the work you intend to write about. A hasty, superficial reading is not good enough; you must read it so that you put something of yourself into the reading. A fast read-through may be fine for a start, but then you need to go back and study the people, the movement, and the ideas of the story or poem. Jot down brief notes as you go—notes about the pattern of development and the juxtaposition of events, notes about the characters and the tensions within them and the conflicts between them, notes about the writer's techniques and features of his or her style, notes on your own reaction to the characters, events, and ideas. That kind of careful study gives you the best chance of finding a worthwhile thesis.

There are usually many approaches to writing about any given work; in fact, your choice among a great number of possibilities may prove to be your first problem in getting started. What you want to avoid is just retelling the story or restating the ideas in an essay or verse, for that does not provide the kind of anaylsis most instructors want. Unless you are specifically asked to write a book review or a synopsis of a story, start with the assumption that your readers already know the story; what they expect is an intelligent analysis of some aspect of the story from your particular point of view. What most instructors hope for is some evidence of genuine insight on your part. Thus, your specific goal in writing ought to be that of finding for yourself something significant in the poem or story and then sharing that discovery with your readers.

RHETORIC

The Bases of Judgment

The term *criticism* comes from a Greek word meaning *judgment*. When you write criticism, you are making a judgment, an evaluation of some artistic work. Before the judgment can be made, however, it is imperative to make clear on what basis the judgment is to be made.

It is generally agreed that there are four bases: (1) the work itself; (2) the maker of the work (the artist); (3) the subject of the work—what it "is about"; and finally, (4) the audience to whom the work must relate.

Modern criticism tends to emphasize the work itself as the ground for criticism. The work exists for itself, not for its maker, not for the audience, not for the world it represents as its subject. It has a self-contained existence in which the critic can judge only the parts and the relationships of the parts that make up the whole. As Archibald MacLeish says, "A poem does not mean, but is."

Romantic criticism tends to emphasize the feelings of the artist. The romantic poet William Wordsworth said, "All good poetry is the spontaneous overflow of powerful feelings." Critics writing from this basis must judge the intention of the maker. They must find what the writer intends; they must see it as their responsibility to understand the writer.

The third basis of criticism concerns the subject, what the work is about. This, one of the oldest theories of criticism, comes from the Greeks who considered all art, including literature, as a representation of life. Art refers to "real" things and people, but their "reality" is modified by the individual vision of the maker. Aristotle, for example, says that tragedy presents people "as better than they are"; comedy presents people as "worse than they are." At its simplest, this type of criticism approves of works that are "true to life."

The final basis of criticism in this analysis is the relationship between the work and the audience. The critic writing from this basis attempts to establish that the work is enjoyable and that the pleasure it creates in the audience leads that audience to right (or wrong) thinking. Even so modern a thinker as George Bernard Shaw said that art which did not teach was not art at all.

Approaches to Criticism

After having established the basis on which judgments are to be made, the critical writer finds that there are many approaches to literary criticism: moral, psychological, sociological, aesthetic, or archetypal. The moral approach is concerned with the relationship between work and audience. The psychological approach offers insight into characters as well as into the creative processes of the makers. The sociological approach emphasizes that the artist/maker is an important, because articulate, member of society. The sociological critic wants to illuminate the way in which artists present and respond to their social milieu. The sociological approach was defined most precisely by Hippolyte Taine, who said that literature was the product of "the moment, the race, and the milieu." The sociological approach is thus based on subject, what the work "is about". The aesthetic approach (sometimes called formalistic approach) to literary criticism is concerned only with the work itself. The critic searches for *intrinsic* meaning in the work, downplaying the artist, the society in which the artist lives and works, and the audience to whom the artist speaks. The archetypal approach includes psychological, sociological, and historical elements. In essence, the archetypal critic searches for plots, characters, themes, and symbols that appear first in mythology and reappear through centuries of writings that are seemingly unlike but are really unified through the repetition of these abiding archetypes. The story of Cinderella, the character of the wicked stepmother, the theme of the quest for love, and the symbol of the river are all examples of archetypes.

Approaches through the Elements

Because you cannot, in a short essay, discuss all aspects of a work, you should choose a relatively narrow topic. One starting point is to consider the elements of fiction: plot, character, theme, or setting. Or you might consider devices used by the author: point of view, tone, symbolism, or irony.

Plot

Plot, the sequence of action, is the easiest element to understand. After all, anyone who reads a story knows what happens in it, but just retelling the story is ineffective. However, discussing the author's handling of the action, the use of flashbacks, motivation, coincidences, or other techniques can make a fine essay.

Central to any plot is *conflict* between the main character (the protagonist) and the natural world or between the protagonist and other people or within the protagonist. Conflict *within* the protagonist is sometimes called *tension*. As the conflict without and the tension within intensify, action and reaction speed the plot to its climax. A character who is at war within himself or herself may break loose at any moment and lash out at an opponent or at society as a whole.

The most obvious examples of tension occur in psychological stories. But even in a story or novel that offers little outward action, tension may be at work, subtly doing violence from within or, in some instances, impelling a character toward some brave new world.

You may choose to examine a specific work either on the basis of some central conflict or in terms of those inner tensions that propel the characters toward their destinies. When the tensions that energize the story are finally brought to a resolution, the reader sees the world, or at least some aspect of it, in a new light. Through an analysis of conflict or tension, perhaps you may help to show how this revelation has been brought about.

Character

The people in the story frequently make an effective topic. If the author is seriously trying to depict life, the characters, like real people, may be ambiguous, they may have good and bad points, they may think and act differently, or they may have values different from ours. However, in writing about character, such differences make a good way to "get into" a story. You might discuss whether the character represents all of us or some of us or is one of a kind. In *The Death of Ivan Ilych*, for example, Tolstoy's Ivan represents all of us. The author here shows the reader the typical stages of a person's life in a job, in marriage, in the quality of friendships, and in sickness and death, which we must all ultimately face.

In many stories the author shows how a particular type of person will act. In "And the Rock Cried Out," Ray Bradbury's main characters exemplify upper-class Americans and their actions when traveling in "developing" or poor countries. In many others, authors show us unique characters dealing with unique situations. Huck in Mark Twain's *Adventures of Huckleberry Finn* and Bartleby in Herman Melville's "Bartleby the Scrivener" are examples of such characters.

Theme

Theme is the unifying element in a work, the author's view of some truth about life. In serious fiction, theme is the author's reason for writing the story. The author writes to reveal some aspect of the human condition. Since the author does not state the theme explicitly but lets it unfold through the other elements and their relationships to each other, you must discover the theme. You may do this by reading closely, paying careful attention to details, and noting the following tips:

1. Check the title for a clue.
2. Check the major conflict and its outcome.
3. If there is a change in the protagonist, check this change and the motivation for it.
4. Examine any symbols that are dominant in the work.

Remember that theme must explain *all* the major incidents in the work. If your version explains only some of them, you probably have only a subtheme. And *no* incident can contradict the theme. If one does, your analysis of the theme is wrong.

Once you have discovered the theme, many topics for an essay emerge. The theme of Joseph Conrad's "Youth" may be stated in different words, but it is basically this.

> There is no time of life as great as youth; at this time, danger is exciting, hardship is a challenge, life is glamorous and romantic, and one feels he can do anything; but all too soon this attitude is gone, and middle age, with its fears and anxieties, dominates our lives, and the magic is gone.

An essay on this theme, developed by examples or contrast, would be relatively easy to write. On the other hand, perhaps you do not accept the theme. Perhaps you believe that youth is a trying and stressful time of life, that only in middle age does a person gain the wisdom and serentiy to enjoy life. An explanation of your disagreement could also become a good essay.

Setting

Setting may also provide subject matter for an essay. The time, the place, the atmosphere which make up setting can influence plot, character, and even theme. For example, the deteriorating old house, isolated and austere, illuminated only by flashes of lightning, sets the stage for Edgar Allan Poe's "The Fall of the House of Usher." Likewise, the silhouettes of leafless branches against the dead, predawn light of gray sky prepares the reader for an ominous happening in Ambrose Bierce's "An Occurrence at Owl Creek Bridge." The opening description of William Faulkner's "A Rose for Emily" helps establish the theme of Emily's inability to bridge the gap between the old days and modern life. Phrases like "heavily lightsome" and "coquettish decay" foreshadow Emily's character, a character which, in turn, determines the theme of the story.

> It was a big, squarish frame house that had once been white, decorated with cupolas and spires and scrolled balconies in the heavily lightsome style of the seventies, set on what had once been our most select street. But garages and cotton gins had encroached and obliterated even the august names of that neighborhood; only Miss Emily's house was left, lifting its stubborn and coquettish decay above the cotton wagons and the gasoline pumps—an eyesore among eyesores.

Sometimes the setting influences a character's actions. In "Defender of the Faith," Nathan Marx's reactions to a fellow Jew exploiting him were certainly affected by the setting. Marx "feared he had acquired an infantryman's heart" and therefore was no longer moved by the suffering of others. He had just returned from Nazi Germany and had seen the prison camps and ovens where six million Jews had been systematically and efficiently killed. Surely, the time and his past experiences affected Marx's actions.

Point of View

The point of view the author uses may also provide good subject matter for a critical essay. If the author tells the story, you can believe that the story illustrates the truth as the author sees it. If, however, the author uses a character to tell the story, this narrator will *reflect* the happenings as *the narrator* sees them. A young child is often an *unreliable* narrator. An unreliable narrator, however, often adds much to the story. For example, one of the delights of *Adventures of Huckleberry Finn* is that Huck, who narrates the story, is completely unaware of the deceits and conventions of "the gentry." He accepts as truth everything adults say and accepts as right everything they do. Therefore, although the reader sees Huck as an extremely bright, clever, and virtuous boy, Huck sees himself as ignorant and wicked. This is dramatic irony. Huck sees himself as stupid because society demands the schooling that Huck lacks. Huck accepts the idea of slavery without question because that's what the adults say is right. A critical essay on *Huck Finn* could focus on any one of several variations on point of view: the unconscious humor evoked by Huck's naiveté, Huck's misconception of himself as evil, Huck's knack of doing the right things for the wrong reasons, Huck's acceptance of the "southern gentry," or the stupidities of adult conventions, when seen through a child's eye.

Analyzing point of view can reveal previously hidden approaches to the author's purpose. You may find the narrator misinformed, prejudiced, or dense; from this discovery, you gain insight into the writer's purpose. Imagine "Cinderella" as told by the cruel stepmother or "Little Red Riding Hood" as narrated by the wolf. You would ask, "Why did the author create a narrator like this?"

Tone

Tone is an important element because it creates style and influences meaning. Except for news writing, in which writers strive to eliminate attitude and stick only to the facts, tone is the expression of the writer's feelings and opinions about the subject and toward the audience. To read well, you must interpret the writer's tone; to write well, you must project a convincing and consistent tone of your own.

Since the essay is so personal a creation, the writer's personality forms its groundwork. Tone expresses how the author feels at this time, under these circumstances, with this audience, about this subject. There is almost no end to the varieties of tone; it may be formal or casual, sentimental or satiric, comic or serious—possibilities without end. Tone is achieved in many ways: through choice of topic, word choice, sentence structure, use of figurative language, organization and order of materials, or combinations of all these.

GREEN IVORY

In the following essay, complete though very brief, the tone is unusual, even though it is consistent with this writer. The essayist, Logan Pearsall Smith, developed an image of himself and for himself through his tone and maintained it through a long, successful career. Even today, fifty years after he wrote, his books remain in print, and he has loyal readers, all because of his characteristic tone. Even the titles of Smith's books identify his tone; he called them *Trivia, More Trivia,* and *All Trivia,* indicating that his attitude was mocking at gravity and self-importance.

> What a bore it is, waking up in the morning always the same person. I wish I were unflinching and emphatic, and had big, bushy eyebrows and a Message for the Age. I wish I were a deep Thinker, or a great Ventriloquist.
>
> I should like to be refined-looking and melancholy, the victim of a hopeless passion; to love in the old, stilted way, with impossible Adoration and Despair under the palefaced Moon.
>
> I wish I could get up; I wish I were the world's greatest living Violinist. I wish I had lots of silver, and first Editions, and green ivory.
>
> Logan Pearsall Smith

Since his essay is only three tiny paragraphs long, he begins with his thesis statement. His topic is the frequent, if not universal, desire sometimes to escape the limitations of one's own personality. This is a subject that could be treated in a technical, psychological manner or in a serious, theological sense. The reader, however, immediately knows that Smith's tone is lighthearted because of the word *bore,* which conveys superficiality. It might be serious to wish to be unflinching or even emphatic, but surely the eyebrows are purposely trivial. In like fashion, he contrasts the deep Thinker with a great Ventriloquist, emphasizing the joke by capitalizing *ventriloquist*.

In the second paragraph, he is highly romantic, but his romance is so stereotyped it's obviously a spoof. And his final paragraph juxtaposes a series of romantic wishes against his humble desire to get out of bed. In fewer words than it took to describe, Smith creates a tone that communicates a gentle joke about human desires and limitations.

An awareness of tone can deepen your pleasure in others' writing and add individuality to your own; but, even more important, tone enhances communication, making your writing clear and effective.

Symbolism

Symbolism also makes a fine subject for the analysis of a critical essay. In brief, symbols are words, objects, or events within a literary work that stand for something else as well as for what they are. That something else that the symbol signifies is usually an abstraction, such as truth, love, beauty, honor; or it might just as easily be greed, corruption, ruthlessness, moral disintegration. But keep in mind that the symbolic word, object, or event is not something tacked on to the story. It is, first of all, a concrete element within the story, yet it is so placed or utilized as to take on another meaning or identity. Thus, an oak tree in a poem or story is, first of all, an oak tree; the author of the poem or story, however, may strongly suggest to the reader that the oak tree does indeed represent something else— perhaps an abstraction such as steadfastness, moral strength, or stubborn endurance.

Yet the symbolic relationship established in a given work may not be that simple. For example, one symbolic detail, let us say snow, may suggest not just a single meaning but a whole cluster of meanings: innocence, purity, freshness, or quiet, merciful oblivion. In a different poem or story, snow might come to signify ambiguity, blurred moral vision, or a mind gone blank. This is not to say, however, that snow (or some other detail in the story) means any old thing that we want it to mean. Its meaning is limited and controlled by the whole context out of which it arises. Usually, when authors intend something to have a symbolic meaning, they send out some clear signals. A certain detail of action or setting, for instance, may be given a prominent position at the beginning, at the end, or at the climax of the story. Or perhaps it may reappear at strategic points throughout the story. Thus, if you discuss symbolism, you must pay close attention to all of the clues that the author gives you and then be prepared to defend your interpretation on the basis of what is to be found in the poem or story itself.

Irony

In the general sense, irony refers to both words and situations that carry a double meaning. In *verbal irony*, the simplest form, the meaning may be the opposite of what the words are saying, or at least incongruous with the usual meaning of the words. For instance, when the husband is nursing a hangover and his wife says, "Darling, you look wonderful," the words are going one way and the meaning is going another. In speech, the tone of voice alone may signal a reversal of meaning; in writing, however, there must be some other clear signal of ironic intention. Situations too may be ironic, in that they bring out some discrepancy between expectation and fulfillment or appearance and reality. In a soap-opera situation, you might have a formerly wealthy widow marrying a confidence man who she believes will provide her with the luxuries to which she has become accustomed, while he is marrying her in the mistaken notion that she is still rich.

In a strict literary sense, *dramatic irony* refers to those situations in which the reader or viewer is aware of something that is at the time unknown to the character. In Sophocles's great tragedy *Oedipus the King*, Oedipus vows to find the villain who has brought a plague upon Thebes, but the viewer or reader already knows that Oedipus himself is the evildoer he has sworn to apprehend.

Irony may range from gentle, good-humored chiding to bitter denunciation. Mark Twain's posthumously published "The War Prayer" lashes out at the hypocrisy of so-called Christian nations in time of war.

> O Lord our Father, our young patriots, idols of our hearts, go forth to battle—be Thou near them! With them—in spirit—we also go forth from the sweet peace of our beloved firesides to smite the foe. O Lord our God, help us to tear their soldiers to bloody shreds with our shells; help us to cover their smiling fields with the pale forms of their patriot dead; help us to drown the thunder of the guns with the shrieks of their wounded, writhing in pain; help us to lay waste their humble homes with a hurricane of fire; help us to wring the hearts of their unoffending widows with unavailing grief; help us to turn them out roofless with their little children to wander unfriended the wastes

of their desolated land in rags and hunger and thirst, sports of the sun flames of summer and the icy winds of winter, broken in spirit, worn with travail, imploring Thee for the refuge of the grave and denied it—for our sakes who adore Thee, Lord, blast their hopes, blight their lives, protract their bitter pilgrimage, make heavy their steps, water their way with their tears, stain the white snow with the blood of their wounded feet! We ask it, in the spirit of love, of Him who is the Source of Love, and who is the ever-faithful refuge and friend of all that are sore beset and seek His aid with humble and contrite hearts. Amen.

ORGANIZATION

The organization of a critical paper is like that of all the other essay types you have been reading about. It has a relatively brief introduction, ending with the thesis statement that announces your narrowed subject and shows your attitude toward it. Almost any of the introductory techniques can be used successfully, but among the best is the use of pertinent quotation from the work or a lively or perceptive comment or anecdote about the work or the author. The thesis statements in critical essays are always interpretative, for interpretation and explanation are what your essay is about.

The body of the essay, as always, is support for your thesis statement, support that comes from the work itself. You will use quotations and paraphrases from the work you read to support your generalizing thesis statement and the topic sentences of the body paragraphs.

The conclusion of your critical essay is a return to the thesis statement, a reaffirmation of the interpretation you have made about the work. Don't weaken your conclusion by trailing off in some vague approval of your author ("Shakespeare is a good writer"). Don't shift attention from your interpretation to your reaction ("I was fascinated by this book. I couldn't put it down"). Remember that the conclusion is your final opportunity to convince your reader and that you do this best when you focus on *your* interpretation of a narrowed topic from the work.

Developing the Critical Essay

Alone or in combination, several of the methods of development you have already studied will supply you with effective means of presenting your critical judgments. Examples, dividing and classifying, and defining—all are appropriate for a critical essay.

Among the most successful methods is the use of comparison and contrast. Almost every literary work offers some qualities that lend themselves to comparison/contrast, one of the easiest and most natural methods of development. Do you see specific points of comparison between two characters in different works by the same author? Do you find a sharp contrast between one story and another that deals with the same general subject? Between two writers who, for example, both write about the Civil War era, the Gilded Age, the Great Depression, or Paris in the twenties?

You need, first, to find an underlying purpose for your comparison. Describing two things, events, or people side by side may be a futile exercise unless your comparison/contrast reveals something worth recognizing. If you can show how two talented writers have looked at the same sort of environment—London's Soho, New Orleans's Vieux Carre, or whatever—and have seen two different worlds, then you may assume that you have something worth writing about. That is not to say that the comparison/contrast must involve exotic subjects, but it must reveal something that the reader might otherwise fail to appreciate.

Another excellent developmental method for criticism is causal analysis. Reality does not conform to the principle of probability; fiction does. In the real world, things just happen without apparent reason, but in fiction, things don't just happen; they are made to happen. Whereas reality is made up, for the most part, of bits and pieces without necessary connection, good ficton must be carefully molded through selection and shaping, so that, in the end, it conforms to rigorous demands of cause and effect. If a writer expects readers to accept a fictive world, even if it is set in outer space, it must conform to probability and the rules of cause and effect.

With this principle of probability in mind, then, you may rightly apply causal analysis to characters and their actions within the fictive world of which they are a part. One of the sharpest accusations hurled at modern fiction and drama is "gratuitous violence." If, for example, a brutal axe murder is committed by an otherwise kindly and gentle lady, perhaps her action could be explained, but the author would need to build a powerful case to demonstrate adequate causation and motivation for such unlikely action. Causal analysis is a tool of logical thinking, and probability is a logical demand that we make of fiction. In most respects, we apply that demand far more rigorously to works of fiction than we do to the reality of everyday events—the traffic slaughter, arson, and murder that fill so much of the daily news.

If you are to apply causal analysis to fiction, you must first read carefully to be sure that you have not overlooked some idea that the author may have stressed; then, you must carefully weigh the various forces at work and try to take into account all the shreds of evidence that contribute to the dynamics of the story.

The Reviewer and the Critic

Two different purposes lead to two widely differing ways to write about literature. One way is the review, which attempts to answer a very specific question in the reader's mind. The reader wants to know if the book being reviewed (or the play or movie or concert or art exhibit) is worth the time and money to read or see it. The reviewer writes about what it is and how good a member of its kind it is. The reviewer's work generally appears in newspapers and popular magazines, for it is a kind of news.

The critic, on the other hand, discusses, explains, or challenges some aspect of the work. Critics usually assume that their readers are already familiar with the work being considered. Critics do not tell readers what the work is about, but they attempt to illuminate something in it. Almost always in your academic work, you will be asked to be a critic.

Use of Others' Writings

In writing a critical paper, you make use of the writings of others, either just the work you are criticizing or that work and the judgments on it by other critics. In either case, you must learn the accepted ways of summarizing, paraphrasing, and quoting. These techniques allow you to include the writings of others in your essays without committing the crime of plagiarism. In all of these, you give credit to the original writer by footnote, parentheses, or reference.

Before beginning to write any of these, however, you must first make sure that you understand exactly what the author means. Read the passage as many times as is necessary to feel confident that you know the author's purpose and tone as well as his or her meaning. Once you have a clear idea of the meaning, you must decide which of the devices you wish to use: the summary, the paraphrase, or the quotation.

The Summary

The use of the summary is not new to you. You used it in high school when you wrote a book review; you used it when you told your friend the plot of a book you read or a movie or a TV program you watched. You probably have used the summary to answer essay questions. The summary is a brief recounting given in your own words. It is usually less than one half as long as the original work, and it follows the same order as the original and includes its major points, major supporting details, any key facts, and examples.

The Paraphrase

A paraphrase is a restatement, in your own words, of what someone else has written. The paraphrase may be shorter than the original, or it may be as long as or longer than the original, for the purpose here is not so much to condense, as is the case with the summary, but to retell the work in your own words and your own style. Paraphrase allows the writer to concentrate on only one part of the original work or to shift the point of emphasis in the original. However, paraphrase only what the author says, not what you think he or she is implying.

You may, if you wish, quote key words or phrases if they seem better than anything you can come up with. However, the quotations should be clearly marked as such and should be blended into your writing so that the sentences are not choppy. Again, you must have a clear understanding of what the original author is saying, and you must completely reword what he or she writes. Changing the order of the words, changing direct quotation to indirect quotation, or moving a few phrases around is not paraphrasing—it's plagiarizing.

The Quotation

A direct quotation is the use of another's writing exactly as it was written, word for word. You may use a phrase, a clause, a sentence, or even a group of sentences and put it in your paper verbatim. The quotation should be used primarily if the material is written brilliantly or if the material is controversial or unknown. Otherwise, the paraphrase is usually better, as it is in your style and the writing remains smoother. However, the careful use of quotations can enhance your writing and provide excellent support for your thesis. Generally, phrases, sentences, and short passages are preferable to long passages. Long quotations from various authors which are strung together with only brief introductions and comments from you make for choppy, unclear writing which shows little thought. Quotation is not a substitute for your own thoughts in your own words but a support for those thoughts. Used as a support, quotations can be convincing. To make sure that they are used for support only, many instructors restrict the use of quotation to no more than 20 percent of your paper. If your instructor writes "good use of quotation" in the margin of your paper, it is sincere praise. It means you have had the perception to see what is good and to incorporate it into your thinking.

Techniques of Quoting. The quotations that you use (a few words or part of a sentence) must fit with the rest of the sentence; that is, the sentence must make sense. A sentence such as "Shakespeare's *Henry V* is a good history play with 'its splendors and its secondary attractions, but the forces in it are not unified' "is unclear. In this sentence, the quotation not only does not support but denies the point to be made. To make the meaning clear, the sentence should read: "Shakespeare's *Henry IV* is a better play than *Henry V*, which 'has its splendors and its secondary attractions, but the forces in it are not unified.' "

The Long Quotation. Any quotation of three lines or more is indented five spaces and single-spaced. No quotation marks are necessary; the indentation and single-spacing show that it is a direct quotation.

With all quotations, and especially with long ones, you must make clear to the reader the relationship between the quotation and the point you are making. This is usually done in your introduction to the quotation. If, for example, you are attempting to prove that the work you were discussing was, contrary to popular opinion, a tragedy, you might write:

> This work is a tragedy because it has the classical properties of a tragedy. John Dryden defined the qualities of tragedy in a 1679 essay: It ought to be great, and to consist of great persons, to distinguish it from comedy, where the action is trivial and the persons of inferior rank . . . it ought to be probable, as well as admirable and great . . . the end or scope of tragedy . . . is, to rectify or purge our passions, fear and pity.

Then you would show that the work has all of these qualities. Notice that in the text of the paper the writer has given credit to the author. Mentioning the author immediately before using his or her ideas or words is useful in showing where your idea ends and the author's begins.

Documentation

You may document (give credit to your sources) either formally or informally. If you are writing formally (a research paper, a thesis, or a dissertation) or if you are using many sources, you should use formal documentation. In a theme based on a single work, you may use informal documentation. Your instructor will usually tell you what type of documentation is required.

Formal Documentation. Formal documentation requires footnotes. A superscript number in your text following the ideas or words of the writer you are using lets the reader know that the material comes from a source other than you. The reader can then look at the footnote to see where the material came from originally.

The first footnote for any work should include the following information (if appropriate) in this order:

- The footnote number that corresponds with the superscript number in your text.
- Author's first and last name, followed by a comma.
- The title of the story, poem, or article, enclosed in quotation marks if it is a separate part of but not the whole work.
- The name of the book, magazine, or newspaper (the whole work), underlined.
- The edition, if given.
- The name or names of the editor, followed by *ed.* or *eds.*, if given.
- The place of publication (the city), followed by a colon.
- The name of the publisher, followed by a comma.
- The date of publication. The above three—place of publication, publisher, and date of publication—are enclosed in parentheses.
- The page number or numbers. Do not write out *page* or use a *p.*
- When quoting poetry, include line numbers with other material.

For example, if you were using material from this book, the first footnote would read

[1]Robert B. Donald et al., *Models for Clear Writing* (Englewood Cliffs, N.J.: Prentice-Hall, Inc., 1988), 93.
Or the first footnote for "Miss Brill" could read
[2]Katherine Mansfield, "Miss Brill," *Studies in Fiction*, 3rd ed., Blaze O. Bonazza, Emil Roy, Sandra Roy, eds. (New York: Harper and Row, 1982), 563–67.

In your footnote, include only information not given in the text of your essay. If you identify the author within your essay, then start your footnote with the name of the work. If you name both the author and the work within the text, your footnote needs to contain only the information not already given.

> In Katherine Mansfield's short story "Miss Brill," the protagonist has a sudden vision of her appearance to others. . . .[3]
> [3]*Studies in Fiction*, 3rd ed., Blaze O. Bonazza, Emil Roy, Sandra Roy, eds. (New York: Harper and Row, 1982), 163–67.

Once you have made the initial reference to a work, which always includes full documentation, all subsequent references need only identify the work by author. For example, the second (and subsequent footnotes) for the works mentioned earlier could be shortened to

> Donald, 21.
> Mansfield, 140.

If two or more works by the same author are cited, an abbreviated title must be used.

> Donald, *Paragraphs*, 112.
> Donald, *Models*, 19–21.

You should note that Latin abbreviations, such as *ibid.* and *op. cit.*, are infrequently used.

There are, of course, many other forms of documentation besides these basic ones. Every scholarly discipline has its preferred style manual. The *MLA Handbook for Writers of Research Papers* is widely used in humanities disciplines and is easily available in most college libraries and bookstores. The following instructions are taken from the *MLA Handbook*.

Footnotes are numbered consecutively throughout the paper and are usually placed at the bottom of the page where the material is used. They may also be placed at the end of the paper or put in the text in parentheses immediately following the material used. Your instructor will tell you which placement to use.

Informal Documentation. Informal documentation is used when you are writing about only one literary work and using only one source. You identify your source in a single footnote, and thereafter you include the necessary information (usually just the page number) in parentheses in the text of your essay.

For example:

> The casual cruelty of the young couple spoiled Miss Brill's joy. "On her way home she usually bought a slice of honey cake. It was her Sunday treat. . . . But today she passed the baker's by." (376) Her pathetic pleasures were dashed from her when the young couple sneered at her beloved fur necklet. "She unclasped the necklet quickly; quickly, without looking, laid it inside [its box]. But when she put the lid on she thought she heard something crying." (376)

In quoting other people's writing, you must follow them word for word. The only acceptable ways to make changes are

> If you are omitting something, make your omission clear by using dots. . . .
> If you are adding something, show your additions by putting your material in square brackets.[]

Do not run two separate quotations back-to-back; some intervening material of your own should come between them, as it does in the preceding sentences about Miss Brill.

Exercise

Discuss the effectiveness of each of the following paraphrases. Point out specific errors, such as plagiarism, omission, misunderstanding of the original, and so on.

Passage to Be Paraphrased

A literary symbol means itself plus more. It stands for what it is and other things that it brings to mind. The flag is a symbol: it stands for a flag plus all the feelings of patriotism, honor, bravery, freedom, and love of country that the flag may bring to mind. Other symbols such as the cross, the swastika, the Statue of Liberty, and the skull and crossbones evoke their own connotations. In any given story, however, the symbol could take on a different meaning. Certain literary symbols have been used so often that they are almost standardized.

> journey = life
> spring, summer, fall = youth, adulthood, old age

morning, afternoon, night = youth, adulthood, old age
crossing a bridge = changing your life
water = purification, life-giving force
light = good, hope, civilization
dark = evil, despair, primitiveness
star = hope

Other symbols have unique meanings; they have a special meaning only in the story in which they appear. The raft, for example, in *Adventures of Huckleberry Finn* represents a kind of Eden, a Paradise, but the raft is not a universal symbol. In other stories, it might represent danger or impermanence or something else or nothing else.

Paraphrase A

If something means itself plus something else, it is a literary symbol. It stands for what it is and other things that it brings to mind. A military uniform, for example, means a uniform plus all the feelings a uniform brings forth—feelings of patriotism and bravery and honor. The same is true of many things, like a skull and crossbones, which makes you think of poison or pirates. Light usually means good things, and dark means bad things, but symbols don't always mean the same things. Sometimes a raft might mean good, but sometimes it might mean evil.

Paraphrase B

"A literary symbol means itself plus more."[1] There are two types of literary symbols; one type of symbol has a traditional meaning because it has been used so often: light, for example, has come to symbolize hope or civilization or goodness, while dark represents the opposite. Seasons and times of day have come to be recognized as also representing ages of man. Feelings of patriotism are often evoked by the flag, and other symbols evoke other emotions. Sometimes "symbols are unique; they have a meaning only in the story in which they appear."[2] In the *Adventures of Huckleberry Finn*, for example, Twain uses a raft as a symbol of Paradise, or it may mean the opposite. Or it may mean just a raft, having no symbolic meaning at all.

The Contest

JACK MATTHEWS

Literary criticism sometimes discusses a theme that deals with an element important in many different kinds of literary works. Other criticism focuses on an individual work. The next two models exemplify these two approaches to literary criticism. Jack Matthew's "The Contest" discusses the archetypal plot of the contest. On the other hand, R. F. Dietrich presents a detailed analysis of a single short story. These two essays, along with the other models in this section, give at least a slight indication of the breadth of literary criticism.

"The Contest" undoubtedly includes as examples titles that not everyone is familiar with. However, since the subject is so broad, you will be able to get the meaning.

In the second example, The Use of Force, *since the critical points are so specific, we have included the short story which is analyzed.*

In spite of recent experimentation, all stories must have conflict of some kind, or we don't refer to them as stories at all—we call them tone poems, or essays, or mood pieces, or something else. In one important sense, conflict *is* the story; it forms the vortex of interest in the story, and it is often the force that propels the narrative movement.

Since it is an essential feature of stories, conflict cannot reasonably be considered a theme. In one of its forms, however—the Contest motif—it constitutes a primordial situation, a truly archetypal theme. While a single character may experience "inner conflict," it would be strange indeed to speak of his "inner contest." In the Contest, there are two characters of comparable power who more or less knowingly enter some sort of arena in a struggle with each other. Often this struggle is highly symbolic, insofar as the characters themselves seem vested with larger meaning.

David and Goliath, Hector and Achilles, Dimmesdale and Chillingworth, Eliza and W. O. Gant (in Thomas Wolfe's *Look Homeward, Angel*), Fast Eddie and Minnesota Fats (in Walter

Tevis's *The Hustler*) are all participants in contests, are all Contest figures. Sometimes the contest is overt and physical; at other times it is concealed and confused, as in the marriage of Eliza and W. O. Gant—a marriage that is itself an arena of strife between two life styles.

Much more than a conflict between life styles is at stake in Herman Melville's strange and fascinating story, "Bartleby the Scrivener." The lawyer and Bartleby come together in the arena of an office of law—a place that exists in service of dialectic, of rational debate for the sake of truth. But Bartleby's challenge is a deeper, more unsettling one: he does not seem to care for reason, or dialectic, or truth. He is a spirit of awesome negation, and the Contest is entered upon the instant his employer (the narrator of the story) determines to force Bartleby not simply to go to work but to "see things his way." In the playing out of the long, strange drama of struggle, Bartleby's insistent preference "not to" makes us feel that he achieves a kind of humble nobility, even though our social and rational sentiments must belong to the kindly but exasperated lawyer who tells the story.

The variations on the Contest theme seem almost endless. Joyce Carol Oates claims that most of her stories have to do with the Contest motif. Her "Love and Death," like Eudora Welty's hauntingly subtle "Circe," involves one of the oldest contests around (and still, at this writing, undecided)—that between man and woman. William Sansom's story, on the other hand, is a colorful and honest journey into the implications of two old men entering the whimsical arena of who-can-out-miser-the-other, and the whimsical triumph of a protagonist who is suddenly deprived of his antagonist.

A few of the many classic short stories that are concerned with the theme of the Contest are "The Pupil" by Henry James, "The Short Happy Life of Francis Macomber" by Ernest Hemingway, "The Bride Comes to Yellow Sky" by Stephen Crane, and "The Secret Sharer" by Joseph Conrad.

The Use of Force

WILLIAM CARLOS WILLIAMS

They were new patients to me, all I had was the name Olson. Please come down as soon as you can, my daughter is very sick.

When I arrived I was met by the mother, a big startled looking woman, very clean and apologetic who merely said, Is this the doctor? and let me in. In the back, she added. You must excuse us, doctor, we have her in the kitchen where it is warm. It is very damp here sometimes.

The child was fully dressed and sitting on her father's lap near the kitchen table. He tried to get up, but I motioned for him not to bother, took off my overcoat and started to look things over. I could see that they were all very nervous, eyeing me up and down distrustfully. As often, in such cases, they weren't telling me more than they had to, it was up to me to tell them; that's why they were spending three dollars on me.

The child was fairly eating me up with her cold, steady eyes, and no expression to her face whatever. She did not move and seemed, inwardly, quiet; an unusually attractive little thing, and as strong as a heifer in appearance. But her face was flushed, she was breathing rapidly, and I realized that she had a high fever. She had magnificent blonde hair, in profusion. One of those picture children often reproduced in advertising leaflets and the photogravure sections of the Sunday papers.

She's had a fever for three days, began the father and we don't know what it comes from. My wife has given her things, you know, like people do, but it don't do no good. And there's been a lot of sickness around. So we tho't you'd better look her over and tell us what is the matter.

As doctors often do I took a trial shot at it as a point of departure. Has she had a sore throat?

Both parents answered me together, No . . . No, she says her throat don't hurt her.

Does your throat hurt you? added the mother to the child. But the little girl's expression didn't change nor did she move her eyes from my face.

Have you looked?

I tried to, said the mother, but I couldn't see.

As it happens we had been having a number of cases of diphtheria in the school to which this child went during that month and we were all, quite apparently, thinking of that, though no one had as yet spoken of the thing.

Well, I said, suppose we take a look at the throat first. I smiled in my best professional manner and asking for the child's first name I said, come on, Mathilda, open your mouth and let's take a look at your throat.

Nothing doing.

Aw, come on, I coaxed, just open your mouth wide and let me take a look. Look, I said opening both hands wide, I haven't anything in my hands. Just open up and let me see.

Such a nice man, put in the mother. Look how kind he is to you. Come on, do what he tells you to. He won't hurt you.

At that I ground my teeth in disgust. If only they wouldn't use the word "hurt" I might be able to get somewhere. But I did not allow myself to be hurried or disturbed but speaking quietly and slowly I approached the child again.

As I moved my chair a little nearer suddenly with one cat-like movement both her hands clawed instinctively for my eyes and she almost reached them too. In fact she knocked my glasses flying and they fell, though unbroken, several feet away from me on the kitchen floor.

Both the mother and father almost turned themselves inside out in embarrassment and apology. You bad girl, said the mother, taking her and shaking her by one arm. Look what you've done. The nice man. . . .

For heaven's sake, I broke in. Don't call me a nice man to her. I'm here to look at her throat on the chance that she might have diphtheria and possibly die of it. But that's nothing to her. Look here, I said to the child, we're going to look at your throat. You're old enough to understand what I'm saying. Will you open it now by yourself or shall we have to open it for you?

Not a move. Even her expression hadn't changed. Her breaths however were coming faster and faster. Then the battle began. I had to do it. I had to have a throat culture for her own protection. But first I told the parents that it was entirely up to them. I explained the danger but said that I would not insist on a throat examination so long as they would take the responsibility.

If you don't do what the doctor says you'll have to go to the hospital, the mother admonished her severely.

Oh yeah? I had to smile to myself. After all, I had already fallen in love with the savage brat, the parents were contemptible to me. In the ensuing struggle they grew more and more abject, crushed, exhausted while she surely rose to magnificent heights of insane fury of effort bred of her terror of me.

The father tried his best, and he was a big man but the fact that she was his daughter, his shame of her behavior and his dread of hurting her made him release her just at the critical moment several times when I had almost achieved success, till I wanted to kill him. But his dread also that she might have diphtheria made him tell me to go on, go on though he himself was almost fainting, while the mother moved back and forth behind us raising and lowering her hands in an agony of apprehension.

Put her in front of you on your lap, I ordered, and hold both her wrists.

But as soon as he did the child let out a scream. Don't, you're hurting me. Let go of my hands. Let them go I tell you. Then she shrieked terrifyingly, hysterically. Stop it! Stop it! You're killing me!

Do you think she can stand it, doctor! said the mother.

You get out, said the husband to the wife. Do you want her to die of diphtheria?

Come on now, hold her, I said.

Then I grasped the child's head with my left hand and tried to get the wooden tongue depressor between her teeth. She fought, with clenched teeth, desperately! But now I also had grown furious—at a child. I tried to hold myself down but I couldn't. I know how to expose a throat for inspection. And I did my best. When finally I got the wooden spatula behind the last teeth and just the point of it into the mouth cavity, she opened up for an instant but before I could see anything she came down again and gripping the wooden blade between her molars she reduced it to splinters before I could get it out again.

Aren't you ashamed, the mother yelled at her. Aren't you ashamed to act like that in front of the doctor?

Get me a smooth-handled spoon of some sort, I told the mother. We're going through with this. The child's mouth was already bleeding. Her tongue was cut and she was screaming in wild hysterical shrieks. Perhaps I should have desisted and come back in an hour or more. No doubt it would have been better. But I have seen at least two children lying dead in bed of neglect in such cases, and feeling that I must get a diagnosis now or never I went at it again. But the worst of it was that I too had got beyond reason. I could have torn the child apart in my own fury and enjoyed it. It was a pleasure to attack her. My face was burning with it.

The damned little brat must be protected against her own idiocy, one says to one's self at such times. Others must be protected against her. It is social necessity. And all these things are true. But a blind fury, a feeling of adult shame, bred of a longing for muscular release are the operatives. One goes on to the end.

In a final unreasoning assault I overpowered the child's neck and jaws. I forced the heavy silver spoon back of her teeth and down her throat till she gagged. And there it was—both tonsils covered with membrane. She had fought valiantly to keep me from knowing her secret. She had been hiding that sore throat for three days at least and lying to her parents in order to escape just such an outcome as this.

Now truly she *was* furious. She had been on the defensive before but now she attacked. Tried to get off her father's lap and fly at me while tears of defeat blinded her eyes.

The Use of Force

R. F. Dietrich

As is often the case with thesis stories, the author's first clue that he has written a thesis story (rather than a story of character or plot) occurs in the title. The title states an idea, and that idea is the subject of the story. If "the use of force" is the general subject (the use of force in a doctor-patient encounter being the specific subject), the theme is what the author has to say about "the use of force". Williams seems to be saying that the use of force, in however noble a cause, inevitably compromises the humanity of the person using it. (Such theme-stating should be treated as only tentative, to be tested against the reality of the story itself.)

Characterization, in the sense of a detailed presentation of character, is not especially important to this thesis story. While the situation in which the characters are placed is concrete enough, the characters themselves seem rather abstract. The doctor is perhaps more perceptively aware of his situation than most doctors would be, the result of his having lived through this eye-opening experience, but there is nothing else distinguishing about him. In all other things he plays the role of the conventional doctor. He tells the story in a very casual and frank manner, fashioning himself in the familiar image of the family doctor, who achieves great villainy only when he collects an exorbitant fee. In our rather settled image of a doctor, he is supposed to be cool and calm on all occasions, disciplined to evince only one emotion—sympathetic cheerfulness. When children refuse to open their mouths, he is supposed to make a funny face, and "abracadabra" the innermost depths of Johnny's being are exposed to view. The reader expects as much of the doctor of this story. When the Olsons show how little help they are going to be, the doctor's good-humored response and time-honored bedside manner make us feel confident that he is going to be the doctor we expect, rather than a person who is going to disturb us with manifestations of individuality.

The Olsons too are "representative" characters rather than "individual." The mother and father are stereotyped as "anxious parents" bewildered by the presence of disease in their household. They represent an adult world rendered helpless by the introduction of the irrational into their ordinarily closed world of family habit. Although their daughter is given a few individualizing strokes of characterization, she too remains rather abstractly "a sick child." "Kindly doctor," "anxious parents," and "sick child" are thus types of people involved in a typical conflict for the sake of putting strong emphasis upon the story's idea. The reader will never lose the theme of this story in a deep well of thorough characterization or involved plot, since the people and actions are significant here not in and for themselves but for their thematic functions alone.

But why does Williams use, specifically, a doctor-patient encounter to express his particular theme? He wants to show that even the noblest of human endeavors can end in compromising the nobility of both the cause and the person pursuing it if the conditions call for ignoble means: that even the most civilized cause can be corrupted if uncivilizing means are used to achieve it. Confronted with the problem of how best to convey this theme, Williams chose as his natural antagonists a person in a state of civilization and another person in a state of nature. What more noble and civilized occupation than that of doctor, the curer of disease, and what more noble and civilized cause than the curing of a sick child? Beyond this, the doctor's profession has, since the Enlightenment, stood for reason and disciplined emotion. The doctor is the man called upon to give rational answers to irrational problems, the man who will make everything all right by restoring order to the disordered human organism. To adults he is, then, the very emblem of civilization, standing for man's proud ability to control rationally the forces of unreason (especially disease) opposed to civilization. The child, on the other hand, is a force of nature, as yet untamed by adult attempts to train her into civilized ways. The doctor-patient conflict thus opposes the two extremes of the man of reason and the child of unreason in a test of priority that exposes the inability of man to contest the irrational except on its own brutalizing terms.

The stages in the doctor's regression from the civilized to the uncivilized are subtly developed. At first the doctor displays his best bedside manner. When his coaxing fails to open the child's mouth, he phrases her lack of reaction in tones of good-humored understanding—"nothing doing." However, when the mother helpfully promises that the doctor will not hurt her, the doctor grinds his teeth "in disgust" at this false promise. This is the first indication of an excessive reaction on the part of the doctor (significantly inspired by the apparent falsity of an adult), and as if to balance it he insists that he did not allow himself "to be hurried or disturbed," that he spoke "quietly and slowly" as he approached the child again. But then the doctor's determined effort at rationality encounters a very unexpected challenge. The girl knocks his glasses off, and when the mother admonishes her and tells her what a "nice man" the doctor is, the doctor curiously realizes that he is not at all a nice man to the sick child and that her having diphtheria and possibly dying of it is not the real issue ("nothing to her"). He senses that there is something more important at stake here than merely dying.

The doctor does not suddenly abandon all reason. He sees that "the battle" is on, but is quite cool and professional in explaining the alternatives to the parents. It was entirely up to them. "He would not insist upon a throat examination so long as they would take the responsibility." At the mention of responsiblity the mother threatens the girl with going to the hospital, thus putting the responsibility back upon the doctor. The doctor's attitude now takes another strange turn. He scoffs at the mother's threat ("oh yeah?") in words the child herself might have used. An identification has begun to take place, not with the adult world as represented by the parents, for they were "contemptible" to him, but with the irrational world of the "savage brat." He reacts to the challenge of the girl in a quite elemental fashion, scorning the parents who in the ensuing struggle "grew more and more abject, crushed, exhausted." They are crushed by the vital powers of unreason, in which the doctor finds only glory. The encounter with the screaming denial of his symbolic status loosens the structures of his medical discipline and renews the admiration for that force that is the primitive antagonist of man's pretensions of rationality, and before which the ordinary adult is cowed. Thus, seemingly, the doctor lends himself to the "immortal struggle," with respect for the enemy, and scorn for those who surrender meekly to it.

But this makes the conflict sound a bit too heroic. The point of the story is not that hero vanquishes villain but that the hero loses his human status, and thus his status as a hero, when he deigns to fight on the villain's terms. Furthermore, it is all right to speak of "immortal struggle" on the heroic plane, but objectively we are still faced with the picture of a small, sick child being brutally handled by a full-sized furious adult. The doctor, in responding to the elemental nature of their conflict, has allowed its emotional current to sweep him along in an obsession. He is rationally aware of contending with a sick child and yet allows himself to be drawn into a violent contest of wills. The brutal methods of the doctor in discovering the nature of the illness expose with rare honesty (seldom found in medical journals) how a supposedly disciplined adult can be easily overwhelmed by the subrational wells of impulse within him. He "had got beyond reason. . . . A blind fury, a feeling of adult shame, bred of a longing for muscular release are the operatives. One goes on to the end."

The mention of "adult shame" is especially significant. The increasing attraction of the child's world to the doctor is apparently in direct proportion to (and perhaps the result of) his increasing feeling of repulsion toward the adult world. As the attack upon their daughter continues, the parents become beside themselves with shame and "agony of apprehension." Part of their adulthood lies in their being tame and disciplined in the expression of emotion. The assumption of reason has only made them timid. Violent, unashamed expressions of emotion produce in them the discomforts of embarrassment, since only the pathetic and sentimental are socially allowed in the adult world. Such scenes of passion remind the adults that they have been cast out of the child's garden of spontaneity, with the curse of shame as the penalty for their "original sin." The doctor quite spontaneously "had grown furious at a child," but the parents know only one response to fury. "Aren't you ashamed," the mother yelled at her. "Aren't you ashamed to act like that in front of the doctor?"—but especially in front of the doctor. The doctor is the human symbol of that discipline that is at once the idol-god and the frustration of the ordinary, civilized adult, and nothing is more unseemly, more shameful, than to express the fundamental unreason of humanity before this correct and condescending god.

Thus the parents' helpless response to the challenge of the irrational provides an important qualification of the general theme. The encounter with unreason may reduce one's humanity and expose all sorts of unrealized beastliness, but the potentially harmful irrational cannot for that reason be ignored or disguised behind a screen of seemliness. If the cause is noble, it is better to engage the destructive irrational in combat, however debasing the outcome, than to stupidly ignore its presence and allow it to deal out death without contest. Better yet is to engage the foe informed with the knowledge that even a limited success will require sacrifices of one's humanity, for such knowledge will protect the innocent from total defeat or surrender. Perhaps for just such a purpose of informing was this story written. . . .

At the conclusion the doctor triumphantly discovers the membrane upon the tonsils, symptoms of the disease he had suspected, but there is something about this revelation of inner being that qualifies his sense of triumph. The image of hidden disease is strongly suggestive of another kind of disease, that which lies beneath the surface of human rationality. Just as the use of force exposes the disease in the child, so too the use of force exposes that disease in human nature capable of lowering man to the level of a beast.

The attitude of the doctor as narrator toward his experience is curiously mixed. The tone of the narration is variously wry, frank, casual, smooth, and confident. The whole affair is treated as a momentary lapse of an eventually restored discipline, the event reflected upon with an ironic eye. In the opening sentences the doctor is careful to reassure us of his conventional role and essential innocence. We might get the wrong idea later on that he is a villain of some sort, or at least a nasty man, so he is careful to forestall this judgment by making the point that, in all his innocence, he had never met any of the Olsons before (perhaps Williams made the Olsons "new" because he wanted the conflict to be impersonal and spontaneous) and was just an ordinary doctor trying to do his job in the ordinary way with nothing but the noblest of motives. The story follows the pattern of the sort of anecdote that begins, "I was walking along minding my own business when," and so on. But obviously this is more than a humorous anecdote about a man who innocently fell through a manhole while chasing a lady's wind-blown hat. If the tone seems casual, it is achieved by the doctor's wry awareness of his own lapse of discipline. He realizes that the original experience was not at all a casual affair, and in revealing deep truths about himself perhaps did permanent damage to his conventional role. The ironic reflection, thus turned upon himself, seems tinged with a bit of awe, the wry tone and comic effects less for purposes of entertaining than for gaining control of an overpoweringly emotional experience, a disturbing revelation of inner being. Certainly the realization that one has within oneself the potential of savagery would breed new respect for the powers of darkness, and such a realization is not to be tossed off lightly in a breezy anecdote. On the other hand, if the doctor is going to continue as a civilized person fulfilling his professional function, he must gain enough control of and detachment from the disturbing experience to prevent either a maniacal raving about the horror of life or an equally harmful withdrawal from life. By telling the story in the wry manner he does, he is able to appreciate its lesson all the better for holding it at arm's length.

Fenimore Cooper's Literary Offenses

MARK TWAIN

Mark Twain, who once said that he never used metropolis *when he could use* city *because the pay was the same, takes issue with the writing style of James Fenimore Cooper, who had, Twain says, "in the restricted space of two-thirds of a page . . . scored 114 offenses against literary art out of a possible 115. It breaks the record."*

The Pathfinder *and* The Deerslayer *stand at the head of Cooper's novels as artistic creations. There are others of his works which contain parts as perfect as are to be found in these, and scenes even more thrilling. Not one can be compared with either of them as a finished whole. The defects in both of these tales are comparatively slight. They are pure works of art.—Prof. Lounsbury.*

The five tales reveal an extraordinary fullness of invention. . . . One of the very greatest characters in fiction, Natty Bumppo. . . .

The craft of the woodsman, the tricks of the trapper, all the delicate art of the forest, were familiar to Cooper from his youth up.—Prof. Brander Matthews.

Cooper is the greatest artist in the domain of romantic fiction yet produced by America.—Wilkie Collins.

It seems to me that it was far from right for the Professor of English Literature in Yale, the Professor of English Literature in Columbia, and Wilkie Collins to deliver opinions on Cooper's literature without having read some of it. It would have been much more decorous to keep silent and let persons talk who have read Cooper.

Cooper's art has some defects. In one place in *Deerslayer,* and in the restricted space of two-thirds of a page, Cooper has scored 114 offenses against literary art out of a possible 115. It breaks the record.

There are nineteen rules governing literary art in the domain of romantic fiction—some say twenty-two. In *Deerslayer* Cooper violated eighteen of them. These eighteen require:

That a tale shall accomplish something and arrive somewhere. But the *Deerslayer* tale accomplishes nothing and arrives in the air.

They require that the episodes of a tale shall be necessary parts of the tale and shall help to develop it. But as the *Deerslayer* tale is not a tale and accomplishes nothing and arrives nowhere, the episodes have no rightful place in the work, since there was nothing for them to develop.

They require that the personages in a tale shall be alive, except in the case of corpses, and that always the reader shall be able to tell the corpses from the others. But this detail has often been overlooked in the *Deerslayer* tale.

They require that the personages in a tale, both dead and alive, shall exhibit a sufficient excuse for being there. But this detail also has been overlooked in the *Deerslayer* tale.

They require that when the personages of a tale deal in conversation, the talk shall sound like human talk, and be talk such as human beings would be likely to talk in the given circumstances, and have a discoverable meaning, also a discoverable purpose and a show of relevancy, and remain in the neighborhood of the subject in hand, and be interesting to the reader, and help out the tale, and stop when the people cannot think of anything more to say. But this requirement has been ignored from the beginning of the *Deerslayer* tale, to the end of it.

They require that when the author describes the character of a personage in his tale, the conduct and conversation of that personage shall justify said description. But this law gets little or no attention in the *Deerslayer* tale, as Natty Bumppo's case will amply prove.

They require that when a personage talks like an illustrated, giltedged, tree-calf, hand-tooled, seven-dollar Friendship's Offering in the beginning of a paragraph, he shall not talk like a Negro minstrel in the end of it. But this rule is flung down and danced upon in the *Deerslayer* tale.

They require that crass stupidities shall not be played upon the reader as "the craft of the woodsman, the delicate art of the forest," by either the author or the people in the tale. But this rule is persistently violated in the *Deerslayer* tale.

They require that the personages of a tale confine themselves to possibilities and let miracles alone, or, if they venture a miracle, the author must so plausibly set it forth as to make it look possible and reasonable. But these rules are not respected in the *Deerslayer* tale.

They require that the author shall make the reader feel a deep interest in the personages of his tale and in their fate, and that he shall make the reader love the good people in the tale and hate the bad ones. But the reader of the *Deerslayer* tale dislikes the good people in it, is indifferent to others, and wishes they would all get drowned together.

They require that the characters in a tale shall be so clearly defined that the reader can tell beforehand what each will do in a given emergency. But in the *Deerslayer* tale this rule is vacated.

In addition to these large rules there are some little ones. These require that the author shall

Say what he is proposing to say, not merely come near it.

Use the right word, not its second cousin

Eschew surplusage.

Not omit necessary details.

Avoid slovenliness of form.

Use good grammar.

Employ a simple and straightforward style.

Even these seven are coldly and persistently violated in the *Deerslayer* tale.

Cooper's gift in the way of invention was not a rich endowment but such as it was he liked to work it, he was pleased with the effects, and indeed he did some quite sweet things with it. In his little box of stage-properties he kept six or eight cunning devices, tricks, artifices for his savages and woodsmen to deceive and circumvent each other with, and he was never so happy as when he was working these innocent things and seeing them go. A favorite one was to make a moccasined person tread in the tracks of the moccasined enemy, and thus hide his own trail. Cooper wore out barrels and barrels of moccasins in working that trick. Another stage-property that he pulled out of his box pretty frequently was his broken twig. He prized his broken twig above all the rest of his effects, and worked it the hardest. It is a restful chapter in any book of his when somebody doesn't step on a dry twig and alarm all the reds and whites for two hundred yards around. Every time a Cooper person is in peril and absolute silence is worth four dollars a minute, he is sure to step on a dry twig. There may be a hundred handier things to step on but that wouldn't satisfy Cooper. Cooper requires him to turn out and find a dry twig, and if he can't do it, go and borrow one. In fact, the Leatherstocking Series ought to have been called the Broken Twig Series.

I am sorry there is not room to put in a few dozen instances of the delicate art of the forest, as practised by Natty Bumppo and some of the other Cooperian experts.

For instance, one of his acute Indian experts, Chingachgook (pronounced Chicago, I think), has lost the trail of a person he is tracking through the forest. Apparently that trail is hopelessly lost. Neither you nor I could ever have guessed out the way to find it. It was very different with Chicago. Chicago was not stumped for long. He turned a running stream out of its course and there, in the slush in its old bed, were that person's moccasin tracks. The current did not wash them away, as it would have done in all other like cases—no, even the eternal laws of Nature have to vacate when Cooper wants to put up a delicate job of woodcraft on the reader. . . .

If Cooper had been an observer his inventive faculty would have worked better, not more interestingly but more rationally, more plausibly. Cooper's proudest creations in the way of "situations" suffer noticeably from the absence of the observer's protecting gift. Cooper's eye was splendidly inaccurate. Cooper seldom saw anything correctly. He saw nearly all things as through a glass eye, darkly. Of course a man who cannot see the commonest little everyday matters accurately is working at a disadvantage when he is constructing a "situation." In the *Deerslayer* tale Cooper has a stream which is fifty feet wide where it flows out of a lake; it presently narrows to twenty as it meanders along for no given reason, and yet when a stream acts like that it ought to be required to explain itself. Fourteen pages later the width of the brook's outlet from the lake has suddenly shrunk thirty feet and become "the narrowest part of the stream." This shrinkage is not accounted for. The stream has bends in it, a sure indication that it has alluvial banks and cuts them, yet these bends are only thirty and fifty feet long. If Cooper had been a nice and punctilious observer he would have noticed that the bends were oftener nine hundred feet long than short of it.

Cooper made the exit of that stream fifty feet wide in the first place for no particular reason; in the second place, he narrowed it to less than twenty to accommodate some Indians. He bends a "sapling" to the form of an arch over this narrow passage and conceals six Indians in its foliage. They are "laying" for a settler's scow or ark which is coming up the stream on its way to the lake; it is being hauled against the stiff current by a rope whose stationary end is anchored in the lake; its rate of progress cannot be more than a mile an hour. Cooper describes the ark, but pretty obscurely. In the matter of dimensions "it was little more than a modern canal-boat." Let us guess, then, that it was about one hundred and forty feet long. It was of "greater breadth than common." Let us guess, then, that it was about sixteen feet wide. This leviathan had been prowling down bends which were but a third as long as itself and scraping between banks where it had only two feet of space to spare on each side. We cannot too much admire this miracle. A low-roofed log dwelling occupies "two-thirds of the ark's length"—a dwelling ninety feet long and sixteen feet wide, let us say, a kind of vestibule train. The dwelling has two rooms, each forty-five feet long and sixteen feet wide, let us guess. One of them is the bedroom of the Hutter girls, Judith and Hetty; the other is the parlor in the daytime, at night it is pap's bed-chamber. The ark is arriving at the stream's exit now, whose width has been reduced to less than twenty feet to accommodate the Indians—say to eighteen. There is a foot to spare on each side of the boat. Did the Indians notice that there was going to be a tight squeeze there? Did they notice that they could make money by climbing down out of that arched sapling and just stepping aboard when the ark scraped by? No, other Indians would have noticed these things but Cooper's Indians never notice anything. Cooper thinks they are marvelous creatures for noticing but he was almost always in error about his Indians. There was seldom a sane one among them.

The ark is one hundred and forty feet long; the dwelling is ninety feet long. The idea of the Indians is to drop softly and secretly from the arched sapling to the dwelling as the ark creeps along under it at the rate of a mile an hour, and butcher the family. It will take the ark a minute and a half to pass under. It will take the ninety-foot dwelling a minute to pass under. Now, then, what did the six Indians do? It would take you thirty years to guess and even then you would have to give up, I believe. Therefore, I will tell you what the Indians did. Their chief, a person of quite extraordinary intellect for a Cooper Indian, warily watched the canal-boat as it squeezed along under him and when he had got his calculations fined down to exactly the right shade, as he judged, he let go and dropped. And *missed the house*! That is actually what he did. He missed the house and landed in the stern of the scow. It was not much of a fall, yet it knocked him silly. He lay there unconscious. If the house had been ninety-seven feet long he would have made the trip. The fault was Cooper's, not his. The error lay in the construction of the house. Cooper was no architect.

There still remained in the roost five Indians. The boat has passed under and is now out of their reach. Let me explain what the five did—you would not be able to reason it out for yourself. No. 1 jumped for the boat but fell in the water astern of it. Then No. 2 jumped for the boat but fell in the water still farther astern of it. Then No. 3 jumped for the boat and fell a good way astern of it. Then No. 4 jumped for the boat and fell in the water *away* astern. Then even No. 5 made a jump for the boat—for he was a Cooper Indian. In the matter of intellect, the difference between a Cooper Indian and the Indian that stands in front of the cigarshop is not spacious. The scow episode is really a sublime burst of invention but it does not thrill, because the inaccuracy of the details throws a sort of air of fictitiousness and general improbability over it. This comes of Cooper's inadequacy as an observer.

How Does the Author Make His Point?

1. What is the thesis statement?
2. What is the author's tone? How does this tone affect the audience?
3. Give five examples of Twain's use of exaggeration. What do these contribute to the story?
4. How does Twain support his comments about Cooper's specific failings?
5. Discuss several of the techniques Twain uses to make this critical essay funny.

What Do You Think?

1. Do you think the "rules" that Twain lists are basic rules of rhetoric or Twain's own?
2. Do you think Twain is fair in his criticism of Cooper?
3. Are the actions of the Indians described in paragraphs 10 and 11 believable? Can you think of any other examples of unbelievable behavior in stories you have read?

How Does a Poem Mean?

John Ciardi

In the following passage, poet and literary critic John Ciardi discusses the use of symbolism and other elements in Robert Frost's "Stopping by Woods on a Snowy Evening":

Whose woods these are I think I know.
His house is in the village though;
He will not see me stopping here
To watch his woods fill up with snow.

My little horse must think it queer
To stop without a farmhouse near
Between the woods and frozen lake
The darkest evening of the year.

He gives his harness bells a shake
To ask if there is some mistake.
The only other sound's the sweep
Of easy wind and downy flake.

The woods are lovely, dark and deep.
But I have promises to keep,
And miles to go before I sleep,
And miles to go before I sleep.*

   Note that the poem begins as a simple description of events, but that it ends in a way that suggests meanings far beyond the specific description. This movement *from the specific to the general* is one of the basic formulas of poetry. Such a poem as Yvor

Winters' "Before Disaster" . . . and Holmes's "The Chambered Nautilus" . . . follow exactly this progression from the specific to the general, but the generalization in these poems is, in a sense, divided from the specific description or narration, and even seems additional to the specific action rather than intrinsically part of it. It is this sense of division that is signified when one speaks of "a tacked-on moral." Frost, however, is painstakingly careful to avoid the tacked-on moral. Everything in the poem pretends, on one level, to be part of the incident narrated. Yet one cannot miss the feeling that by the end of the poem, Frost has referred to something much more far-reaching than stopping by woods or than driving home to go to bed. There can be little doubt, in fact, that part of Frost's own pleasure in this poem was in making the larger intent *grow out* of the poem rather than in tacking it on. It is in the poem's own performance of itself that the larger meaning is made to emerge from the specific incident. A careful look at that performance will teach a great deal about the nature of poetry.

The poem begins with a situation. A man—knowing Robert Frost, we know it is a Vermont or New Hampshire man—is on his way somewhere at night-fall. It is snowing and as he passes a patch of woods he stops to watch the easy down-drift of the snow into the dark woods. We are told two other things: first that the man is familiar with these parts (he knows who owns these woods and where he lives) and second that no one sees him stop. More could be read into this opening (for example: why doesn't he say what errand he is on? why does he say he knows whose woods these are? what is the significance of watching another man's woods in this way?). Such questions can be multiplied almost endlessly without losing real point, but for present purposes let us assume that we have identified scene one of the poem's performance without raising these questions.

Note that the scene is set in the simplest possible terms. We have no trouble sensing that the man stopped because the scene moved him, but he neither tells us that it is beautiful nor that it moved him. A student writer, always ready to overdo, might have said that he was moved to stop and "to fill his soul with the slow steady stately sinking of that crystalline loveliness into the glimmerless profundities of the hushed primeval wood." Frost prefers to avoid such a spate of words, and to speak the incident in the simplest terms.

His choice illustrates two basic principles of writing of which every sensitive reader should be aware. Frost stated the first principle himself in "The Mowing" . . . when he wrote, "Anything *more* than the truth would have seemed too *weak.*" (italics mine) Understatement is one of the principal sources of power in English poetry.

The second principle here illustrated is to let the action speak for itself. A good novelist who wishes us to know a character does not tell us that charcter is good or bad and leave it at that. Rather, he introduces the character, shows him in action, and lets his actions speak for him. This process is spoken of as *characterization in action.* One of the skills of a good poet is to enact his experiences rather than to talk about having had them. "*Show* it, don't *tell* it," he says, "make it happen, don't talk about its happening."

One part of this poem's performance, in fact, is to *act out* (and thereby to make us act out—i.e., *feel out*—i.e., *identify with*) just why the speaker did stop. The man is the principal actor of this little "drama of why" and in scene one he is the only character. In scene two (starting with the beginning of stanza two), however, a "foil" is introduced. In drama, a "foil" is a character who "plays against" a more important character; by presenting a different point of view or an opposed set of motives, the foil moves the more important character to react in ways that might not have found expression without such opposition. The more important character is thus more fully revealed, to the reader and to himself. The foil here is the horse.

The horse forces the first question in the drama of why. Why did the man stop? Until he comes to realize that his "little horse must think it queer" to stop this way, he has not asked himself why he stopped; he simply did. But he senses that the horse is confused by the stop. He imagines how the horse must feel about it—what is there to stop for out here in the cold, away from bin and stall and all that any self-respecting horse would value on such a night?

In imagining the horse's question, the man is of course led to examine his own reasons. In stanza two this question arises only as a feeling within the man. In stanza three, however, the horse acts definitely. He gives his harness bells a shake. "What's wrong," he seems to say, "what are we doing here?"

By now, obviously, the horse, without losing its identity as a horse has also become a symbol. A symbol is something that stands for something else. That something else may, perhaps, be taken as the order of life that does not understand why a man stops in the wintry middle of nowhere to watch snow come down. (Could the dark and the snowfall symbolize a death wish? that hunger for the last rest that man may feel, but not a beast?) So there is the man, there is that other order of life, and there is the third presence—the movement of the inanimate wind and snow (the all-engulfing?) across both their lives—with the difference that the man knows the second darkness of the dark while the horse does not.

The man has no ready answer to this combination of forces. They exist and he feels them—all three of them, himself included. We sense that he would like to remain here longer to ponder these forces, perhaps to yield to their total. But a fourth force prompts him. That fourth force can be given many names. It is almost certainly better, in fact, to give it many names than attempt to limit it to one. Social obligation, responsibility, personal commitment, duty, or just the realization that a man cannot indulge a mood forever—all of these things and more. He has a long way to go and it is time to be getting there (so there's something to be said for the horse, too). We find the man's inner conflict dramatized to this point by the end of scene two (which coincides with the end of stanza three).

Then and only then—his feelings dramatized in the cross tug of motives he has given form to—does the poet, a little sadly, venture on the comment of his final scene. "The woods are lovely, dark and deep." The very sound of the syllables lingers over the thought. But there is something to do yet before he can yield to the lovely dark-and-deep. "Not yet," he seems to say, "not yet." He has a long way to go—miles to go before he can sleep. Yes, miles to go. He repeats the line and the performance ends.

But why the repetition? The first time Frost writes "And miles to go before I sleep" there can be little doubt that he means, "I have a long way to go yet before I can get to bed tonight." The second time he says it, however, "miles to go" and "sleep" are suddenly transformed into symbols. What is the "something else" these symbols stand for? Hundreds of people have asked Mr. Frost that question in one form or another, and Mr. Frost has always turned the question away with a joke. He has turned it away primarily *because he cannot answer it*. He could answer some part of it. But some part is not enough.

For a symbol is like a rock dropped into a pool: it sends out ripples in all directions, and the ripples are in motion. Who can say where the last ripple disappears? One may have a sense that he at least knows approximately the center point of all those ripples, the point at which the stone struck the water. Yet even then he has trouble marking it precisely. How does one make a mark on water? Oh, very well—the center point of "miles to go" is probably approximately in the neighborhood of being close to meaning, perhaps, "the road of life," and "before I sleep" is maybe that close to meaning "before I take my final rest." (That rest-in-darkness that seemed so temptingly "lovely dark-and-deep" for the moment of the mood.) But the ripples continue to move and the light to change on the water and the longer one watches the more changes he sees.

How Does the Author Make His Point?

1. What is the thesis statement?
2. Ciardi uses an extended metaphor—the poem is likened to drama—in this essay. Pick out specific details that support this metaphor.
3. Find all the examples of definition in this essay.
4. Discuss the metaphor used in paragraph 13. Is it effective? Why?

What Do You Think?

1. Discuss the differences between the words the student writer uses and the words Frost uses to tell why the man stopped (paragraph 13).
2. Why do you think Frost uses a horse for the "foil"? Would the poem have been more or less effective if the foil had been a man?
3. Do you agree with the author's interpretation of the stopping as a death wish?
4. Do you agree that man's social obligations should force him to forgo his pleasures?

The Organic Nature of Poetry

CLEANTH BROOKS
and ROBERT PENN WARREN

This essay is an excerpt from the highly influential textbook
Understanding Poetry, *which explicitly states the aesthetic basis for
judgment of poetry by the "New Critics." The authors have dismissed a
number of conventional ideas about the bases of poetic criticism, including
"message bearing" and making poetry "pretty."*

We have seen, then, that a poem is not to be thought of as
merely a bundle of things which are "poetic" in themselves. Nor is
it to be thought of, as the "message hunters" would seem to have
it, as a kind of box, decorated or not, in which a "truth" or a "fine
sentiment" is hidden.

Certainly it is not to be thought of as a group of *mechanically*
combined elements—meter, rhyme, figurative language, idea, and
so on—put together to make a poem as bricks are put together to
make a wall. The relationship among the elements in a poem is
what is all important: it is not a mechanical relationship but one
which is *far more intimate and fundamental.* If we must compare a
poem to the make-up of some physical object it ought not to be to
a wall but to something organic like a plant.

We may investigate this general principle by looking at some
particular examples. The following lines could scarcely be called
melodious. Indeed, they may be thought to have a sibilant, hissing
quality rather than that of melody.

> If it were done when 'tis done, then "twere well
> It were done quickly: if the assassination
> Could trammel up the consequence, and catch,
> With his surcease, success, that but this blow
> Might be the be-all and the end-all here,
> But here, upon this bank and shoal of time,
> We'd jump the life to come.

This is the speech of Macbeth at the moment when he is debating the murder of Duncan; innumerable critics and readers have considered the passage to be great poetry. We are not to consider that the passage is great poetry *in spite* of its lack of ordinary melodious effects; but rather we are to see that the broken rhythms and the tendency to harshness of sound are essential to the communication that Shakespeare wished. For instance, the piling up of the s sounds in the second, third, and fourth lines help give an impression of desperate haste and breathless excitement. The lines give the impression of a conspiratorial whisper. The rhythm and sound effects of the passage, then, are poetic in the only sense which we have seen to be legitimate: they are poetic because they contribute to the total significance of the passage.

Or we may approach the general problem in another way. Here are two lines by Robert Burns which have been greatly admired by the poet William Butler Yeats:

> The white moon is setting behind the white wave,
> And Time is setting with me, O!

Let us suppose that the lines had been written as follows:

> The white moon is setting behind the white wave,
> And Time, O! is setting with me.

Literally considered, the two versions would seem to say exactly the same thing: they describe a scene and give an exclamation provoked by it. If one will, however, read the two versions carefully with an ear for the rhythm he will discover that the transposition of the word O has made a great difference in the movement.

But this difference is not finally important *merely* because the first version may be in itself more melodious than the second. The movement of the first version is superior primarily because it contributes to the total effect, or to what we might call the total interpretation, of a scene. The placing of the cry at the emphatic position of a line-end implies that the speaker had scarcely realized the full force of his own statement until he had made it. The lingering rhythm caused by the position of the exclamation at the end of the second line coincides with the fact that the poet sees in the natural scene a representation of the pathos of the passing of Time and his own life. By placing the exclamation anywhere else we impair this relationship between the rhythm and the other elements involved—the image of the moonset and the poet's statement about the passing of Time. Yeats has summarized the general effect of the passage and the relationship of the parts as follows:

> Take from them [the lines] the whiteness of the moon and of the waves, whose relation to the setting of Time is too subtle for the intellect, and you take from them their beauty. But, when all are together, moon and wave and whiteness and setting Time and the last melancholy cry, they evoke an emotion which cannot be evoked by any other arrangement of colors and sounds and forms.

The remarks by Yeats here apply, as we can see, to the elements of the scene itself as well as to the rhythm. He is not praising the lines merely because the scene of the white moon setting behind the white wave gives in itself a pretty picture. As a matter of fact, a white moon may not appear as beautiful as a golden moon, but if we rewrite the lines with a golden moon we have lost something from them:

> The gold moon is setting behind the gold wave,
> And Time is setting for me,O!

The "something" that has been lost obviously depends on the relationship of the color to the other elements in the general effect. The whiteness of the moon and the wave in connection with the idea of "setting" and then more specifically in connection with the idea of the irrevocable passage of Time, suggests, even though unconsciously to most readers, a connection with the paleness of something waning or dying. The connection is not a logical connection, as Yeats intimates when he says the "relation . . . is too subtle for the intellect," but it is nonetheless a powerful one. All of this merely means that Yeats is saying that the beauty—by which he means the total poetic effect—of the lines depends on the relationship of the parts to each other.

How Do the Authors Make Their Point?

1. Where is the authors' thesis statement?
2. What is the authors' main method of development?
3. What other method do they employ in the example and their explanation?

What Do You Think?

1. Why do you think the authors chose such sharply contrasting examples?
2. What do the authors mean when they say that a poem ought to be "something organic like a plant"?
3. Do the authors make clear to you something about poetry that you did not recognize previously?

The Maturing of Huckleberry Finn

ROBERT STATTI (student)

Here is an early draft of a student's critical paper.

In Mark Twain's masterpiece, *Adventures of Huckleberry Finn*, one cannot help but be impressed by the awesome influence of the Mississippi on the lives of the people both on the river and along its banks. The author, with explicit detail, takes the main character, Huck Finn, and his Negro partner, Jim, down that river on a journey to freedom. Huck's destination is the new frontier where he would be free of civilization. Jim's mistaken destination is the free states of the Ohio. It is on this journey that Twain transforms Huck from a disreputable, illiterate, irresponsible fourteen-year-old vagabond into a boy gaining respect for the laws and morality of civilization, although the full extent of this transformation is ultimately left to the imagination of the reader.

Huck's contempt for civilization and his attitude toward morality are quickly established in the novel: "The widow she cried over me, and called me a poor lost lamb, and she called me a lot of other names, too, but she never meant no harm by it. She put me in them new clothes again, and I couldn't do nothing but sweat and sweat, and feel all cramped up. Well then, the old thing commenced again." Huck's idea of the ideal life was lying around in tattered rags, smoking his pipe, fishing, and no books. As for morality, the river is Huck's god. The good fortunes it brings and the dangers it holds are something he can comprehend and accept, but he cannot understand or accept civilized religion: "After supper she got out her book and learned me about Moses and the Bullrushers, and I was in a sweat to find out about him; but by-and-by she let it out that Moses had been dead a considerable long time; so then I didn't care no more about him; because I don't take no stock in dead people."

The first sign of change in Huck appears when he learns of the woman's husband's plan to go to Jackson's Island to catch that "runaway nigger." Obviously, Huck was thinking mainly of his own escape but here Jim's role as "Miss Watson's nigger" changes. In Huck's own words—"Git up and hump yourself, Jim! There ain't a minute to lose. They're after us!" Thus, the partnership was formed and Huck would assume the responsibility for his friend's safety and lead him to freedom. Huck's true inner character surfaces during the trash incident: "It was fifteen minutes before I could work myself up to go and humble myself to a nigger; but I done it, and I warn't sorry for it afterward, neither." It must be remembered that the story takes place in the 1830's and for Huck to humble himself was to go against everything he ever had been taught about relationships between white men and Negroes. Huck's sensitivity to Jim's feelings leads to trust, respect, and true friendship with the black slave. This friendship is severely tested as Huck struggles with his conscience over whether or not to turn Jim in to the authorities. "I was paddling off, all in a sweat to tell on him," but when it came down to a final decision, friendship won out: "I didn't answer up prompt. I tried to for a second or two, to brace up and out with it, but I warn't man enough—hadn't the spunk of a rabbit. I see I was weakening so I just give up trying, and up and says—He's white."

It is ironic that Twain takes Huck ashore to teach him love and compassion, for it is this very type of civilization from which Huck is fleeing. During his stay with the Grangerfords, Huck found contentment in family life. Forgotten was Jim, and their escape down the river for the Grangerford-Shepherdson feud provided him with a new adventure. It is here, however, that Huck realizes the profound consequence of real life adventure: "I ain't agoing to tell all that happened—it would make me sick again if I was to do that. I wished I hadn't ever come ashore that night." If showing concern for others is a measure of social development, then Huck was maturing. His decision not to let the king and Duke rob the Wilks girls of their money came from his heart: "It made my eyes water a little, to remember her crying there all by herself in the night, and them devils laying there right under her own roof, shaming her and robbing her." Respectability and pride are now a part of the character, Huck.

By revolving the story around the awesome flow of the mighty Mississippi, Twain gives coherence and color to the adventures of the journey. Had the escape been by any other route, the achievements of Huck and his endeavors to free an already free slave would have been lost for he would have known how deep into the South they were going. The river was good to Huck. It gave him a solid foundation upon which to build his life. Though he still rejects civilization, "I reckon I got to light out for the territory ahead of the rest, because Aunt Sally she's going to adopt me and civilize me and I can't stand it," the reader knows that Huck will turn out to be good, just as sure as he will grow out of his britches.

Rereading his paper, the student saw that in the writing he had moved somewhat away from his thesis statement that Huck gained "respect for laws and morality of civilization." Since the paper did not say what he had expected it to say, he went back to his thesis statement and rewrote it.

It is on this journey that Huck, a disreputable, illiterate, irresponsible fourteen-year-old vagabond wages an inner battle between his moral feelings and the morality and laws of civilization.

How Does the Author Make His Point

1. Discuss the author's use of direct quotation. Does this to add or detract from the essay?
2. Even if you have not yet read *The Adventures of Huckleberry Finn*, would the author's essay convince you that Huck was growing in responsibility and respectability?
3. Does the author succeed in making the setting a unifying factor?

What Do You Think

1. In what way is the revised thesis statement an improvement over the first one?
2. Since Huck rejects conventional respectability, what does the author mean when, in the conclusion, he says Huck "will turn out to be good . . . .?
3. Remembering that Mark Twain once said (The Literary Offenses of James Fenimore Cooper) that one of an author's jobs was to make his readers like some of his characters and dislike others, what is the effect of Huck's method of speaking, his use of dialect? Does this make you like Huck more or less?

INTEGRATING READING SKILLS WITH WRITING SKILLS: FORM AND CONTENT

Although teaching the skills of imaginative writing is beyond the scope of this book, the writing of criticism of imaginative writing, like other expository writing, is a learnable skill. More than any other type of writing you have yet tried, writing about literature depends upon your response to others' writing. The prewriting that you do here depends upon reading carefully and noting your responses to what your author has to say and how he says it. As you criticize (which really means to appreciate), you pay close attention to what your author has to say—his content—and the way he chooses to say it—his form.

All expository writing, of course, has form: it has a beginning, a middle, and an end; it has a topic sentence, a body of development, and a conclusion. But in imaginative literature, a great deal more attention is paid to form than in the expository genre. The content of all writing is what the author has to say, his thesis statement in an essay, his theme in fiction or poetry. In imaginative literature, the theme is frequently not openly stated but must be perceived through indirect methods. In expository writing, the thesis statement is overtly announced, usually very early in the development of the essay.

In imaginative literature, the form itself is one of the methods of communicating the theme. The theme is revealed by many indicators. Part of the effect of imaginative literature is intensified because of the pleasure the reader receives from following these indicators or clues to an understanding of the author's theme. Participation in the discovery gives the reader a sense of pleased achievement.

The form comes about because the author creates characters, places them somewhere in a setting, motivates them into action—the plot. The author also expresses an attitude toward his characters, which he reveals by his description of them, by the way he lets them speak, by the way he lets them react with other characters. The way he chooses to tell his story through all these elements makes up the form of his story.

The reader, responding to what the writer has done in choosing his content and constructing his form, creates a form himself. Through his responses to the original writing, he selects a thesis idea and supports it, usually with references of direct quotations from the original work. He then restates his thesis idea in his conclusion.

Thus, there is a direct line of communication from the author's imaginative original to the responsive presentation of the critic's ideas. The critic's writing is only as effective as his response to the writing of the original author.

The Wonderful Adventures of Nils

KAREN SECREST (student)

Here is an example of a student essay that reflects careful reading and wise response.

In 1906, the National Teachers' Association of Sweden asked former teacher and distinguished author Selma Lagerlof to write a book with a two-fold purpose: to teach children the geography and folklore of their counry. The resulting two volumes, *The Wonderful Adventures of Nils* and *The Further Adventures of Nils*, are, according to *The Oxford Companion to Children's Literature*, "a strikingly original work." The books were instant best sellers and were quickly translated into English, German, and Danish. In 1909, Selma Lagerlof became the first woman to win the Nobel Prize for Literature.

Nils Holgersson, the main character, is a mischievous, lazy, callous, and ill-tempered boy who is magically changed into a tiny, sprite-like creature as punishment for tormenting an elf. The main theme deals with the boy's change in personality and values as he learns to show compassion for animals, especially a group of wild geese with whom he makes an amazing journey through the Swedish countryside. The ultimate physical goal is Lapland; the ultimate behavioral goal is a change in attitude by Nils toward the animals as he learns to trust, love, and help them on several occasions.

The story utilizes many of the motifs typical of fairy tales: a dangerous physical journey or quest, negative characters representing evil forces, helpers in the form of talking animals who represent the forces of goodness and positive values to be acquired by the main character as he successfully completes various tasks. The result is a highly entertaining and informative book as Nils struggles to regain his human form. Each chapter is a tale in itself, with carefully researched folklore and accurate and entertaining descriptions of the geographic, economical, and social features of Lagerlof's Sweden.

Nils' transformation into a helpless "Thumbietot," or Tom

Thumb, puts him at the mercy of the animals he so mercilessly tormented when he was a human being. He becomes dependent upon their good will for his very survival. Nils is fortunately befriended by a tame gander whose life he saves on several occasions. Nils learns humility, compassion, and courage as they journey together and struggle to keep up with the wild geese on their difficult odyssey. He learns to trust the gander as he must snuggle into the warm down under its wing each night to keep from perishing in the cold.

Several of the talking animals serve as teachers to Nils. A threatening cat chooses to release him out of respect for the boy's mother—a satiric move since the cat has more respect for the mother than the boy does. Akka, the female leader of the wild geese, is wise and fearless and a strict disciplinarian with her flock and with Nils, but she shows compassion as she sees that the boy has something to eat. Nils repays her kindness by saving her flock from the wicked Smirre Fox who is the evil force behind many of their misadventures. Enraged, the fox vows vengeance upon Nils who has kept him from feasting on the geese. He reappears in tale after tale and uses his cunning to persuade other animals, such as an otter and a martin, to attack the geese. All are foiled by Nils' courage and quick-thinking.

Infected with the freedom and beauty of flying on the gander's back, Nils makes a fateful decision to continue on the journey to Lapland. He learns a great deal about the geography of Sweden. Never an enthusiastic scholar in the past, Nils, nevertheless, is fascinated by such tales as those explaining why salmon swim upstream and how the town of Bliking was formed of gigantic rock steps and falling water. Lagerlof uses extensive and descriptive imagery in teaching Nils and the reader about the buildings, rivers, and products of farm and industry.

One example of Miss Lagerlof's exquisite empathy is revealed in her tale, "On the Farm," a tender story of a captured mother squirrel whose shrill, agonized cries as she mourns her lost babies arouse the curiosity of Grandma. Imagine the old lady's surpise as the unfortunate babies are brought to the mother one-by-one by a tiny, elf-like creature who is, of course, Nils. When the farmer observed this act, he said, "One thing is certain, we have behaved in such a manner that we are shamed before both animals and human beings." And he returned the squirrel family to its home in the hazel-grove.

One interesting tale involves a band of vagabond crows. They kidnap little Nils because they have a treasure concealed in a sealed jar and they need his help in opening the jar. Nils battles their treacherous leader and kills him. Revengeful crows lead Smirre Fox to him, but he escapes by starting a fire in the cabin. The demolished cabin belongs to friends, and Nils feels so guilty that he vows to repay them for the loss. His maturing ability to show love is evident as he mourns the death of Fumle-Drumle, a crow who saved his life.

An important milestone in the book is the experience Nils has with an elderly farm woman, whose children have grown up and left home. Her loneliness and longing for them impresses upon Nils the fact that his own parents might be missing him—not the boy he was but the boy "he might become."

Another major theme of the book is expressed in the last chapter, "Home At Last." Akka, the wild goose, tells Nils:

> If you have learned anything from us, Thumbietot, you no longer think that humans should have the whole earth to themselves. All my days, I have been hounded and hunted. It would be a comfort to know that there is a refuge somewhere for someone like me.

While reading about animal fantasies in *Children's Literature from A to Z*, I found the following three guidelines for well-developed tales:,

1. How convincing are the characters' actions and thoughts?
2. Are they presented consistently?
3. Are they appropriate for the story being told?

Applying these guidelines to *The Wonderful Adventures of Nils*, I found that Miss Lagerlof's is a unique animal fantasy. Each animal character behaves in accepted manner. Foxes are cunning, cruel and sly; bears are ferocious when aroused; geese are freedom-loving jokesters; cats are aloof and independent; and all are consistent in behavior throughout the book.

Since the main theme is that Nils must learn to love and care for the animals, I think that they were appropriate characters for this book. They alternate reprimands with moral lessons and loving concern for Nils, and he repays their teachings by his self-sacrificing attitude at the end of the book. There are 43 stories in all and each one could stand by itself, but it's much more fun to read them all, one after another, after another . . . .

IMPROVING YOUR VOCABULARY: METAPHOR

The vocabulary section of chapter 9 discussed limitation and extension, two of the major ways in which meanings change. When meanings change through extension, the change tends to be away from literal meaning to figurative meaning. Literal language points to definite objects, actions, or ideas, like a boat, sailing a boat, or navigation. It is factual in content and specific in style.

Figurative language, on the other hand, is imaginative. It is closely related to connotative language (see chapter 4) because they both have emotional overtones. In addition, figurative language usually depends on the extended meanings of a word rather than the primary meaning. For example, in a line from a poem by Christina Rosetti, she says, "My heart is like a singing bird," which is certainly not literal. She uses the word *heart* not in the literal sense of the cardiac muscle but in the imaginative sense of her emotions. She conveys her happiness in an imaginative comparison with a singing bird. She intensifies her feeling later, "The birthday of my life has come because my love has come to me." She doubles her meanings in two key words: *birthday* and *love*. *Birthday* has one connotative sense of happy days and another of beginnings. *Love* is possibly used both in its primary sense of the emotion or in the extended sense of the beloved one. Through the use of figurative language, the poet has achieved brevity, clarity, and intensity.

Metaphor is the most important form of figurative language. The other figures of speech are really just subdivisions of metaphor. Based on comparison, metaphor means *transfer*—the transfer of one kind of meaning to another through comparison. Through these transfers, language can be almost endlessly extended by association.

ASSIGNMENTS

A. Read the following poem and write a critical essay on it, using any of the approaches discussed in this chapter:

THE MAN HE KILLED

"Had he and I but met
By some old ancient inn,

We should have sat us down to wet
Right many a nipperkin!

But ranged as infantry,
And staring face to face,
I shot at him as he at me,
And killed him in his place.

I shot him dead because—
Because he was my foe,
Just so—my foe of course he was;
That's clear enough; although

He thought he'd 'list, perhaps,
Off-hand like—just as I—
Was out of work—had sold his traps—
No other reason why.

Yes, quaint and curious war is!
You shoot a fellow down
You'd treat if met where any bar is,
Or help to half-a-crown."

Thomas Hardy

B. Read any of the short stories listed below or one suggested by your
instructor. Write a critical essay on some aspect of the work. To help
you get started, look at some of the possible topics suggested below.

"Barn Burning"—William Faulkner
"Miss Brill"—Katherine Mansfield
"The Rocking-Horse Winner"—D.H. Lawrence
"Hands"—Sherwood Anderson
"The Catbird Seat"—James Thurber
"Why I Live at the P.O."—Eudora Welty
"The Basement Room"—Graham Greene
"The Patented Gate and the Mean Hamburger"—Robert
   Penn Warren
"The Spinoza of Market Street"—Isaac Bashevis Singer
"First Confession"—Frank O'Connor
"A Wagner Matinee"—Willa Cather
"My Kinsman, Major Molineux"—Nathaniel Hawthorne
"The Portable Phonograph"—Walter Van Tilburg Clark
"The Enormous Radio"—John Cheever
"Death in the Woods"—Sherwood Anderson

POSSIBLE TOPICS:

On plot
1. Does Faulkner make plausible the moral decision made by Sarty in "Barn Burning"?
2. Discuss the plot of "My Kinsman, Major Molineux" from its historical basis. Although the story is set in prerevolutionary Salem, it can also be interpreted as a modern story. What ideas in the story make it modern?
3. Discover and discuss the antagonist in "Hands."
4. In "Death in the Woods," how is the narrator changed by the experience?

On character
1. Discuss the details that characterize the protagonist and the antagonist as character foils in "The Patented Gate and the Mean Hamburger."
2. In "The Spinoza of Market Street," how does the protagonist embody Spinoza's philosophy?

On theme
1. In "The Basement Room," Graham Greene gives his theme in one short sentence. Find this sentence and discuss Greene's development of his theme.
2. What sociological/psychological truth makes up the theme of the compassionate story, "A Wagner Matinee"? Beyond narrating, what is the function of the narrator?

On devices or techniques
1. In "Miss Brill," what techniques of style does Mansfield use to arouse the compassion of the reader to the extent that never again can he ignore an old woman on a park bench?
2. Discuss the central symbol in either "The Rocking-Horse Winner," "The Portable Phonograph," or "The Enormous Radio."
3. What makes the three comic stories on the list funny? After all, what's funny about being forced out of your home ("Why I Live at the P.O."), losing your job ("The Catbird Seat"), or feeling you're condemned to Hell ("First Confession")?

Author Index

Allen, Frederick Lewis, 72-75
Allen, William, 283-87
Ashe, Arthur, 358-60
Asimov, Isaac, 238-40
Associated Press, 134
Auden, W. H., 261

Baker, Russell, 267-69
Bettmann, Otto L., 220-21
Brooks, Cleanth, 428-30
Burgess, Gellett, 127-29

Catton, Bruce, 194-97
Ciardi, John, 423-27
Clavell, James, 69-70
Cran, William, 355-57

Davies, Robertson, 171-73
Davis, Ossie, 365-68
Dickens, Charles, 68-69
Dietrich, R. F., 411-16
Douglas, William O., 378-79
Fowler, H. W., 127
Frost, Robert, 423

Gallico, Paul, 241-44
Garrity, John A., 123
Gary, Romain, 67-68
Gibson, George, 228-32
Goodman, Ellen, 112-14
Graves, Robert, 350
Greene, Bob, 309-14

Haley, Alex, 161-63
Hall, Mildred and Edward, 97-98
Hardy, Thomas, 440-41
Hayakawa, S. I., 138-40
Hayden, Rose Lee, 352-54
Hemingway, Ernest, 167-70

Hodge, Alan, 350
Hritz, Tom, 50-52

Janko, Edmund, 302-5

Kipling, Rudyard, 262
Krutch, Joseph Wood, 319-20
Kung, Hans, 215-18

Lancaster, Bob, 35-39
Leacock, Stephen, 164-66
Levy, Newman, 28-49

Mace, David and Vera, 199-201
MacNeil, Robert, 355-57
Maddocks, Melvin, 202-5
Malcolm X, 161-63
Matthews, Jack, 405-6
McCrum, Robert, 355-57
Mencken, H. L., 361-64
Mizer, Jean E., 288-90
Moorehead, Alan, 90-91
Morris, Desmond, 329-32
Morris, James, 379-80

Oates, Joyce Carol, 279-81

Perelman, S. J., 136
Petrunkevitch, Alexander, 154-66
Pirsig, Robert, 175-77, 255
Popkin, Roy, 32-33

Rickover, Hyman G., 376-77
Roberts, Paul, 141-53
Rosten, Leo, 321-27

Safire, William, 105-7
Saunders, Lawrence, 68-69
Schulz, Muriel R., 369-72
Sinclair, Upton, 89-90
Smith, Logan Pearsall, 393
Sowell, Thomas, 246-48, 294-95
Steinbeck, John, 76-77
Swift, Bob, 249-50

Taine, Hippolyte, 351
Taylor, Deems, 115-18
Tennyson, Alfred, Lord, 264-65
Thomas, Lewis, 108-10, 206-10
Thompson, Dorothy, 315-17
Thoreau, Henry David, 65-67
Thurber, James, 41-46, 101-4
Trippett, Frank, 270-73

Tuite, James, 79-80
Twain, Mark, 129-30, 395-96, 417-22

Ulmer, Curtis, 334-35

Van Allen, Maurice, W., 275-77
Viorst, Judith, 233-37

Warren, Robert Penn, 428-30,
Williams, William Carlos, 407-10
Woolf, Virginia, 82-84

Yeats, William Butler, 190

Subject Index

Acknowledging use of others' writings,
    398–400
  paraphrasing, 399
  quoting, 399–400
  summarizing, 398–99
Active vocabulary, 336, 339
Addition, as transitional device, 100, 137
Adequate development, 15, 301–5, 396–98
Affective comprehension, 294
Affixes, 258–60
*American Heritage Dictionary of the English
    Language*, 60, 340–42, 381
Analogies, 189–90, 302–4, 348
Analysis, causal, in writing about literature,
    397–98
Analysis desired by instructors in students'
    writings about literature, 397
Anecdote(s), 16, 396
Anticipating reader's questions in process
    essay, 175
Antonyms, 381–82
Approaches to criticism, 388–89
Appropriateness of usage, 178
Attitude toward subject or topic, 6, 25–26,
    382, 396
Audience awareness, 7, 26, 135–37, 227
Audience, intended, of literature, 387–88
Authority, misuse of, 348
Awareness of audience, 7, 26, 135–137, 227

Bases, consistent:
  in comparison and contrast, 183–84
  in division and classification, 224
  of judgment in literature, 387–88
Block method of organizing writing,
    185–86, 188
Body, 8, 14–15
  adequate development of, 15, 301–5,
    395–400
  in cause and effect, 265–66
  in comparing and contrasting, 184–88
  in defining, 308
  in describing, 64–65
  in dividing and classifying, 226
  in explaining by examples, 98
  in explaining a process, 137
  narrating, 28–28
  in persuading, 351
  in writing about literature, 396
Brainstorming for topic, 2–3, 182

Causal analysis, in criticism, 397–98
Cause and effect, 6
  analysis, two directions in, 263
  body, 265–66
  chain of, 264–65
  conclusion, 265–66

contributing, 264
in defining, 302
essay, 262–99
establishing, 262–99
organization in 265–66
proximate, 264
sufficient, 263–64
Cause, necessary and sufficient, 263–64
Central purpose, in comparing and
 contrasting, 182
Chain of cause and effect, 264–65
Challenge, use in summary, 16
Character, 68–69, 390
Charged words, 383
Choosing a topic:
 brainstorming, 2–3, 182
 in comparison and contrast, 182–83
 free writing, 3–4
 journal, 4
 library, 5
Choosing good examples, 96–98, 124
Chronological order, 133
Circular reasoning fallacy, 348
Clarity:
 explaining for, 174–77
 selection of details and, 187–88
Clauses, subordinate, 100, 227
Classifying, See Dividing and classifying
Climatic order, 99–100
Clincher, in summary, 16
Closing metaphor, 16–17
Coherence, 14–15
Combination method of organizing
 comparison and contrast, 185, 187
Combining methods of development, 301–5
Comparing and contrasting, 181–222, 307,
 397
 analogy, use in, 189–90
 bases, same, 183–84
 block method, 185–88
 body, 184–88
 brainstorming, 182
 central purpose in, 182
 choosing topic, 182–83
 combination method of organizing, 185,
 187
 conclusion, 184, 188
 defined, 182
 defining by, 307
 detail, specific, 187–88
 introduction, 184–85
 organization of body, three methods, 185
 outlines for, 186–87
 point-by-point method of organizing,
 185–86, 188
 prewriting for, 182–83
 subjects, two, 184, 188
 thesis statement in, 184
 transitions, adequate, 188
Comprehension, types of reading, 293–94
Conciseness, 381

Conclusion, 8, 15–17, 28, 396
 in cause and effect, 265–66
 in comparison and contrast, 184, 188–89
 in defining, 308
 in describing, 67
 in dividing and classifying, 226
 in explaining a process, 137
 in explaining by examples, 99–100
 in narrative, 28
 in persuading, 351
 re-asserting thesis in, 266, 308, 351
 writing about literature, 396
Connotation, defined, 218–20
Connotative language, 440
Contemporary events, use in introduction,
 13
Conflict, or tension, as central to plot,
 389–90
Content:
 of essay, 18
 form and, 435–36
Contrasting, See Comparing and contrasting
Contributing cause, 264
Context, role in discovering meaning,
 336–45
Controlling idea, 6, 25 See also Thesis
 statement
Crediting sources, See Documentation
Critic, distinguished from reviewer, 398
Critical comprehension, 294
Criticism, bases for, of literature, 387–89
Critical essay, 386–442 See also Literature,
 writing about

Defining, 301–45
 body, 308
 combining methods of development,
 301–5
 by comparing and contrasting, 307
 conclusion, 308
 by examples, 306
 extended definition, 306
 formal definition, 306
 introduction in, 308
 kinds of definitions, 305
 limited definition, 305
 by narrating, 307
 by negation, 307
 by process, 307
 by synonym, 306
 by word origin, 307–8
Denotation, defined, 218–20
Describing, 11–12, 62–94
 as aid to other, non-descriptive, writing,
 67–70
 body, 64–65
 conclusion, 67
 details, specific and pertinent, 63–65, 70,
 88–89

Describing *(cont.)*
  essay, writing, 64–67
  introduction, 64
  observation and, 62–63
  organization for, 62–64
  prewriting for, 62
  setting, 11–12, 391–92
Detail(s), 135
  degree of, needed, 137
  in describing, 63–65, 88–89
  specific, 187–88
  use to form generalizations, 88–89
Development:
  adequate, in body, 15
  in critical essay, 396–400
  method of, combining, 301–5
Diction and structure, revising, 18
Dictionaries, 381–82, 338
  connotation and denotation, 218
  guide to appropriate usage, 178
  reading entire entry, 91–92
  synonyms, 381–82
  types, 59–60
  uses of 58–60
  word meaning, guide to changes in,
    340–42
Direct quotation, 399–400
Direct statement of thesis in introduction,
  13–14
Discourse, modes of, 95
Dispensing with the opposition approach,
  13
Distinguishing between fact and opinion,
  375–81
Dividing and classifying, 223–61
  awareness of audience, 227
  basis for, consistent and sensible, 224
  body, 226
  conclusion, 226
  defining by, 307
  guidelines for, 224
Dividing and classifying *(cont.)*
  introduction, 226
  subordinate clause transitions, 227
  thesis statement, 226
  two steps in organizing, 225
Documentations:
  formal, 401–2
  informal, 402–3
Dramatic irony, 395

Editing and revising:
  guidelines for, 17–20
Either-or fallacy, 347
Elements of fiction, 389–96
  character, 390
  plot, 389–90
  setting, 391–92
  theme, 390–91, 435
Emotional appeals in persuading, 346

English:
  formal, 178
  informal, 178
  nonstandard, 178
Enumeration, 100, 137
Essay(s):
  audience and, 7, 135–37, 227
  balanced development, need for, 225
  cause and effect, establishing, 262–99
  coherence, 14–15
  comparing and contrasting, 181–222
  critical, *See* Literature, writing about
  defining, 301–45
  describing, 62–94
  dividing and classifying, 223–61
  editing and rewriting, 17–20
  explaining a process, 133–80
  explaining by examples, 95–132
  establishing a purpose, 5
  about literature, 386–442
  mechanics, guidelines for, 20
  narrating, 23–61
  outlining, 8–10, 183, 186–87
  parts of, *See* Body, Conclusion,
    Introduction, Thesis statement
  persuading, 346–85
  proofreading, 20–21
  rewriting, guidelines for, 18–20
  title, effective, 17
  topic, choosing, 2–5
  unity, 14
Etymology, 256–61
Events, contemporary, use in introduction,
  13
Examples:
  choosing good, 96–98
  defining by, 306
  explaining by, 95–132
Experience, own, as aid in narrating, 23
Explaining a process, 133–80
  audience and, 135–37
  body, 137
  clarity in, 174–77
  degree of detail, 137
  five key steps in, 135
  introduction, 137
  logical sequence, 135
  necessary detail, 135
  organization in, 136–37
  step-by-step nature, 136
  thesis statement, 135
  transitions, clear, 135
Exposition, basic forms, 133
Extended definition, 305
Extension:
  as method of change in word meanings,
    340–43

Fact(s):
  distinguishing from opinion, 375–81
  use in introduction, 12

Fallacies, 347–49
   circular reasoning, 346
   either-or, 347
   false analogy, 348
   hasty generalization, 347
   large numbers, 349
   majority-is-always-right, 349
   misuse of authority, 348
   Post hoc, 347–48
False analogy, 348
Fiction, elements of, 389–96 *See also*
      Literature, writing about
Figurative analogies, 190
Figurative meaning, 440
Final quotation, in summary, 16
Footnotes, 401–2
Formal definition, 306
Formal English, 178
Form and content, 435–36
Free writing, 3–4

Generalization(s):
   using details to form, 88–89
   hasty, fallacy, 347
   in thesis statement, 96–98
Greek:
   prefixes, 258–59
   suffixes, 259–60
Guidelines for revising and editing essay,
      18–20

Hasty generalization fallacy, 347
"How to" instructions, 135

Ideas:
   main and supporting, 98–99
   for topics, 2–5, 182–3
Indentation of long quotation, 400
Informal documentation, 402–3
Informal English, 178
Integrating reading and writing skills:
   clear purpose, having, 54–58
   details, using to form generalizations,
      88–89
   explaining for clarity, 174–77
   form and content, 135–36
   generalizations, forming, 88–89
   meaning through context, discovering,
      336–45
   prewriting and prereading, 214
   reading for comprehension, 174–77
   recognizing cause and effect
      relationships, 293–94
   recognizing patterns of organization,
      254–56
Introduction(s), 8, 10–11

in cause and effect, 265–66
   in comparison and contrast, 184–85
   in defining, 308
   in describing, 64
   in division and classification, 226
   in explaining a process, 350
   in narrating, 26–27
   in persuading, 350
   thesis statement at end, 100, 266, 308,
      351
Introduction techniques:
   contemporary events, 13
   description, use of, 11–12, 64
   direct statement, 13–14
   dispensing with opposition, 13
   facts, 12
   justification, 13
   narrative, 10–11
   quotations, 12–13
   statement, direct, 13–14
   statistics, 12
   "Why write", 14
Irony, 395–96

Journal keeping, as idea source, 4
Judgments, between fact and opinion,
      375–76
Justification, use in introduction, 13

Language, tone in writing and, 377–81
Large numbers fallacy, 349
Latin:
   abbreviations in footnotes, 402
   prefixes, 258
   roots, 257
   suffixes, 259–60
Levels of usage, 177–78
Library, as aid in topic choice, 5
Limitation, as method of word meaning
      change, 343
Limited definition, 305
Literal comprehension, 293
Literal meaning, 440
Literature, writing about, 386–442
   analysis desired, 387
   body, 396
   character, 390
   criticism bases for, 387–89
   conclusion, 396
   conflict in, 389–90
   developing essay, 396–400
   documentation, 401–3
   elements of fiction, 389–96
   introduction, 396
   irony, 395–96
   metaphor, 440
   modern criticism, 388
   narrowed subject, 396

Literature, writing about (cont.)
  organization of paper, 396–98
  paraphrase, 399
  plot, 389–90
  point of view, 392
  quotations, direct, 399–400
  romantic criticism, 388
  setting, 391–92
  summary, 398–99
  symbolism, 394–95
  theme, 390–91, 435
  tension in, 389–90
  thesis statement, 396
  tone, 392–94
  use of others' writings, 398–400
Logical appeals in persuading, 346
Logical sequence, 135

Meaning:
  changes in word, 440
  connotative, 218–20, 440
  in context, 336–45
  denotative, 218–20
  extension of, 340–41
  limitation of, 342
  literal, 440
Metaphor:
  closing, 16–17
  defining by, 306
  in literature, 440
Methods of development, combining, 301–5
Misuse of authority fallacy, 348
Modern criticism, 388
Modes of discourse, 388

Narrating, 5, 23–61
  body, 27–28
  clear purpose in, 54–58
  conclusion, 28
  defining by, 307
  use of own experiences in, 23
Narrator, in literature, 392
Narrowed subject, 396
Necessary and sufficient cause, 263–64
Negation, defining by, 307
Nonstandard English, 178
Nonverbal analogies, 190

Observation of details, 62–63, 88–89
Opinion, distinguishing from fact, 375–81
Opposition, climatic, 99–100
Organization:
  in cause and effect, 265–66
  in comparing and contrasting, 184–90
  of details, 63–64
  in defining, 308

  in describing, 62
  in dividing and classifying, 225–27
  in explaining a process, 136–37
  in explaining by examples, 98–100
  in narrating, 23–28
  overall, of paper, 10–17
  in persuading, 349–51
  in writing about literature, 396–98
  recognizing different patterns of, 254–56
  of thoughts, 7–10
Outlining, 8–10, 138, 183, 186–87
Oxford English Dictionary, 59

Paper, See Essay
Parallel wording, 100
Paraphrasing, 399
Parentheses, in informal documentation, 403
Passive vocabulary, 336, 339
Patterns of organization, recognizing, 254–56
Persuading, 6, 346–85
  all writing as, 346
  attitude toward topic, 349, 351
  body, 351
  conclusion, 351
  emotional appeals, 346
  fallacies, 347–49
  prewriting, 349
  selecting topic, 349
  thesis statement in, 349–50
Plagirarism, 398
Plot, 389–90
Point of view, 392
Post hoc fallacy, 347–48
Prefixes, 257–59
Prereading, 214
Prewriting:
  describing, 62–64
  comparing and contrasting, 182–83
  form and content, 435
  prereading, 214
Process:
  defining by, 307
  explaining a, 133–80
Proving arguments, use of analogies and, 190
Proofreading, 20–21
Proximate cause, 264
Purpose for comparision, underlying, 397

Questions in reader's mind, in process essay, 175
Quotation(s):
  direct, 399–400
  pertinent, 396
  use in introduction, 12–13

Random House Dictionary of the English Language, 60
Reading comprehension levels, 293–94
Reading critically, reader's failure to, 375
Reading skills, integrating writing and:
  clear purpose, having, 54–58
  details, using to form generalizations, 88–89
  explaining for clarity, 174–77
  form and content, 435–36
  generalizations, forming, 88–89
  prewriting and prereading, 214
  reading for comprehension, 174–77
  recognizing patterns of organization, 254–56
  recognizing cause and effect relationships, 293–94
Reasoning, circular fallacy, 348
Recognizing cause and effect relationships, 293–94
Recognizing patterns of organization, 254–56
Reviewer, distinguished from critic, 398
Rewriting, guidelines for, 18–20
Rhetoric:
  bases of judgment, 387–96
  cause and effect, 262–65
  combining methods of development, 301–5
  comparing and contrasting, 181
  defining, 301–8
  dividing and classifying, 223–25
  persuading, 346–49
  explaining a process, 133–36
  explaining by examples, 95–98
Romantic criticism, 388
Roots of words, 258

Selecting a topic, 2–5, 183
Sentences, revising, 19, *See also* Thesis statement
Setting, 11–12, 391–92
Slanting, 382–84
Specific details and examples, 96–98, 124
Sources, crediting, *See* documentation
Statement, direct, in introduction, 13–14
Statistics, use in introduction, 12
Step by step explanation in process, 136
Structure and diction, revising, 18
Subject(s):
  attitude toward, 382
  of essay, 25
  narrowed, 396
  two, in comparing and contrasting, 184, 188
  of work of literature, as critical basis, 388
Subordinate clause transitions, 100, 227
Sufficient cause, 263–64
Suffixes, 259–60
Summary:
  of essay, 15–16

of writing by another, 398–99
Symbolism, 394–95
Synonyms, 100, 306, 381–81

Theme in literature, 390–91, 435
Thesaurus, 58–60, 382
Thesis statement, 13–14, 25–26, 435
  in comparing and contrasting, 184
  in defining, 302
  re-asserting in conclusion, 100, 266, 308, 351
Time sequence, 133, 347
Titles, choosing effective, 17
Thought:
  causal analysis and, 397
  movement in comparison and contrast, 188
  organizing, 7–10
Tone, 392–94
  impact of language on, 377–81
  importance of, 379
Topic:
  choosing, 2–5
  in persuading, 349
Transitions:
  clear, 135
  devices for, 100, 227

Understanding how language affects tone, 377–81
Unity, 14
Usage, levels of, 177–78
Use of others' writings, 398–99

Vocabulary, *See also* Words
  antonyms, 381–82
  connotation, 218–19
  denotation, 218–19
  dictionary, 58, 91–92
  etymology, 256–61
  levels of usage, 177–78
  meaning and context, 336–45
  metaphor, 440
  synonyms, 381–82
  thesaurus, 58

Webster's Ninth New Collegiate Dictionary, 60
Webster's Third New International Dictionary of the English Language, 59–60
"Why write" approach, 13–14
Words, 19, 381–84
  affixes, 256–61
  appropriateness, 178
  change in meanings, 340–43

Words (*cont.*)
    charged, 383
    denotative and connotative meanings,
        218–20
    etymology, 256–61
    levels of usage, 177–78
    meaning and context, 336–45
    new, 58–60, 91–92, 336, 339–40
    origin, defining by, 307–8
    precision in, 381
    vocabulary, 58–60, 91–92, 336, 339–40
Writing, 1–22 *See also* Writing about
        literature
    audience, 7, 135–37, 227
    body of essay, 8, 14–15, 27–28, 64–65,
        98, 137, 184–88, 226, 301–5, 308, 351,
        395–96, 400
    conclusion of essay, 8, 15–17, 28, 67,
        99–101, 137, 184, 188, 226, 256–66,
        308, 351, 396
    controlling idea, 6, 25 *See also* Thesis
        statement
    description as aid to other writing, 6,
        67–70
    description in introduction, 11–12
    editing and revising, 17–21
    four major types, 67
    free writing, 3–4
    integrating reading skills and, 174–77,
        214, 254–56, 293–94, 336–45, 375–81,
        435–36
    introduction, 8, 10–14, 26–27, 64,
        100,184–85, 226, 265–66, 350
    organizing, 7–17, 23–28, 62, 98–100,
        136–37, 184–90, 225–27, 265–66, 308,
        349–51, 396–98
    outlining, 8–10, 183, 186–87

    parts of essay, 8–17
    thesis statement, 6, 13–14, 25–26, 184,
        302, 435
    topic, choosing, 2–5
Writing about literature, 386–442
    acknowledging sources, 398–400
    analysis desired by instructor, 387
    attitude toward subject, 396
    character, 390
    criticism, bases for, 387–89
    conflict, 389–90
    developing essay, 396–400
    documentation, 401–3
    elements of fiction, 389–96
    form and content, 435–36
    irony, 395–96
    figures of speech, 400
    metaphor, 410
    modern criticism, 388
    organization of essay, 396–98
    paraphrase, 399
    plot, 389–90
    point of view, 392
    quotation, direct, 399–400
    relationship between work and audience
        as critical basis, 388
    romantic criticism, 388
    setting, 391–92
    summary, 398–99
    symbolism, 394–95
    tension in plot, 389–90
    theme, 390–91, 435
    thesis statement, 396
    tone, 392–94
    use of others' writings, 398–400
    work itself as critical basis, 388